TO YOUR ETERNITY

YOSHITOKI OIMA

8

THE STORY SO FAR

On Jananda, with the help of Tonari and her crew, Fushi learns what it is like to have friends worth fighting for, and how painful it is to lose them. After tending to Pioran in her final days, Fushi lives in solitude on a desert island until a brief reunion-turned-farewell with Tonari inspires Fushi to return to society. Now on a journey to discover new friends, Fushi begins living in towns for a time. One day, a man named Kahaku—a descendant of Hayase, and the leader of the Guardians—approaches Fushi. The Guardians built their influence as the protectors of the holy Fushi, source of the Immortal legends. By guarding civilians from Nokker attacks, they attracted more and more followers. From Kahaku, Fushi learns that some people have come to believe that he is an evil that attracts Nokkers. Fushi decides to travel with Kahaku, but the two are soon captured by a prince named Bon, and taken to his kingdom.

CHARACTERS

Fushi

An immortal being created to preserve this world by accumulating data. Over time, Fushi has acquired vessels and can transform into them. Is currently searching for friends who can understand him.

FRIENDS FUSHI HAS MET ALONG THE WAY

March

Gugu

Tonari

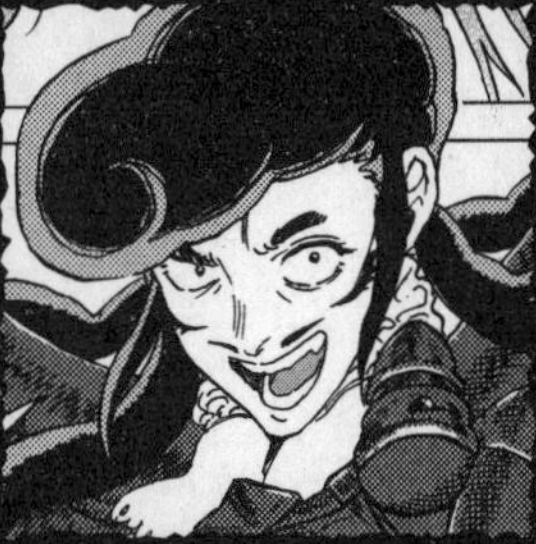

Bonchien Nicoli la Tasty Peach Uralis

The First Prince of the Uralis Kingdom. In order to prove that he is the rightful heir to the throne, he captures Fushi. Has the ability to see what other people cannot.

Uralis Kingdom

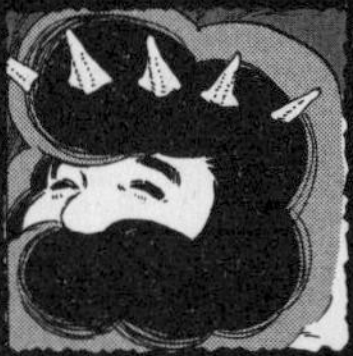

King

Bonchien's father.

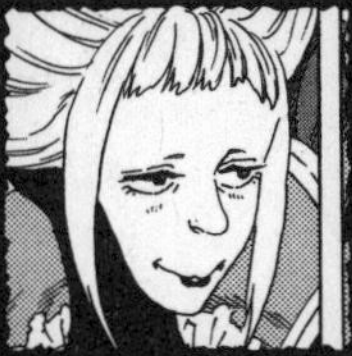

Queen

Bonchien's mother.

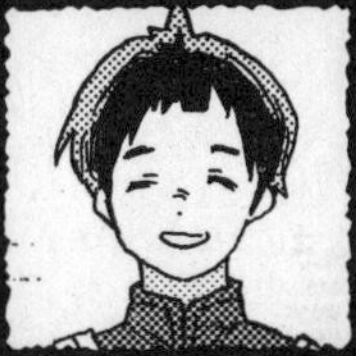

Torta

Bonchien's younger brother.

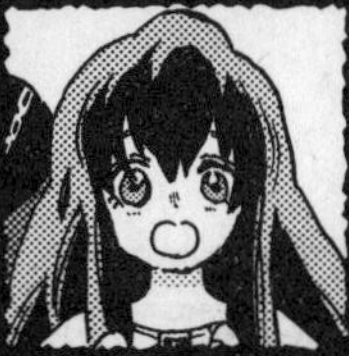

Pocoa

Bonchien's younger sister.

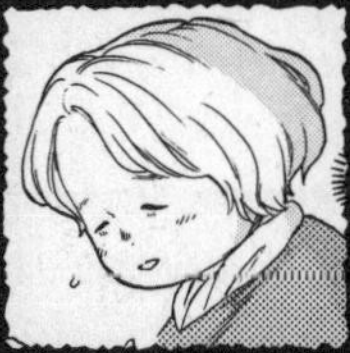

Todo

Bonchien's retainer.

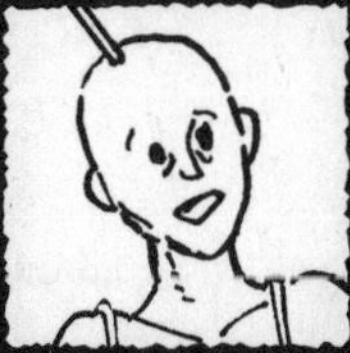

Fen

Lives in the castle's kitchen.

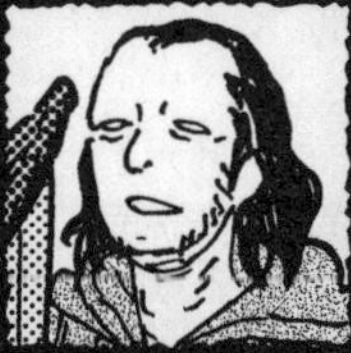

Nixon

A one-armed swordsman.

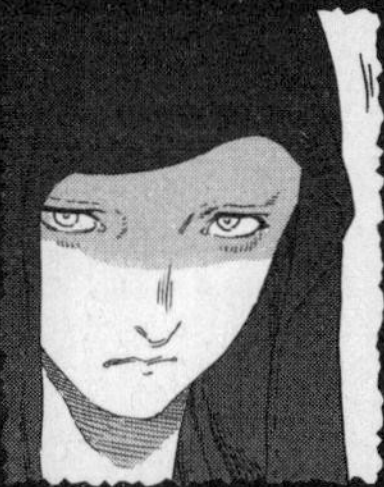

The Beholder

Created Fushi in order to preserve the world. Always watching Fushi from nearby. Can detect Nokkers.

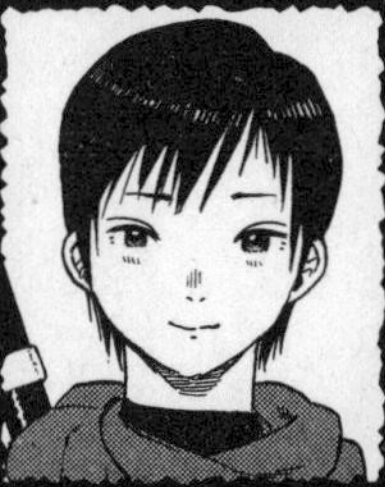

Kahaku

Descendant of Hayase and the sixth successor to carry out her will. A Nokker lives in his left arm. Is attracted to Fushi in Parona's form.

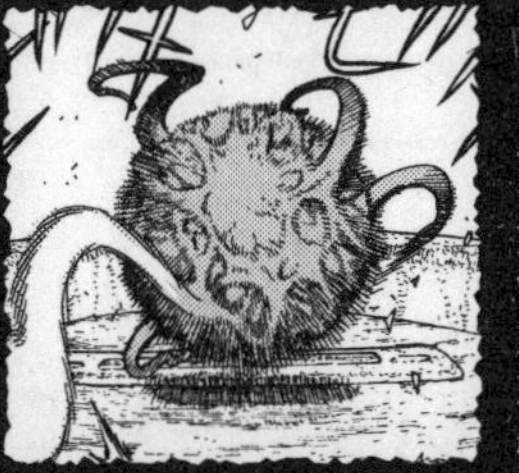

Nokker

Plots to obstruct the Beholder's plans. Was designed not only to steal what Fushi acquires, but also to weaken him. Learns from mistakes and attacks using many different methods.

CONTENTS

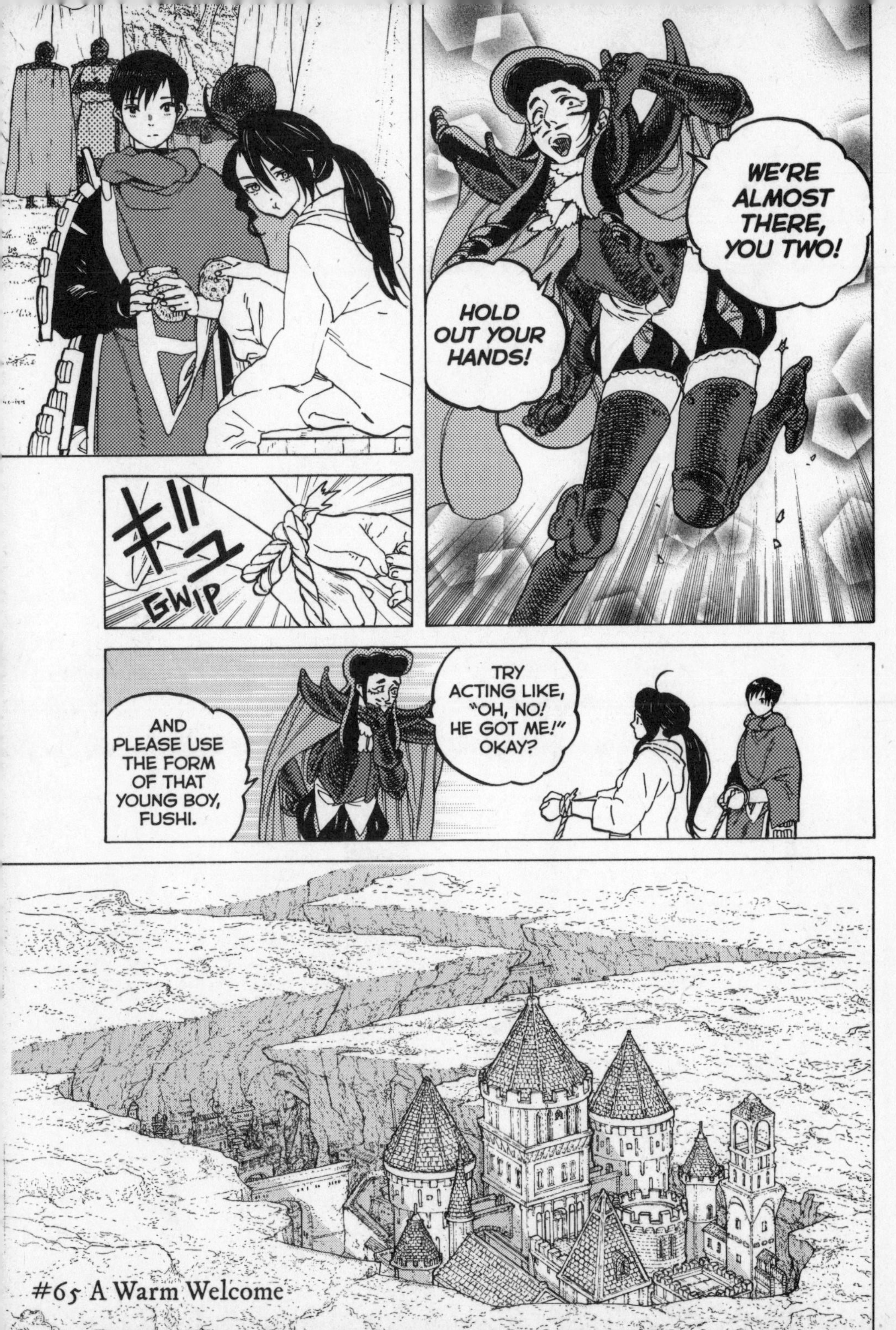
WE'RE ALMOST THERE, YOU TWO!
HOLD OUT YOUR HANDS!
キュ
GWIP
TRY ACTING LIKE, "OH, NO! HE GOT ME!" OKAY?
AND PLEASE USE THE FORM OF THAT YOUNG BOY, FUSHI.
#65 A Warm Welcome

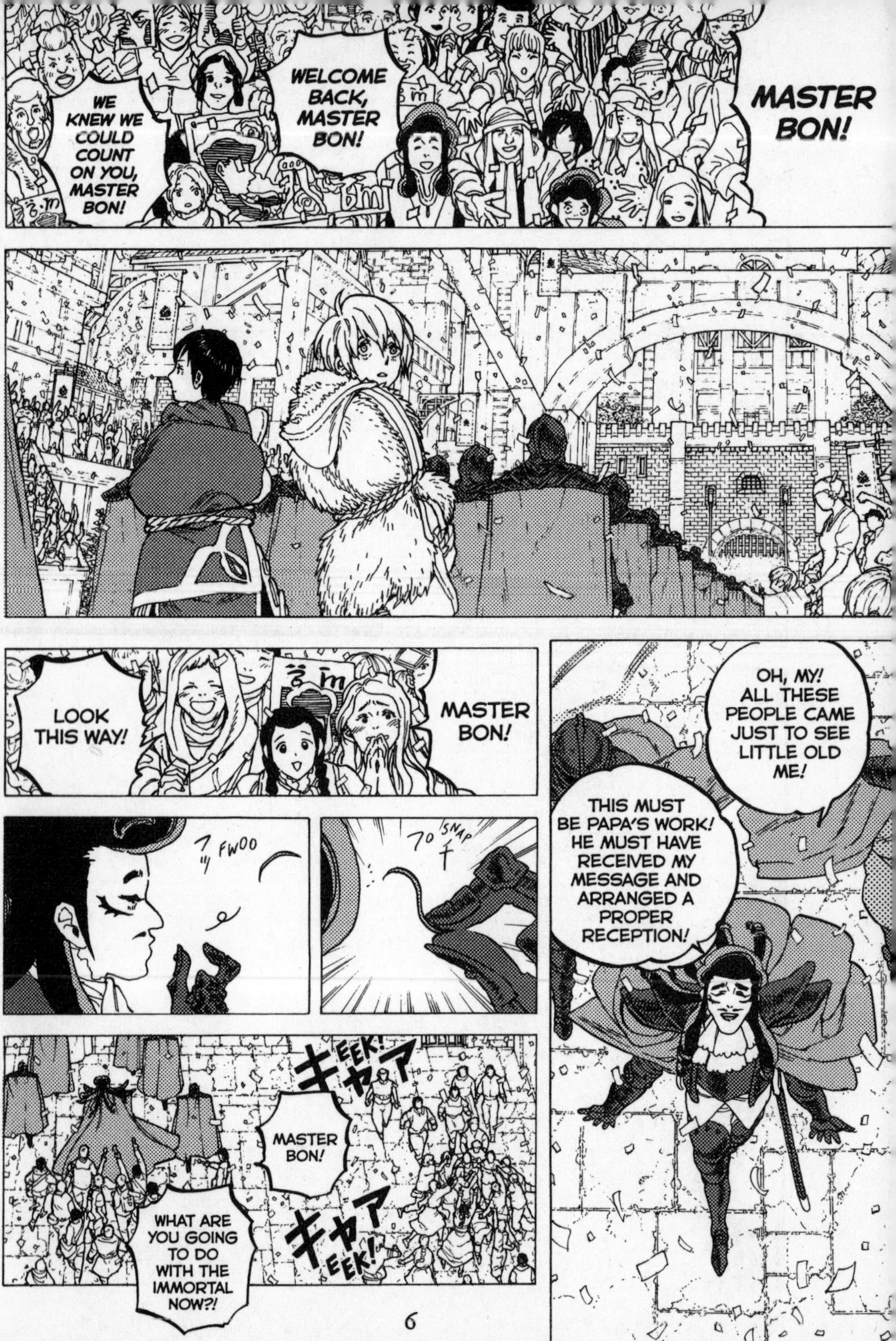
MASTER BON!
WELCOME BACK, MASTER BON!
WE KNEW WE COULD COUNT ON YOU, MASTER BON!
OH, MY! ALL THESE PEOPLE CAME JUST TO SEE LITTLE OLD ME!
THIS MUST BE PAPA'S WORK! HE MUST HAVE RECEIVED MY MESSAGE AND ARRANGED A PROPER RECEPTION!
MASTER BON!
LOOK THIS WAY!
フ SNAP
フッ FWOO
キャア EEK!
MASTER BON!
キャア EEK!
WHAT ARE YOU GOING TO DO WITH THE IMMORTAL NOW?!

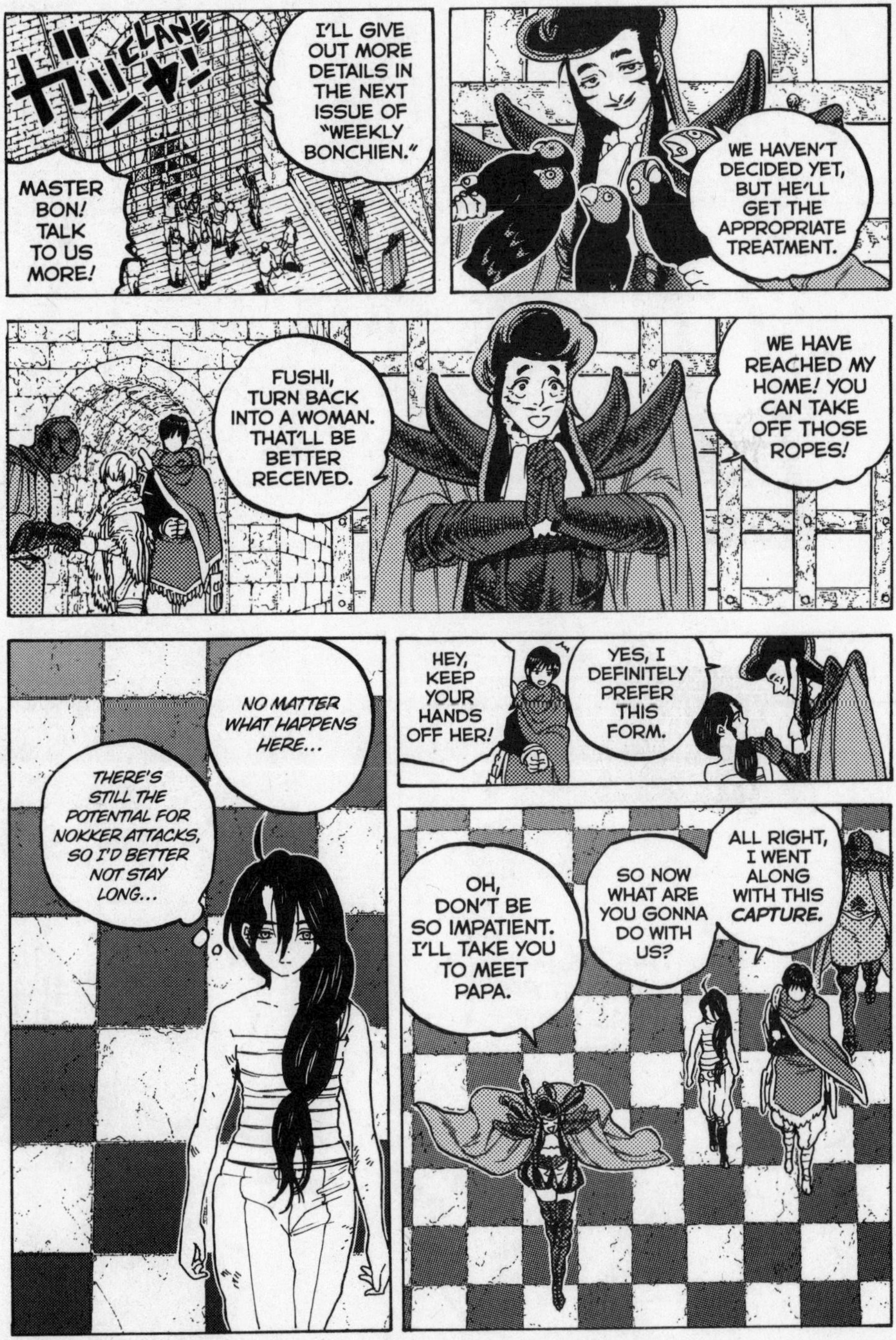
WE HAVEN'T DECIDED YET, BUT HE'LL GET THE APPROPRIATE TREATMENT.
I'LL GIVE OUT MORE DETAILS IN THE NEXT ISSUE OF "WEEKLY BONCHIEN."
ガシャン
CLANE
MASTER BON! TALK TO US MORE!
WE HAVE REACHED MY HOME! YOU CAN TAKE OFF THOSE ROPES!
FUSHI, TURN BACK INTO A WOMAN. THAT'LL BE BETTER RECEIVED.
YES, I DEFINITELY PREFER THIS FORM.
HEY, KEEP YOUR HANDS OFF HER!
ALL RIGHT, I WENT ALONG WITH THIS *CAPTURE.*
SO NOW WHAT ARE YOU GONNA DO WITH US?
OH, DON'T BE SO IMPATIENT. I'LL TAKE YOU TO MEET PAPA.
NO MATTER WHAT HAPPENS HERE...
THERE'S STILL THE POTENTIAL FOR NOKKER ATTACKS, SO I'D BETTER NOT STAY LONG...

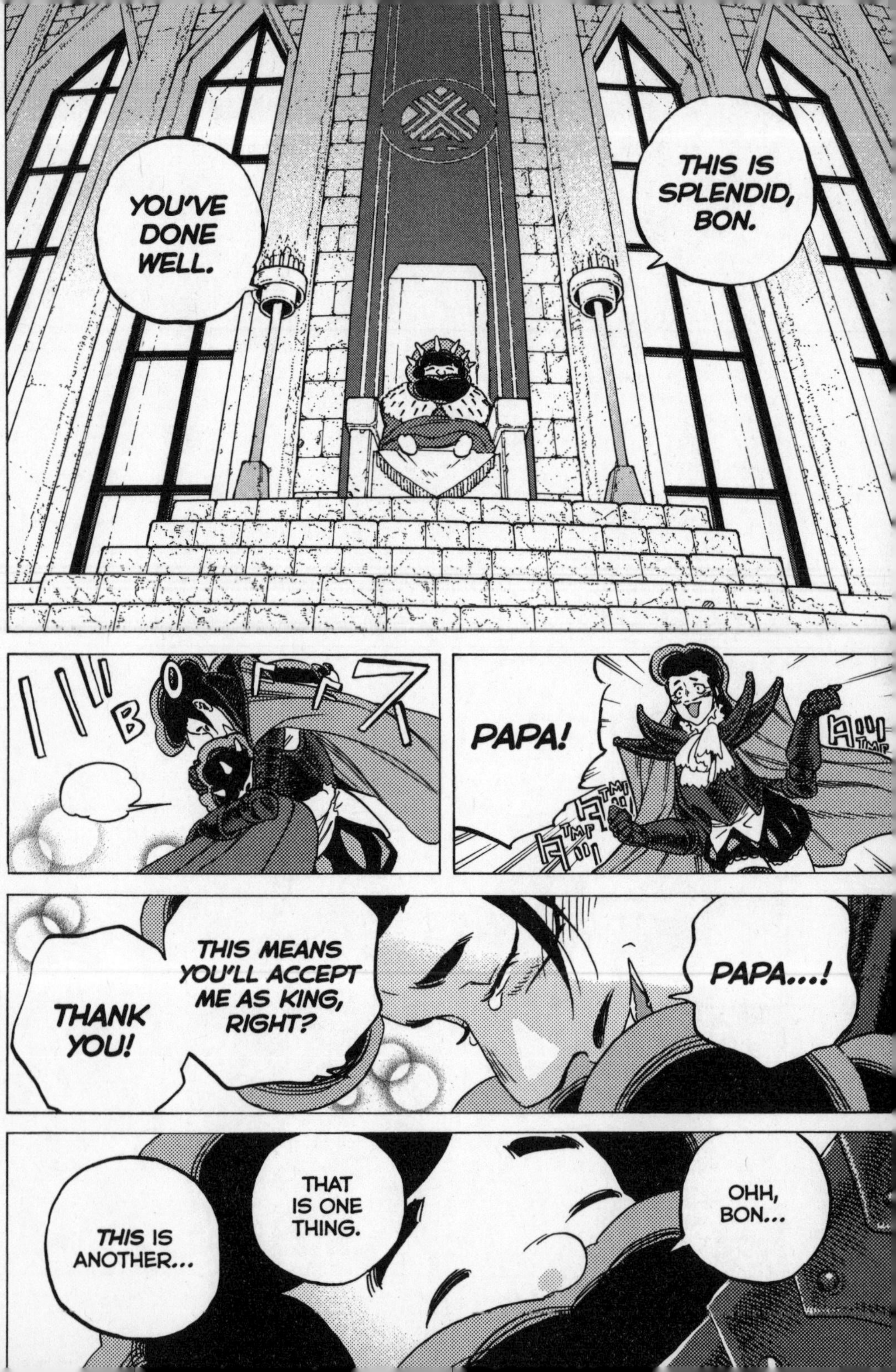
THIS IS SPLENDID, BON.
YOU'VE DONE WELL.
PAPA!
TMP
TMP
TMP
PAPA...!
THIS MEANS YOU'LL ACCEPT ME AS KING, RIGHT?
THANK YOU!
OHH, BON...
THAT IS ONE THING.
THIS IS ANOTHER...

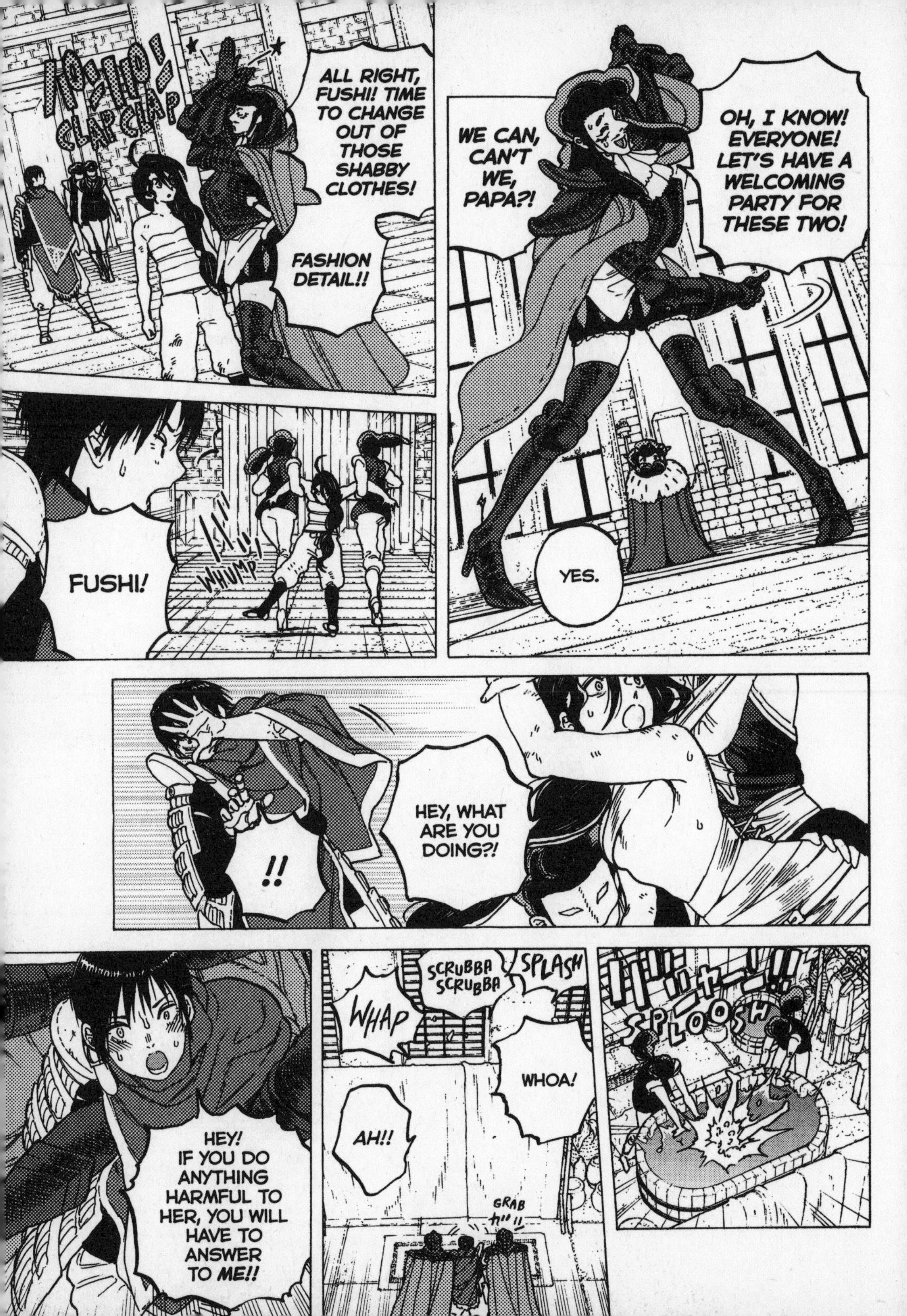
OH, I KNOW! EVERYONE! LET'S HAVE A WELCOMING PARTY FOR THESE TWO!
WE CAN, CAN'T WE, PAPA?!
YES.
CLAP CLAP
ALL RIGHT, FUSHI! TIME TO CHANGE OUT OF THOSE SHABBY CLOTHES!
FASHION DETAIL!!
WHUMP
FUSHI!
HEY, WHAT ARE YOU DOING?!
!!
SPLOOSH
SPLASH
SCRUBBA SCRUBBA
WHAP
WHOA!
AH!!
GRAB
HEY! IF YOU DO ANYTHING HARMFUL TO HER, YOU WILL HAVE TO ANSWER TO *ME*!!

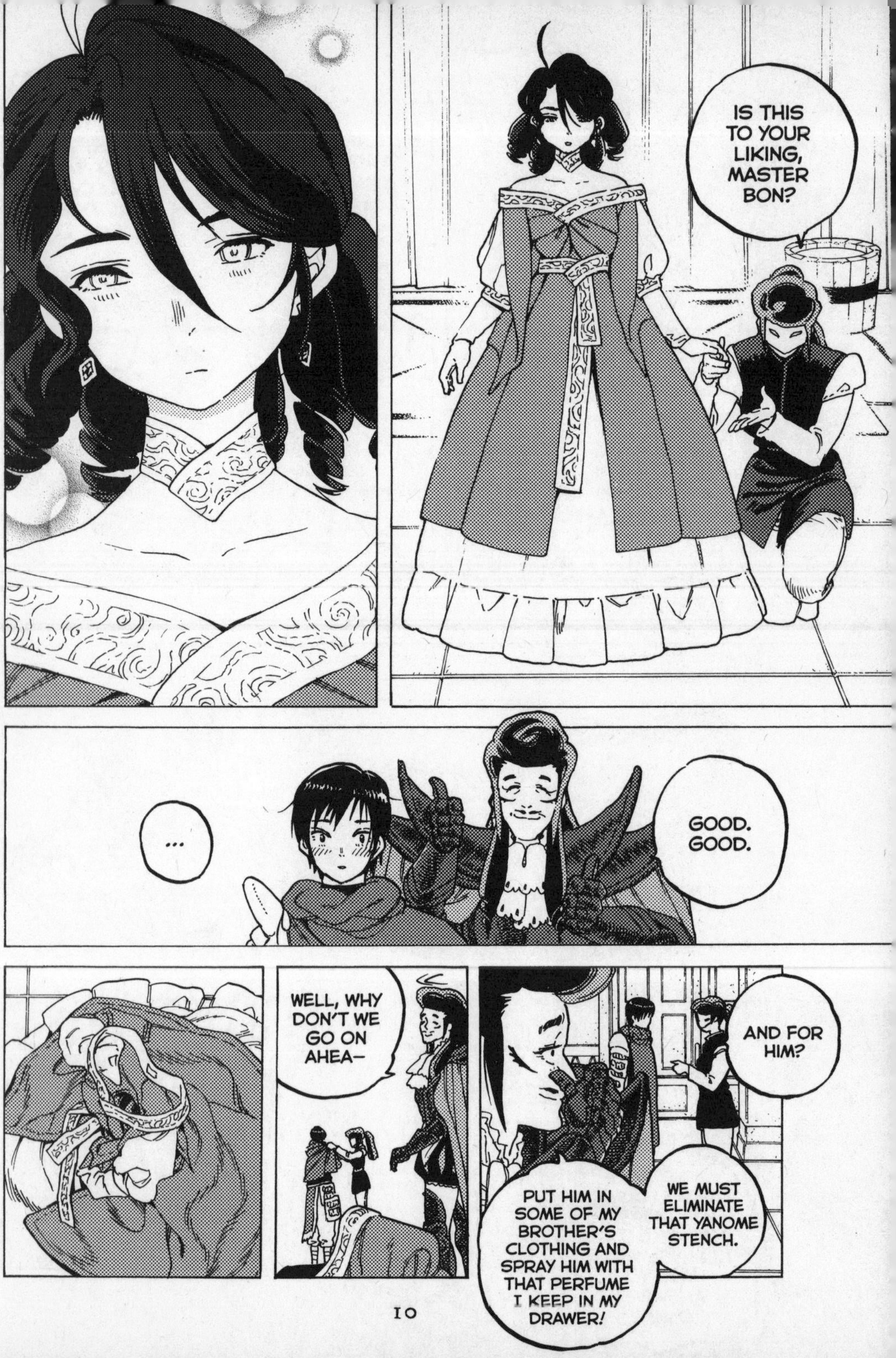
IS THIS TO YOUR LIKING, MASTER BON?
...
GOOD. GOOD.
WELL, WHY DON'T WE GO ON AHEA–
AND FOR HIM?
PUT HIM IN SOME OF MY BROTHER'S CLOTHING AND SPRAY HIM WITH THAT PERFUME I KEEP IN MY DRAWER!
WE MUST ELIMINATE THAT YANOME STENCH.

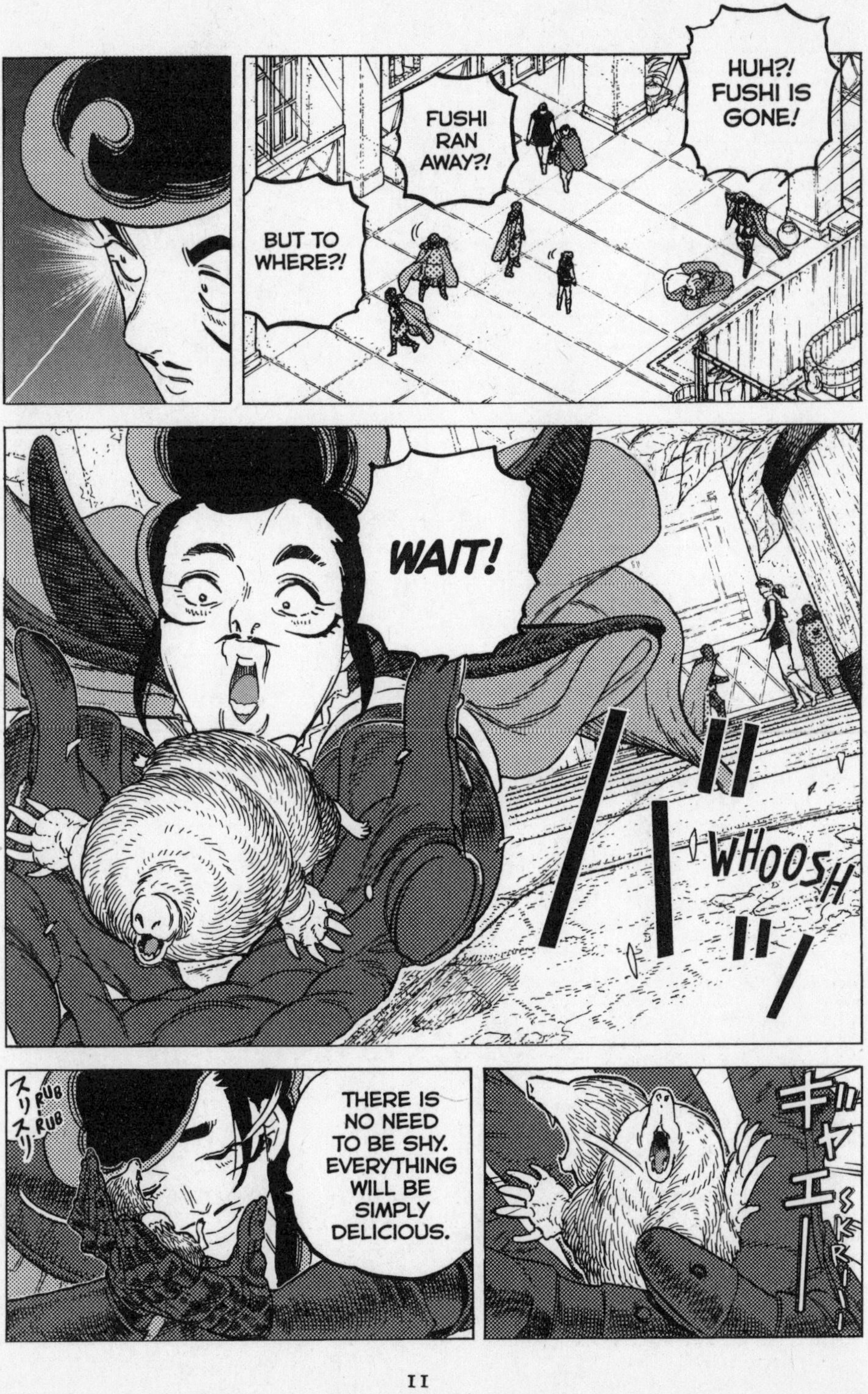
HUH?! FUSHI IS GONE!
FUSHI RAN AWAY?!
BUT TO WHERE?!
WAIT!
WHOOSH
ギャエー
SKRI—
THERE IS NO NEED TO BE SHY. EVERYTHING WILL BE SIMPLY DELICIOUS.
スリスリ
RUB RUB

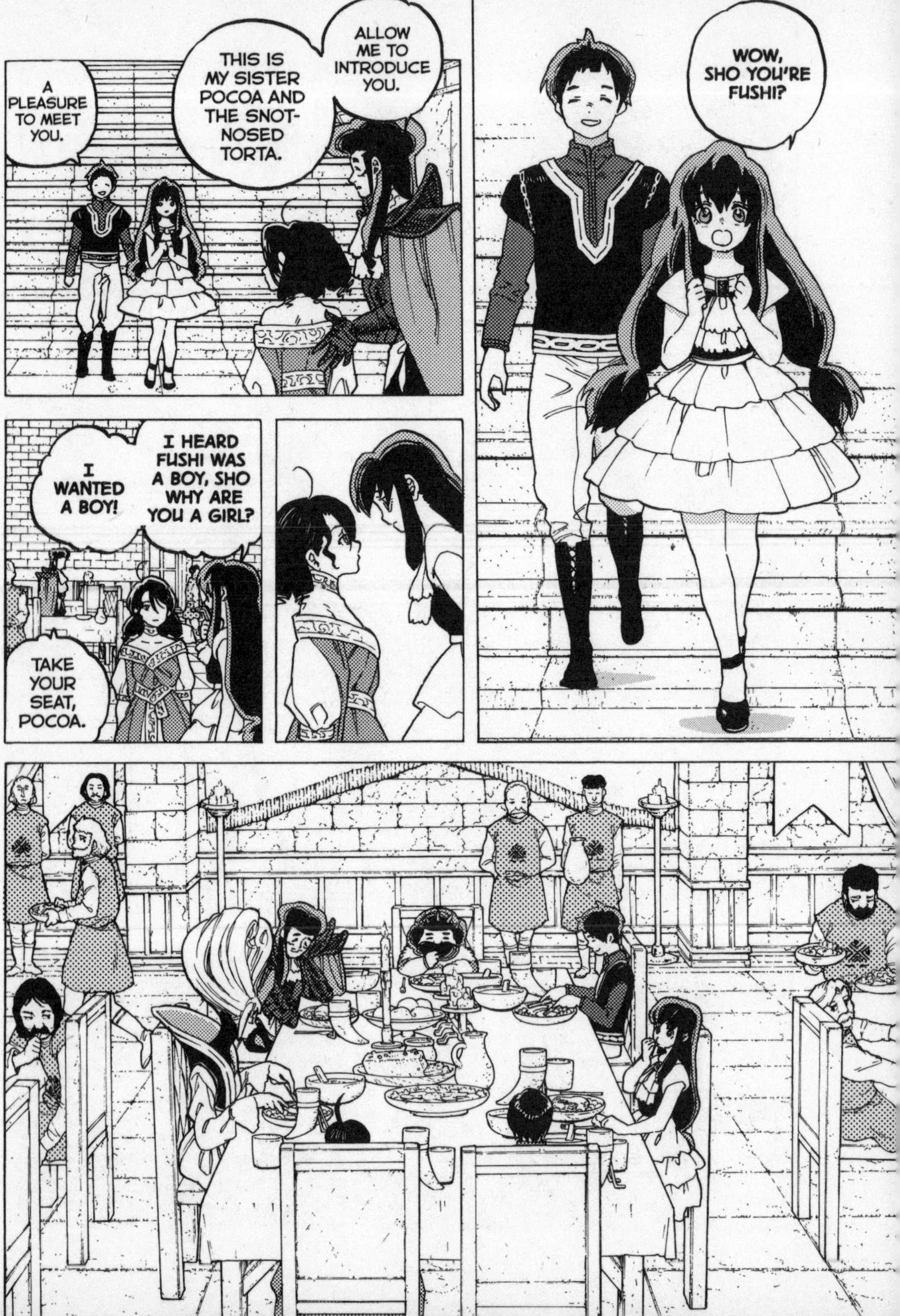
WOW, SHO YOU'RE FUSHI?
ALLOW ME TO INTRODUCE YOU.
THIS IS MY SISTER POCOA AND THE SNOT-NOSED TORTA.
A PLEASURE TO MEET YOU.
I HEARD FUSHI WAS A BOY, SHO WHY ARE YOU A GIRL?
I WANTED A BOY!
TAKE YOUR SEAT, POCOA.

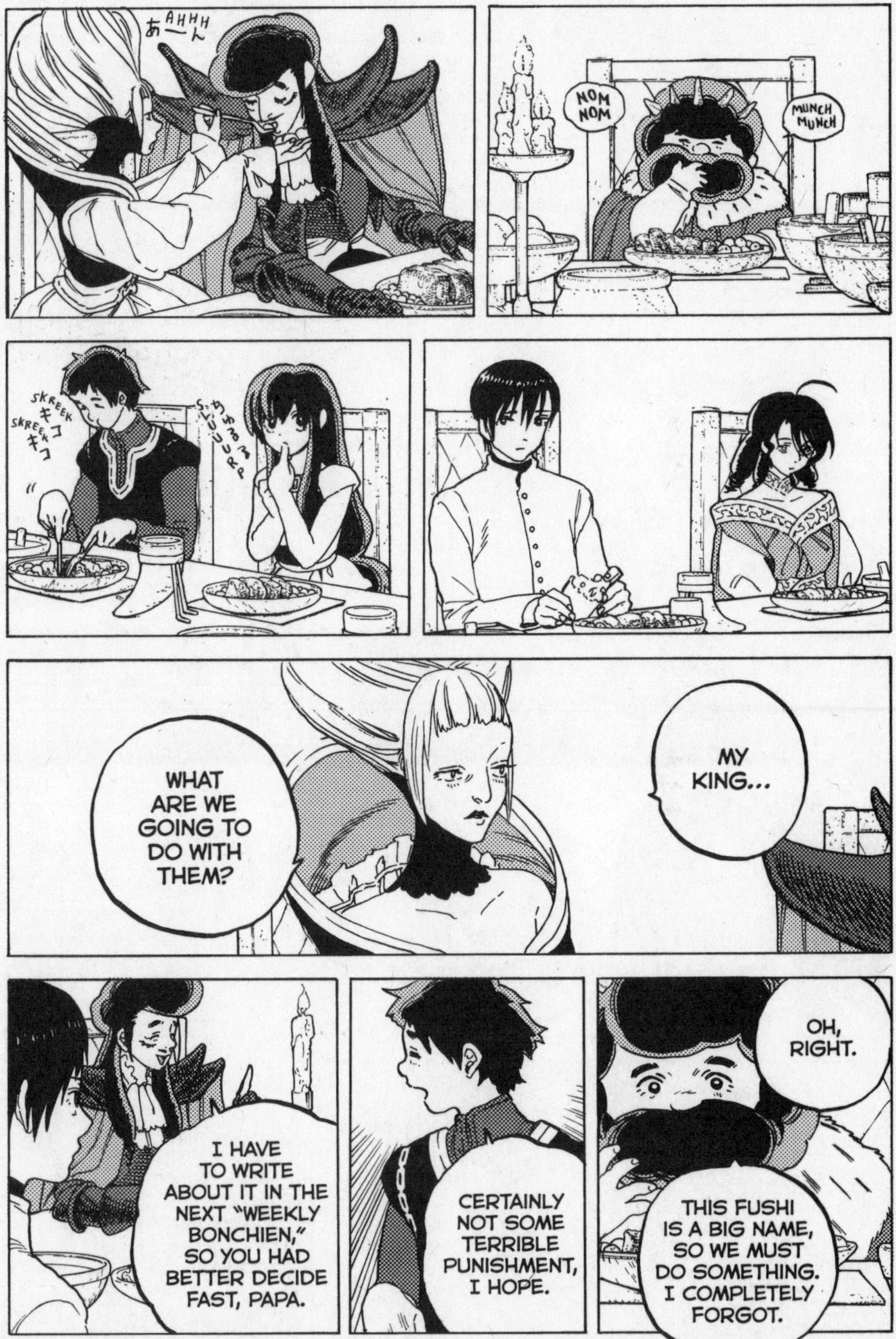
NOM NOM
MUNCH MUNCH
AHHH
あ～ん
SLUUURP
ちゅるるる
SKREEK
キコ
SKREEK
キコ
MY KING...
WHAT ARE WE GOING TO DO WITH THEM?
OH, RIGHT.
THIS FUSHI IS A BIG NAME, SO WE MUST DO SOMETHING. I COMPLETELY FORGOT.
CERTAINLY NOT SOME TERRIBLE PUNISHMENT, I HOPE.
I HAVE TO WRITE ABOUT IT IN THE NEXT "WEEKLY BONCHIEN," SO YOU HAD BETTER DECIDE FAST, PAPA.

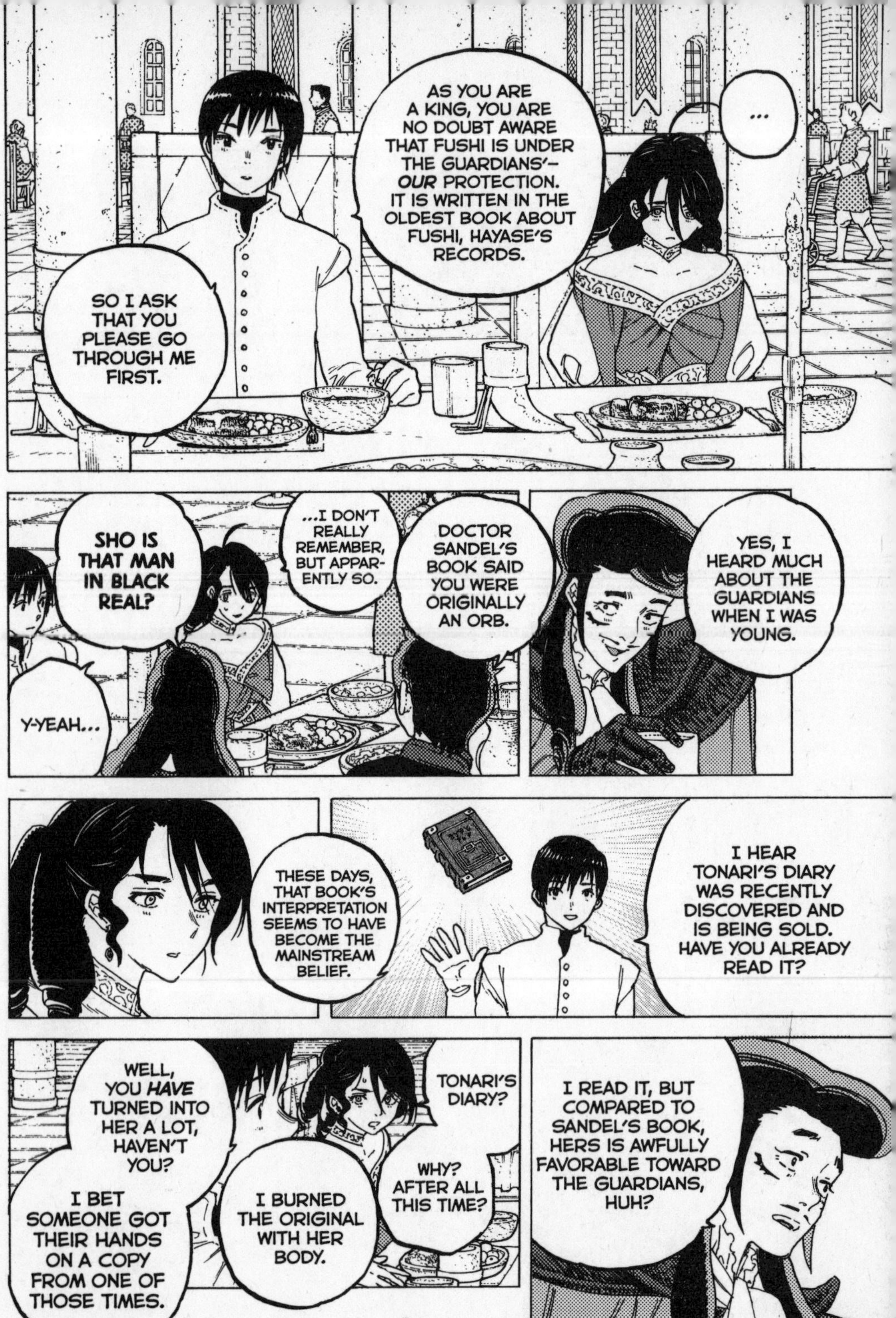
...
AS YOU ARE A KING, YOU ARE NO DOUBT AWARE THAT FUSHI IS UNDER THE GUARDIANS'— *OUR* PROTECTION. IT IS WRITTEN IN THE OLDEST BOOK ABOUT FUSHI, HAYASE'S RECORDS.
SO I ASK THAT YOU PLEASE GO THROUGH ME FIRST.
YES, I HEARD MUCH ABOUT THE GUARDIANS WHEN I WAS YOUNG.
DOCTOR SANDEL'S BOOK SAID YOU WERE ORIGINALLY AN ORB.
...I DON'T REALLY REMEMBER, BUT APPARENTLY SO.
SHO IS THAT MAN IN BLACK REAL?
Y-YEAH...
I HEAR TONARI'S DIARY WAS RECENTLY DISCOVERED AND IS BEING SOLD. HAVE YOU ALREADY READ IT?
THESE DAYS, THAT BOOK'S INTERPRETATION SEEMS TO HAVE BECOME THE MAINSTREAM BELIEF.
I READ IT, BUT COMPARED TO SANDEL'S BOOK, HERS IS AWFULLY FAVORABLE TOWARD THE GUARDIANS, HUH?
TONARI'S DIARY?
WHY? AFTER ALL THIS TIME?
I BURNED THE ORIGINAL WITH HER BODY.
WELL, YOU *HAVE* TURNED INTO HER A LOT, HAVEN'T YOU?
I BET SOMEONE GOT THEIR HANDS ON A COPY FROM ONE OF THOSE TIMES.

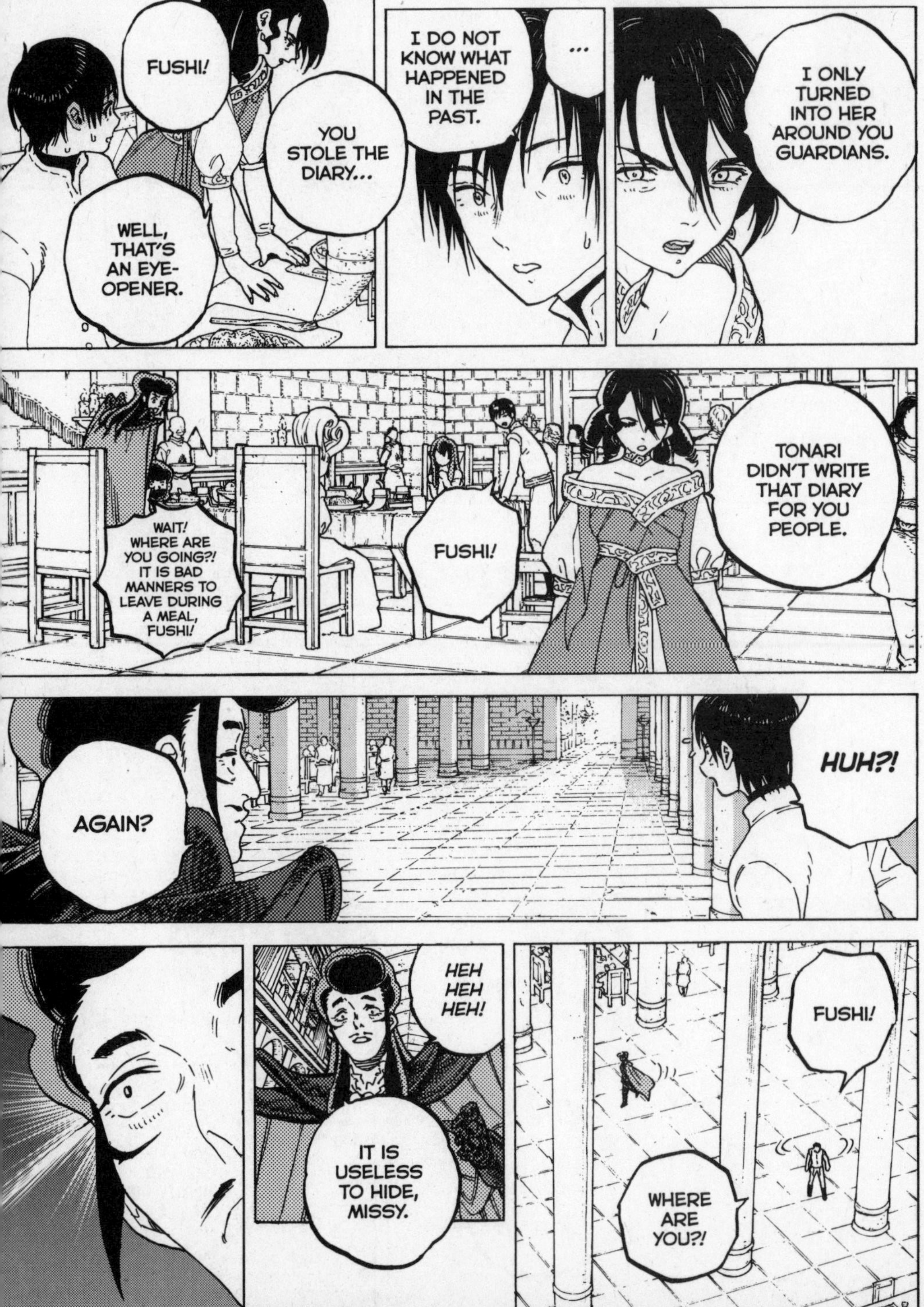
I ONLY TURNED INTO HER AROUND YOU GUARDIANS.
...
I DO NOT KNOW WHAT HAPPENED IN THE PAST.
FUSHI!
YOU STOLE THE DIARY...
WELL, THAT'S AN EYE-OPENER.
TONARI DIDN'T WRITE THAT DIARY FOR YOU PEOPLE.
FUSHI!
WAIT! WHERE ARE YOU GOING?! IT IS BAD MANNERS TO LEAVE DURING A MEAL, FUSHI!
HUH?!
AGAIN?
FUSHI!
WHERE ARE YOU?!
HEH HEH HEH!
IT IS USELESS TO HIDE, MISSY.

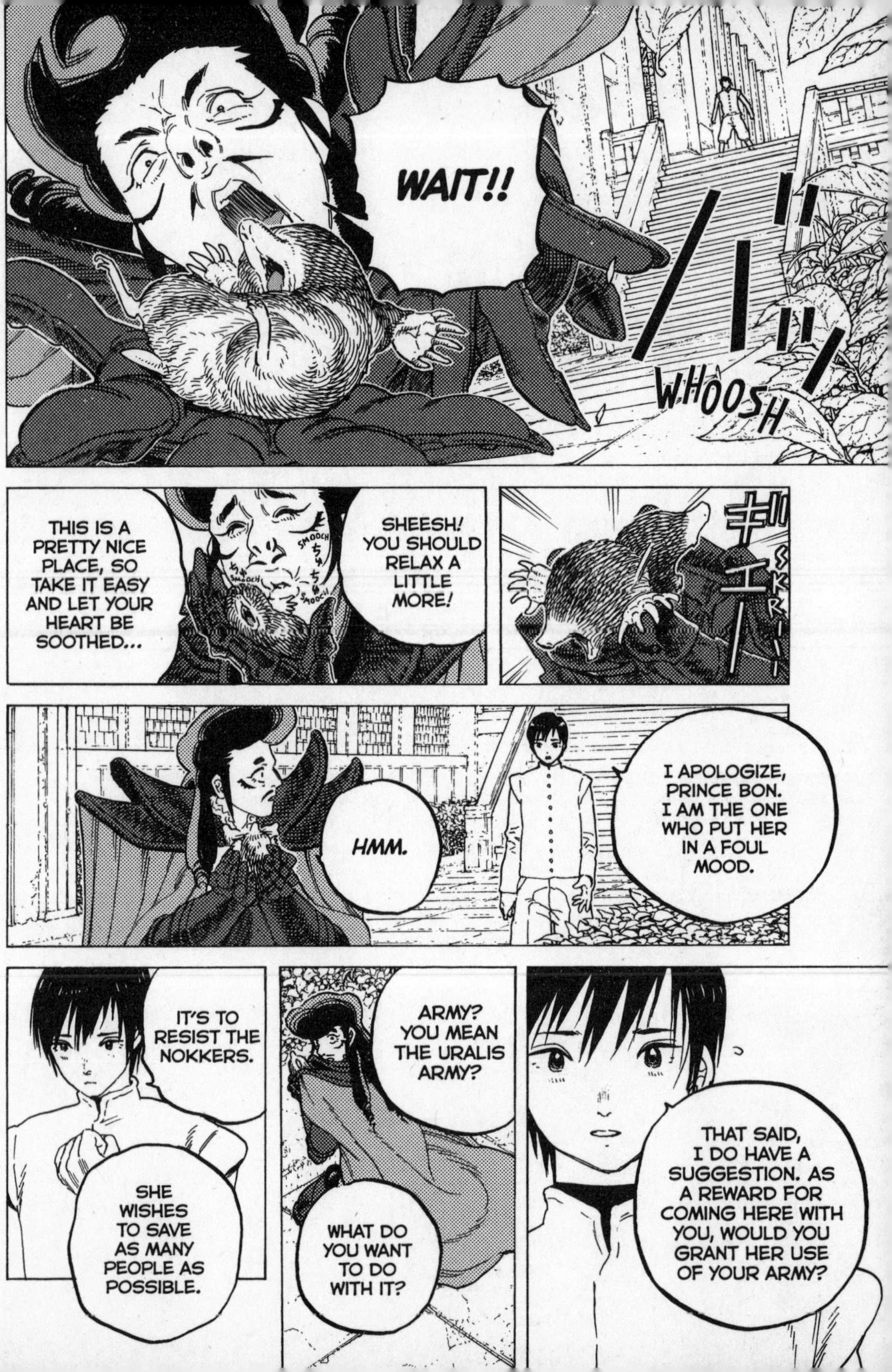
WAIT!!
WHOOSH
SKRI--
SHEESH! YOU SHOULD RELAX A LITTLE MORE!
THIS IS A PRETTY NICE PLACE, SO TAKE IT EASY AND LET YOUR HEART BE SOOTHED...
I APOLOGIZE, PRINCE BON. I AM THE ONE WHO PUT HER IN A FOUL MOOD.
HMM.
THAT SAID, I DO HAVE A SUGGESTION. AS A REWARD FOR COMING HERE WITH YOU, WOULD YOU GRANT HER USE OF YOUR ARMY?
ARMY? YOU MEAN THE URALIS ARMY?
WHAT DO YOU WANT TO DO WITH IT?
IT'S TO RESIST THE NOKKERS.
SHE WISHES TO SAVE AS MANY PEOPLE AS POSSIBLE.

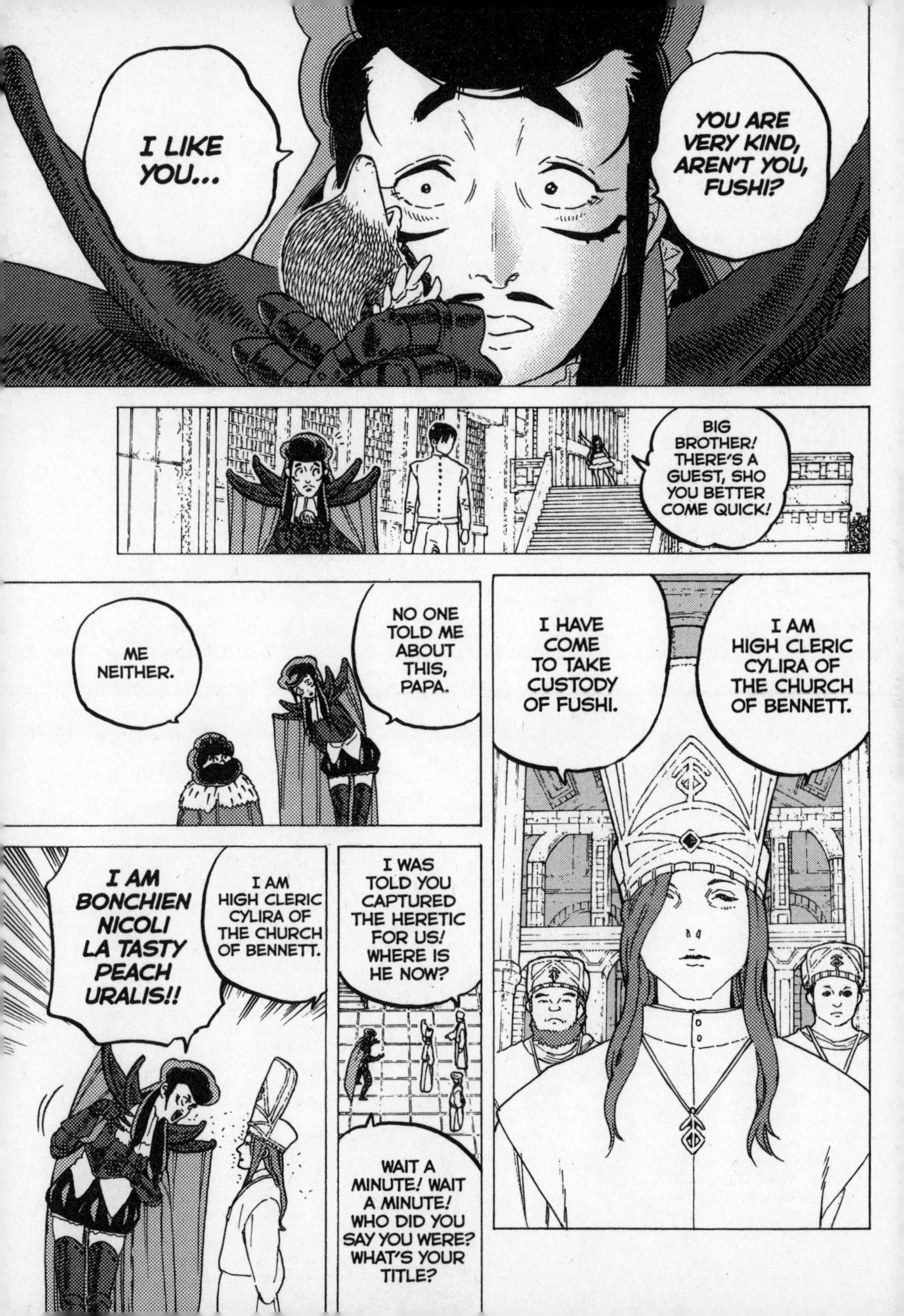
YOU ARE VERY KIND, AREN'T YOU, FUSHI?
I LIKE YOU...
BIG BROTHER! THERE'S A GUEST, SHO YOU BETTER COME QUICK!
I AM HIGH CLERIC CYLIRA OF THE CHURCH OF BENNETT.
I HAVE COME TO TAKE CUSTODY OF FUSHI.
NO ONE TOLD ME ABOUT THIS, PAPA.
ME NEITHER.
I WAS TOLD YOU CAPTURED THE HERETIC FOR US! WHERE IS HE NOW?
WAIT A MINUTE! WAIT A MINUTE! WHO DID YOU SAY YOU WERE? WHAT'S YOUR TITLE?
I AM HIGH CLERIC CYLIRA OF THE CHURCH OF BENNETT.
I AM BONCHIEN NICOLI LA TASTY PEACH URALIS!!

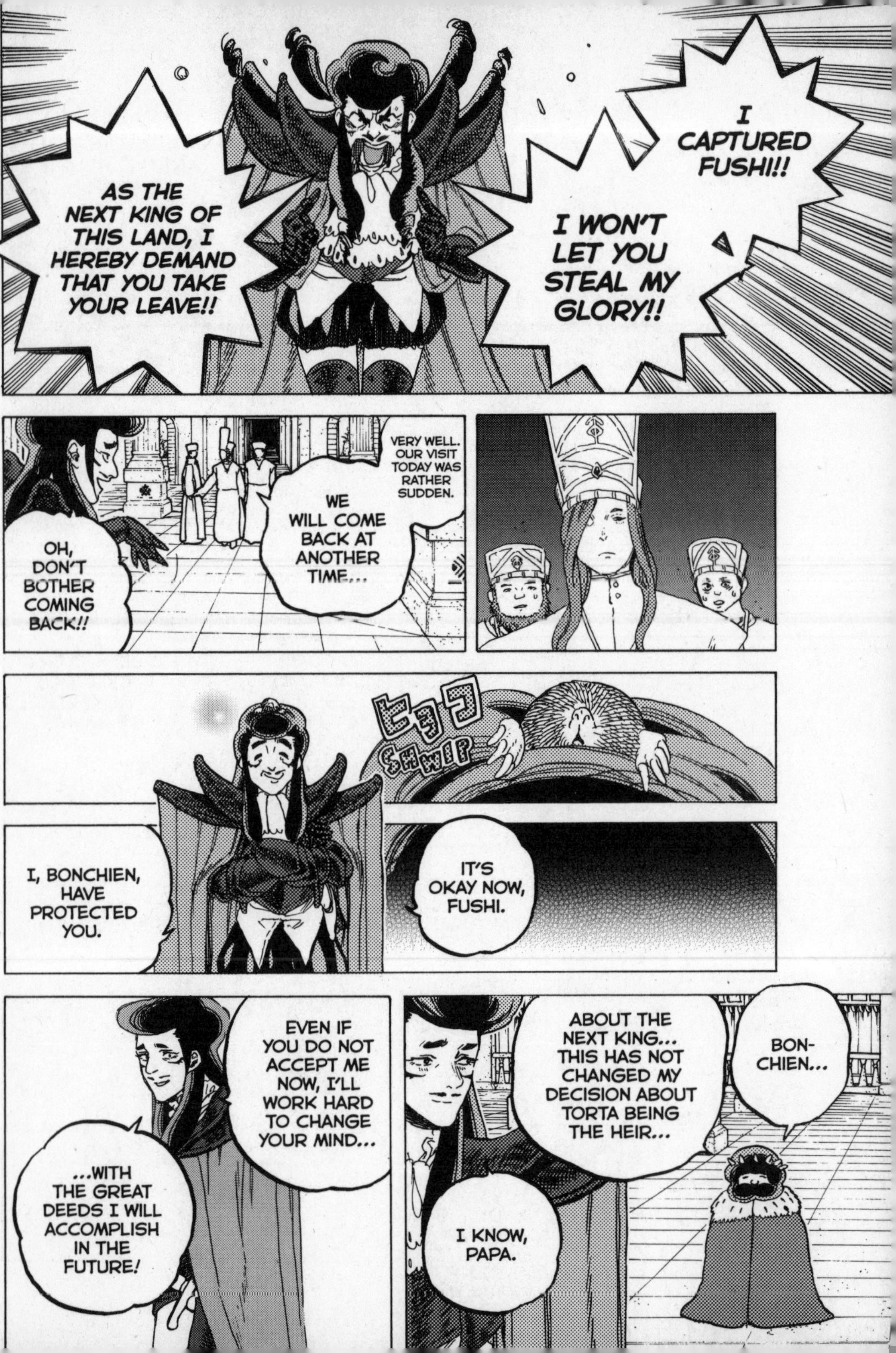
I CAPTURED FUSHI!!
I WON'T LET YOU STEAL MY GLORY!!
AS THE NEXT KING OF THIS LAND, I HEREBY DEMAND THAT YOU TAKE YOUR LEAVE!!
VERY WELL. OUR VISIT TODAY WAS RATHER SUDDEN.
WE WILL COME BACK AT ANOTHER TIME...
OH, DON'T BOTHER COMING BACK!!
ヒョコ
SHWIP
IT'S OKAY NOW, FUSHI.
I, BONCHIEN, HAVE PROTECTED YOU.
BON-CHIEN...
ABOUT THE NEXT KING... THIS HAS NOT CHANGED MY DECISION ABOUT TORTA BEING THE HEIR...
I KNOW, PAPA.
EVEN IF YOU DO NOT ACCEPT ME NOW, I'LL WORK HARD TO CHANGE YOUR MIND...
...WITH THE GREAT DEEDS I WILL ACCOMPLISH IN THE FUTURE!

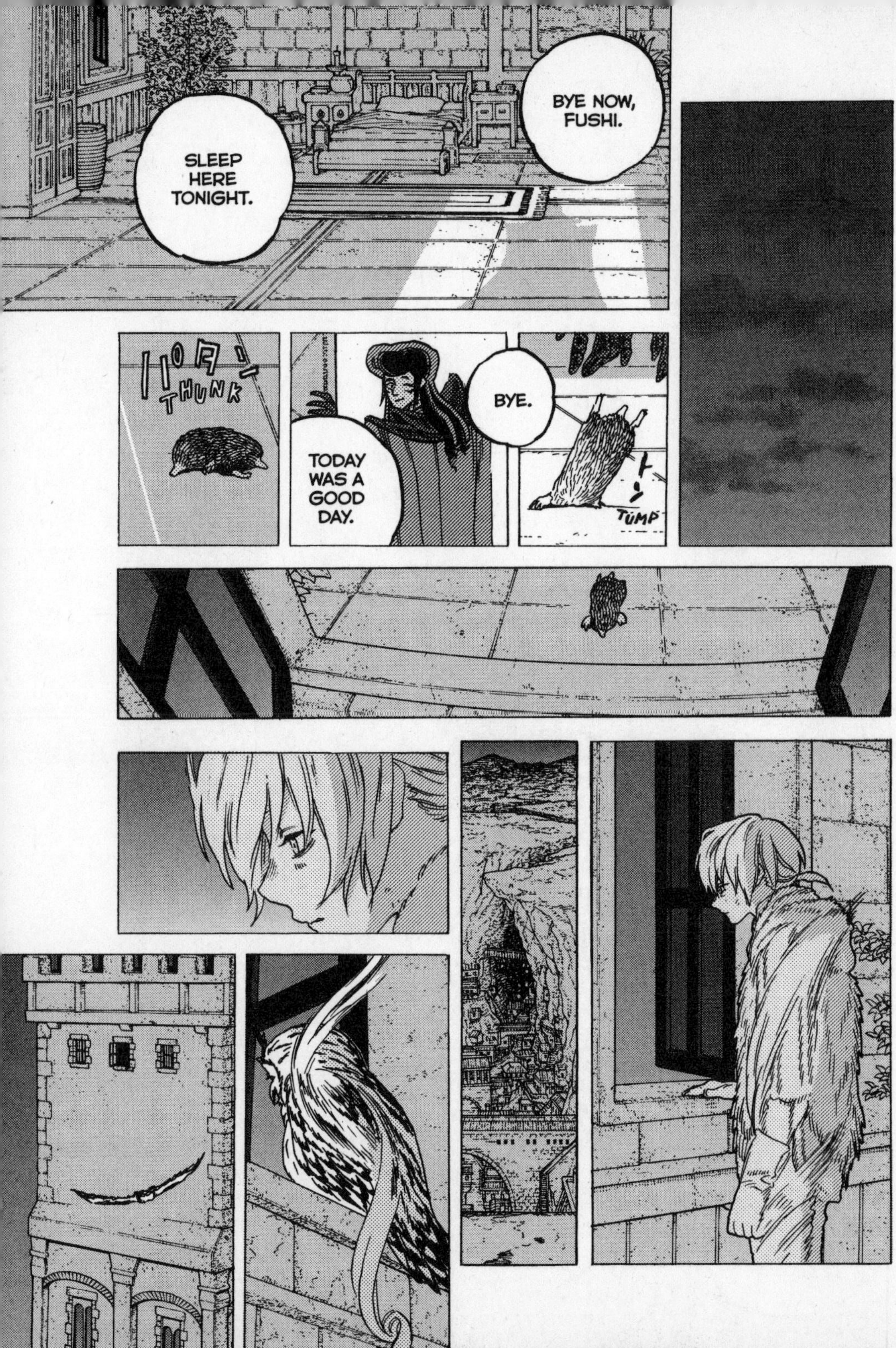

BYE NOW, FUSHI.
SLEEP HERE TONIGHT.
BYE.
TUMP
TODAY WAS A GOOD DAY.
THUNK

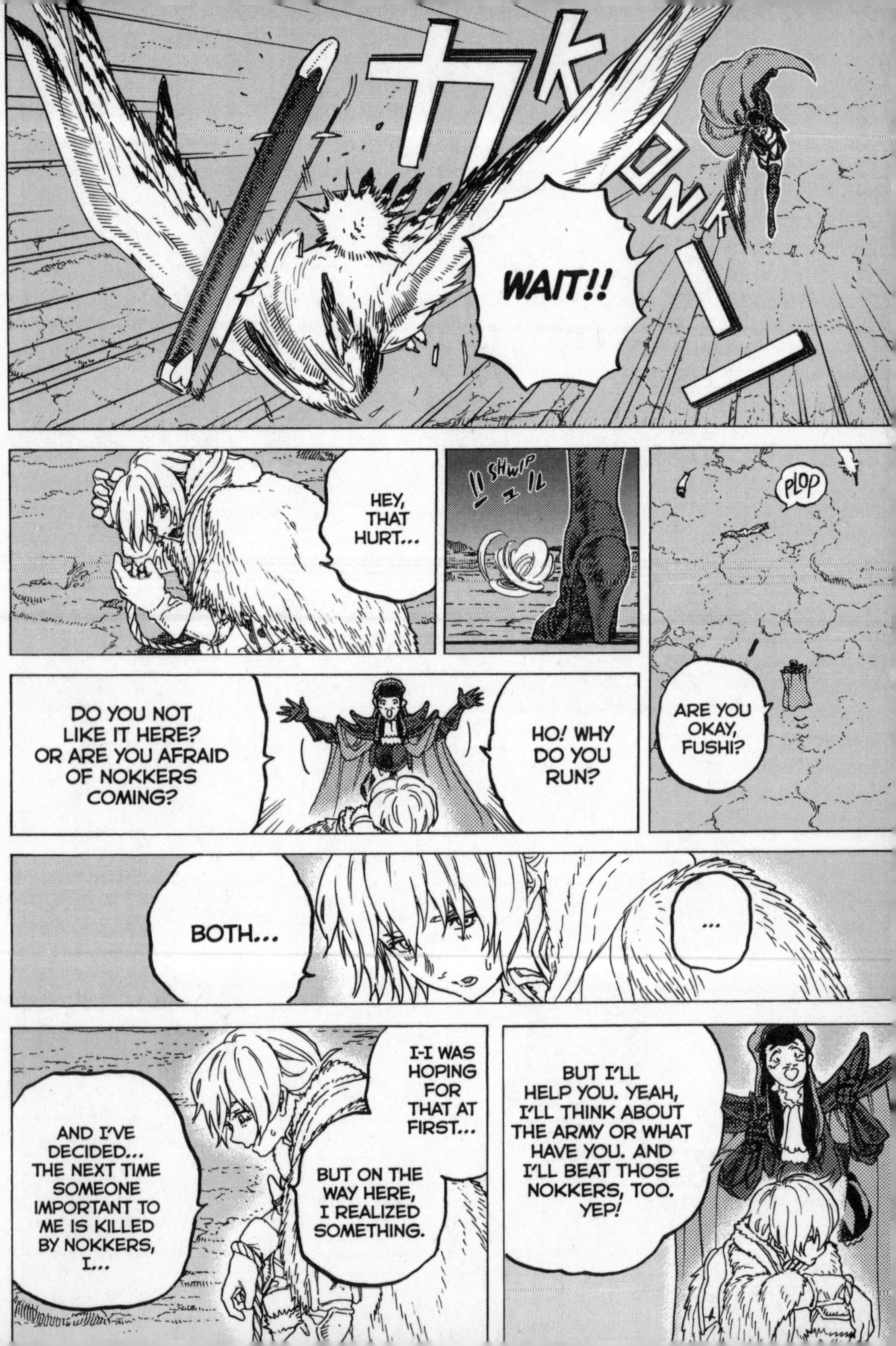
KONK
WAIT!!
PLOP
ARE YOU OKAY, FUSHI?
SHWIP
HEY, THAT HURT...
HO! WHY DO YOU RUN?
DO YOU NOT LIKE IT HERE? OR ARE YOU AFRAID OF NOKKERS COMING?
...
BOTH...
BUT I'LL HELP YOU. YEAH, I'LL THINK ABOUT THE ARMY OR WHAT HAVE YOU. AND I'LL BEAT THOSE NOKKERS, TOO. YEP!
I-I WAS HOPING FOR THAT AT FIRST...
BUT ON THE WAY HERE, I REALIZED SOMETHING.
AND I'VE DECIDED... THE NEXT TIME SOMEONE IMPORTANT TO ME IS KILLED BY NOKKERS, I...

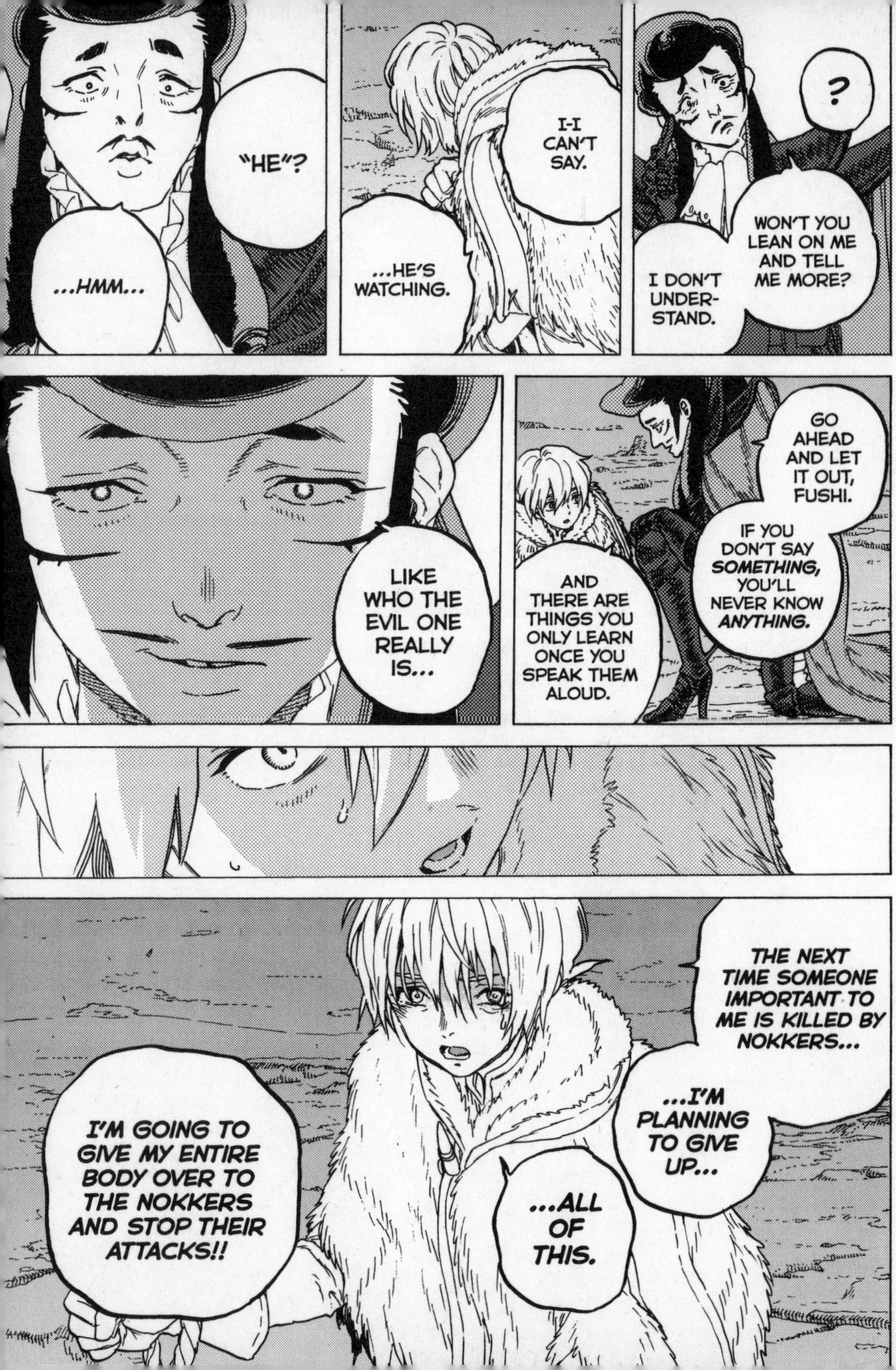
?
WON'T YOU LEAN ON ME AND TELL ME MORE?
I DON'T UNDER-STAND.
I-I CAN'T SAY.
...HE'S WATCHING.
"HE"?
...HMM...
GO AHEAD AND LET IT OUT, FUSHI.
IF YOU DON'T SAY *SOMETHING*, YOU'LL NEVER KNOW *ANYTHING*.
AND THERE ARE THINGS YOU ONLY LEARN ONCE YOU SPEAK THEM ALOUD.
LIKE WHO THE EVIL ONE REALLY IS...
THE NEXT TIME SOMEONE IMPORTANT TO ME IS KILLED BY NOKKERS...
...I'M PLANNING TO GIVE UP...
...ALL OF THIS.
I'M GOING TO GIVE MY ENTIRE BODY OVER TO THE NOKKERS AND STOP THEIR ATTACKS!!

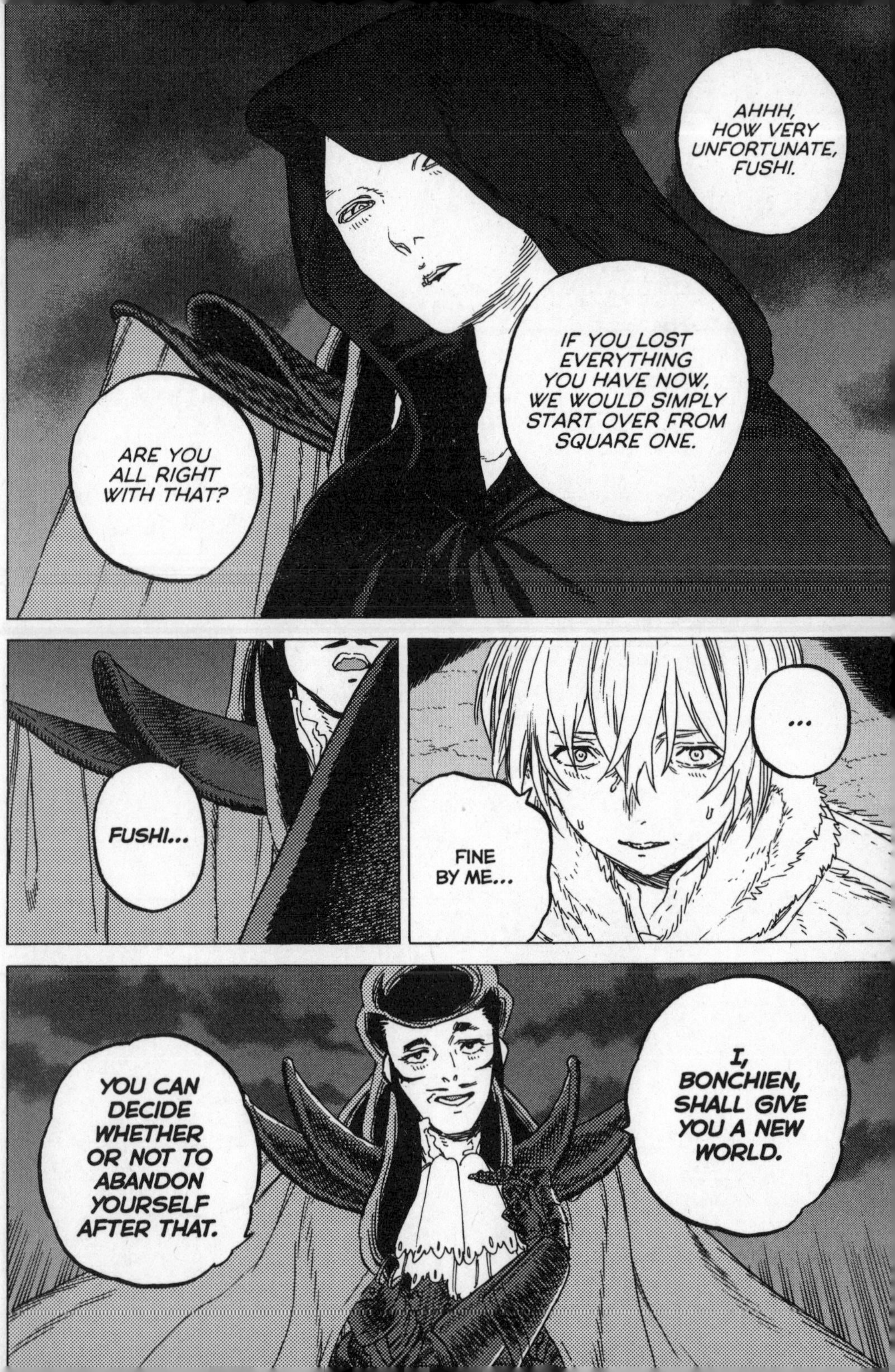
AHHH, HOW VERY UNFORTUNATE, FUSHI.
IF YOU LOST EVERYTHING YOU HAVE NOW, WE WOULD SIMPLY START OVER FROM SQUARE ONE.
ARE YOU ALL RIGHT WITH THAT?
...
FINE BY ME...
FUSHI...
I, BONCHIEN, SHALL GIVE YOU A NEW WORLD.
YOU CAN DECIDE WHETHER OR NOT TO ABANDON YOURSELF AFTER THAT.

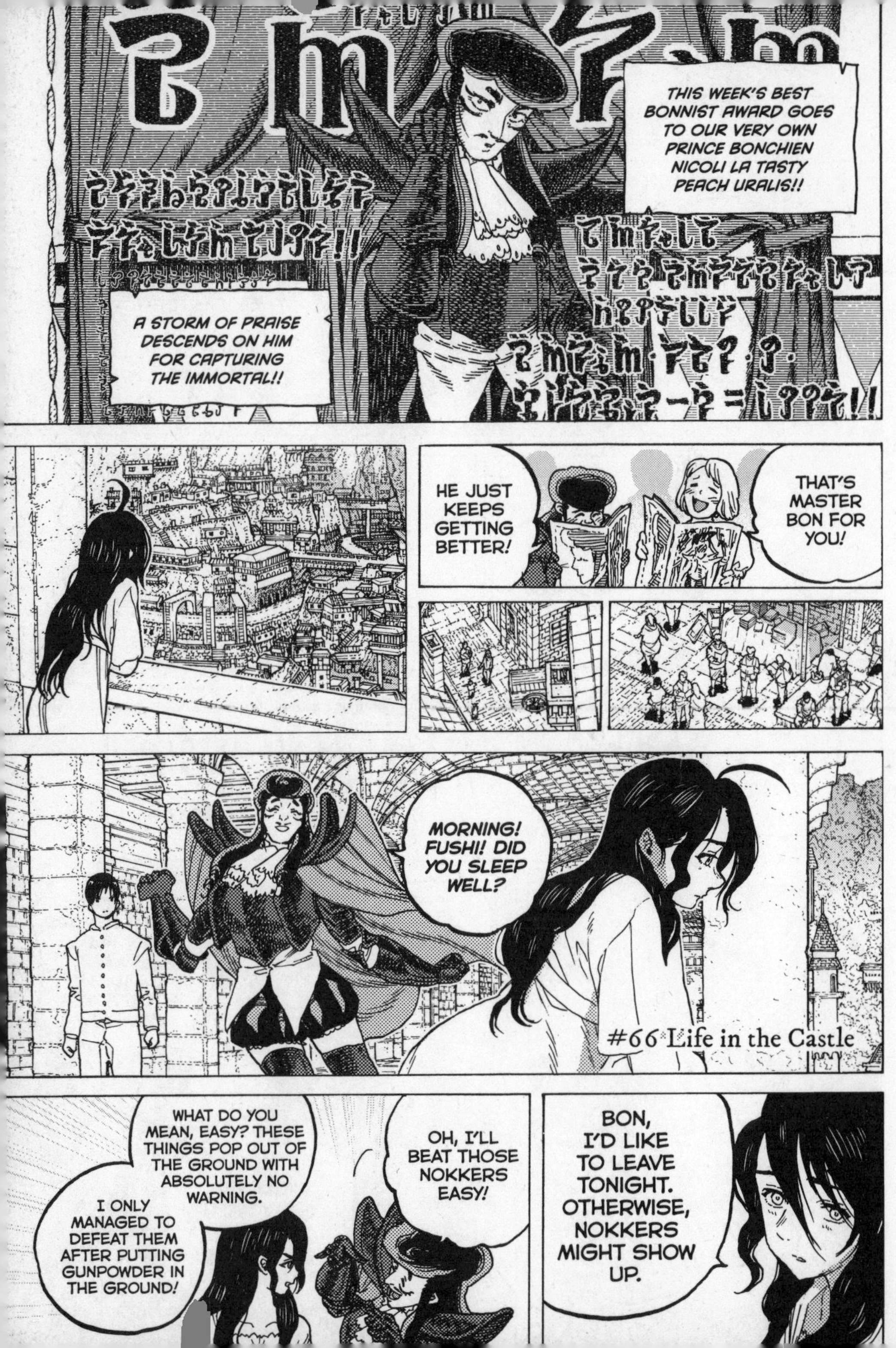
THIS WEEK'S BEST BONNIST AWARD GOES TO OUR VERY OWN PRINCE BONCHIEN NICOLI LA TASTY PEACH URALIS!!
A STORM OF PRAISE DESCENDS ON HIM FOR CAPTURING THE IMMORTAL!!
THAT'S MASTER BON FOR YOU!
HE JUST KEEPS GETTING BETTER!
MORNING! FUSHI! DID YOU SLEEP WELL?
#66 Life in the Castle
BON, I'D LIKE TO LEAVE TONIGHT. OTHERWISE, NOKKERS MIGHT SHOW UP.
OH, I'LL BEAT THOSE NOKKERS EASY!
WHAT DO YOU MEAN, EASY? THESE THINGS POP OUT OF THE GROUND WITH ABSOLUTELY NO WARNING.
I ONLY MANAGED TO DEFEAT THEM AFTER PUTTING GUNPOWDER IN THE GROUND!

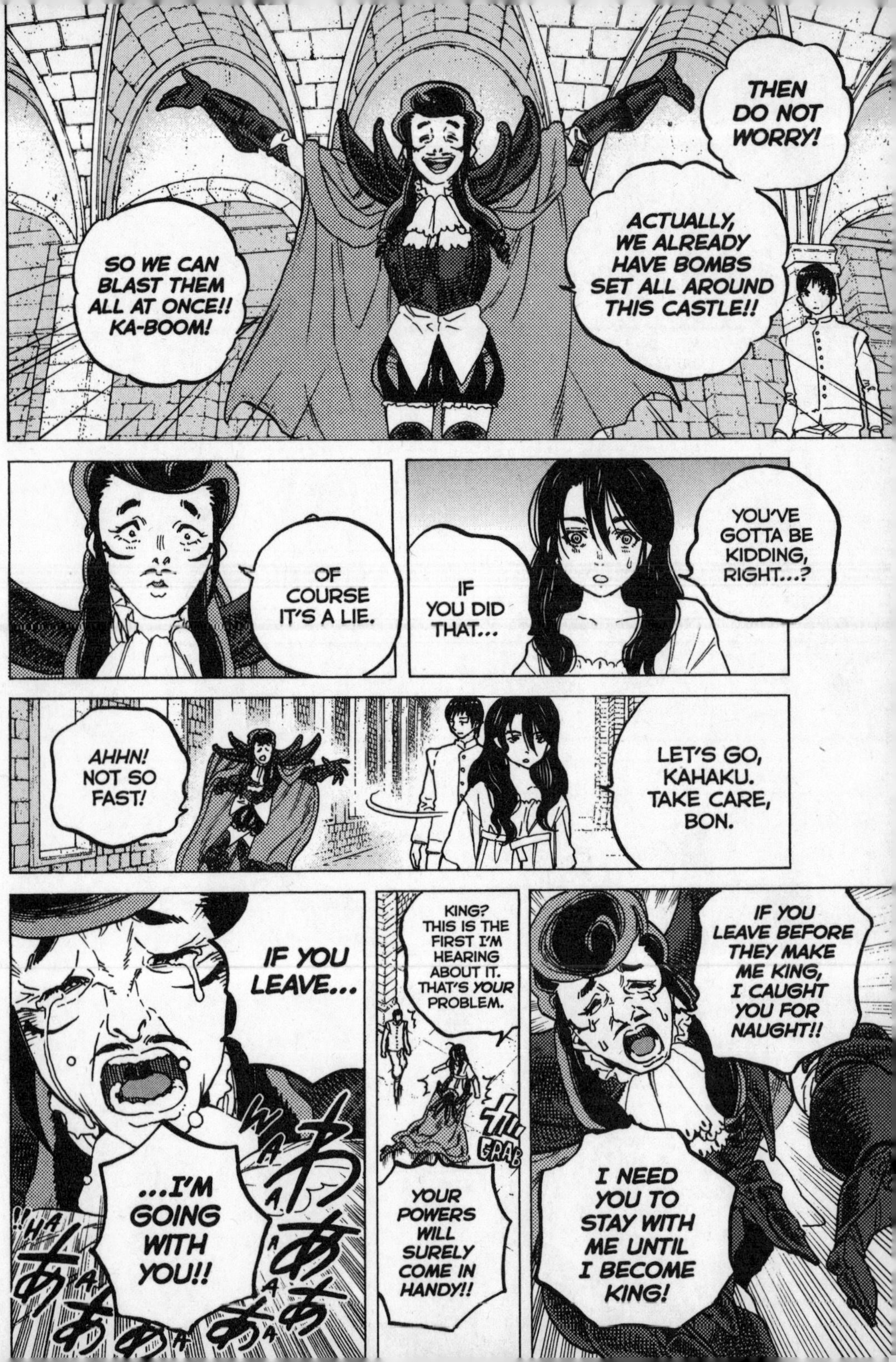
THEN DO NOT WORRY!
ACTUALLY, WE ALREADY HAVE BOMBS SET ALL AROUND THIS CASTLE!!
SO WE CAN BLAST THEM ALL AT ONCE!! KA-BOOM!
YOU'VE GOTTA BE KIDDING, RIGHT...?
IF YOU DID THAT...
OF COURSE IT'S A LIE.
LET'S GO, KAHAKU. TAKE CARE, BON.
AHHN! NOT SO FAST!
IF YOU LEAVE BEFORE THEY MAKE ME KING, I CAUGHT YOU FOR NAUGHT!!
I NEED YOU TO STAY WITH ME UNTIL I BECOME KING!
KING? THIS IS THE FIRST I'M HEARING ABOUT IT. THAT'S YOUR PROBLEM.
GRAB
YOUR POWERS WILL SURELY COME IN HANDY!!
IF YOU LEAVE...
...I'M GOING WITH YOU!!

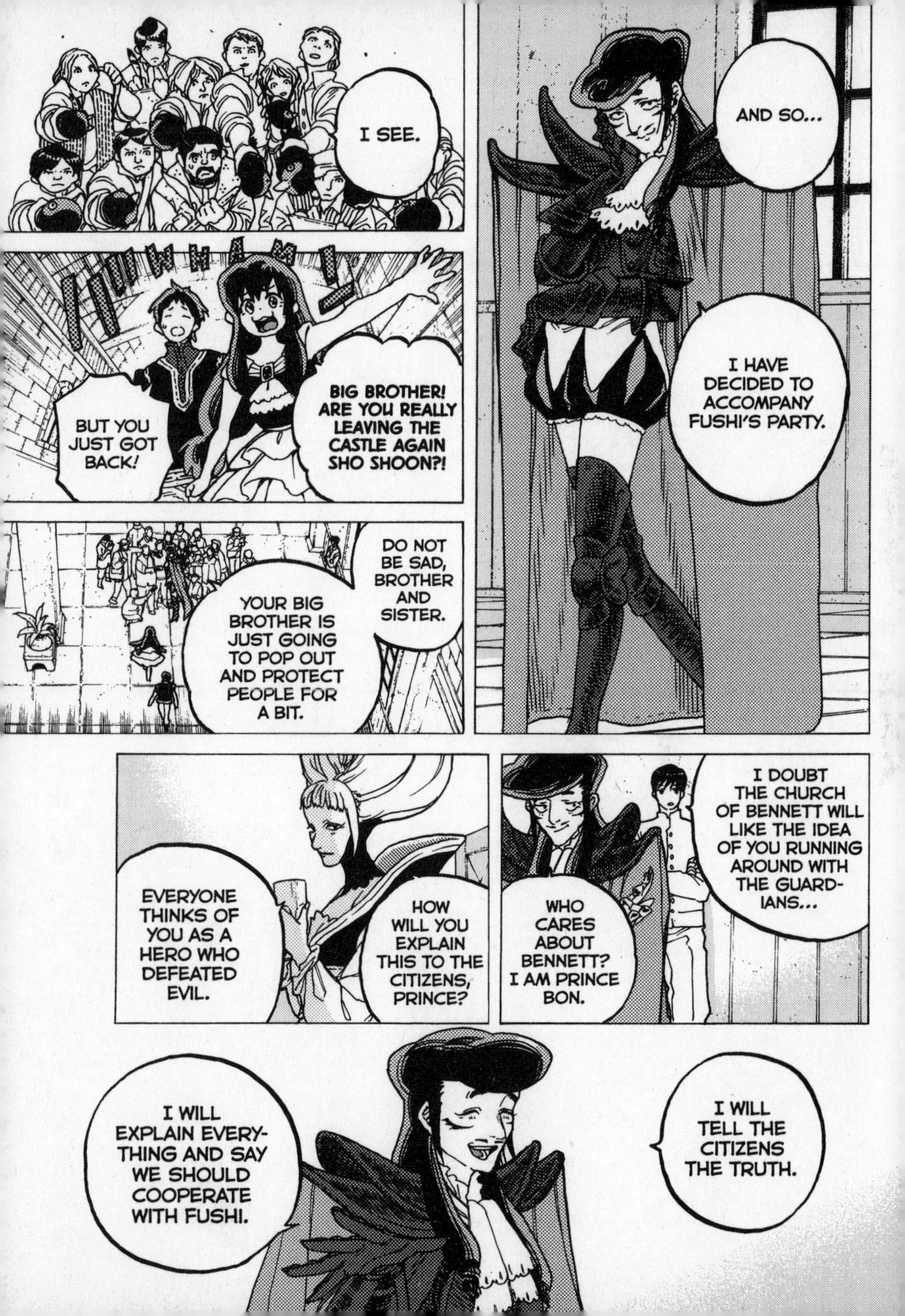
AND SO...
I HAVE DECIDED TO ACCOMPANY FUSHI'S PARTY.
I SEE.
WHAM!!
BIG BROTHER! ARE YOU REALLY LEAVING THE CASTLE AGAIN SHO SHOON?!
BUT YOU JUST GOT BACK!
DO NOT BE SAD, BROTHER AND SISTER.
YOUR BIG BROTHER IS JUST GOING TO POP OUT AND PROTECT PEOPLE FOR A BIT.
I DOUBT THE CHURCH OF BENNETT WILL LIKE THE IDEA OF YOU RUNNING AROUND WITH THE GUARD-IANS...
WHO CARES ABOUT BENNETT? I AM PRINCE BON.
EVERYONE THINKS OF YOU AS A HERO WHO DEFEATED EVIL.
HOW WILL YOU EXPLAIN THIS TO THE CITIZENS, PRINCE?
I WILL TELL THE CITIZENS THE TRUTH.
I WILL EXPLAIN EVERY-THING AND SAY WE SHOULD COOPERATE WITH FUSHI.

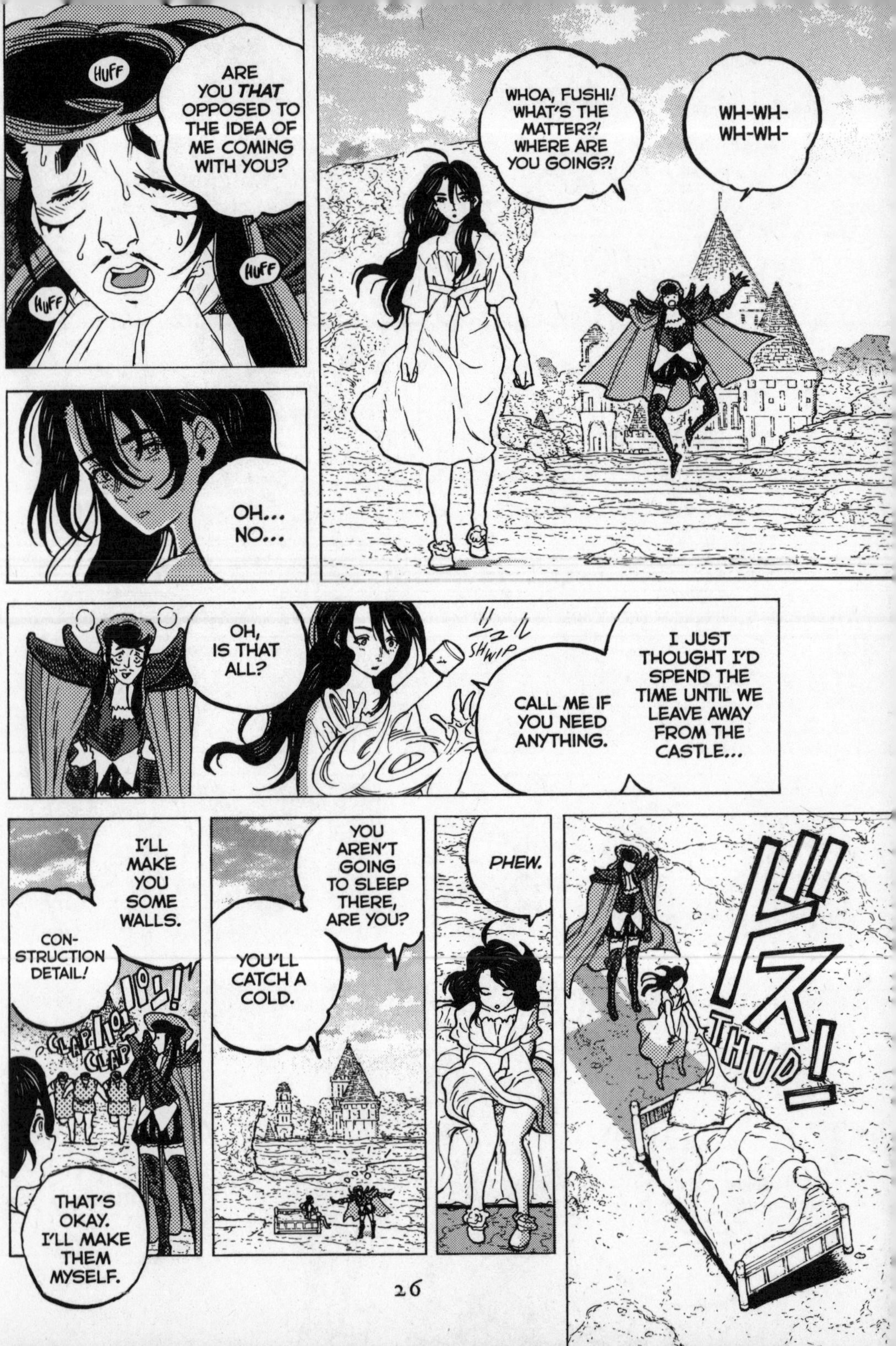
WH-WH-WH-WH-
WHOA, FUSHI! WHAT'S THE MATTER?! WHERE ARE YOU GOING?!
ARE YOU THAT OPPOSED TO THE IDEA OF ME COMING WITH YOU?
HUFF
HUFF
HUFF
OH... NO...
I JUST THOUGHT I'D SPEND THE TIME UNTIL WE LEAVE AWAY FROM THE CASTLE...
CALL ME IF YOU NEED ANYTHING.
SHWIP
OH, IS THAT ALL?
THUD!
PHEW.
YOU AREN'T GOING TO SLEEP THERE, ARE YOU?
YOU'LL CATCH A COLD.
I'LL MAKE YOU SOME WALLS.
CON-STRUCTION DETAIL!
CLAP CLAP
THAT'S OKAY. I'LL MAKE THEM MYSELF.

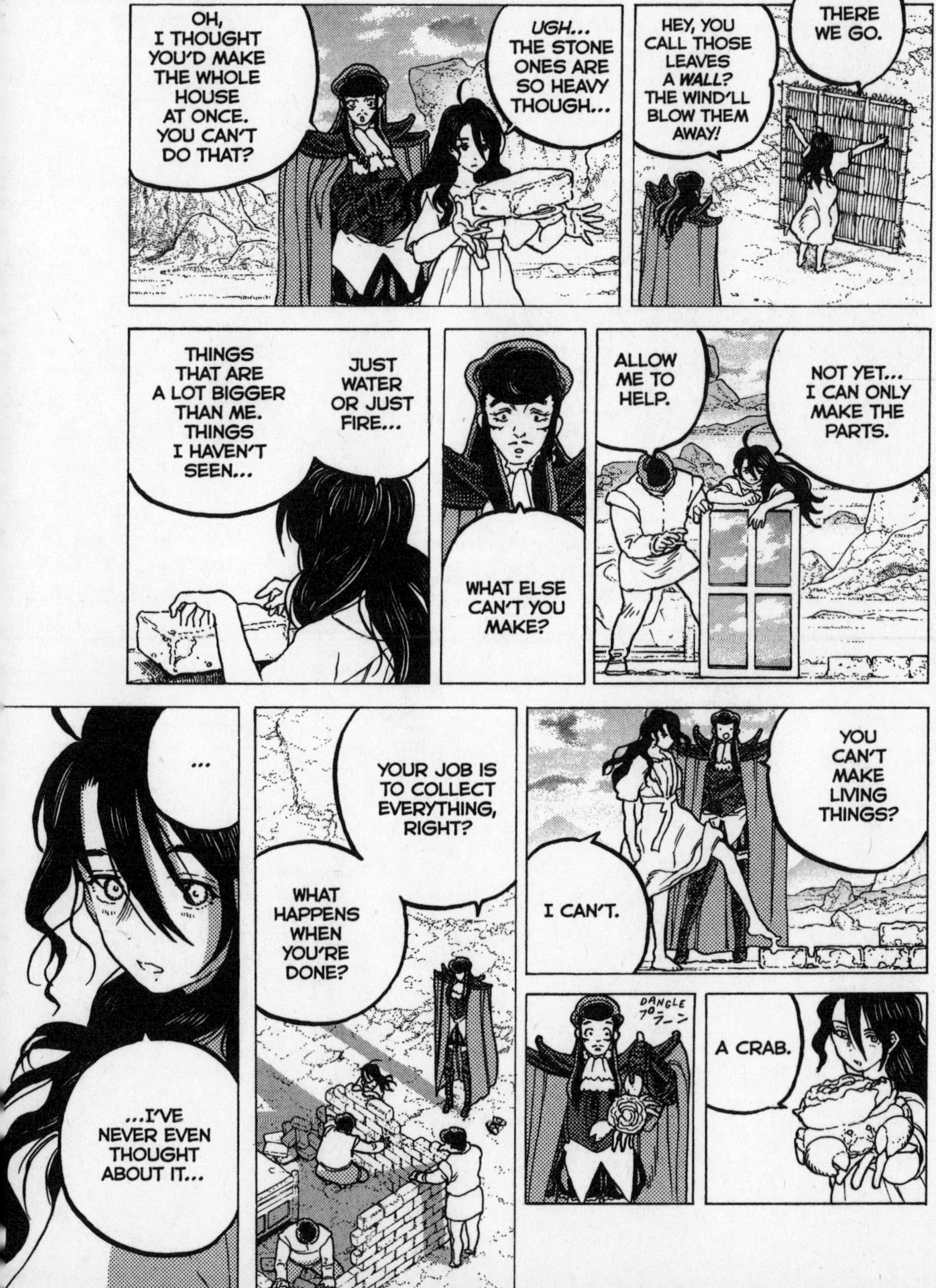
THERE WE GO.
HEY, YOU CALL THOSE LEAVES A *WALL*? THE WIND'LL BLOW THEM AWAY!
UGH... THE STONE ONES ARE SO HEAVY THOUGH...
OH, I THOUGHT YOU'D MAKE THE WHOLE HOUSE AT ONCE. YOU CAN'T DO THAT?
NOT YET... I CAN ONLY MAKE THE PARTS.
ALLOW ME TO HELP.
WHAT ELSE CAN'T YOU MAKE?
JUST WATER OR JUST FIRE...
THINGS THAT ARE A LOT BIGGER THAN ME. THINGS I HAVEN'T SEEN...
YOU CAN'T MAKE LIVING THINGS?
I CAN'T.
A CRAB.
DANGLE
YOUR JOB IS TO COLLECT EVERYTHING, RIGHT?
WHAT HAPPENS WHEN YOU'RE DONE?
...
...I'VE NEVER EVEN THOUGHT ABOUT IT...

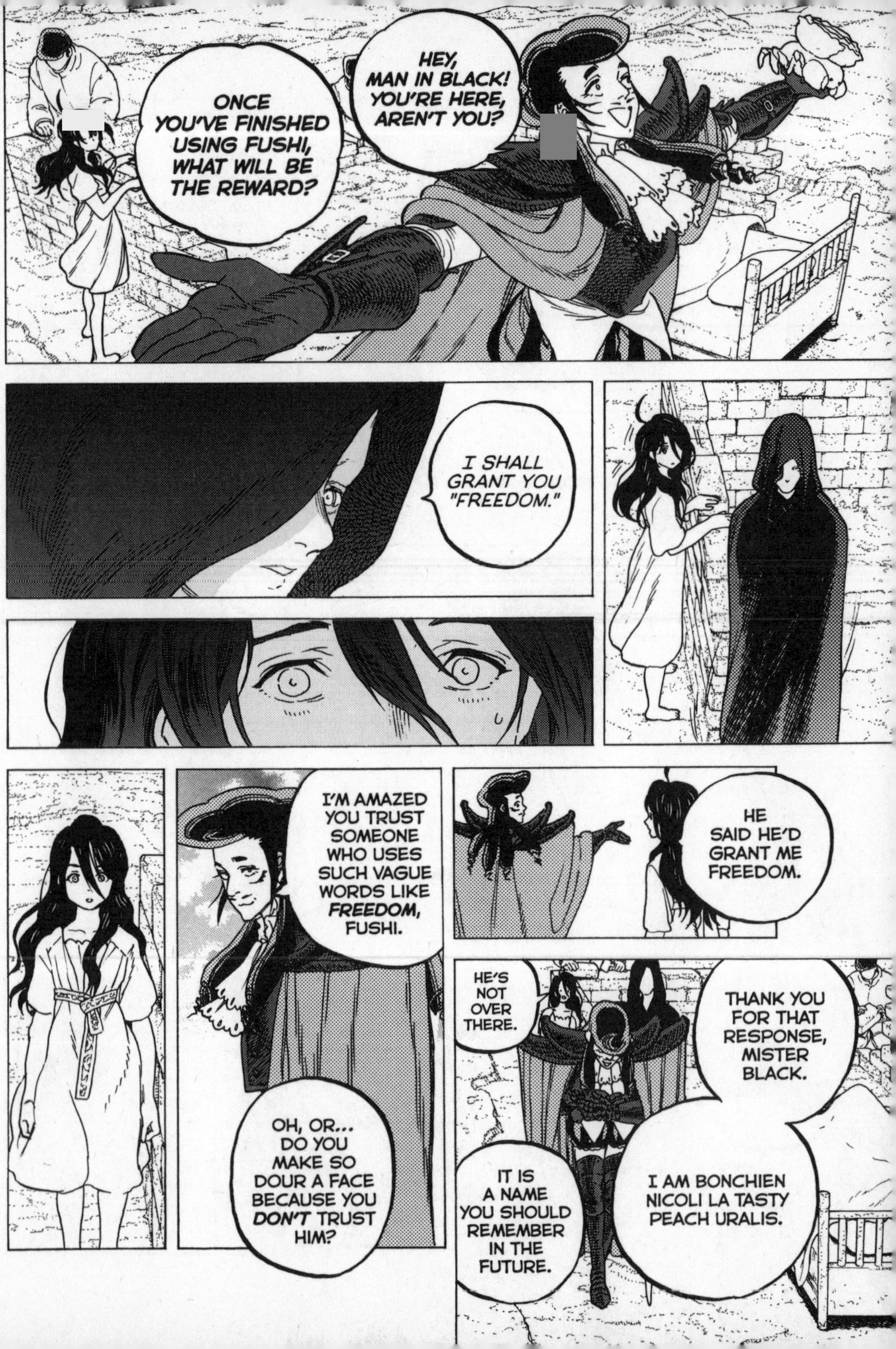
HEY, MAN IN BLACK! YOU'RE HERE, AREN'T YOU?
ONCE YOU'VE FINISHED USING FUSHI, WHAT WILL BE THE REWARD?
I SHALL GRANT YOU "FREEDOM."
HE SAID HE'D GRANT ME FREEDOM.
THANK YOU FOR THAT RESPONSE, MISTER BLACK.
HE'S NOT OVER THERE.
I AM BONCHIEN NICOLI LA TASTY PEACH URALIS.
IT IS A NAME YOU SHOULD REMEMBER IN THE FUTURE.
I'M AMAZED YOU TRUST SOMEONE WHO USES SUCH VAGUE WORDS LIKE ***FREEDOM***, FUSHI.
OH, OR... DO YOU MAKE SO DOUR A FACE BECAUSE YOU ***DON'T*** TRUST HIM?

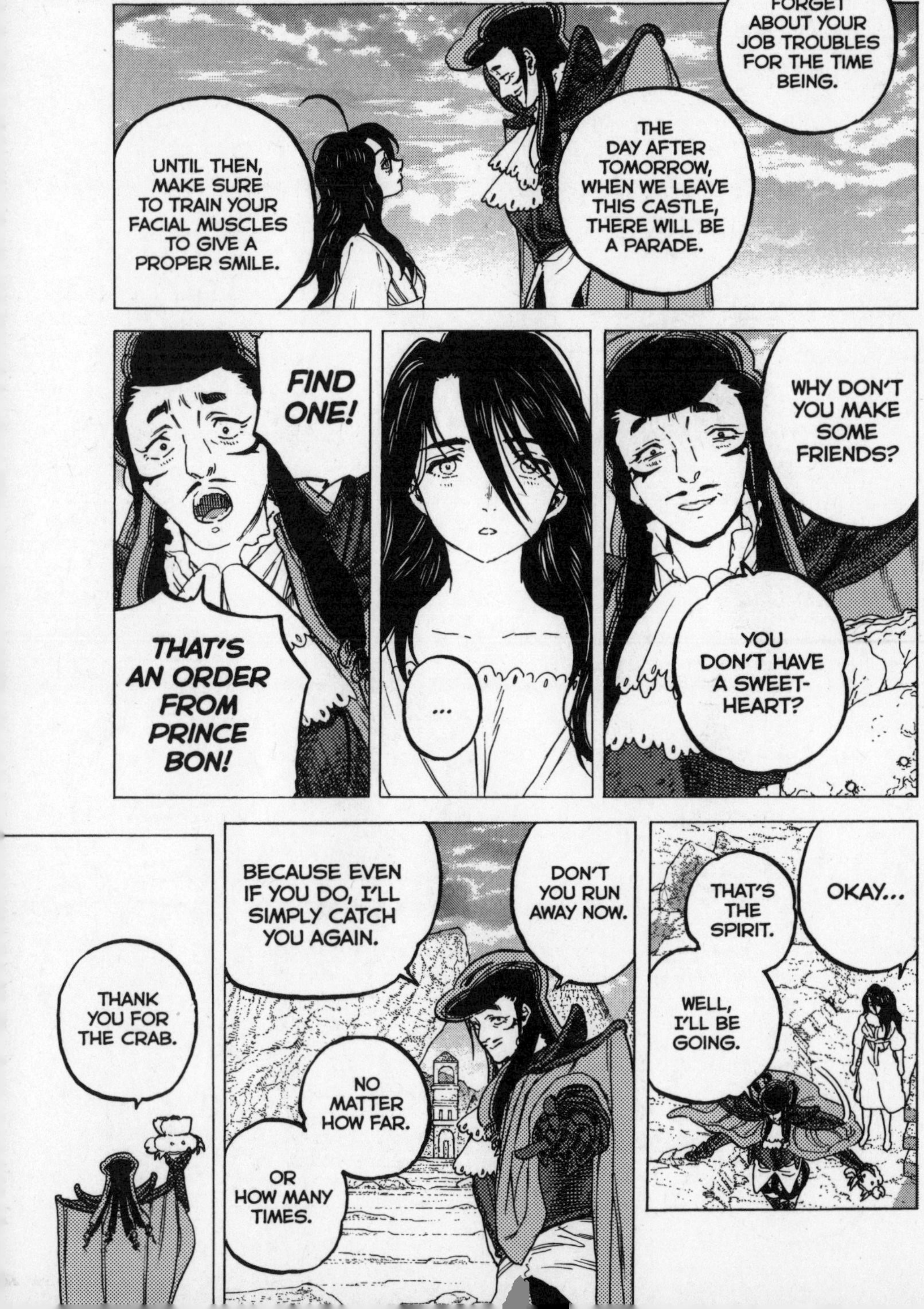
FORGET ABOUT YOUR JOB TROUBLES FOR THE TIME BEING.
THE DAY AFTER TOMORROW, WHEN WE LEAVE THIS CASTLE, THERE WILL BE A PARADE.
UNTIL THEN, MAKE SURE TO TRAIN YOUR FACIAL MUSCLES TO GIVE A PROPER SMILE.
WHY DON'T YOU MAKE SOME FRIENDS?
YOU DON'T HAVE A SWEET-HEART?
...
FIND ONE!
THAT'S AN ORDER FROM PRINCE BON!
OKAY...
THAT'S THE SPIRIT.
WELL, I'LL BE GOING.
DON'T YOU RUN AWAY NOW.
BECAUSE EVEN IF YOU DO, I'LL SIMPLY CATCH YOU AGAIN.
NO MATTER HOW FAR.
OR HOW MANY TIMES.
THANK YOU FOR THE CRAB.

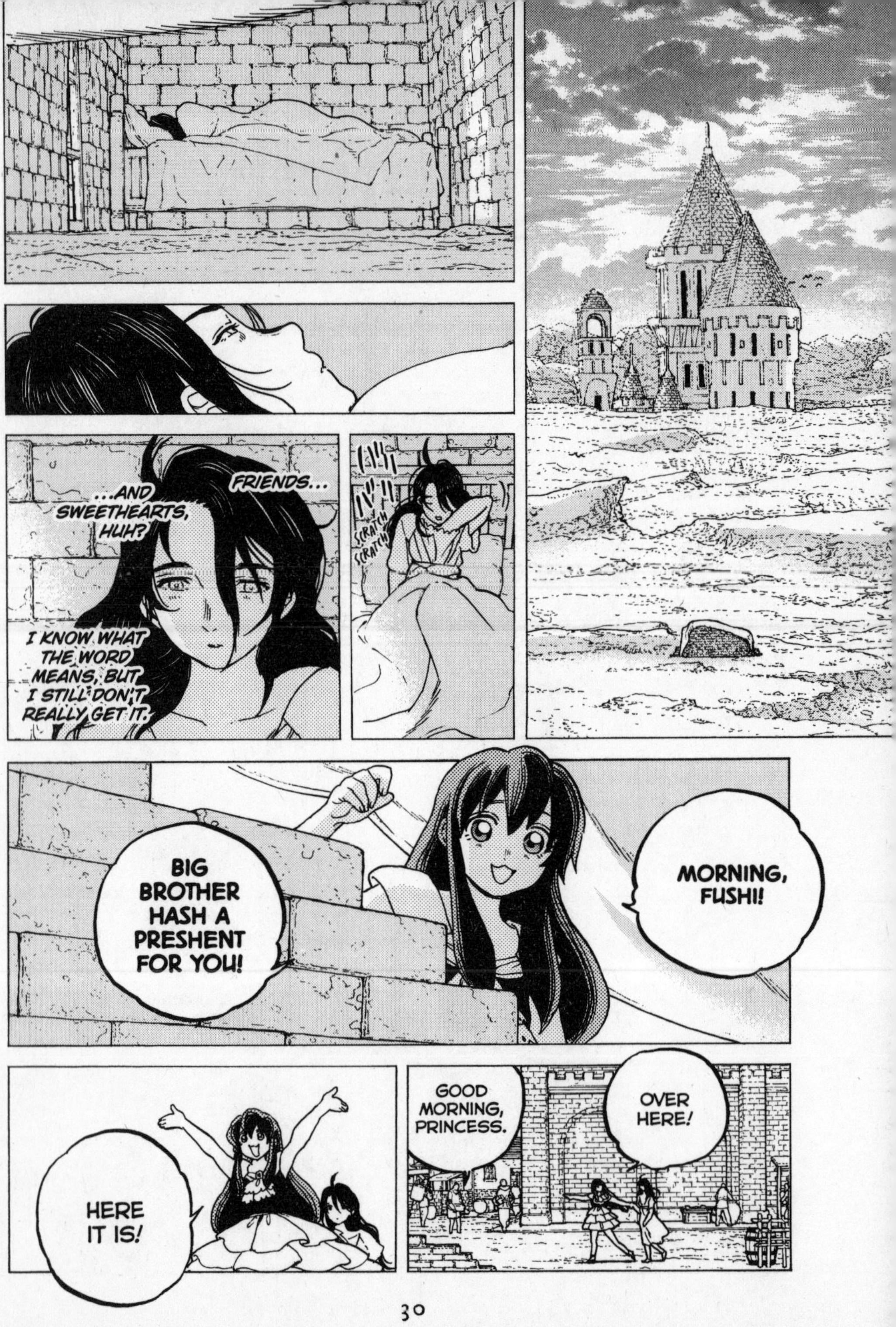
FRIENDS...
...AND SWEETHEARTS, HUH?
I KNOW WHAT THE WORD MEANS, BUT I STILL DON'T REALLY GET IT.
SCRATCH SCRATCH
MORNING, FUSHI!
BIG BROTHER HASH A PRESHENT FOR YOU!
OVER HERE!
GOOD MORNING, PRINCESS.
HERE IT IS!

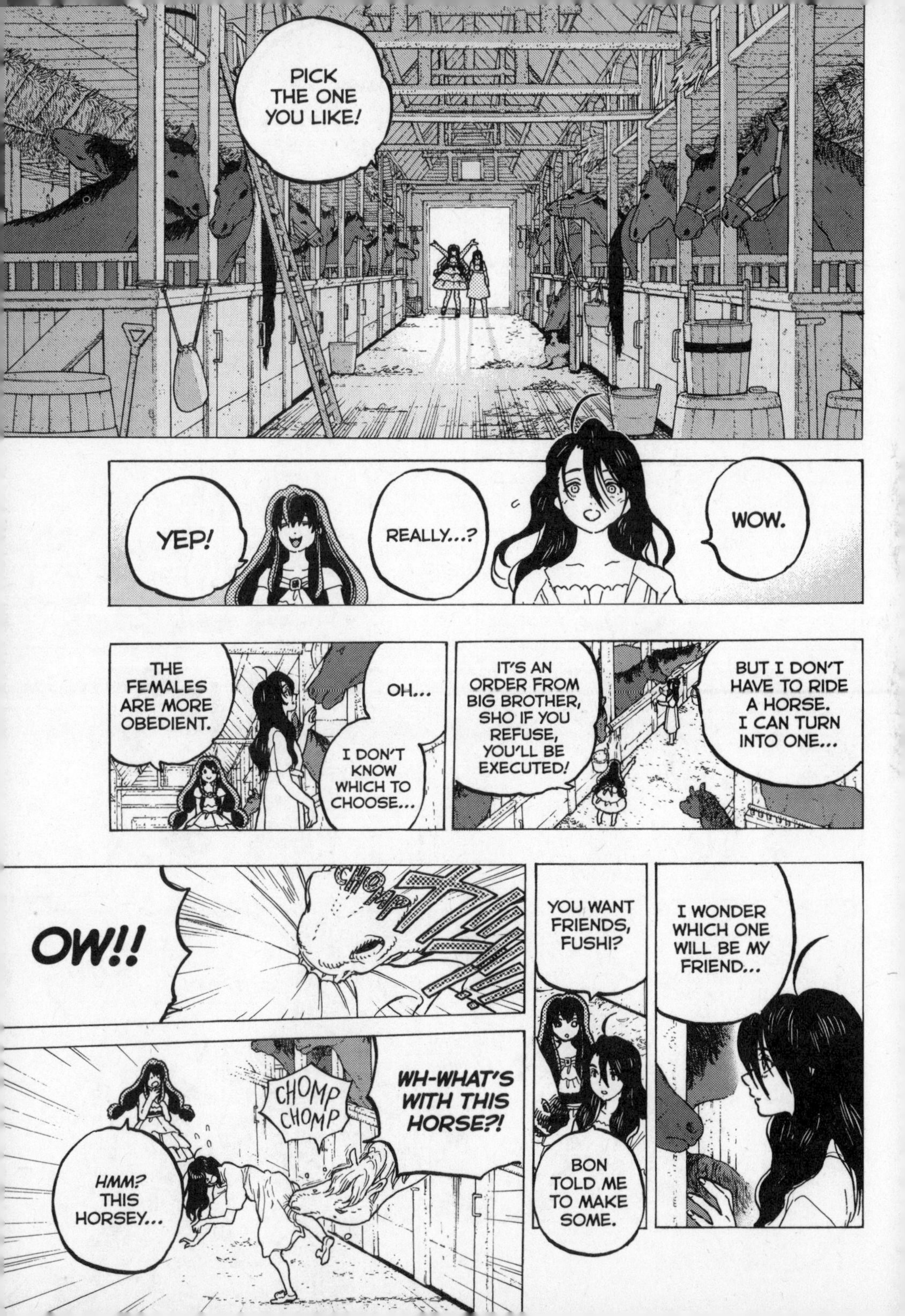
PICK THE ONE YOU LIKE!
WOW.
REALLY...?
YEP!
BUT I DON'T HAVE TO RIDE A HORSE. I CAN TURN INTO ONE...
IT'S AN ORDER FROM BIG BROTHER, SHO IF YOU REFUSE, YOU'LL BE EXECUTED!
OH... I DON'T KNOW WHICH TO CHOOSE...
THE FEMALES ARE MORE OBEDIENT.
I WONDER WHICH ONE WILL BE MY FRIEND...
YOU WANT FRIENDS, FUSHI?
BON TOLD ME TO MAKE SOME.
CHOMP
OW!!
WH-WHAT'S WITH THIS HORSE?!
CHOMP CHOMP
HMM? THIS HORSEY...

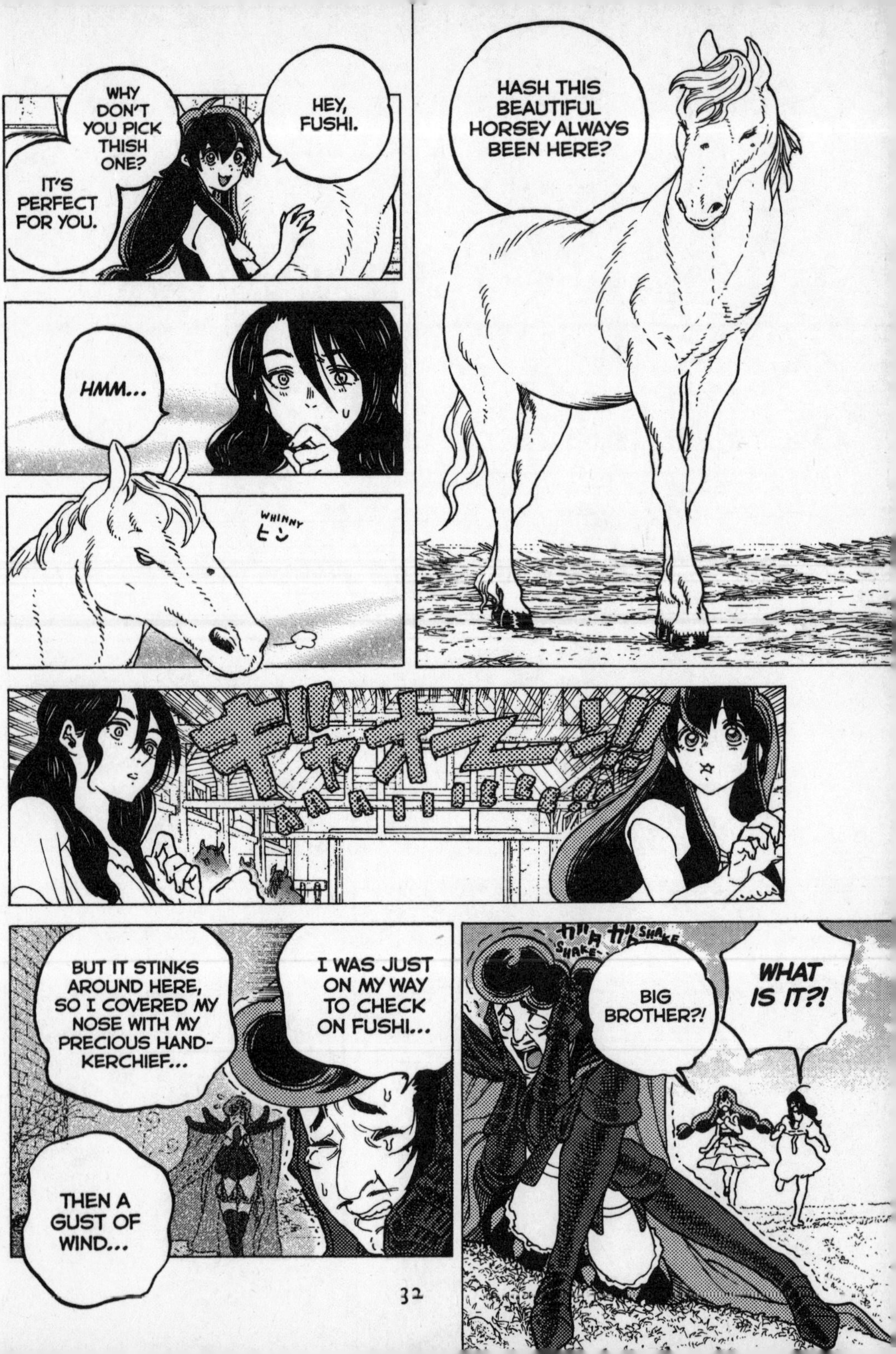
HASH THIS BEAUTIFUL HORSEY ALWAYS BEEN HERE?
HEY, FUSHI.
WHY DON'T YOU PICK THISH ONE?
IT'S PERFECT FOR YOU.
HMM...
WHINNY ヒン
WHAT IS IT?!
BIG BROTHER?!
SHAKE SHAKE
I WAS JUST ON MY WAY TO CHECK ON FUSHI...
BUT IT STINKS AROUND HERE, SO I COVERED MY NOSE WITH MY PRECIOUS HAND-KERCHIEF...
THEN A GUST OF WIND...

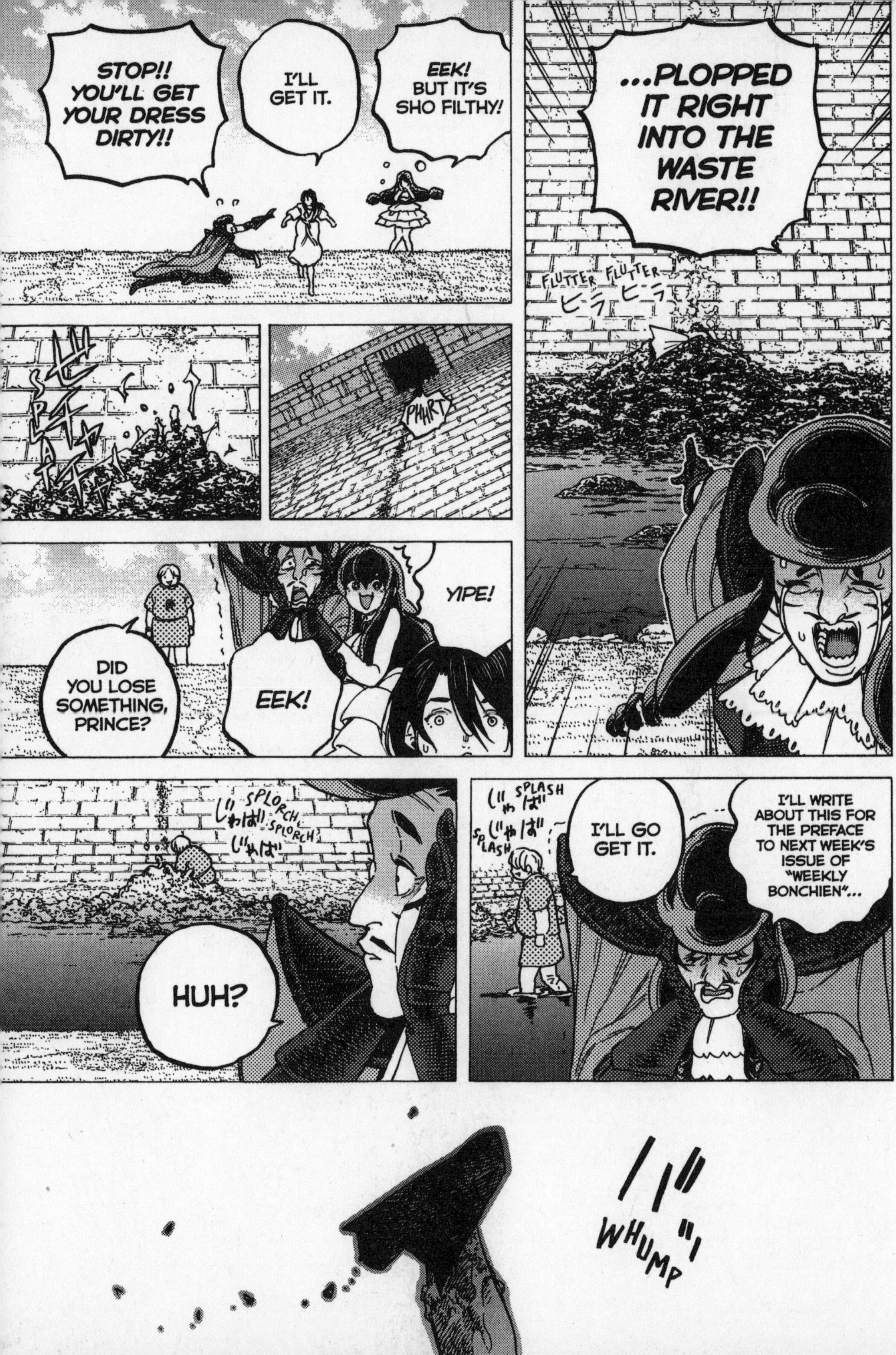
...PLOPPED IT RIGHT INTO THE WASTE RIVER!!
FLUTTER FLUTTER
ヒラヒラ
EEK! BUT IT'S SHO FILTHY!
I'LL GET IT.
STOP!! YOU'LL GET YOUR DRESS DIRTY!!
PHHRT
YIPE!
EEK!
DID YOU LOSE SOMETHING, PRINCE?
I'LL WRITE ABOUT THIS FOR THE PREFACE TO NEXT WEEK'S ISSUE OF "WEEKLY BONCHIEN"...
I'LL GO GET IT.
SPLASH じゃぱ
SPLASH じゃぱ
SPLORCH じゃぱ
SPLORCH じゃぱ
HUH?
WHUMP

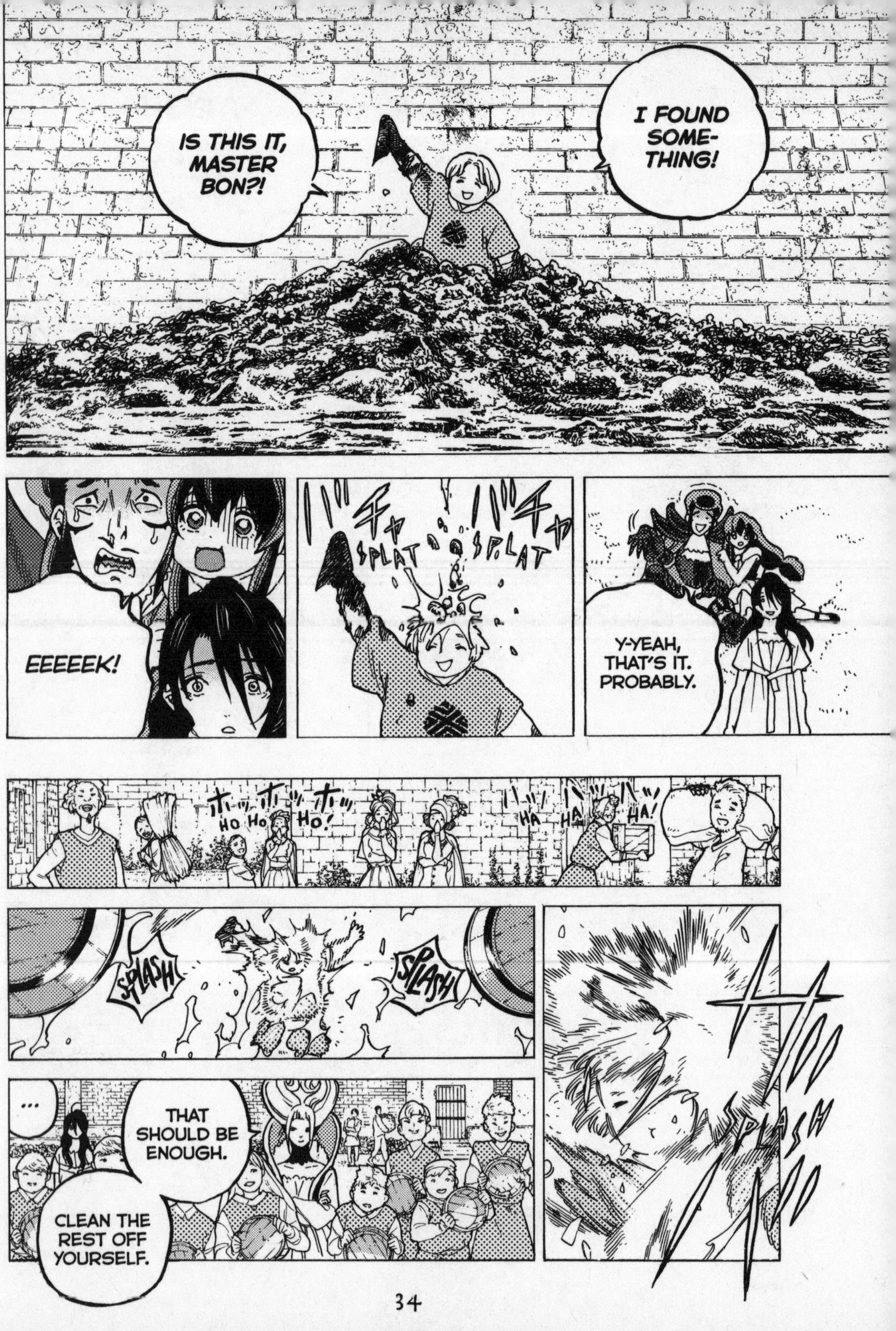
I FOUND SOME-THING!
IS THIS IT, MASTER BON?!
Y-YEAH, THAT'S IT. PROBABLY.
SPLAT SPLAT
EEEEEK!
HA! HA! HA!
HO HO HO!
SPLASH
SPLASH SPLASH
THAT SHOULD BE ENOUGH.
CLEAN THE REST OFF YOURSELF.
...

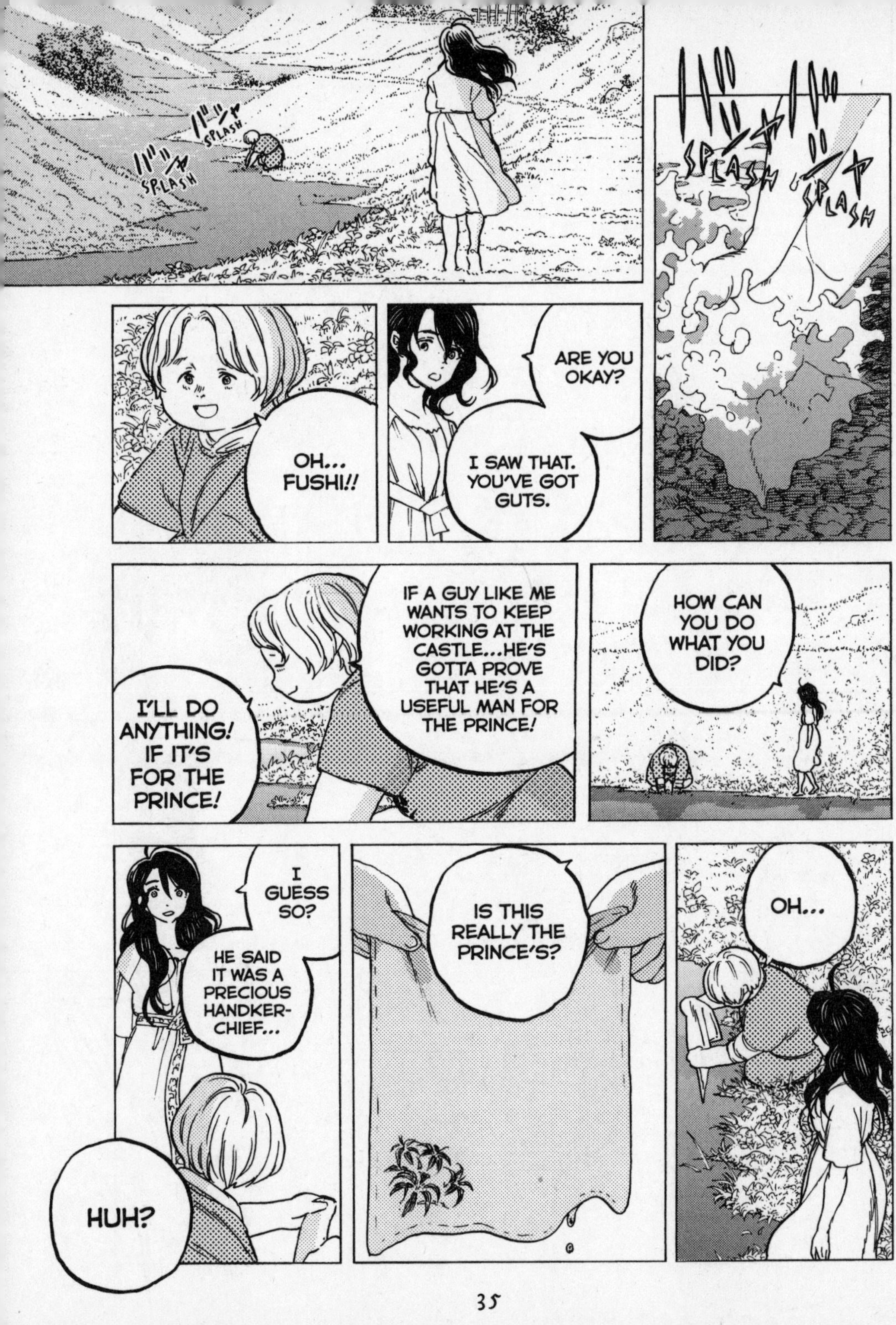
SPLASH
SPLASH
SPLASH
SPLASH
ARE YOU OKAY?
I SAW THAT. YOU'VE GOT GUTS.
OH... FUSHI!!
HOW CAN YOU DO WHAT YOU DID?
IF A GUY LIKE ME WANTS TO KEEP WORKING AT THE CASTLE...HE'S GOTTA PROVE THAT HE'S A USEFUL MAN FOR THE PRINCE!
I'LL DO ANYTHING! IF IT'S FOR THE PRINCE!
OH...
IS THIS REALLY THE PRINCE'S?
I GUESS SO?
HE SAID IT WAS A PRECIOUS HANDKER-CHIEF...
HUH?

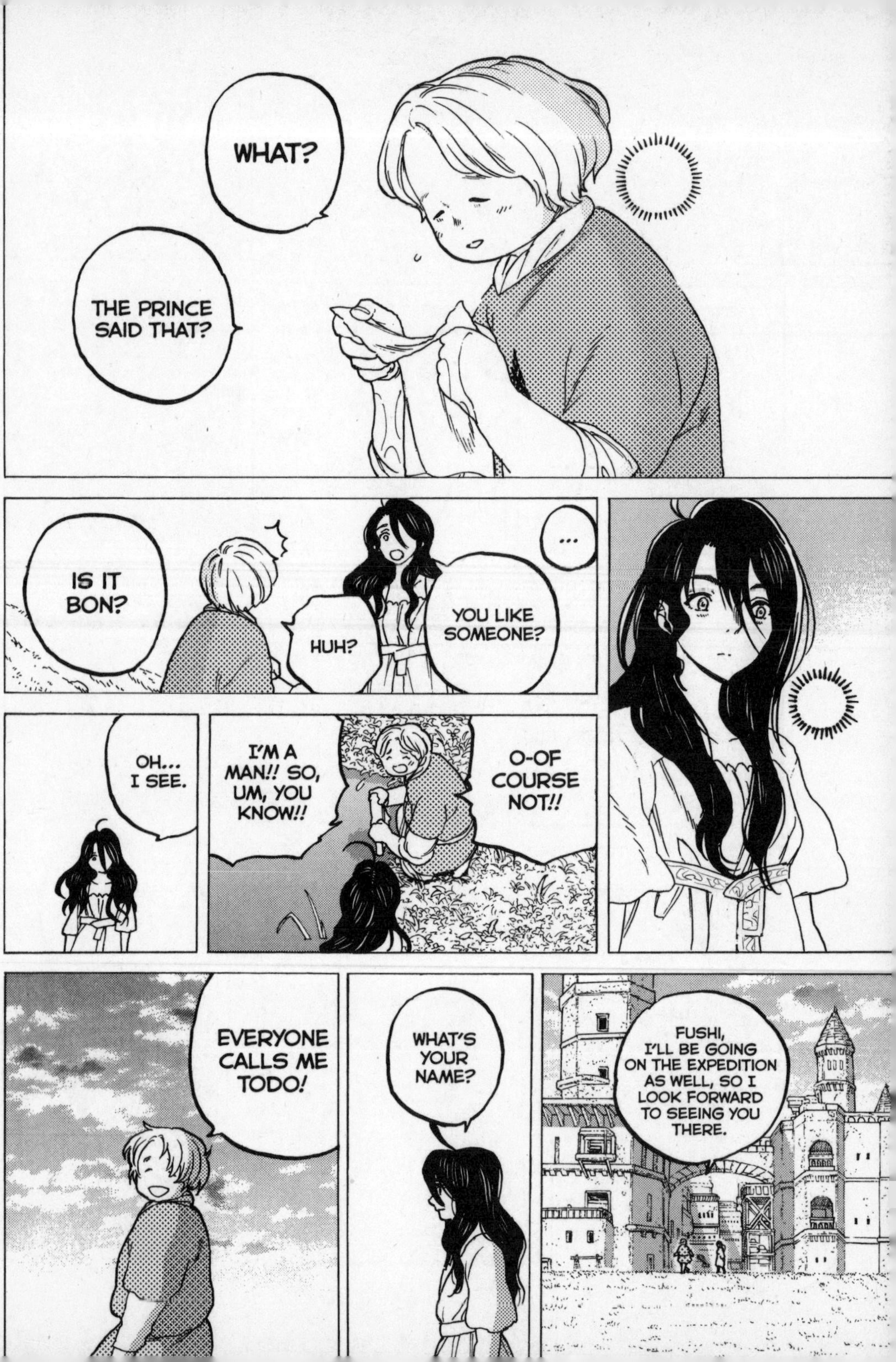
WHAT?
THE PRINCE SAID THAT?
...
YOU LIKE SOMEONE?
HUH?
IS IT BON?
O-OF COURSE NOT!!
I'M A MAN!! SO, UM, YOU KNOW!!
OH... I SEE.
FUSHI, I'LL BE GOING ON THE EXPEDITION AS WELL, SO I LOOK FORWARD TO SEEING YOU THERE.
WHAT'S YOUR NAME?
EVERYONE CALLS ME TODO!

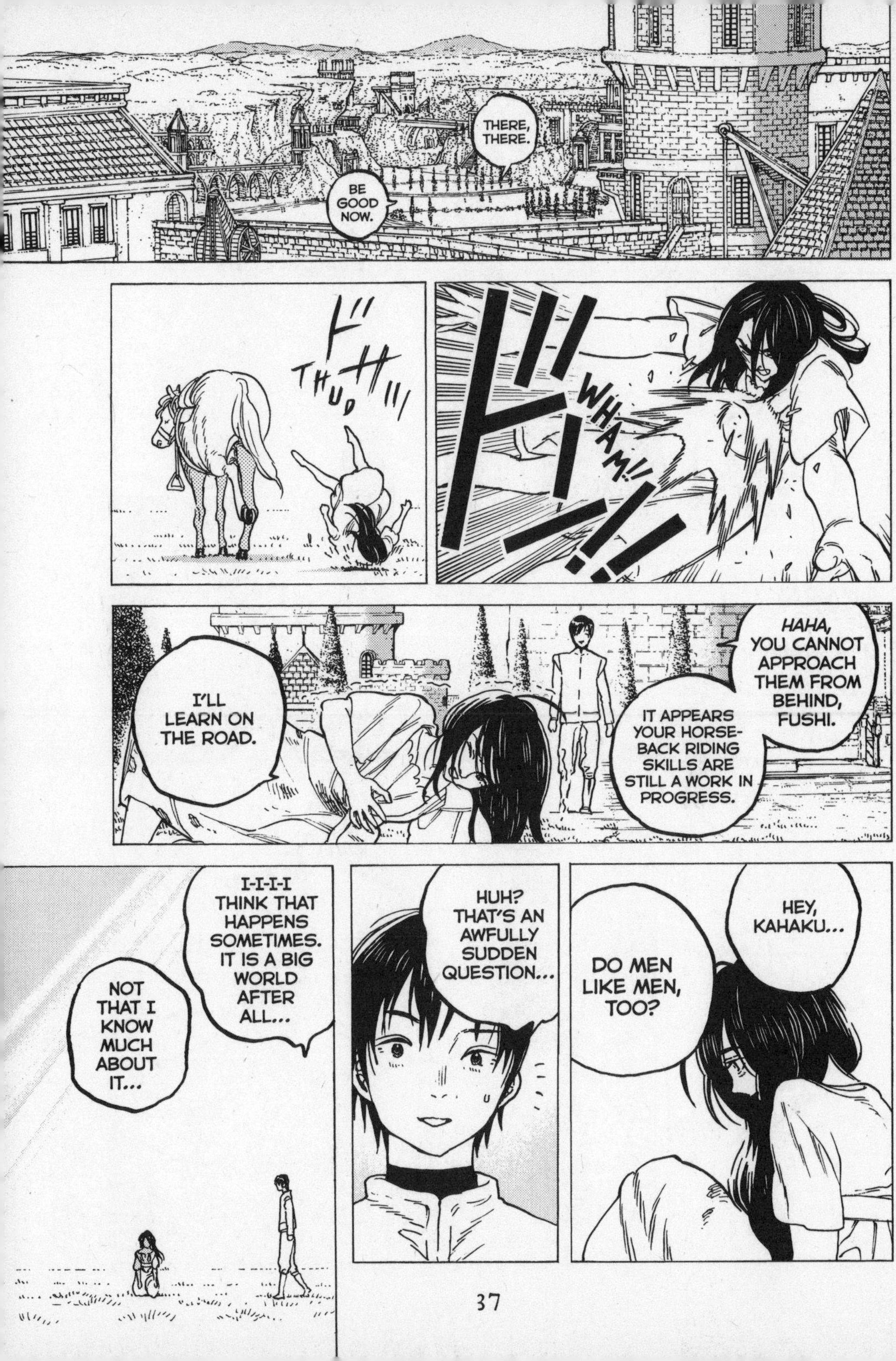
THERE, THERE.
BE GOOD NOW.
WHAM!!
THUD
HAHA, YOU CANNOT APPROACH THEM FROM BEHIND, FUSHI.
IT APPEARS YOUR HORSE-BACK RIDING SKILLS ARE STILL A WORK IN PROGRESS.
I'LL LEARN ON THE ROAD.
HEY, KAHAKU...
DO MEN LIKE MEN, TOO?
HUH? THAT'S AN AWFULLY SUDDEN QUESTION...
I-I-I-I THINK THAT HAPPENS SOMETIMES. IT IS A BIG WORLD AFTER ALL...
NOT THAT I KNOW MUCH ABOUT IT...

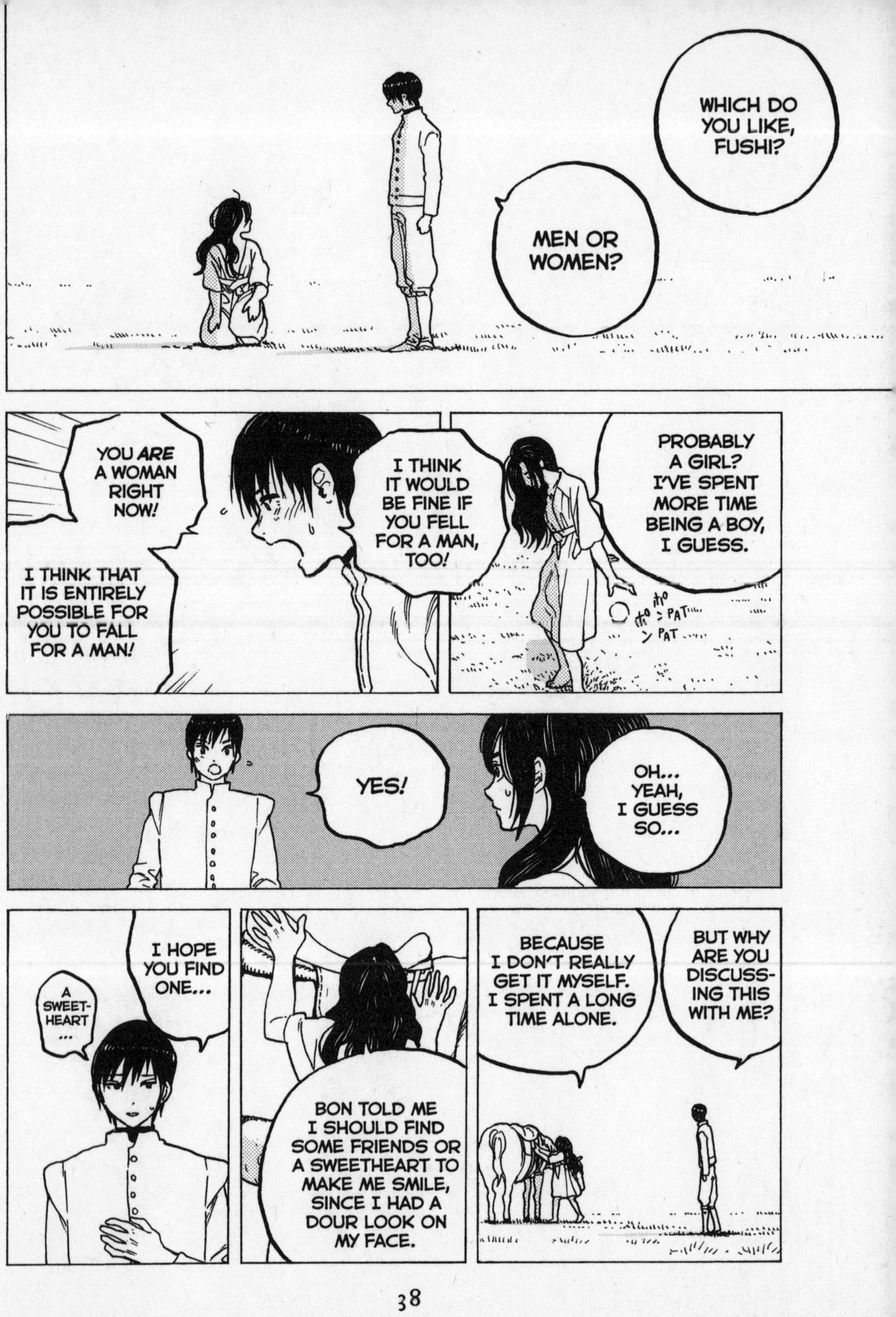
WHICH DO YOU LIKE, FUSHI?
MEN OR WOMEN?
PROBABLY A GIRL? I'VE SPENT MORE TIME BEING A BOY, I GUESS.
PAT PAT
I THINK IT WOULD BE FINE IF YOU FELL FOR A MAN, TOO!
YOU *ARE* A WOMAN RIGHT NOW!
I THINK THAT IT IS ENTIRELY POSSIBLE FOR YOU TO FALL FOR A MAN!
OH... YEAH, I GUESS SO...
YES!
BUT WHY ARE YOU DISCUSSING THIS WITH ME?
BECAUSE I DON'T REALLY GET IT MYSELF. I SPENT A LONG TIME ALONE.
BON TOLD ME I SHOULD FIND SOME FRIENDS OR A SWEETHEART TO MAKE ME SMILE, SINCE I HAD A DOUR LOOK ON MY FACE.
I HOPE YOU FIND ONE...
A SWEETHEART...

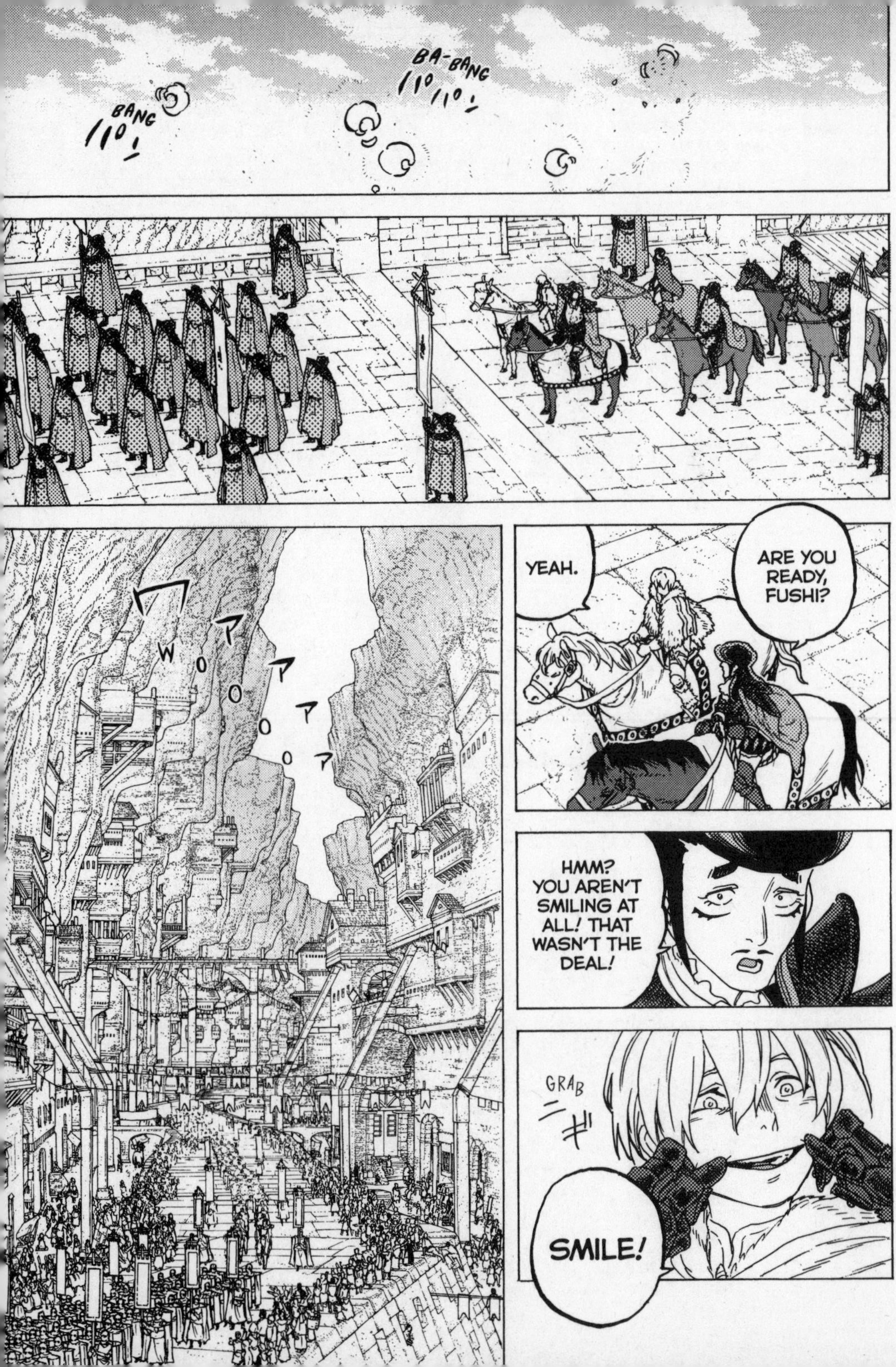
BA-BANG
BANG
ARE YOU READY, FUSHI?
YEAH.
HMM? YOU AREN'T SMILING AT ALL! THAT WASN'T THE DEAL!
GRAB
SMILE!
WOOOO

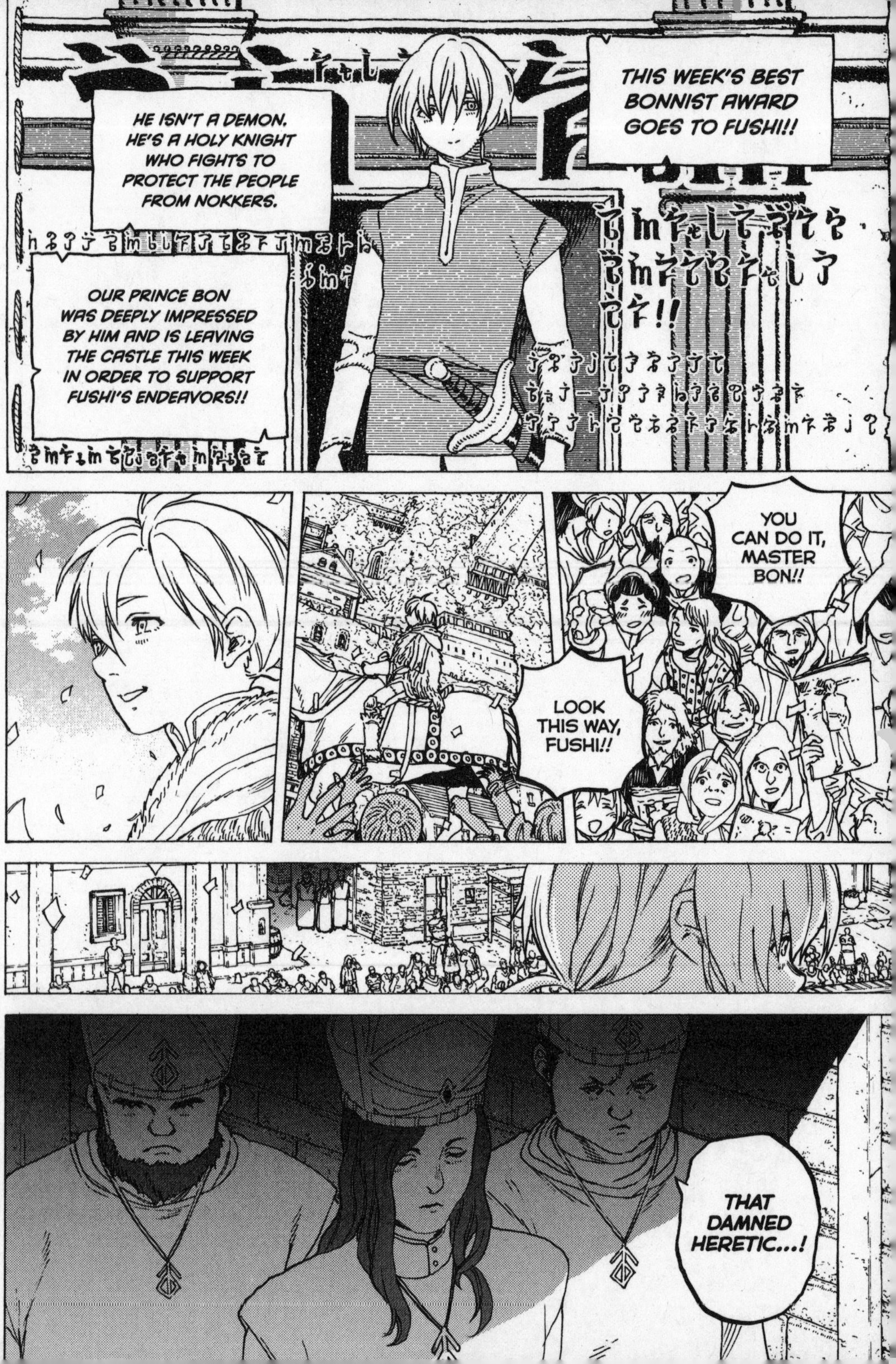
THIS WEEK'S BEST BONNIST AWARD GOES TO FUSHI!!
HE ISN'T A DEMON. HE'S A HOLY KNIGHT WHO FIGHTS TO PROTECT THE PEOPLE FROM NOKKERS.
OUR PRINCE BON WAS DEEPLY IMPRESSED BY HIM AND IS LEAVING THE CASTLE THIS WEEK IN ORDER TO SUPPORT FUSHI'S ENDEAVORS!!
YOU CAN DO IT, MASTER BON!!
LOOK THIS WAY, FUSHI!!
THAT DAMNED HERETIC...!

#67 Expedition of the Holy One

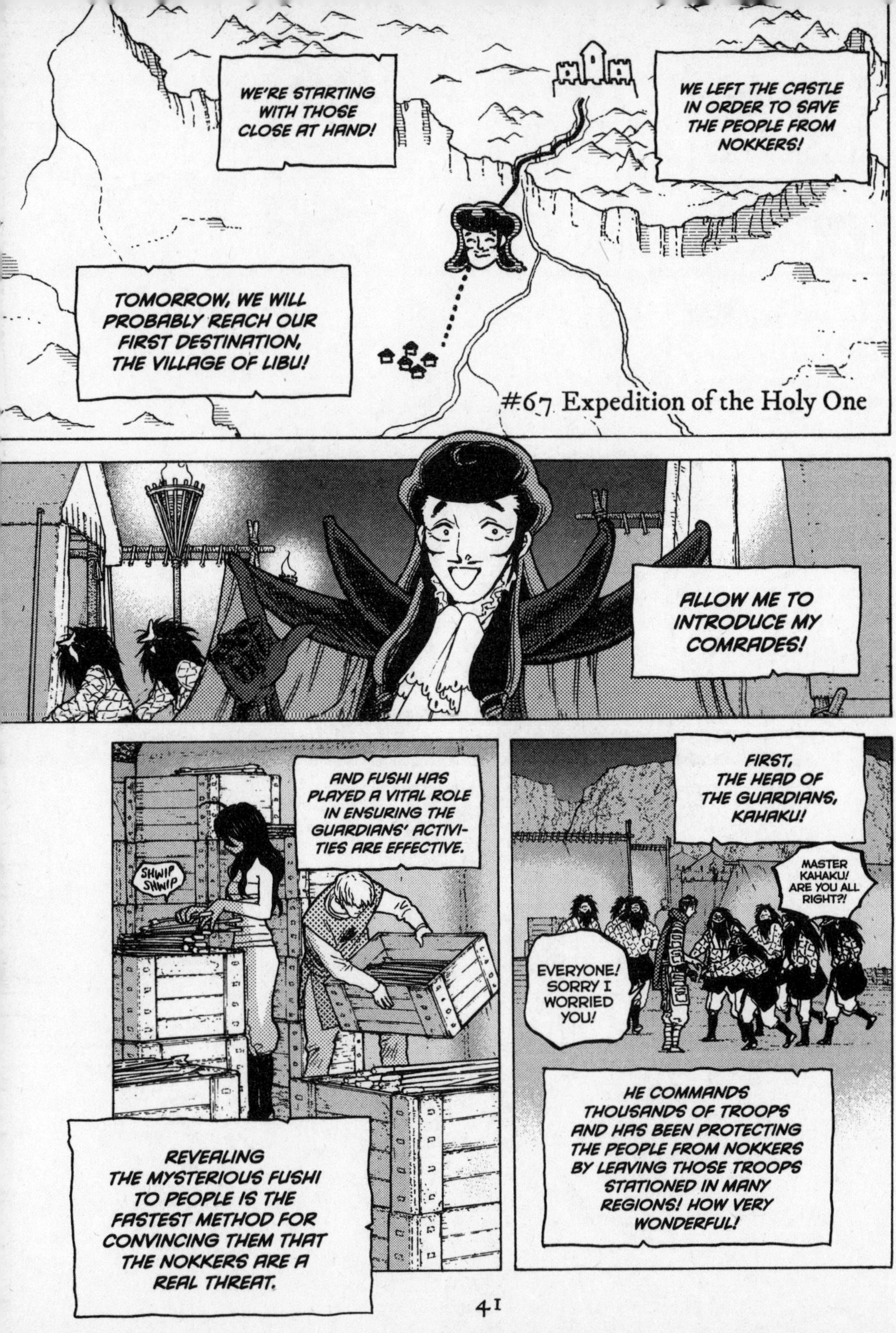

WE LEFT THE CASTLE IN ORDER TO SAVE THE PEOPLE FROM NOKKERS!
WE'RE STARTING WITH THOSE CLOSE AT HAND!
TOMORROW, WE WILL PROBABLY REACH OUR FIRST DESTINATION, THE VILLAGE OF LIBU!
ALLOW ME TO INTRODUCE MY COMRADES!
FIRST, THE HEAD OF THE GUARDIANS, KAHAKU!
MASTER KAHAKU! ARE YOU ALL RIGHT?!
EVERYONE! SORRY I WORRIED YOU!
HE COMMANDS THOUSANDS OF TROOPS AND HAS BEEN PROTECTING THE PEOPLE FROM NOKKERS BY LEAVING THOSE TROOPS STATIONED IN MANY REGIONS! HOW VERY WONDERFUL!
AND FUSHI HAS PLAYED A VITAL ROLE IN ENSURING THE GUARDIANS' ACTIVITIES ARE EFFECTIVE.
SHWIP SHWIP
REVEALING THE MYSTERIOUS FUSHI TO PEOPLE IS THE FASTEST METHOD FOR CONVINCING THEM THAT THE NOKKERS ARE A REAL THREAT.

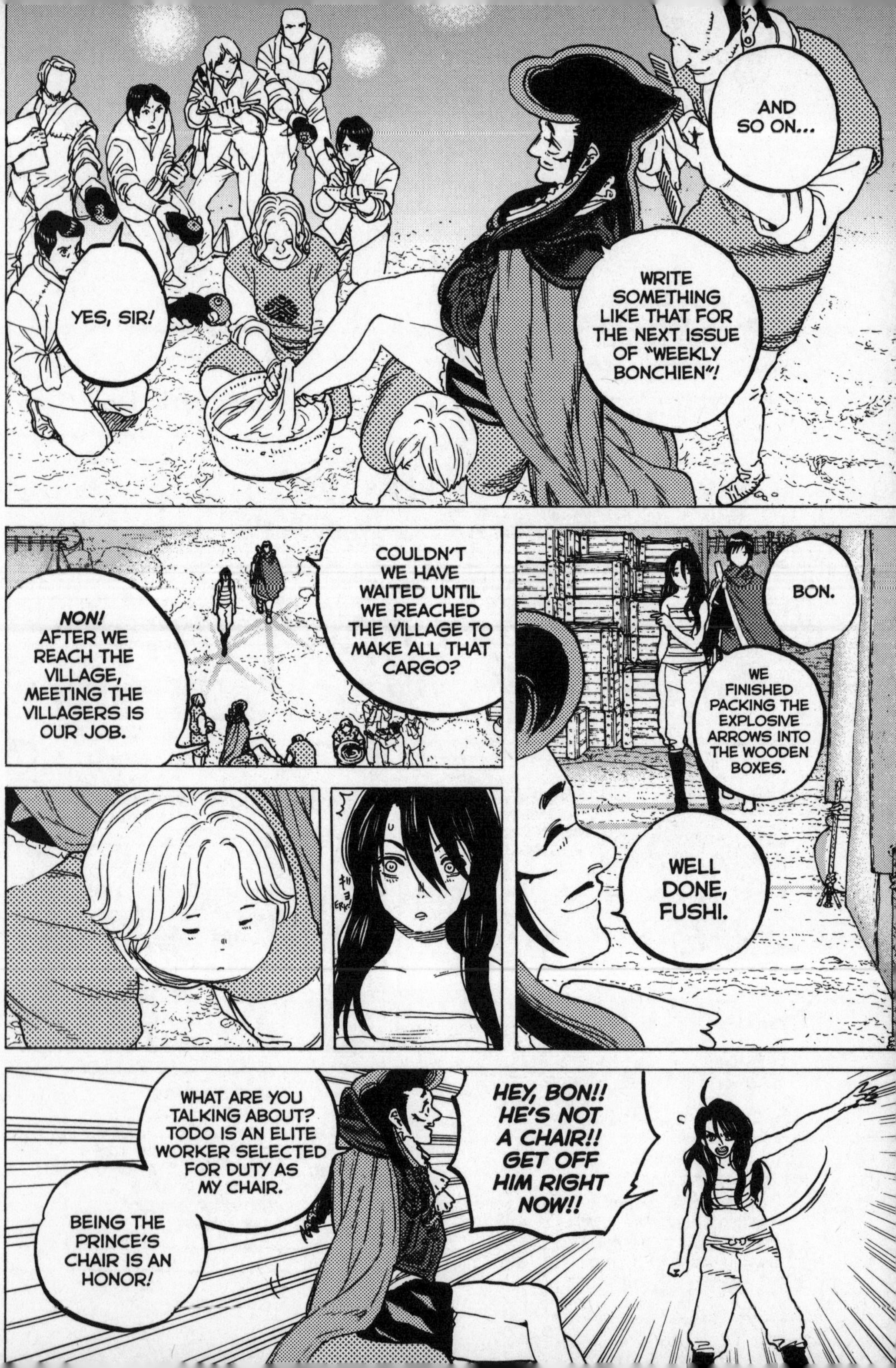
AND SO ON...
WRITE SOMETHING LIKE THAT FOR THE NEXT ISSUE OF "WEEKLY BONCHIEN"!
YES, SIR!
BON.
WE FINISHED PACKING THE EXPLOSIVE ARROWS INTO THE WOODEN BOXES.
WELL DONE, FUSHI.
COULDN'T WE HAVE WAITED UNTIL WE REACHED THE VILLAGE TO MAKE ALL THAT CARGO?
NON! AFTER WE REACH THE VILLAGE, MEETING THE VILLAGERS IS OUR JOB.
ERK
HEY, BON!! HE'S NOT A CHAIR!! GET OFF HIM RIGHT NOW!!
WHAT ARE YOU TALKING ABOUT? TODO IS AN ELITE WORKER SELECTED FOR DUTY AS MY CHAIR.
BEING THE PRINCE'S CHAIR IS AN HONOR!

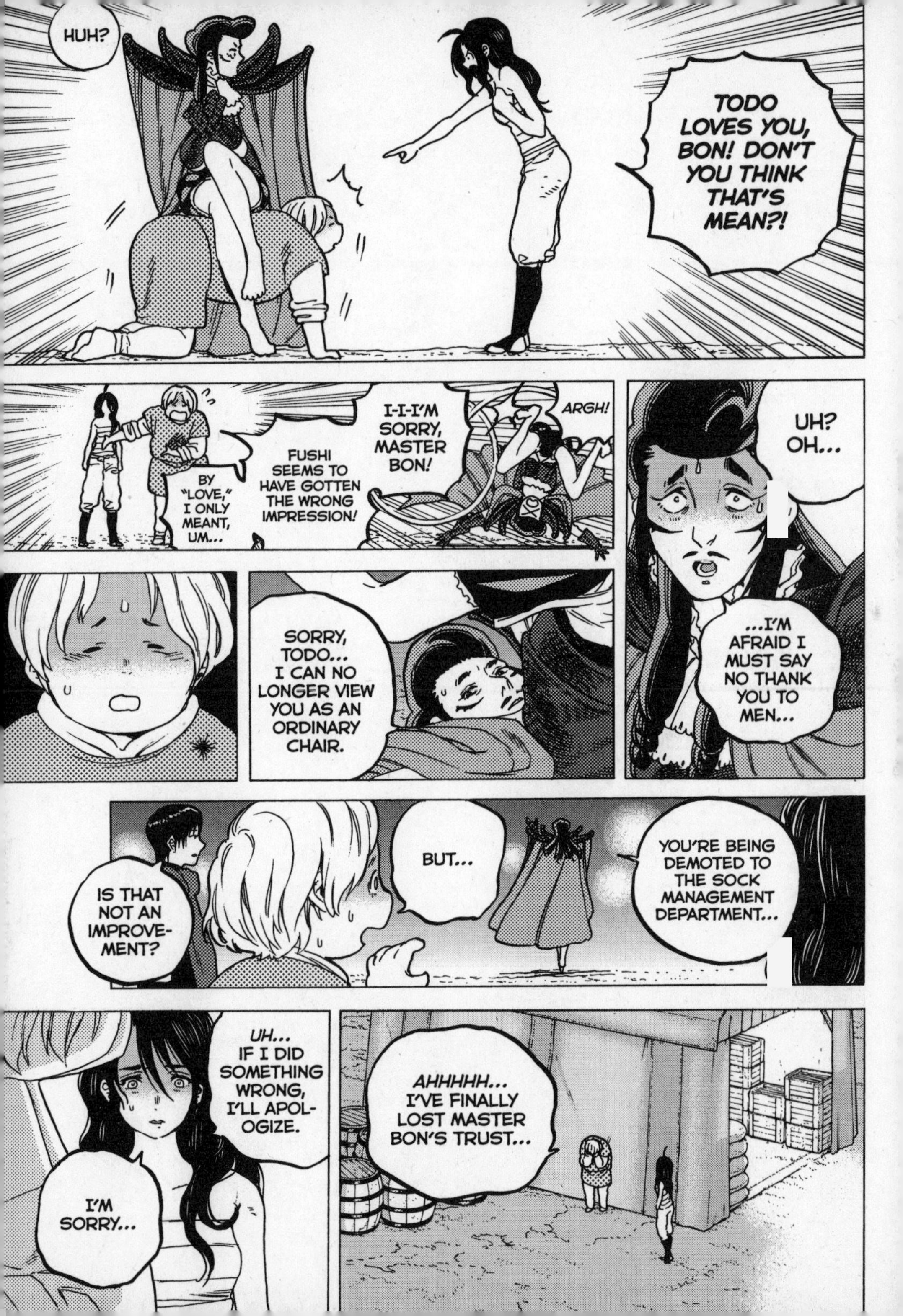
TODO LOVES YOU, BON! DON'T YOU THINK THAT'S MEAN?!
HUH?
UH? OH...
...I'M AFRAID I MUST SAY NO THANK YOU TO MEN...
ARGH!
I-I-I'M SORRY, MASTER BON!
FUSHI SEEMS TO HAVE GOTTEN THE WRONG IMPRESSION!
BY "LOVE," I ONLY MEANT, UM...
SORRY, TODO... I CAN NO LONGER VIEW YOU AS AN ORDINARY CHAIR.
YOU'RE BEING DEMOTED TO THE SOCK MANAGEMENT DEPARTMENT...
BUT...
IS THAT NOT AN IMPROVE-MENT?
AHHHHH... I'VE FINALLY LOST MASTER BON'S TRUST...
UH... IF I DID SOMETHING WRONG, I'LL APOLOGIZE.
I'M SORRY...

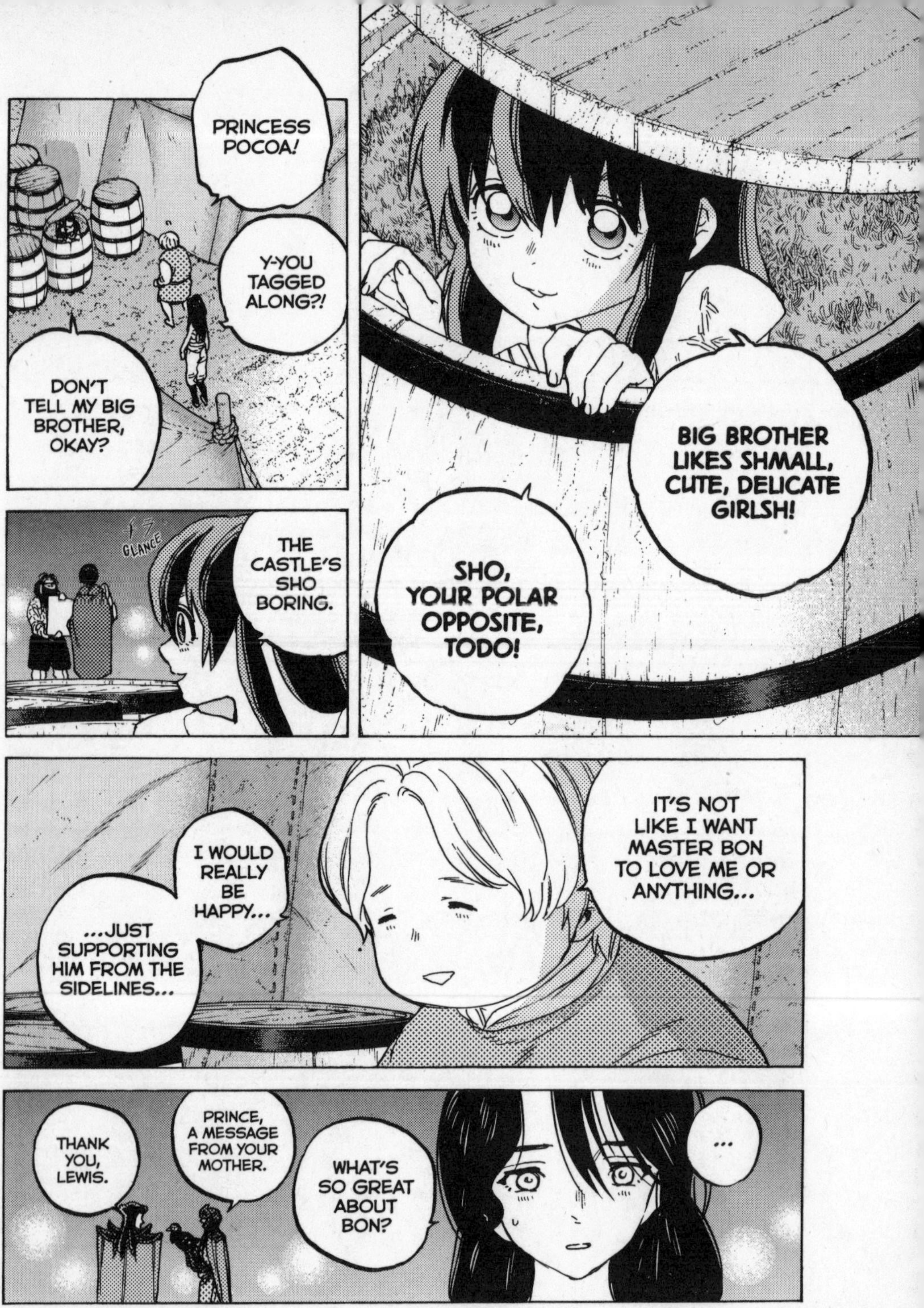
BIG BROTHER LIKES SHMALL, CUTE, DELICATE GIRLSH!
SHO, YOUR POLAR OPPOSITE, TODO!
PRINCESS POCOA!
Y-YOU TAGGED ALONG?!
DON'T TELL MY BIG BROTHER, OKAY?
GLANCE
THE CASTLE'S SHO BORING.
IT'S NOT LIKE I WANT MASTER BON TO LOVE ME OR ANYTHING...
I WOULD REALLY BE HAPPY...
...JUST SUPPORTING HIM FROM THE SIDELINES...
...
WHAT'S SO GREAT ABOUT BON?
PRINCE, A MESSAGE FROM YOUR MOTHER.
THANK YOU, LEWIS.

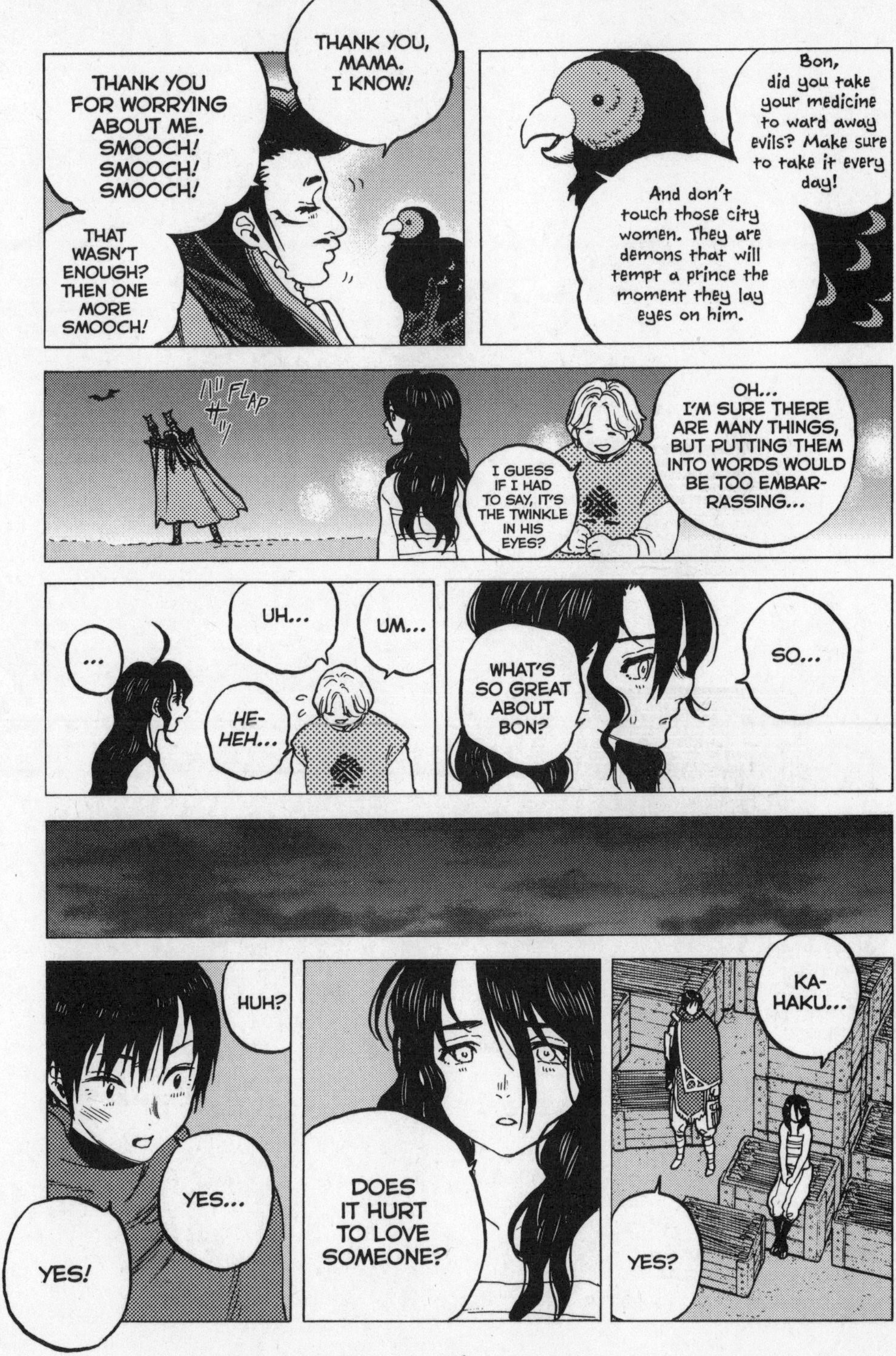
Bon, did you take your medicine to ward away evils? Make sure to take it every day!
And don't touch those city women. They are demons that will tempt a prince the moment they lay eyes on him.
THANK YOU, MAMA. I KNOW!
THANK YOU FOR WORRYING ABOUT ME. SMOOCH! SMOOCH! SMOOCH!
THAT WASN'T ENOUGH? THEN ONE MORE SMOOCH!
OH... I'M SURE THERE ARE MANY THINGS, BUT PUTTING THEM INTO WORDS WOULD BE TOO EMBAR-RASSING...
I GUESS IF I HAD TO SAY, IT'S THE TWINKLE IN HIS EYES?
FLAP
SO...
WHAT'S SO GREAT ABOUT BON?
UM...
UH...
HE-HEH...
...
KA-HAKU...
YES?
DOES IT HURT TO LOVE SOMEONE?
HUH?
YES...
YES!

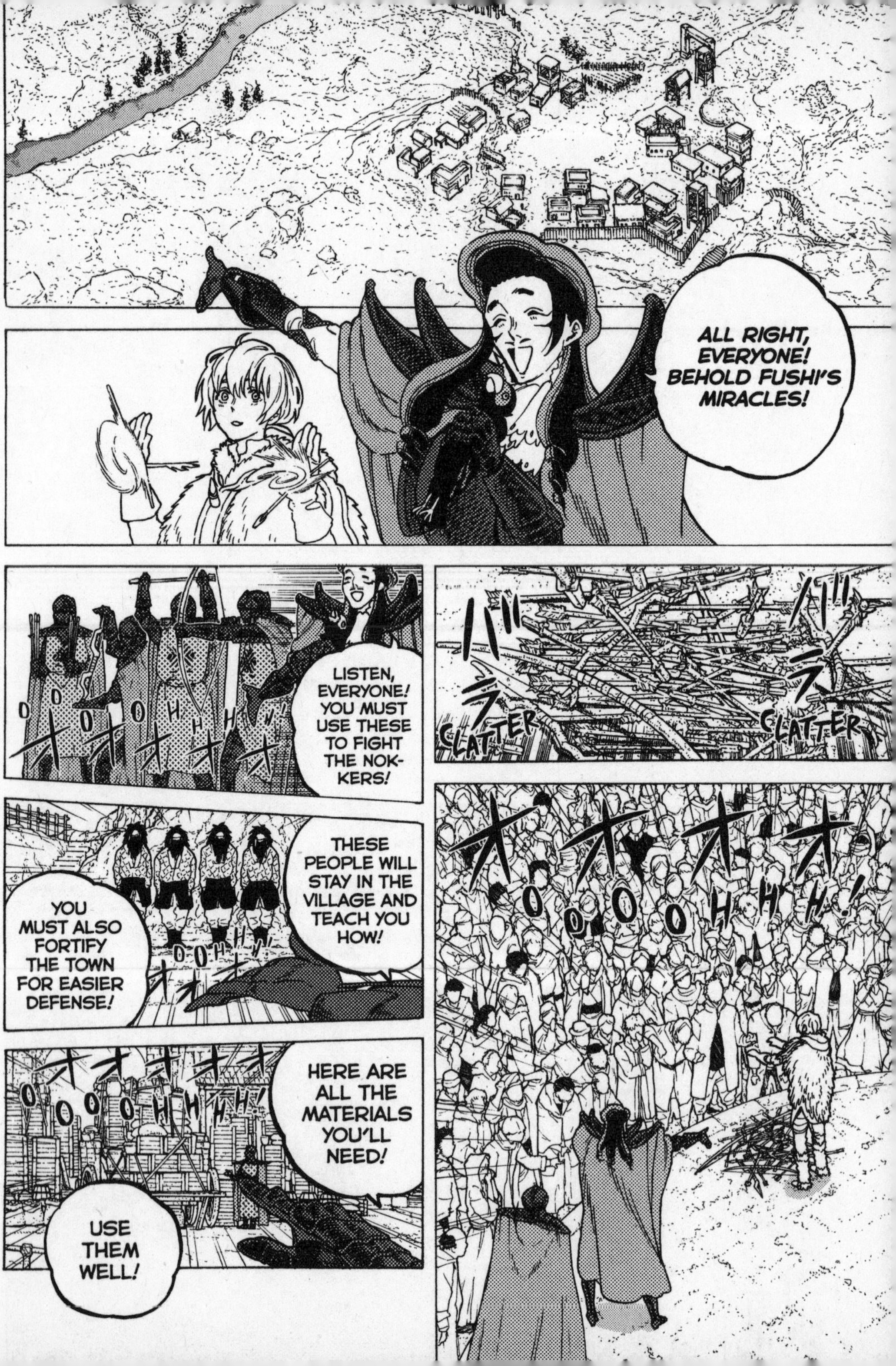
ALL RIGHT, EVERYONE! BEHOLD FUSHI'S MIRACLES!
CLATTER
CLATTER
LISTEN, EVERYONE! YOU MUST USE THESE TO FIGHT THE NOKKERS!
OOOHHH
OOOOOHHH!
THESE PEOPLE WILL STAY IN THE VILLAGE AND TEACH YOU HOW!
YOU MUST ALSO FORTIFY THE TOWN FOR EASIER DEFENSE!
OOOHHH
HERE ARE ALL THE MATERIALS YOU'LL NEED!
OOOOHHHH!
USE THEM WELL!

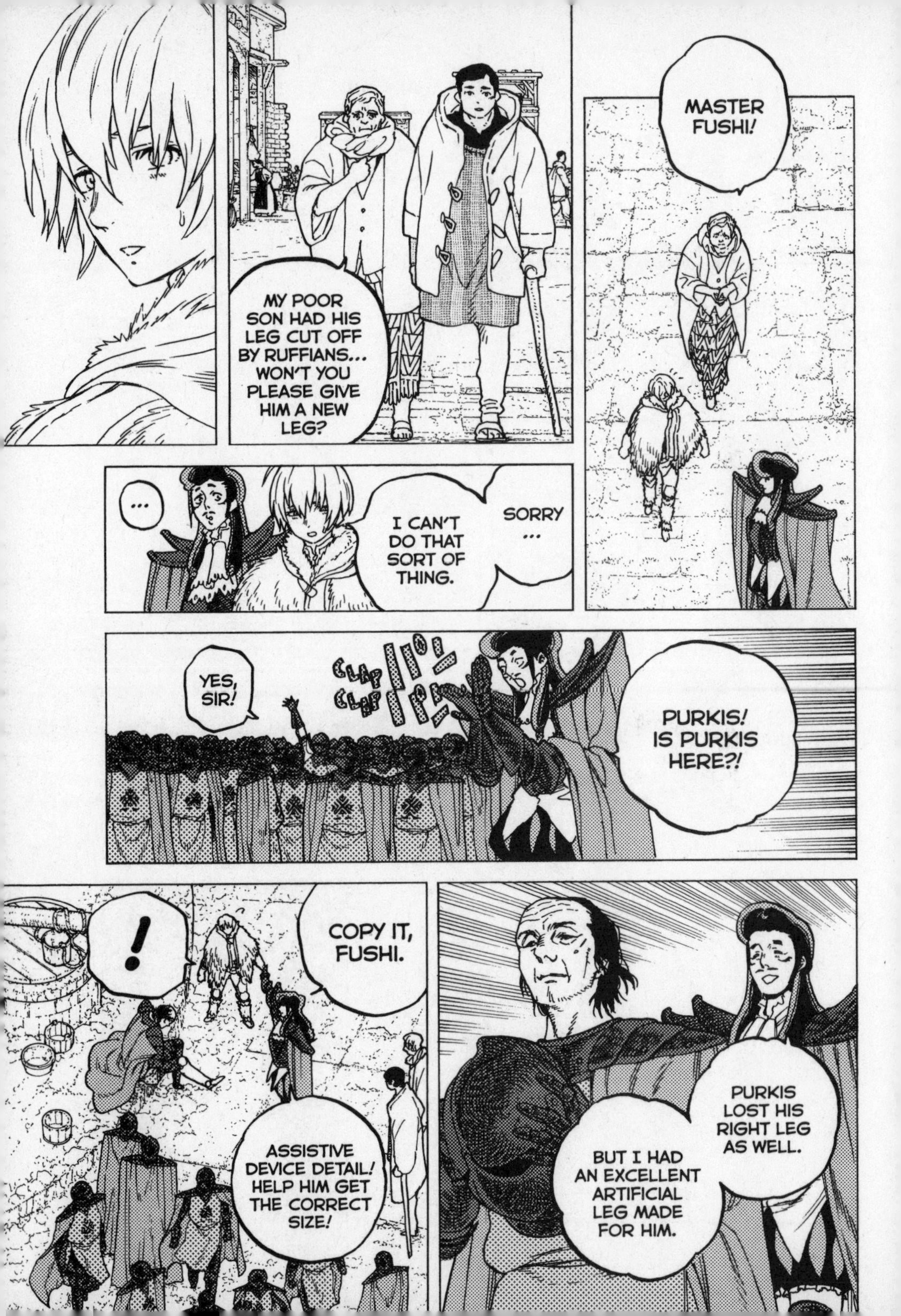
MASTER FUSHI!
MY POOR SON HAD HIS LEG CUT OFF BY RUFFIANS... WON'T YOU PLEASE GIVE HIM A NEW LEG?
SORRY ...
I CAN'T DO THAT SORT OF THING.
...
PURKIS! IS PURKIS HERE?!
CLAP CLAP
YES, SIR!
PURKIS LOST HIS RIGHT LEG AS WELL.
BUT I HAD AN EXCELLENT ARTIFICIAL LEG MADE FOR HIM.
COPY IT, FUSHI.
!
ASSISTIVE DEVICE DETAIL! HELP HIM GET THE CORRECT SIZE!

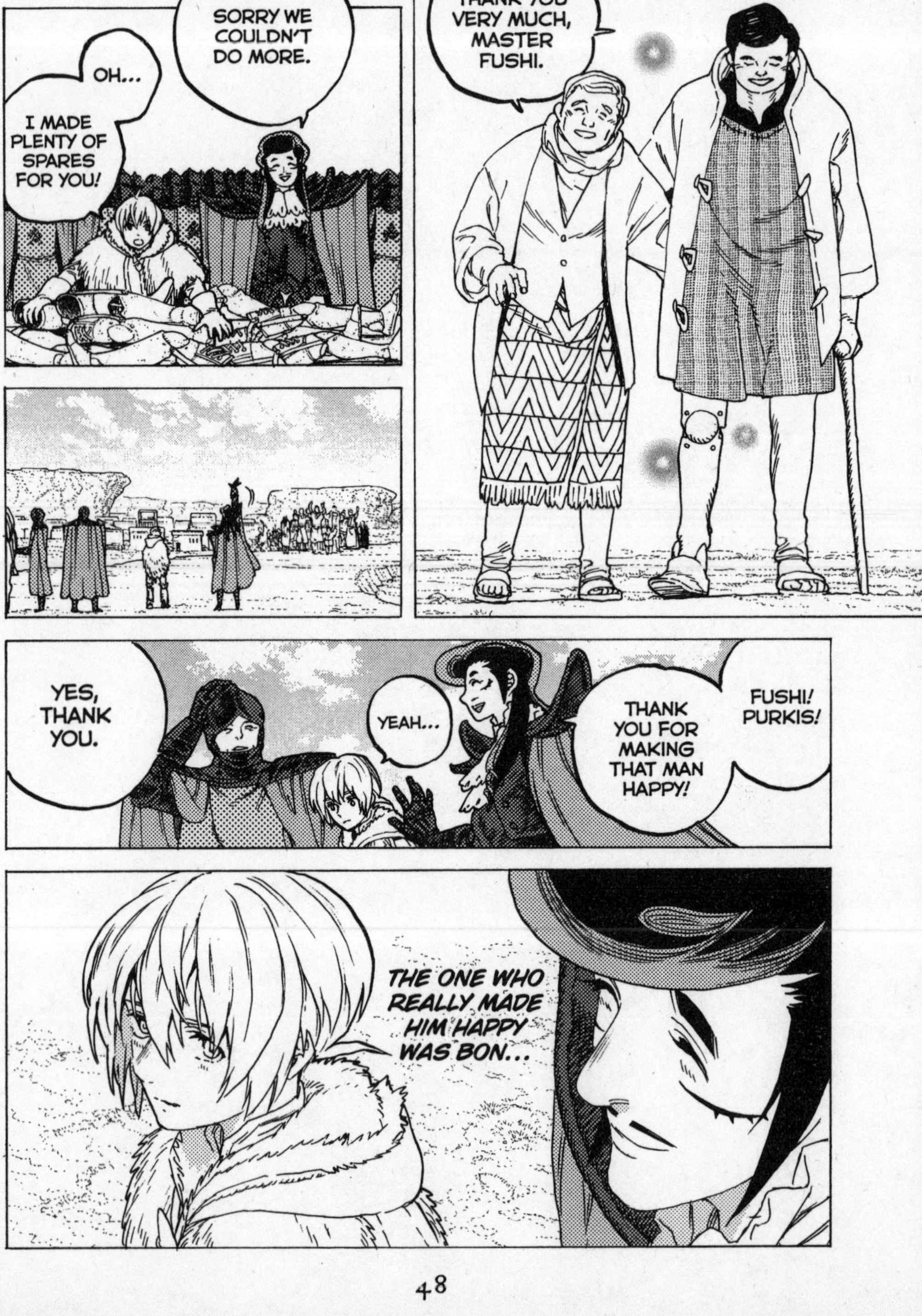
THANK YOU VERY MUCH, MASTER FUSHI.
SORRY WE COULDN'T DO MORE.
OH...
I MADE PLENTY OF SPARES FOR YOU!
FUSHI! PURKIS!
THANK YOU FOR MAKING THAT MAN HAPPY!
YEAH...
YES, THANK YOU.
THE ONE WHO REALLY MADE HIM HAPPY WAS BON...

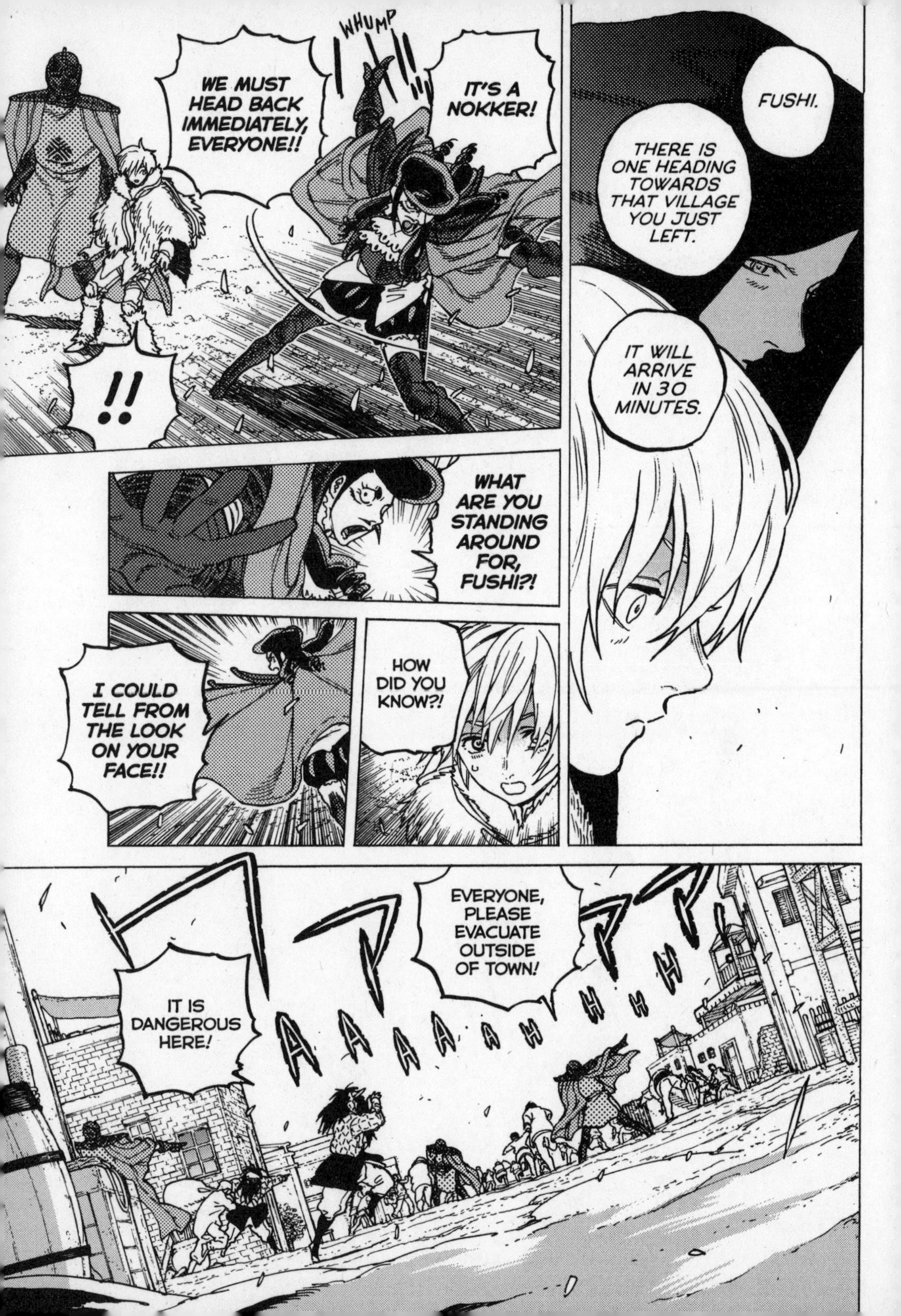
FUSHI.
THERE IS ONE HEADING TOWARDS THAT VILLAGE YOU JUST LEFT.
IT WILL ARRIVE IN 30 MINUTES.
IT'S A NOKKER!
WHUMP
WE MUST HEAD BACK IMMEDIATELY, EVERYONE!!
!!
WHAT ARE YOU STANDING AROUND FOR, FUSHI?!
HOW DID YOU KNOW?!
I COULD TELL FROM THE LOOK ON YOUR FACE!!
EVERYONE, PLEASE EVACUATE OUTSIDE OF TOWN!
AAAAAAHHHHH
IT IS DANGEROUS HERE!

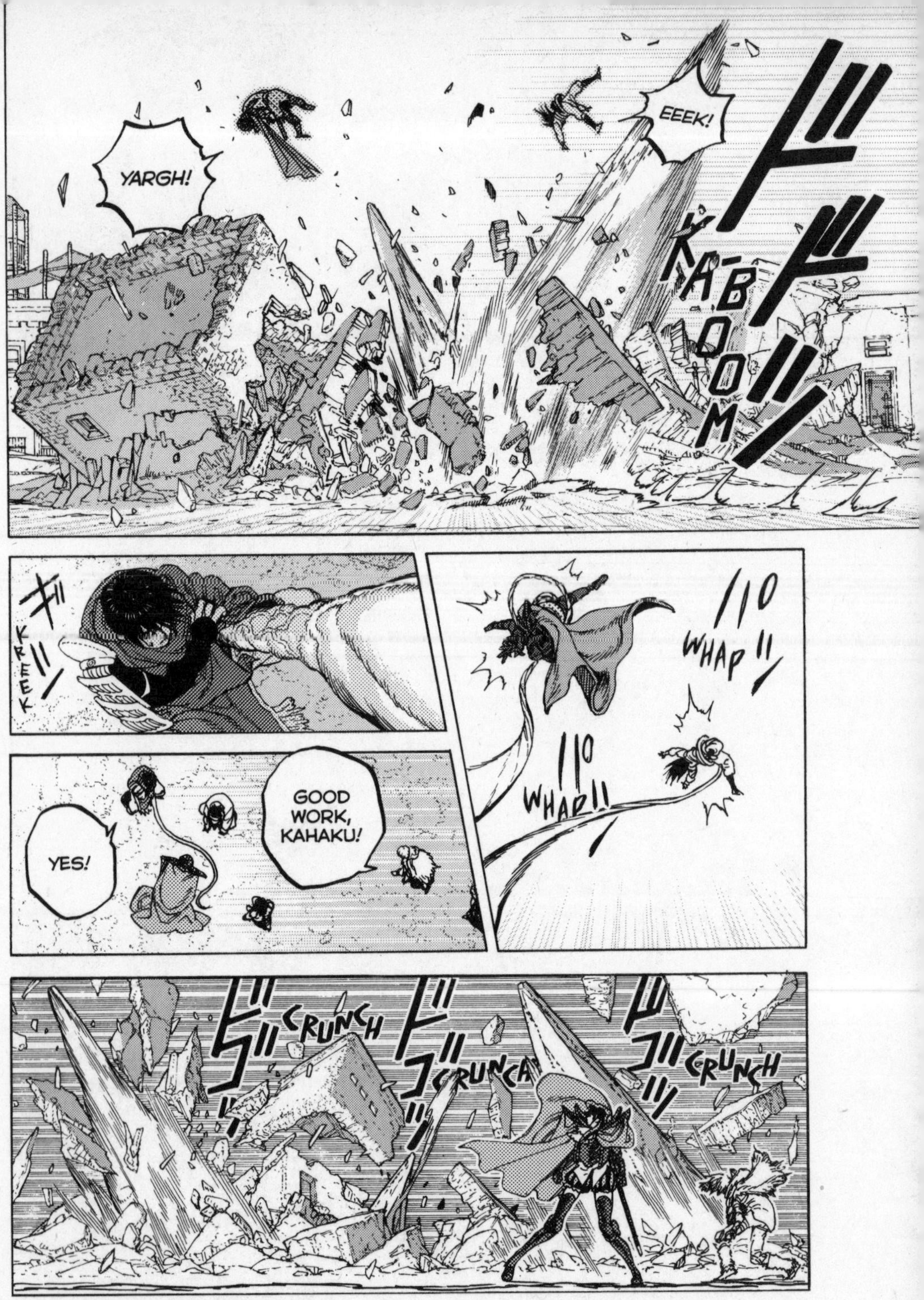
EEEK!
KA-BOOM
YARGH!
WHAP!!
WHAP!!
KREEK
GOOD WORK, KAHAKU!
YES!
CRUNCH
CRUNCH
CRUNCH

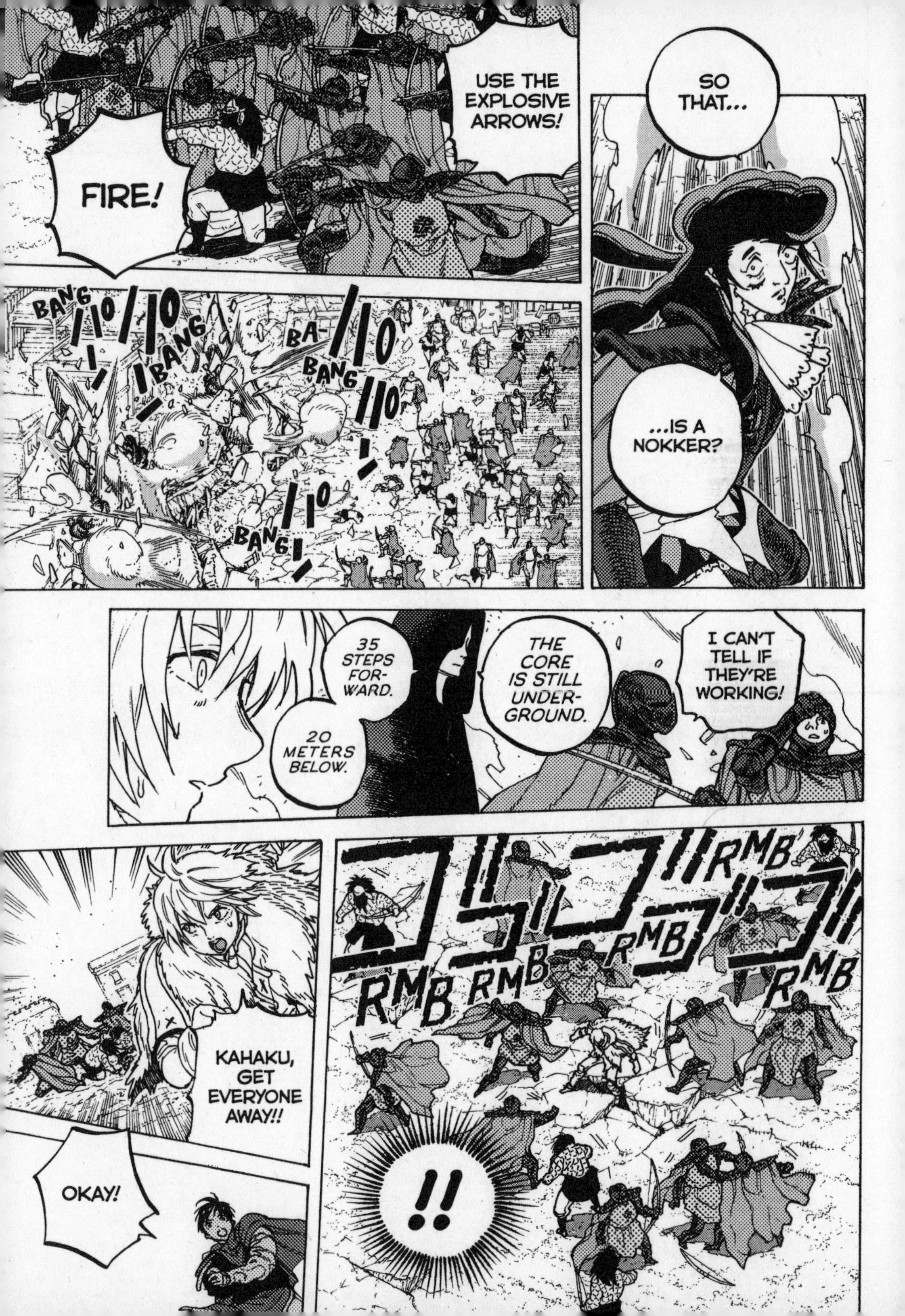
SO THAT...
...IS A NOKKER?
USE THE EXPLOSIVE ARROWS!
FIRE!
BANG
BANG
BA-BANG
BANG
I CAN'T TELL IF THEY'RE WORKING!
THE CORE IS STILL UNDERGROUND.
35 STEPS FORWARD.
20 METERS BELOW.
RMB
RMB
RMB RMB
RMB
!!
KAHAKU, GET EVERYONE AWAY!!
OKAY!

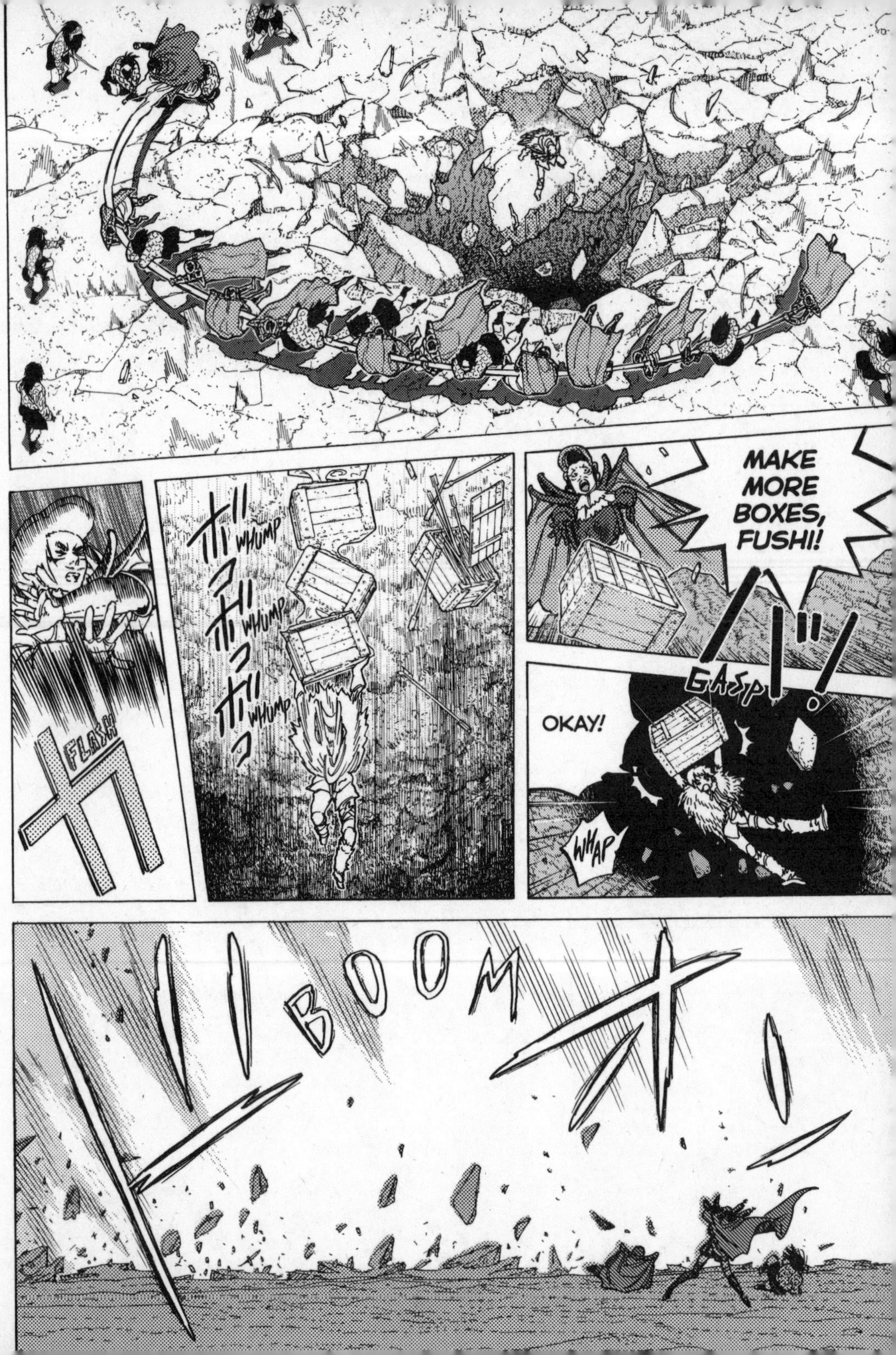
MAKE MORE BOXES, FUSHI!
GASP
OKAY!
WHAP
WHUMP
WHUMP
WHUMP
FLASH
BOOM

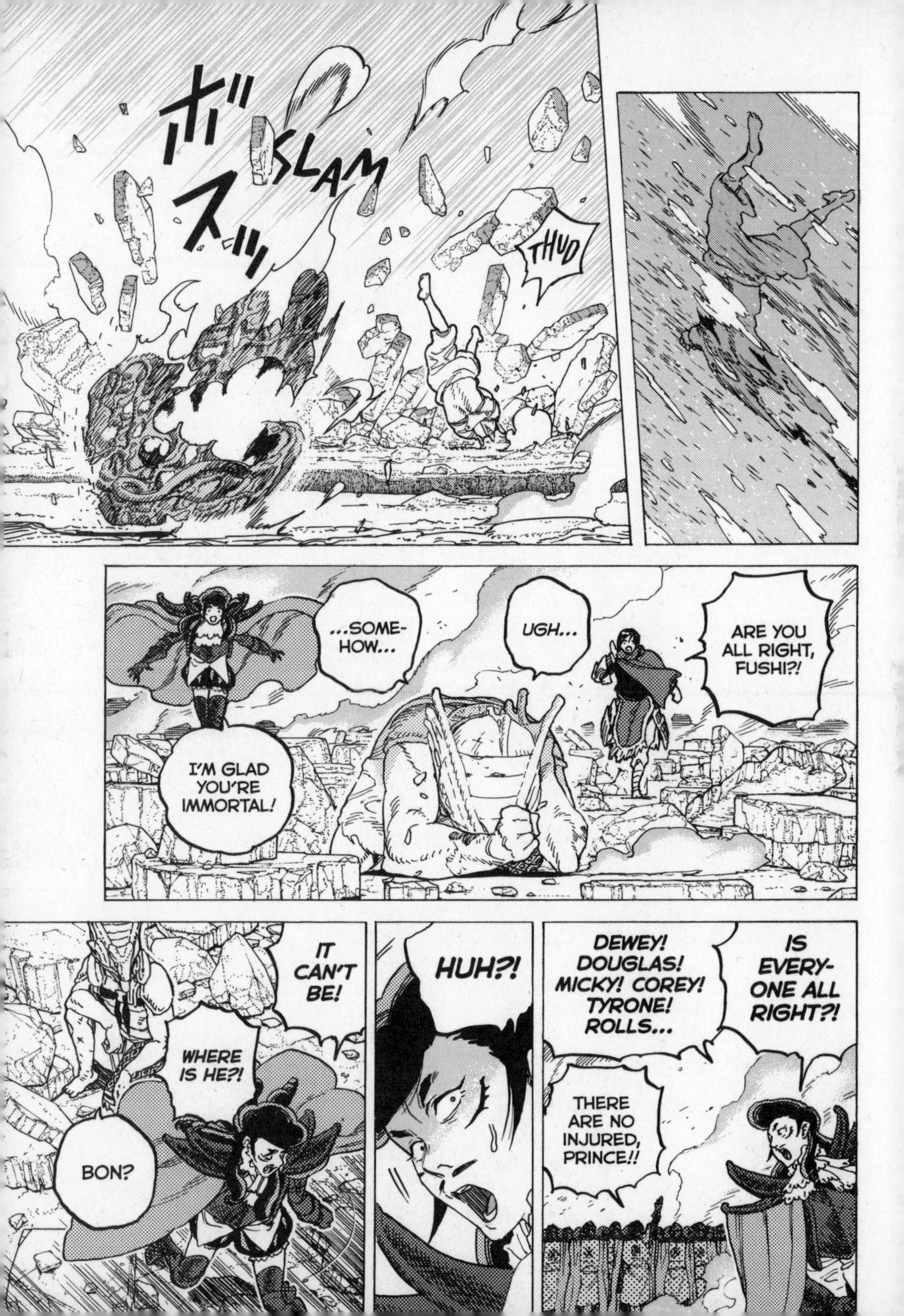
ボスッ
SLAM
THUD
ARE YOU ALL RIGHT, FUSHI?!
UGH...
...SOME-HOW...
I'M GLAD YOU'RE IMMORTAL!
IS EVERY-ONE ALL RIGHT?!
DEWEY! DOUGLAS! MICKY! COREY! TYRONE! ROLLS...
THERE ARE NO INJURED, PRINCE!!
HUH?!
IT CAN'T BE!
WHERE IS HE?!
BON?

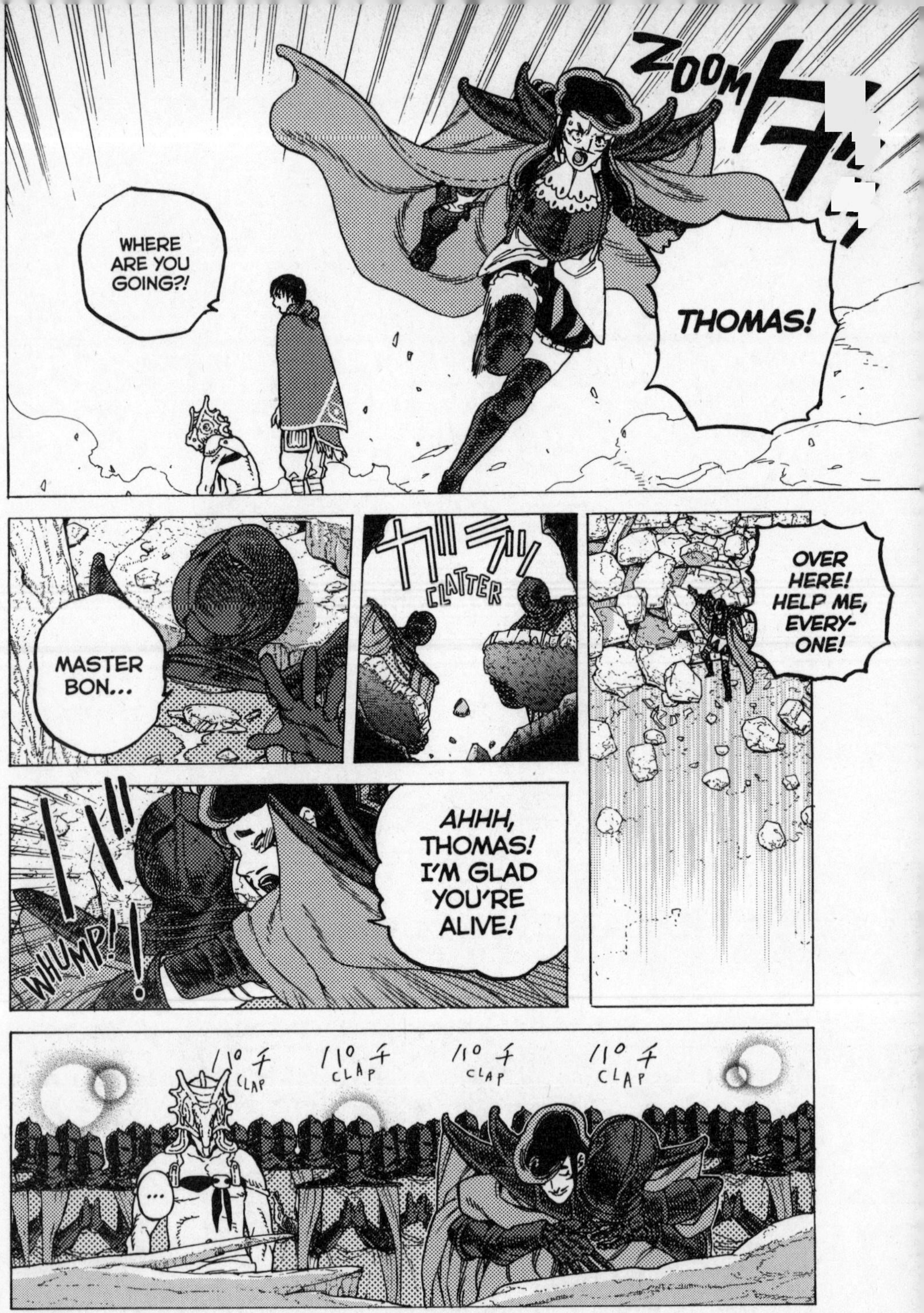
ZOOM
THOMAS!
WHERE ARE YOU GOING?!
OVER HERE! HELP ME, EVERY-ONE!
ガラッ
CLATTER
MASTER BON...
AHHH, THOMAS! I'M GLAD YOU'RE ALIVE!
WHUMP!
パチ
CLAP
パチ
CLAP
パチ
CLAP
パチ
CLAP
...

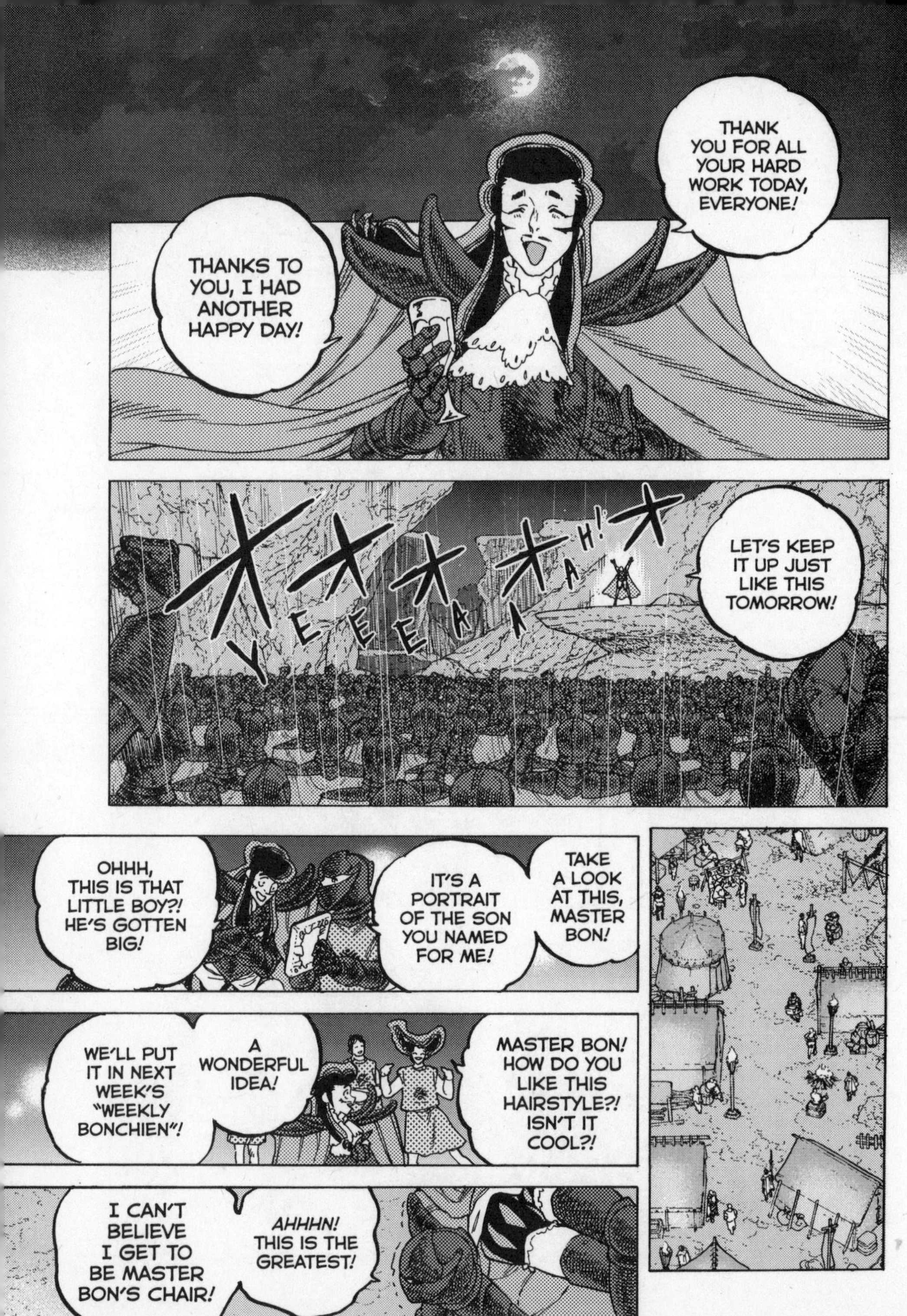
THANK YOU FOR ALL YOUR HARD WORK TODAY, EVERYONE!
THANKS TO YOU, I HAD ANOTHER HAPPY DAY!
LET'S KEEP IT UP JUST LIKE THIS TOMORROW!
YEEEAAAH!
TAKE A LOOK AT THIS, MASTER BON!
IT'S A PORTRAIT OF THE SON YOU NAMED FOR ME!
OHHH, THIS IS THAT LITTLE BOY?! HE'S GOTTEN BIG!
MASTER BON! HOW DO YOU LIKE THIS HAIRSTYLE?! ISN'T IT COOL?!
A WONDERFUL IDEA!
WE'LL PUT IT IN NEXT WEEK'S "WEEKLY BONCHIEN"!
AHHHN! THIS IS THE GREATEST!
I CAN'T BELIEVE I GET TO BE MASTER BON'S CHAIR!

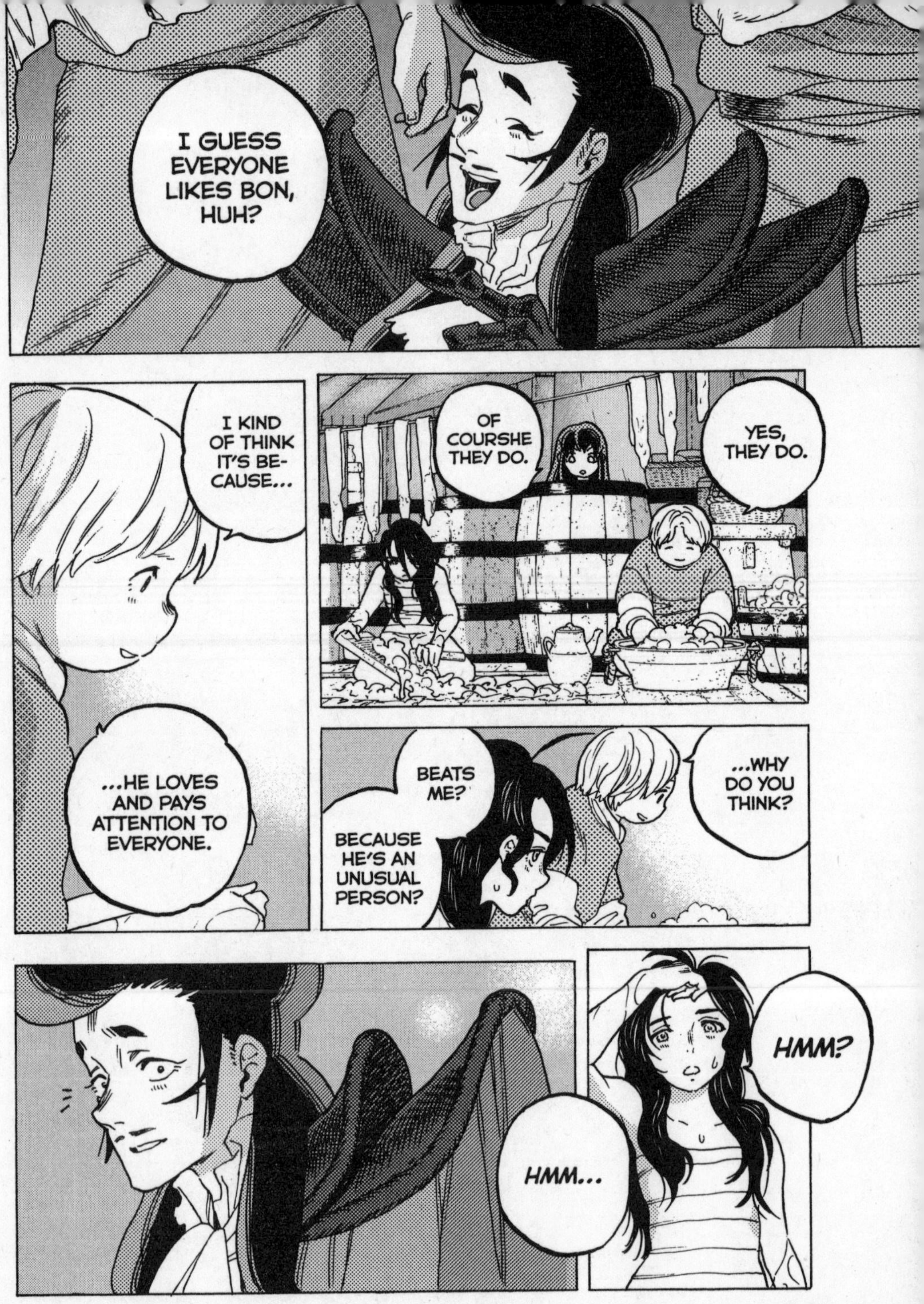
I GUESS EVERYONE LIKES BON, HUH?
YES, THEY DO.
OF COURSHE THEY DO.
...WHY DO YOU THINK?
BEATS ME?
BECAUSE HE'S AN UNUSUAL PERSON?
I KIND OF THINK IT'S BE- CAUSE...
...HE LOVES AND PAYS ATTENTION TO EVERYONE.
HMM?
HMM...

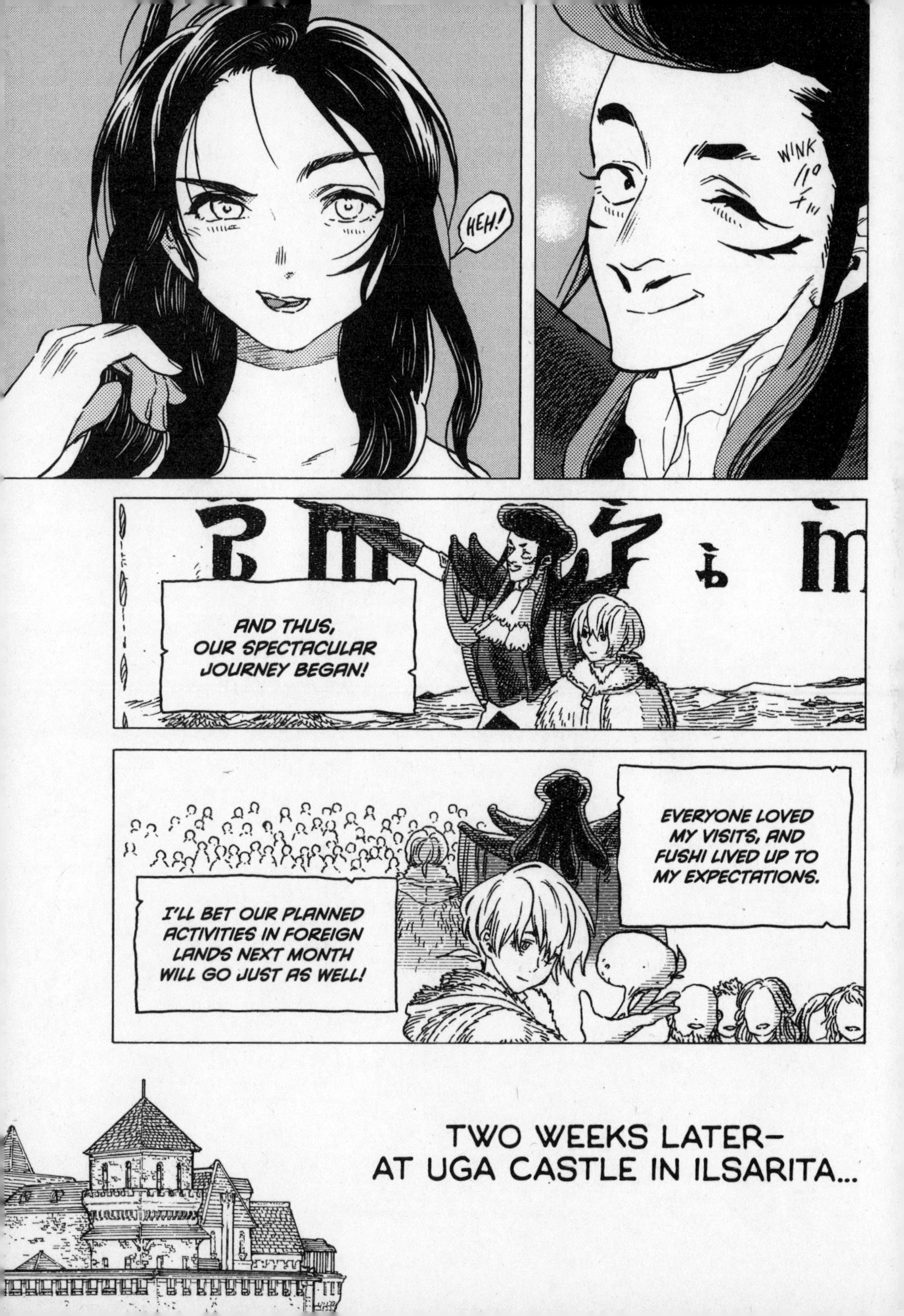
WINK
HEH!
AND THUS, OUR SPECTACULAR JOURNEY BEGAN!
EVERYONE LOVED MY VISITS, AND FUSHI LIVED UP TO MY EXPECTATIONS.
I'LL BET OUR PLANNED ACTIVITIES IN FOREIGN LANDS NEXT MONTH WILL GO JUST AS WELL!
TWO WEEKS LATER—
AT UGA CASTLE IN ILSARITA...

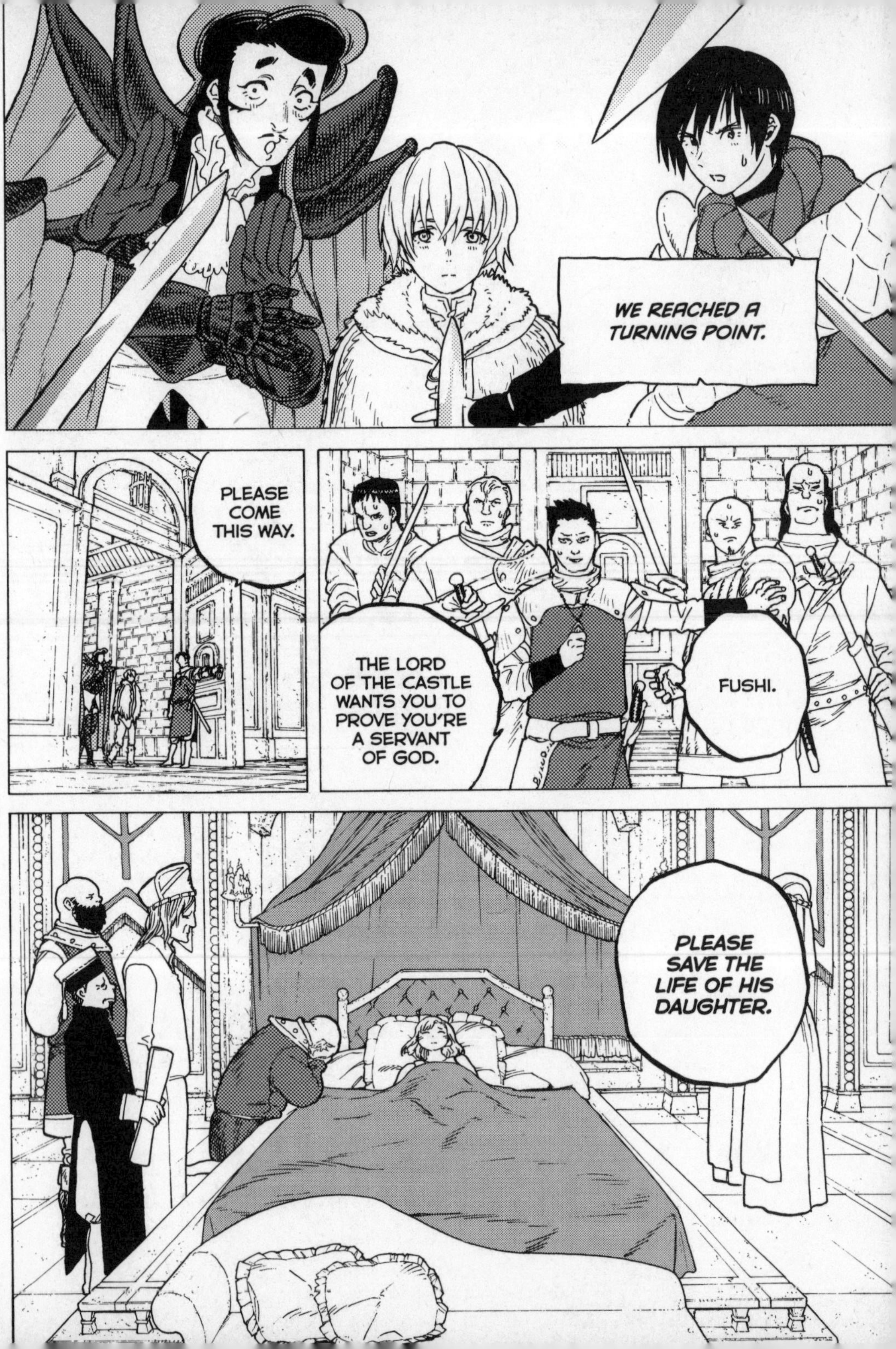
WE REACHED A TURNING POINT.
FUSHI.
THE LORD OF THE CASTLE WANTS YOU TO PROVE YOU'RE A SERVANT OF GOD.
PLEASE COME THIS WAY.
PLEASE SAVE THE LIFE OF HIS DAUGHTER.

#68 Inversion

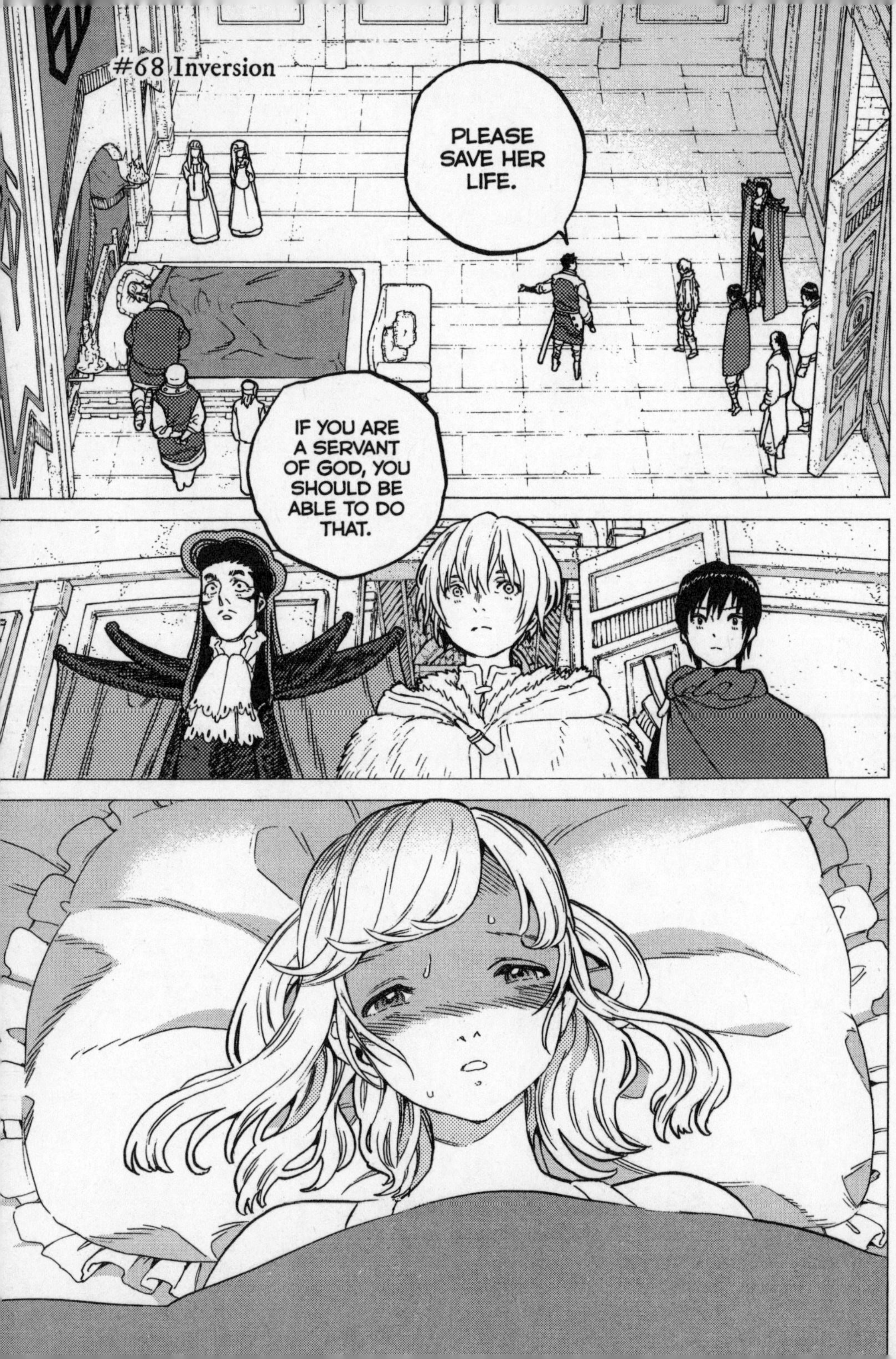
PLEASE SAVE HER LIFE.
IF YOU ARE A SERVANT OF GOD, YOU SHOULD BE ABLE TO DO THAT.

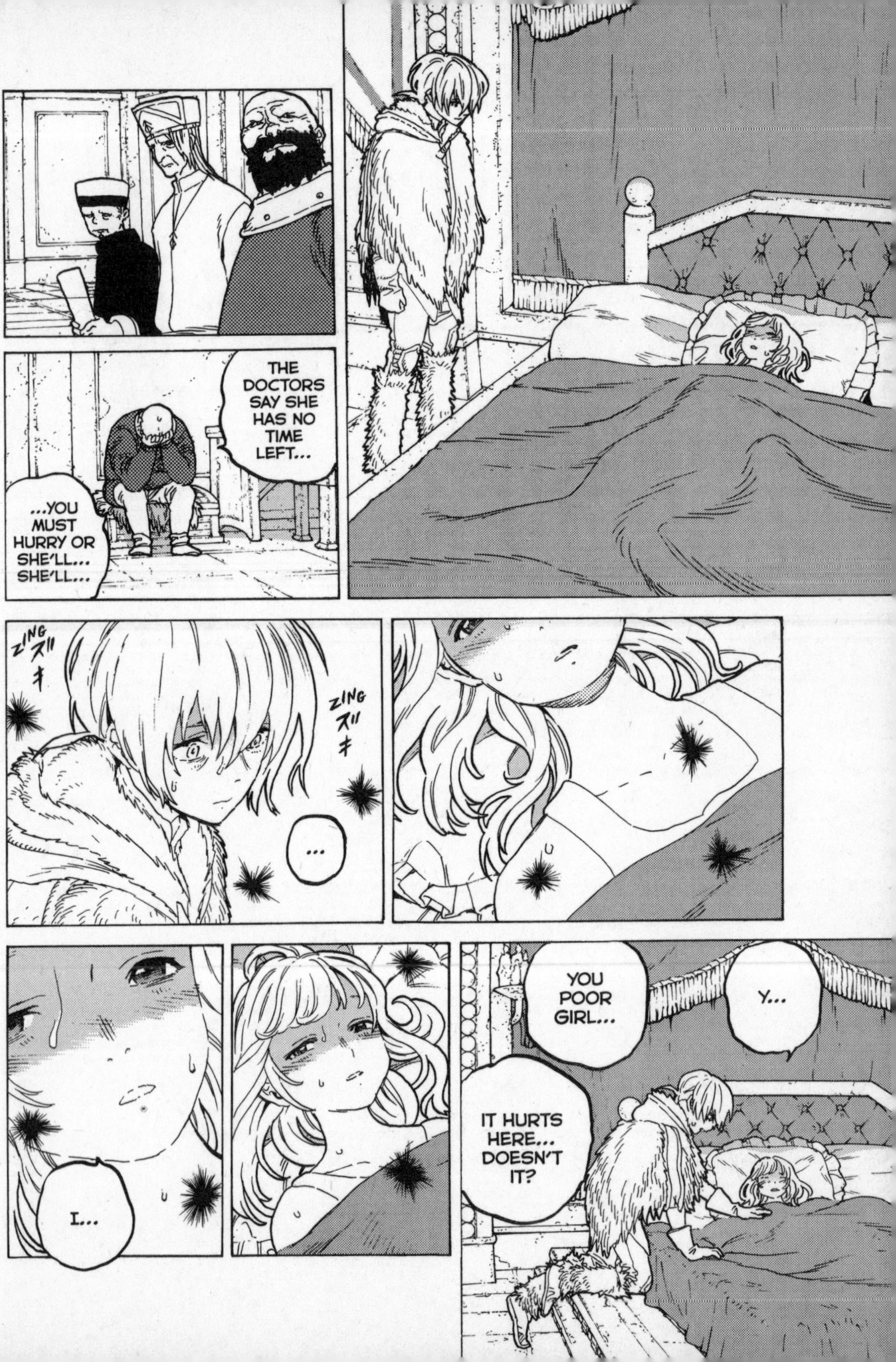
THE DOCTORS SAY SHE HAS NO TIME LEFT...
...YOU MUST HURRY OR SHE'LL... SHE'LL...
ZING ズキ
ZING ズキ
...
Y...
YOU POOR GIRL...
IT HURTS HERE... DOESN'T IT?
I...

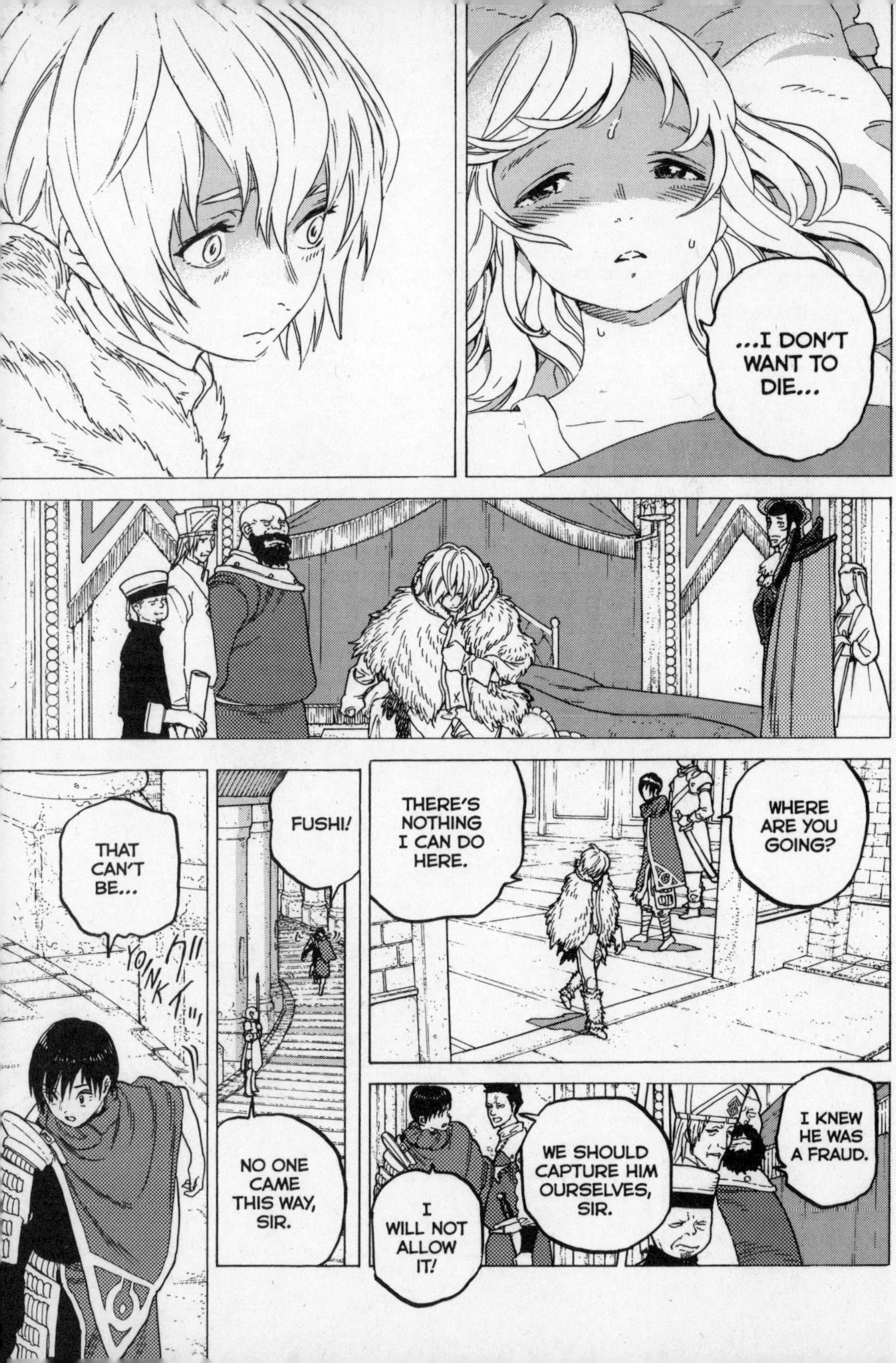
...I DON'T WANT TO DIE...
WHERE ARE YOU GOING?
THERE'S NOTHING I CAN DO HERE.
I KNEW HE WAS A FRAUD.
WE SHOULD CAPTURE HIM OURSELVES, SIR.
I WILL NOT ALLOW IT!
FUSHI!
NO ONE CAME THIS WAY, SIR.
THAT CAN'T BE...
YOINK

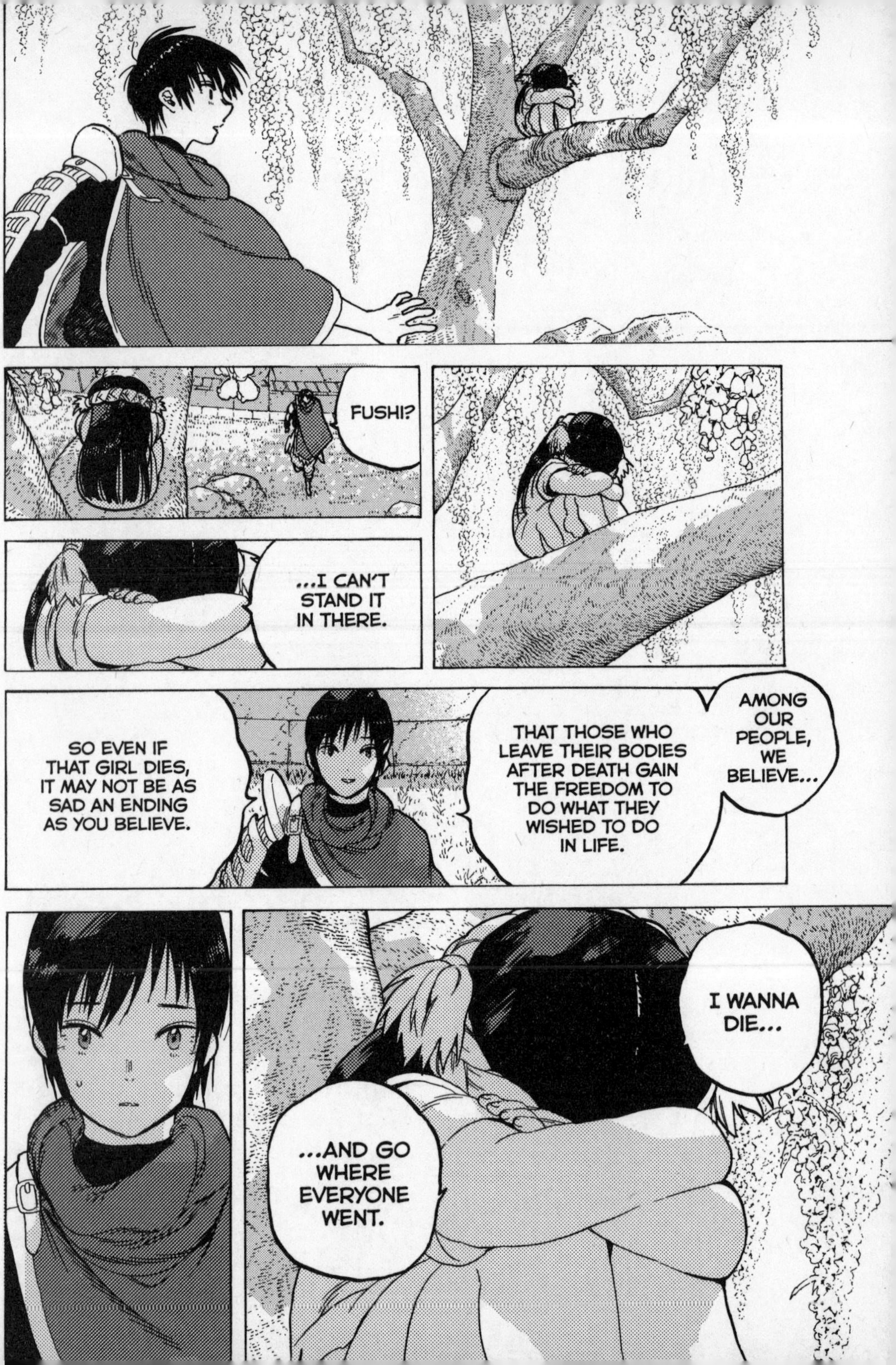
FUSHI?
...I CAN'T STAND IT IN THERE.
AMONG OUR PEOPLE, WE BELIEVE...
THAT THOSE WHO LEAVE THEIR BODIES AFTER DEATH GAIN THE FREEDOM TO DO WHAT THEY WISHED TO DO IN LIFE.
SO EVEN IF THAT GIRL DIES, IT MAY NOT BE AS SAD AN ENDING AS YOU BELIEVE.
I WANNA DIE...
...AND GO WHERE EVERYONE WENT.

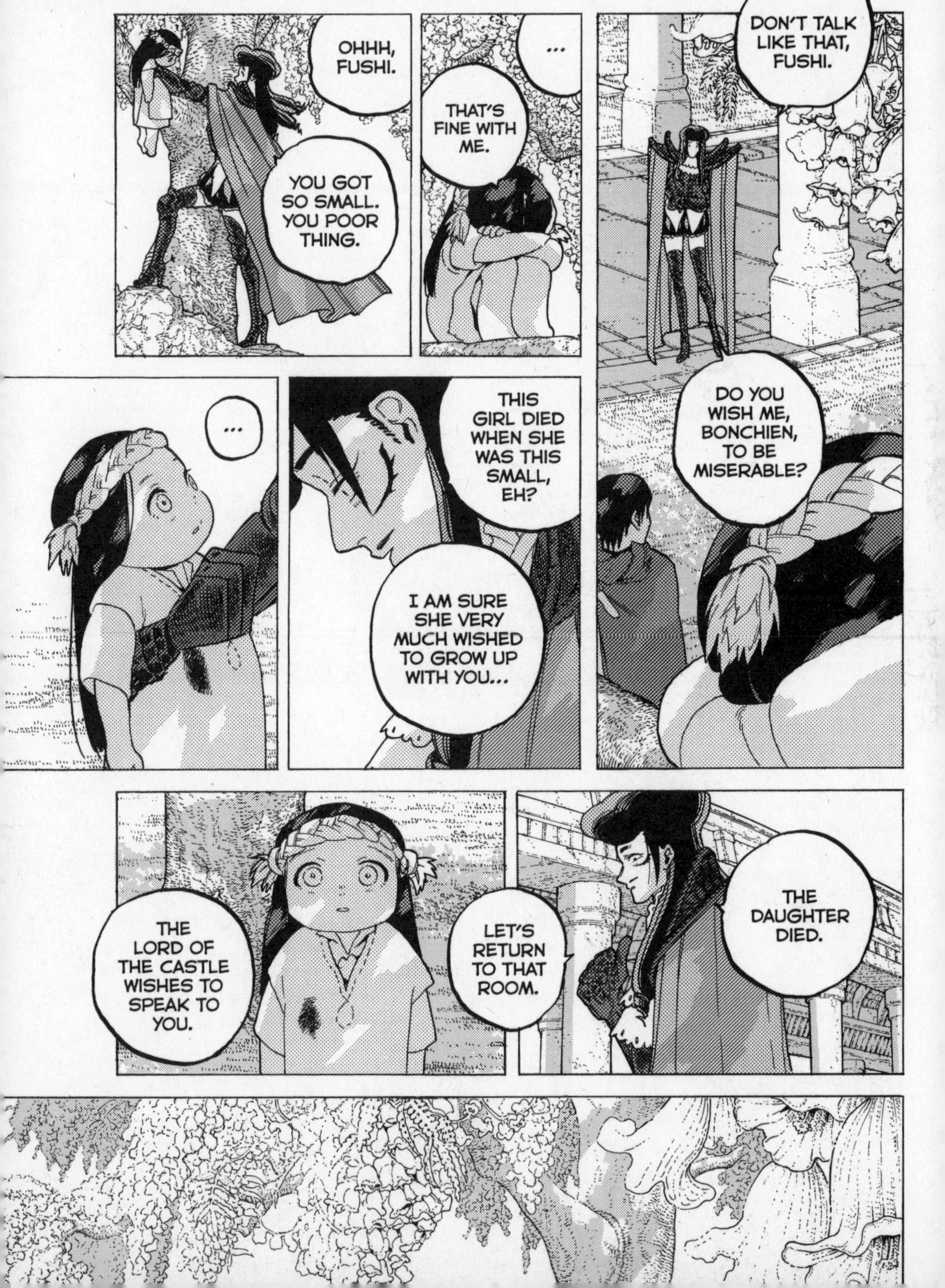
OHHH, FUSHI.
YOU GOT SO SMALL. YOU POOR THING.
...
THAT'S FINE WITH ME.
DON'T TALK LIKE THAT, FUSHI.
...
THIS GIRL DIED WHEN SHE WAS THIS SMALL, EH?
I AM SURE SHE VERY MUCH WISHED TO GROW UP WITH YOU...
DO YOU WISH ME, BONCHIEN, TO BE MISERABLE?
THE LORD OF THE CASTLE WISHES TO SPEAK TO YOU.
LET'S RETURN TO THAT ROOM.
THE DAUGHTER DIED.

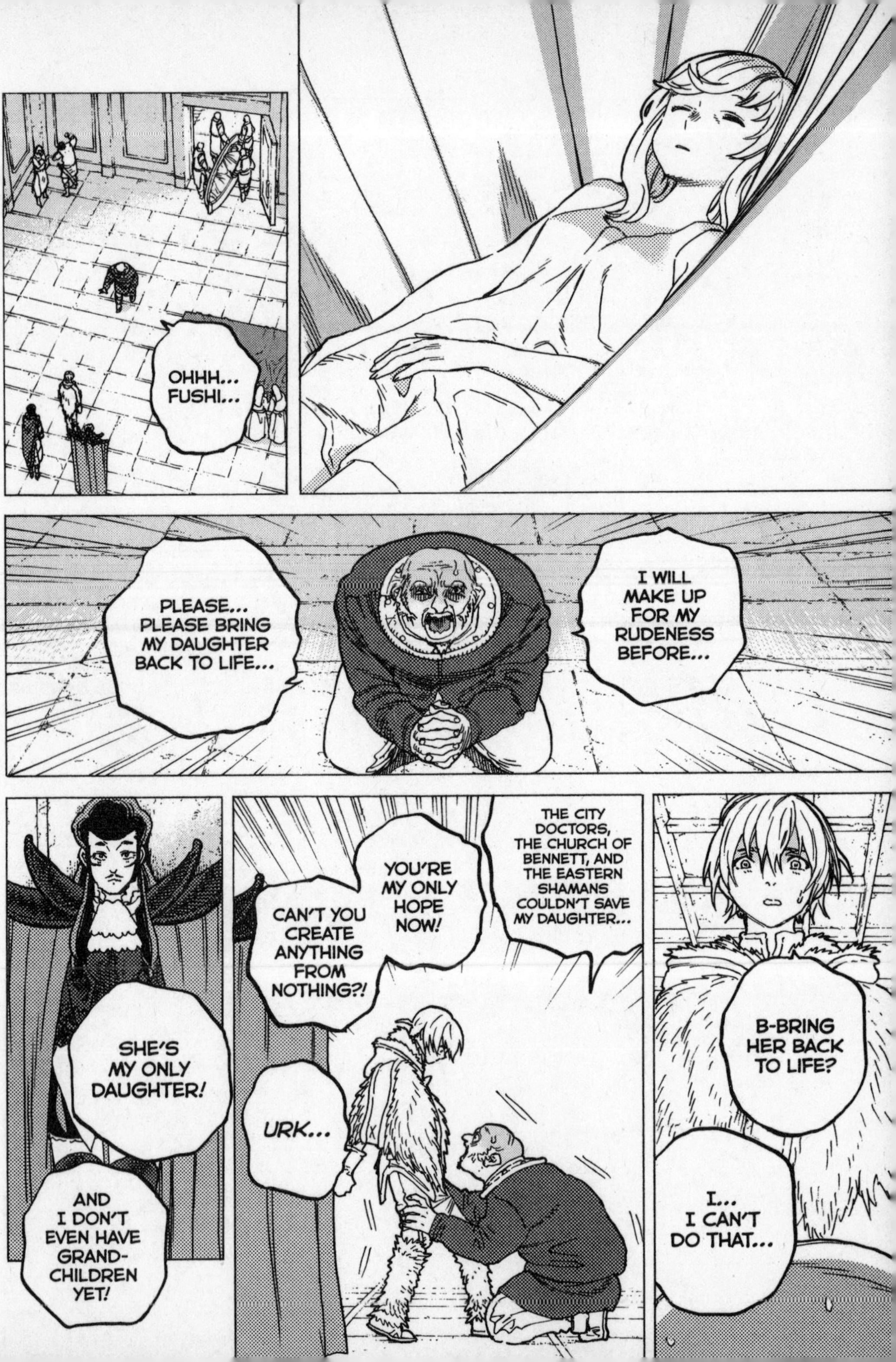
OHHH... FUSHI...
I WILL MAKE UP FOR MY RUDENESS BEFORE...
PLEASE... PLEASE BRING MY DAUGHTER BACK TO LIFE...
B-BRING HER BACK TO LIFE?
I... I CAN'T DO THAT...
THE CITY DOCTORS, THE CHURCH OF BENNETT, AND THE EASTERN SHAMANS COULDN'T SAVE MY DAUGHTER...
YOU'RE MY ONLY HOPE NOW!
CAN'T YOU CREATE ANYTHING FROM NOTHING?!
URK...
SHE'S MY ONLY DAUGHTER!
AND I DON'T EVEN HAVE GRAND-CHILDREN YET!

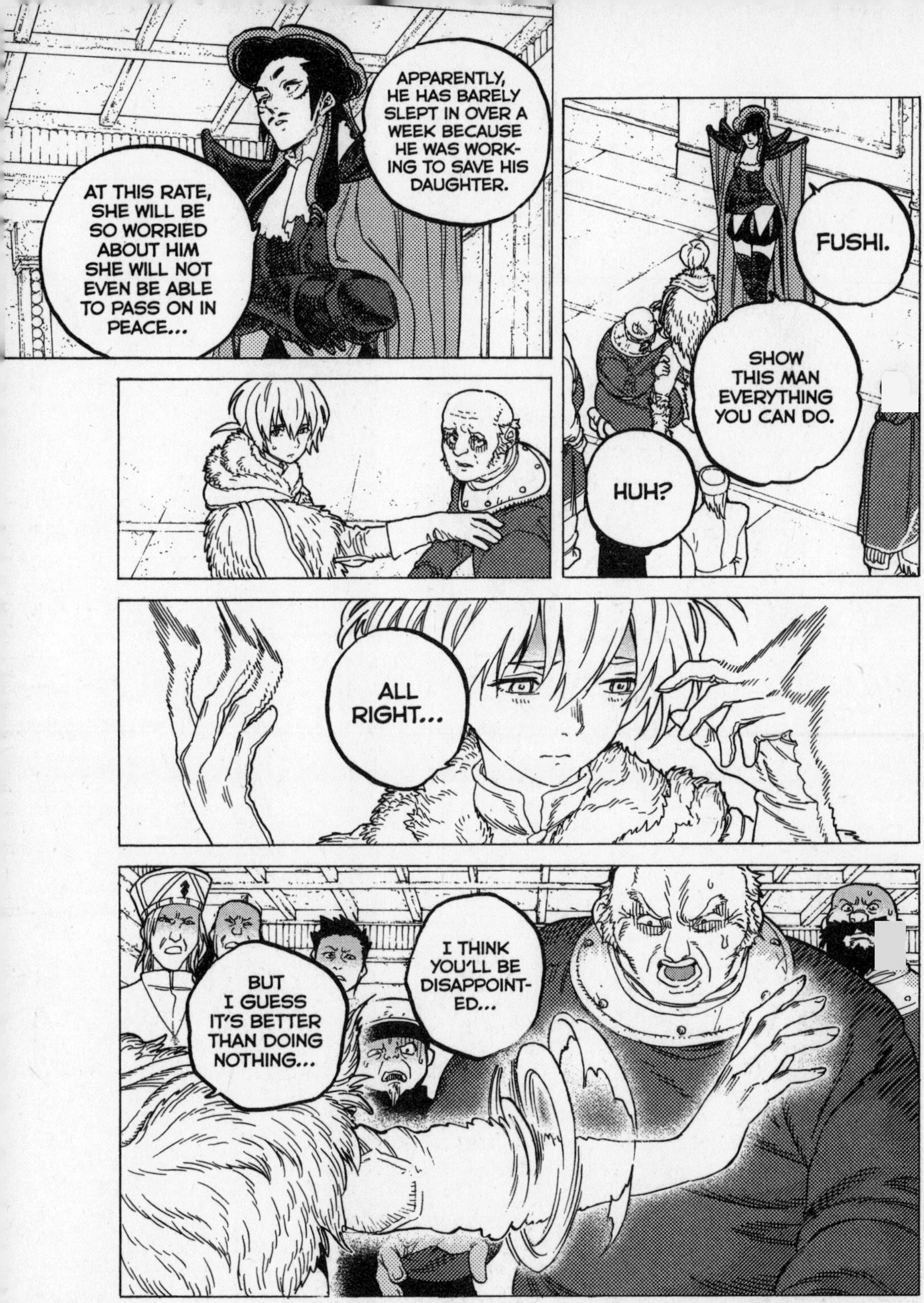
FUSHI.
SHOW THIS MAN EVERYTHING YOU CAN DO.
HUH?
APPARENTLY, HE HAS BARELY SLEPT IN OVER A WEEK BECAUSE HE WAS WORKING TO SAVE HIS DAUGHTER.
AT THIS RATE, SHE WILL BE SO WORRIED ABOUT HIM SHE WILL NOT EVEN BE ABLE TO PASS ON IN PEACE...
ALL RIGHT...
I THINK YOU'LL BE DISAPPOINTED...
BUT I GUESS IT'S BETTER THAN DOING NOTHING...

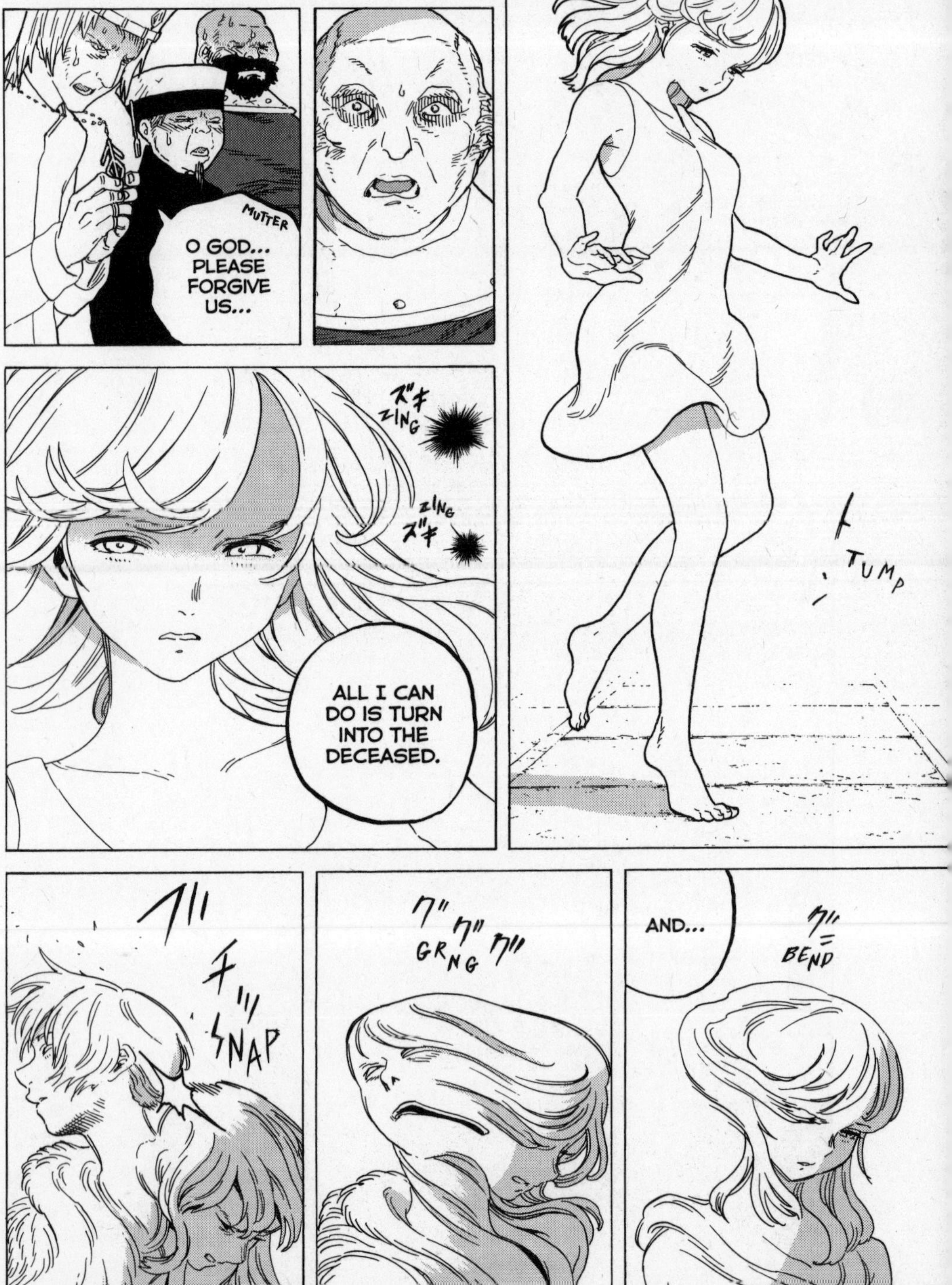
TUMP
MUTTER
O GOD... PLEASE FORGIVE US...
ズキ ZING
ZING ズキ
ALL I CAN DO IS TURN INTO THE DECEASED.
AND...
BEND
GRNG
SNAP

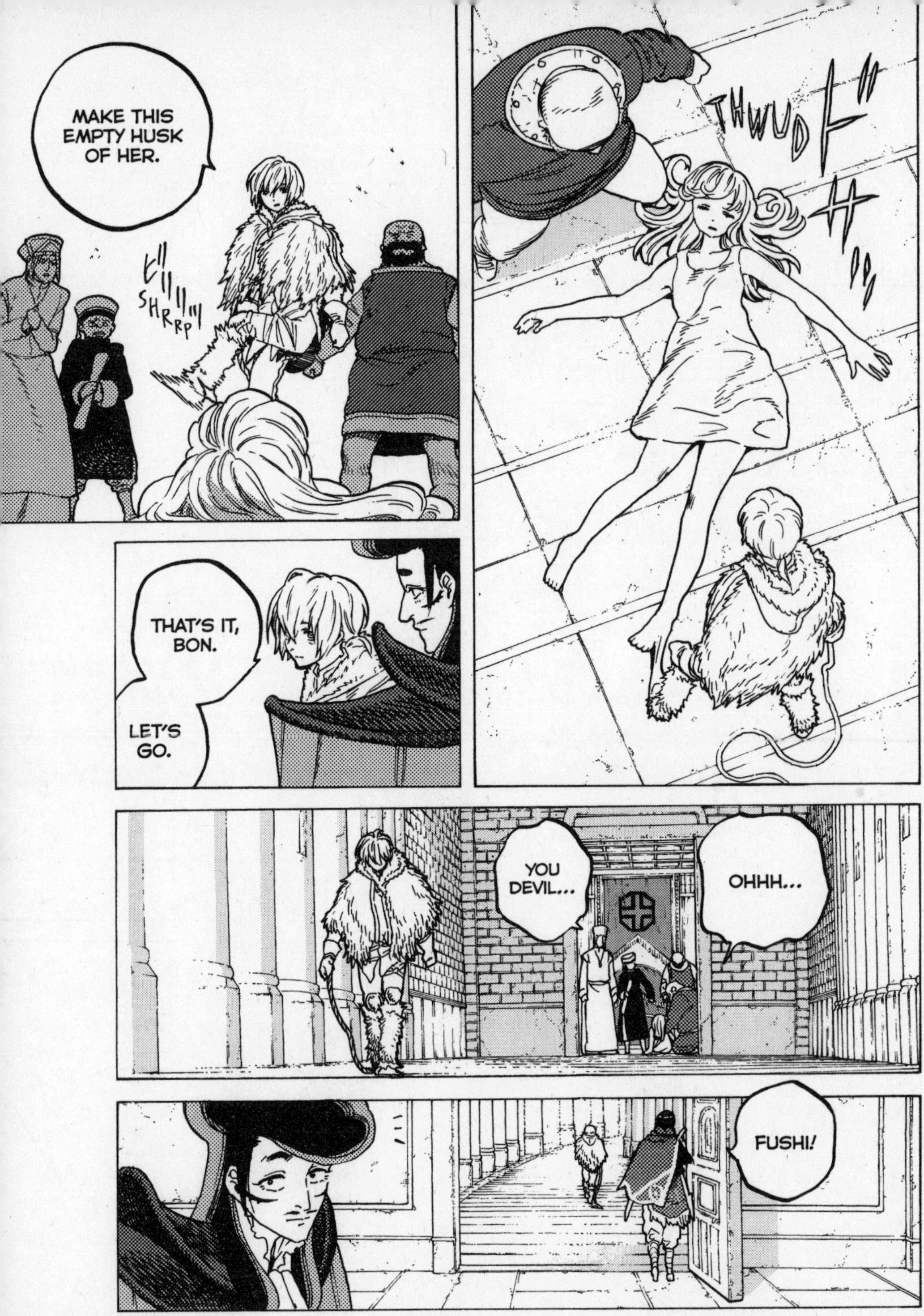
THWUD
MAKE THIS EMPTY HUSK OF HER.
SHRRRP
THAT'S IT, BON.
LET'S GO.
OHHH...
YOU DEVIL...
FUSHI!

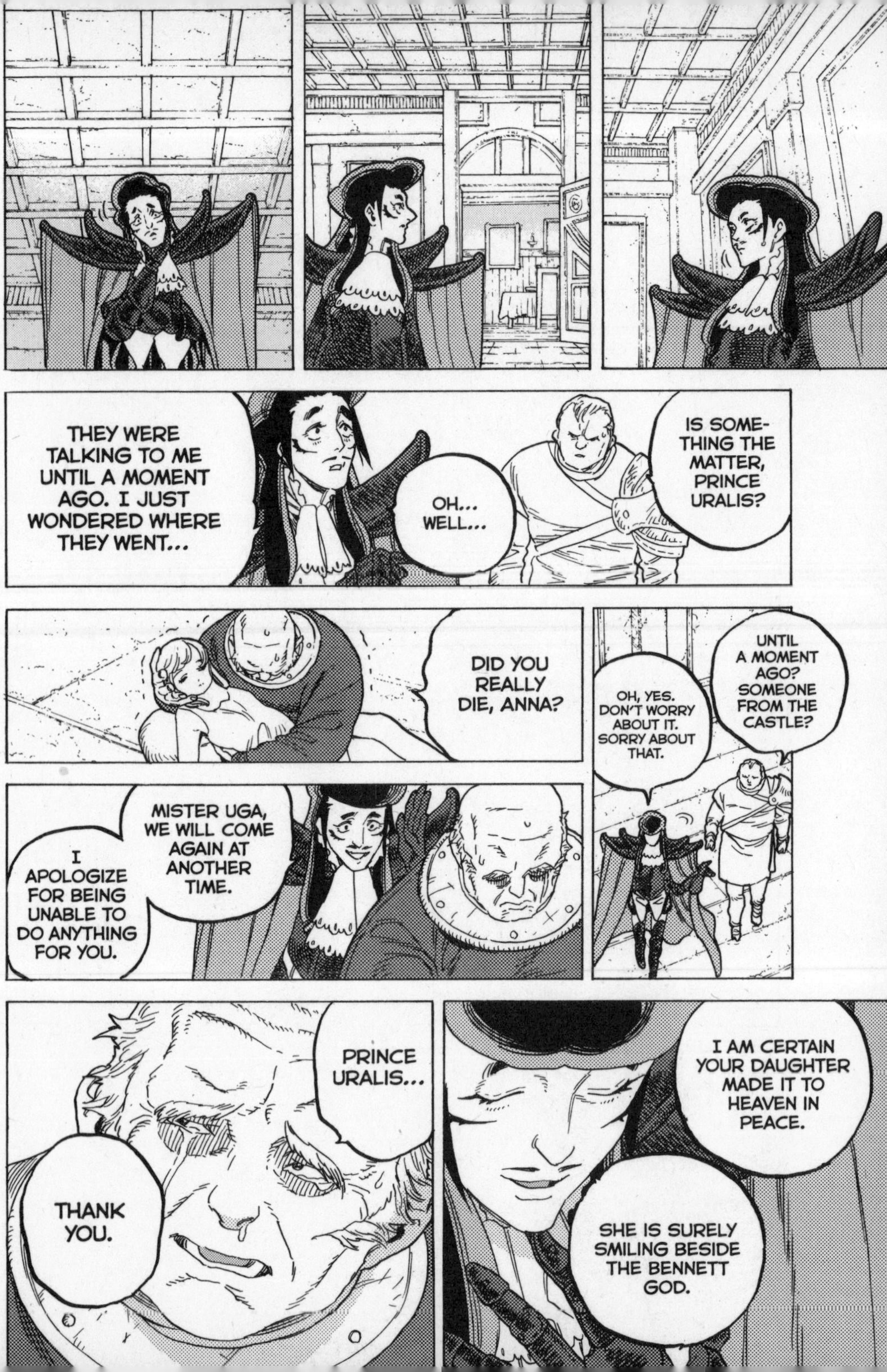
IS SOMETHING THE MATTER, PRINCE URALIS?
OH... WELL...
THEY WERE TALKING TO ME UNTIL A MOMENT AGO. I JUST WONDERED WHERE THEY WENT...
UNTIL A MOMENT AGO? SOMEONE FROM THE CASTLE?
OH, YES. DON'T WORRY ABOUT IT. SORRY ABOUT THAT.
DID YOU REALLY DIE, ANNA?
MISTER UGA, WE WILL COME AGAIN AT ANOTHER TIME.
I APOLOGIZE FOR BEING UNABLE TO DO ANYTHING FOR YOU.
I AM CERTAIN YOUR DAUGHTER MADE IT TO HEAVEN IN PEACE.
SHE IS SURELY SMILING BESIDE THE BENNETT GOD.
PRINCE URALIS...
THANK YOU.

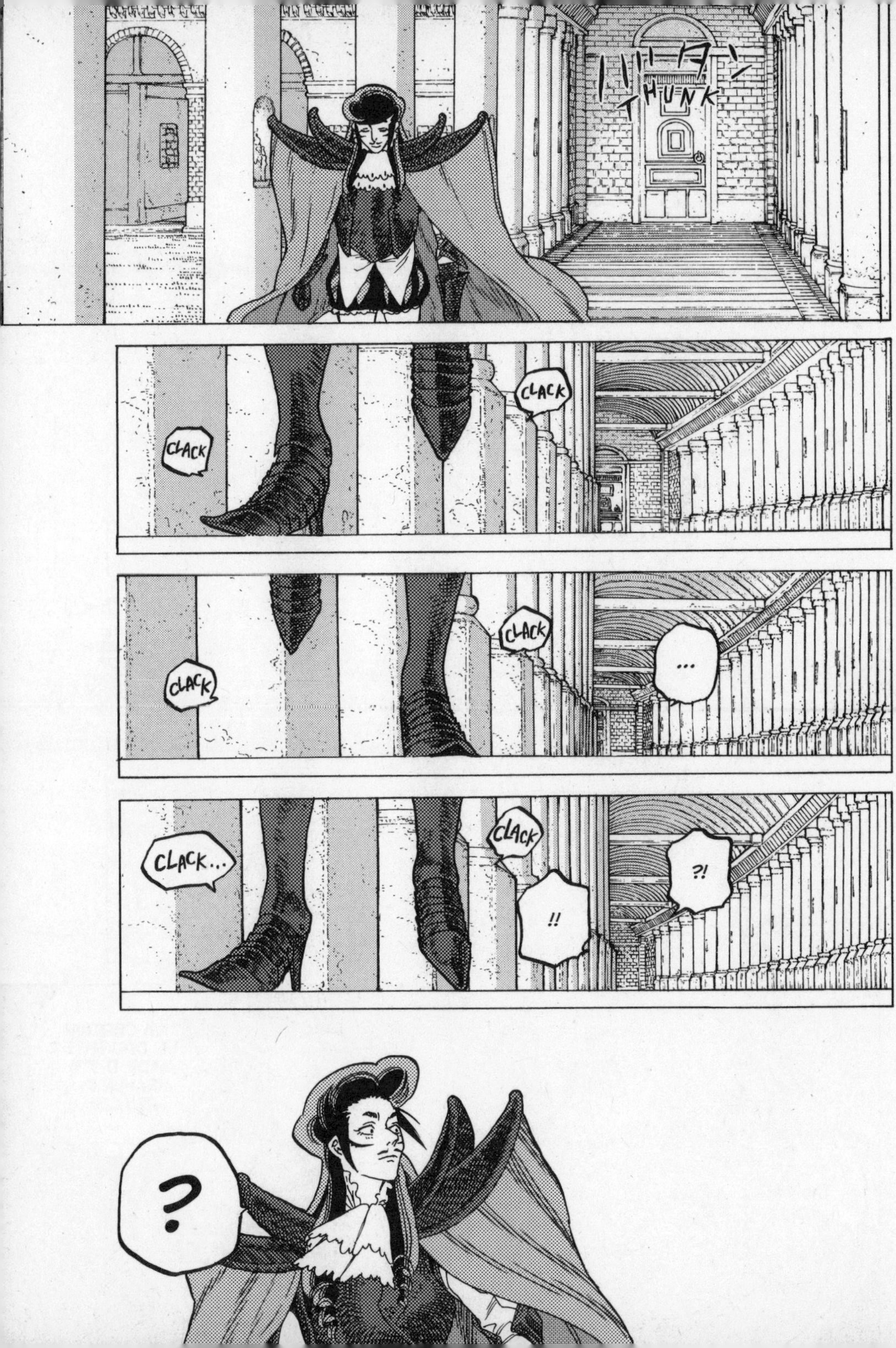
THUNK
CLACK
CLACK
...
CLACK
CLACK
?!
!!
CLACK
CLACK...
?

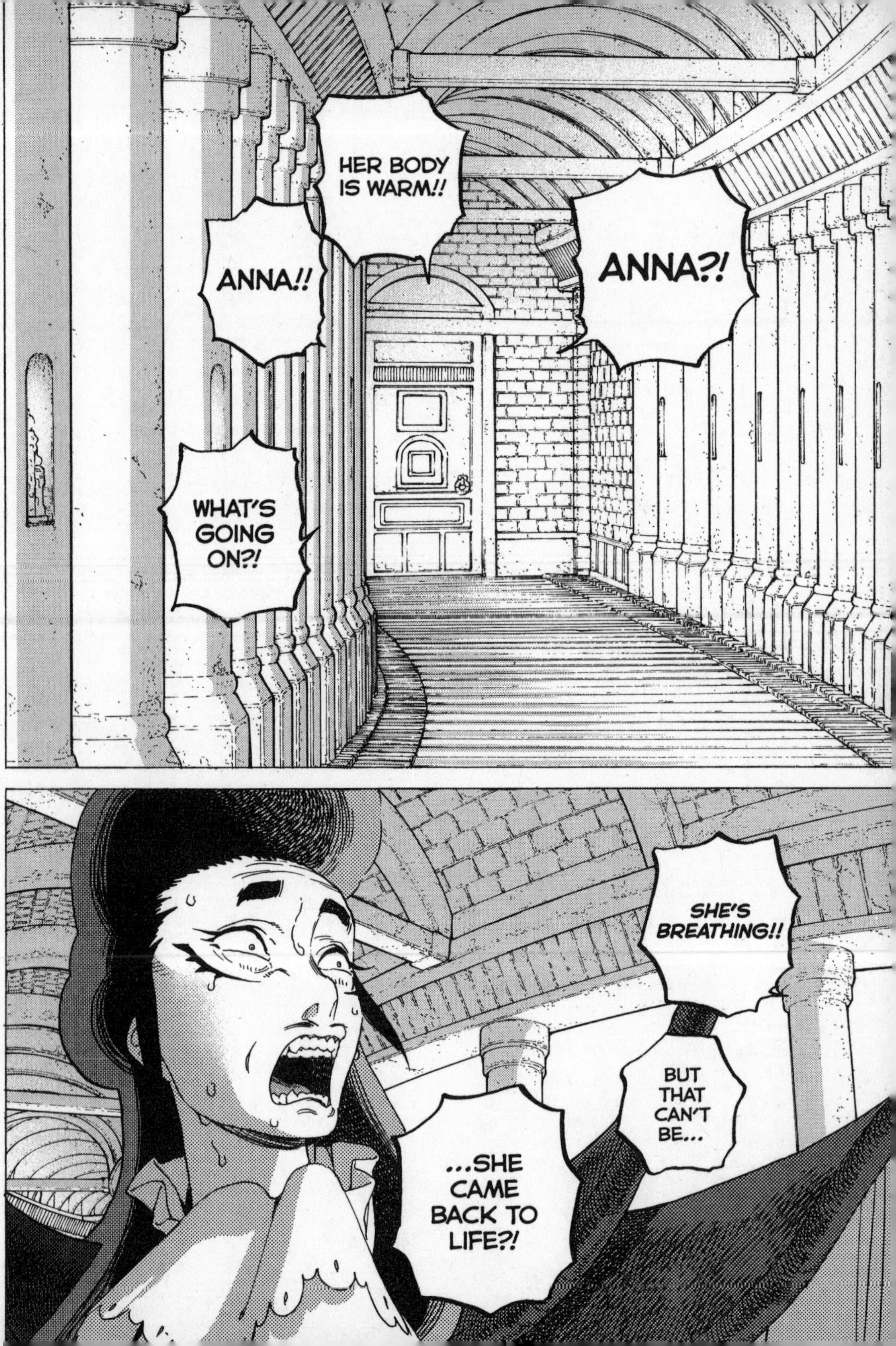
ANNA?!
HER BODY IS WARM!!
ANNA!!
WHAT'S GOING ON?!
SHE'S BREATHING!!
BUT THAT CAN'T BE...
...SHE CAME BACK TO LIFE?!

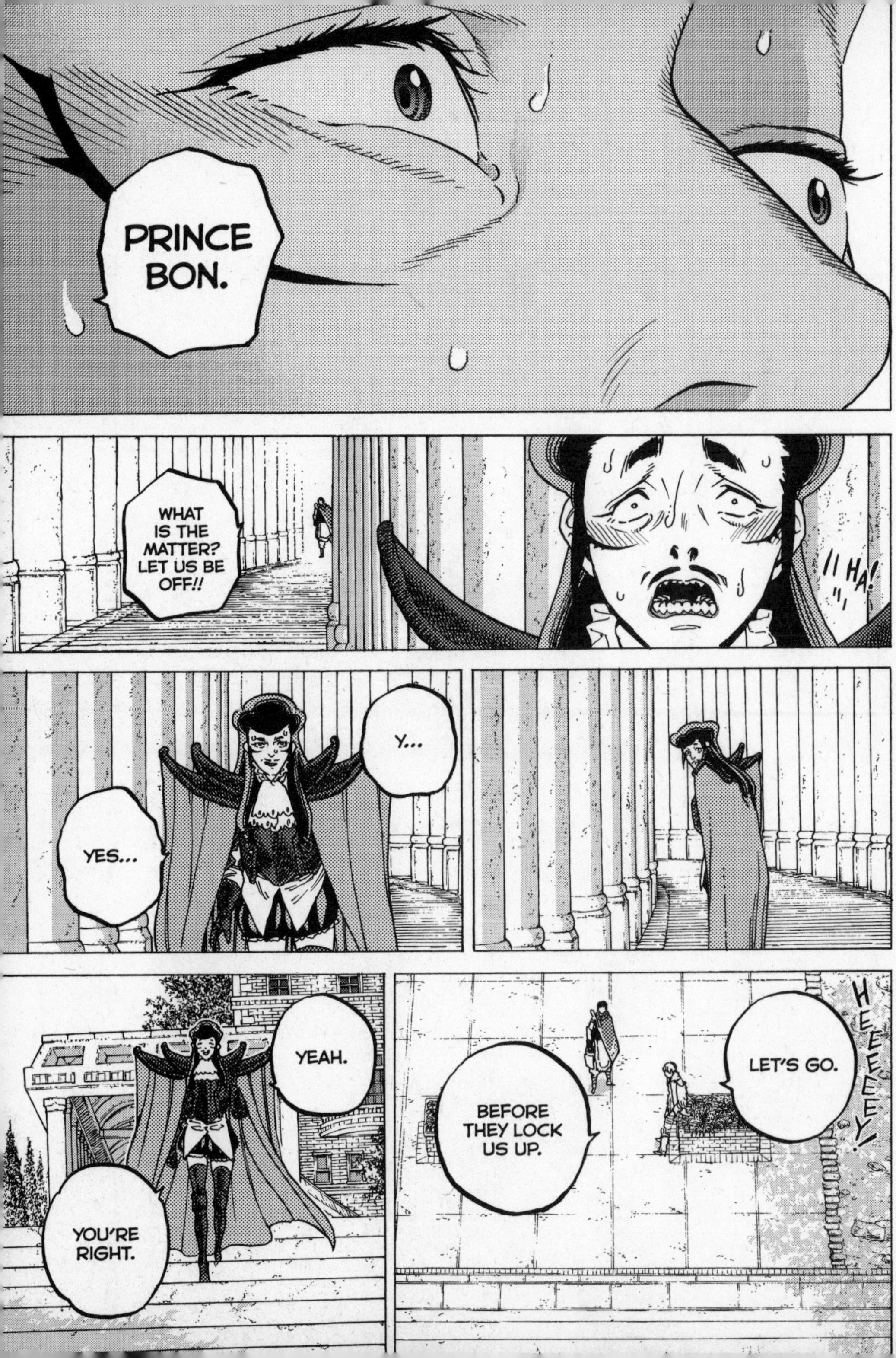
PRINCE BON.
HA!!
WHAT IS THE MATTER? LET US BE OFF!!
Y...
YES...
HEEEEEY!
LET'S GO.
BEFORE THEY LOCK US UP.
YEAH.
YOU'RE RIGHT.

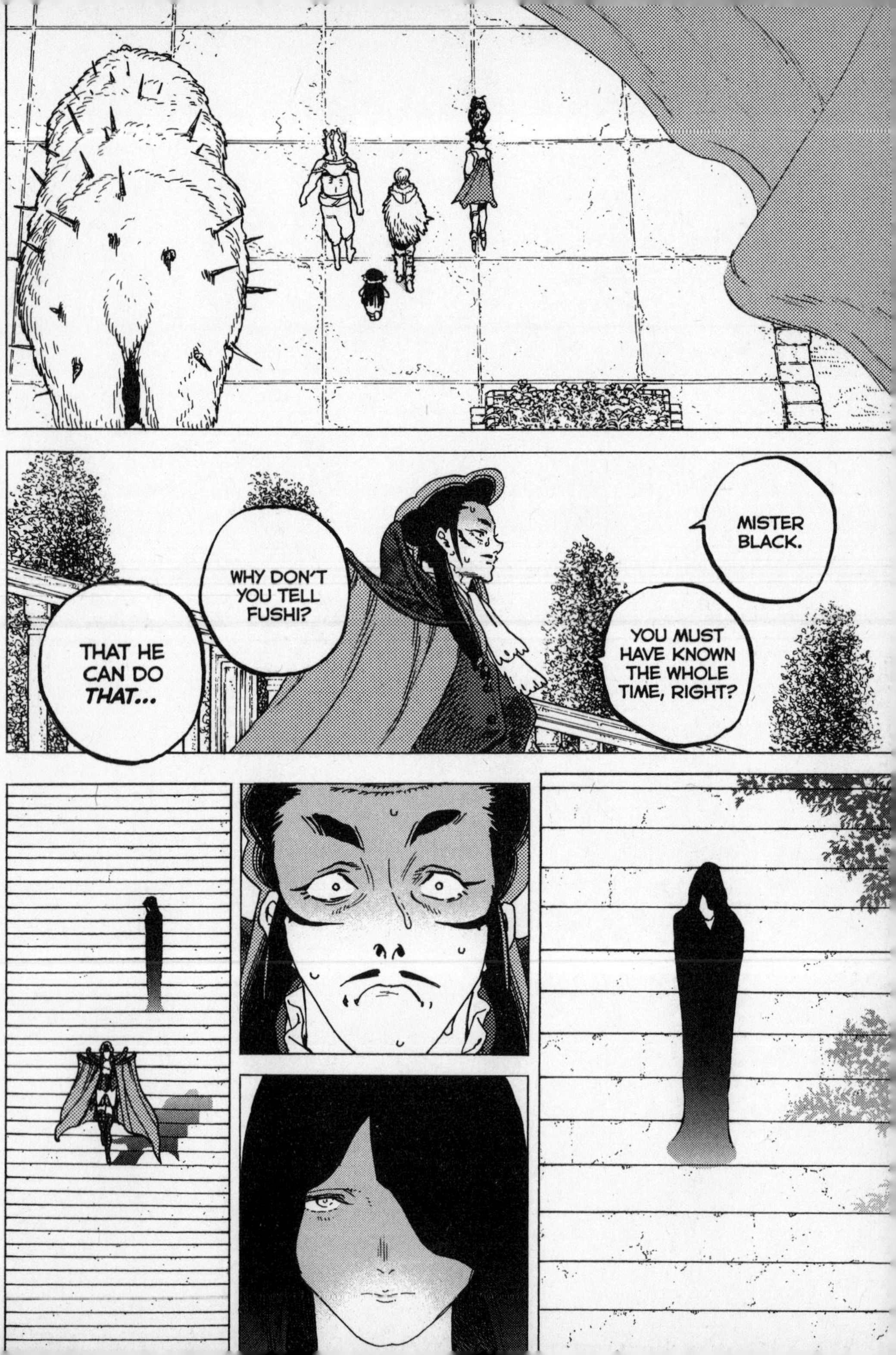
MISTER BLACK.
YOU MUST HAVE KNOWN THE WHOLE TIME, RIGHT?
WHY DON'T YOU TELL FUSHI?
THAT HE CAN DO *THAT*...

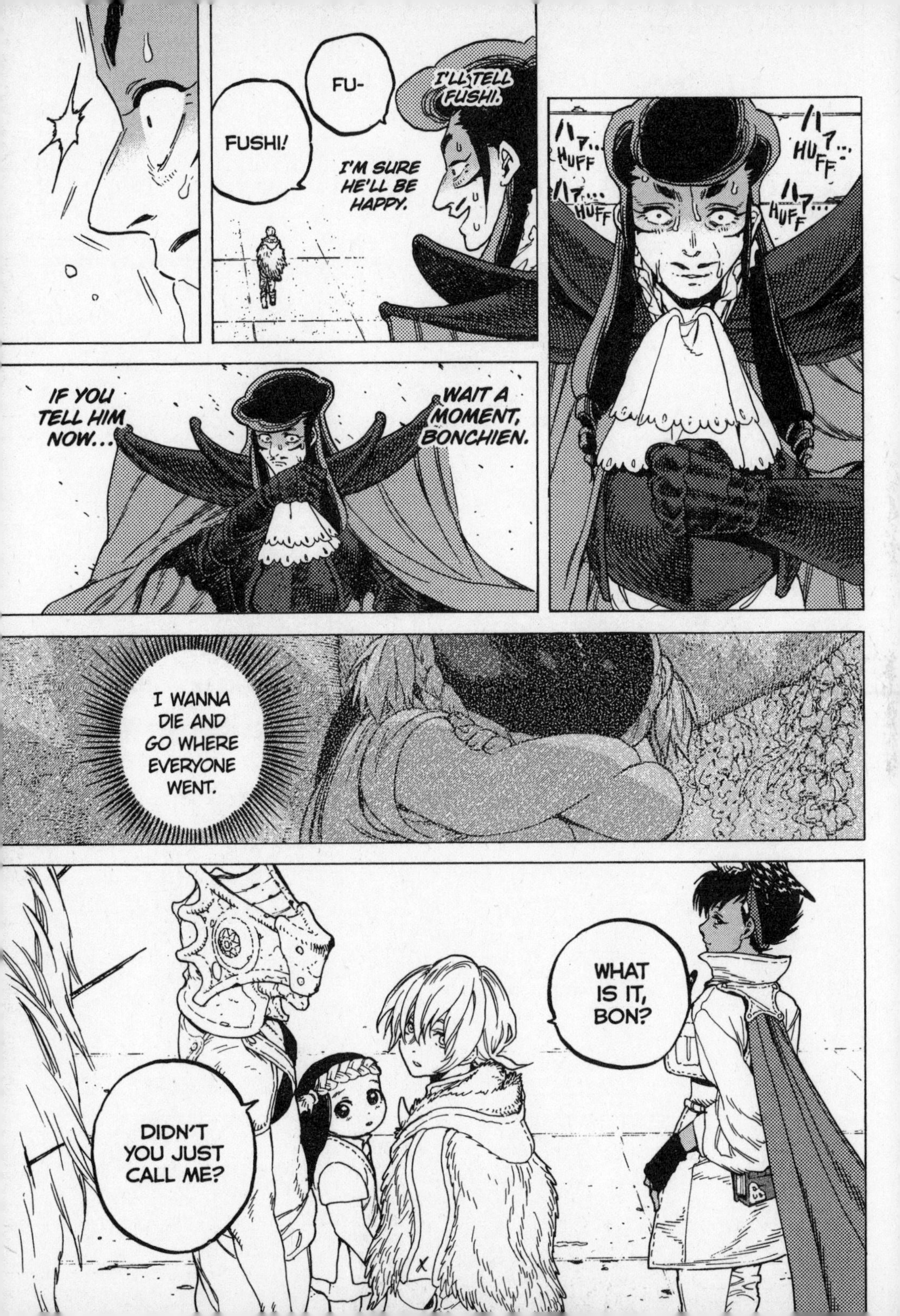

ハァ... HUFF
ハァ... HUFF
ハァ... HUFF
ハァ... HUFF
I'LL TELL FUSHI.
I'M SURE HE'LL BE HAPPY.
FU-
FUSHI!
WAIT A MOMENT, BONCHIEN.
IF YOU TELL HIM NOW...
I WANNA DIE AND GO WHERE EVERYONE WENT.
WHAT IS IT, BON?
DIDN'T YOU JUST CALL ME?

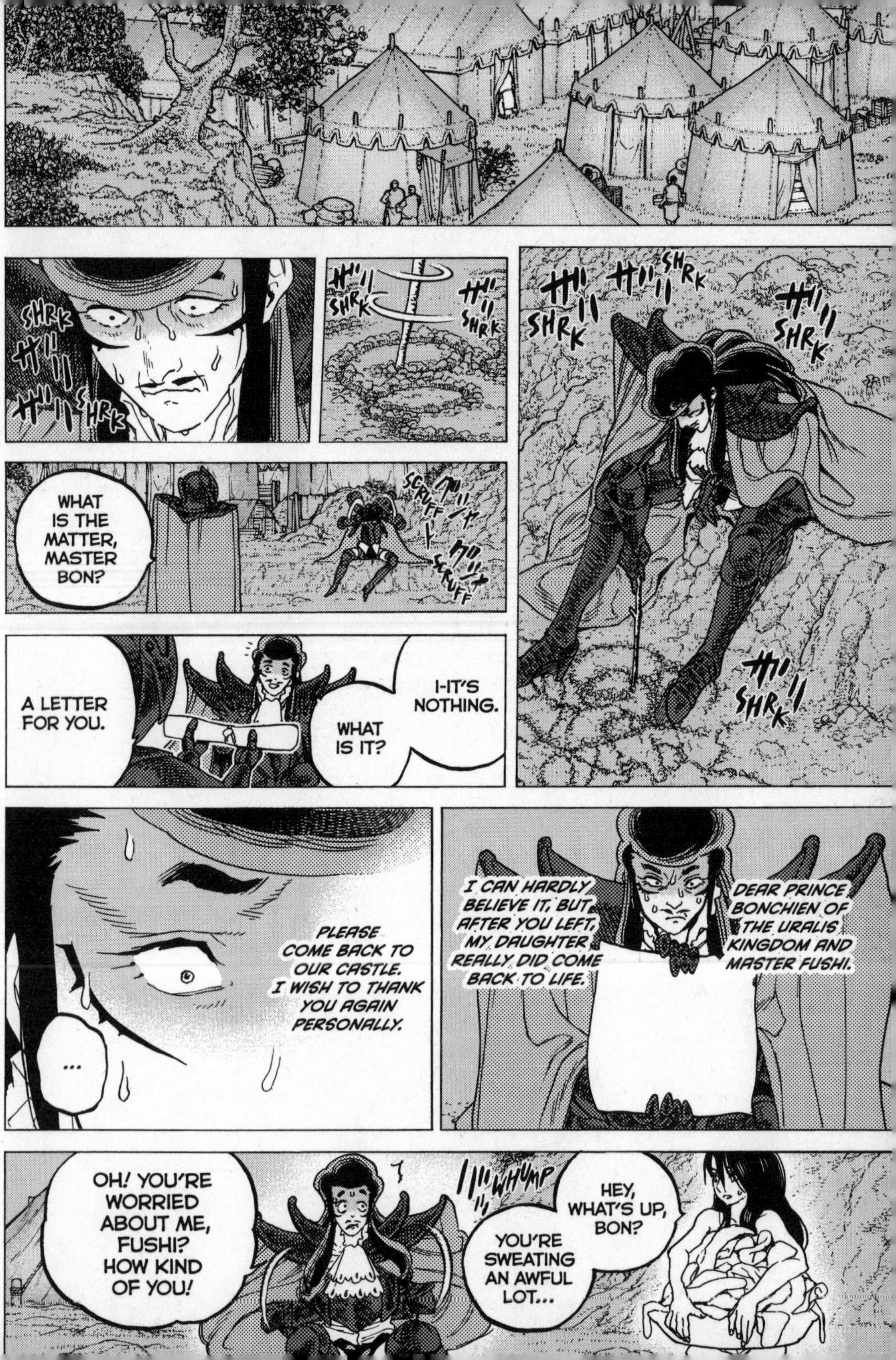
SHRK
SHRK
SHRK
SHRK
SHRK
SHRK
SHRK
SHRK
SCRUFF
SCRUFF
WHAT IS THE MATTER, MASTER BON?
I-IT'S NOTHING.
WHAT IS IT?
A LETTER FOR YOU.
DEAR PRINCE BONCHIEN OF THE URALIS KINGDOM AND MASTER FUSHI.
I CAN HARDLY BELIEVE IT, BUT AFTER YOU LEFT, MY DAUGHTER REALLY DID COME BACK TO LIFE.
PLEASE COME BACK TO OUR CASTLE. I WISH TO THANK YOU AGAIN PERSONALLY.
...
HEY, WHAT'S UP, BON?
YOU'RE SWEATING AN AWFUL LOT...
WHUMP
OH! YOU'RE WORRIED ABOUT ME, FUSHI? HOW KIND OF YOU!

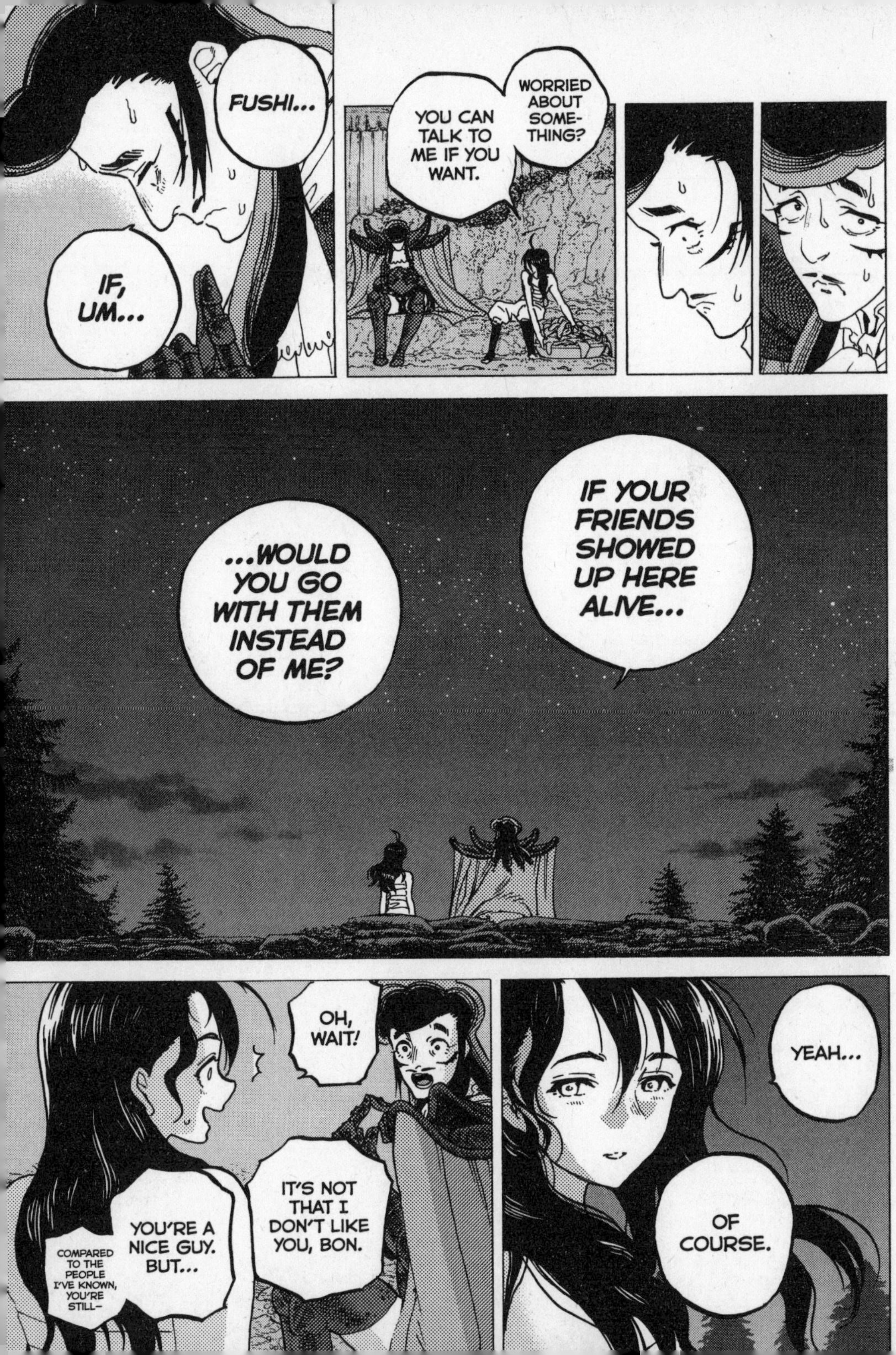
WORRIED ABOUT SOME-THING?
YOU CAN TALK TO ME IF YOU WANT.
FUSHI...
IF, UM...
IF YOUR FRIENDS SHOWED UP HERE ALIVE...
...WOULD YOU GO WITH THEM INSTEAD OF ME?
YEAH...
OF COURSE.
OH, WAIT!
IT'S NOT THAT I DON'T LIKE YOU, BON.
YOU'RE A NICE GUY. BUT...
COMPARED TO THE PEOPLE I'VE KNOWN, YOU'RE STILL–

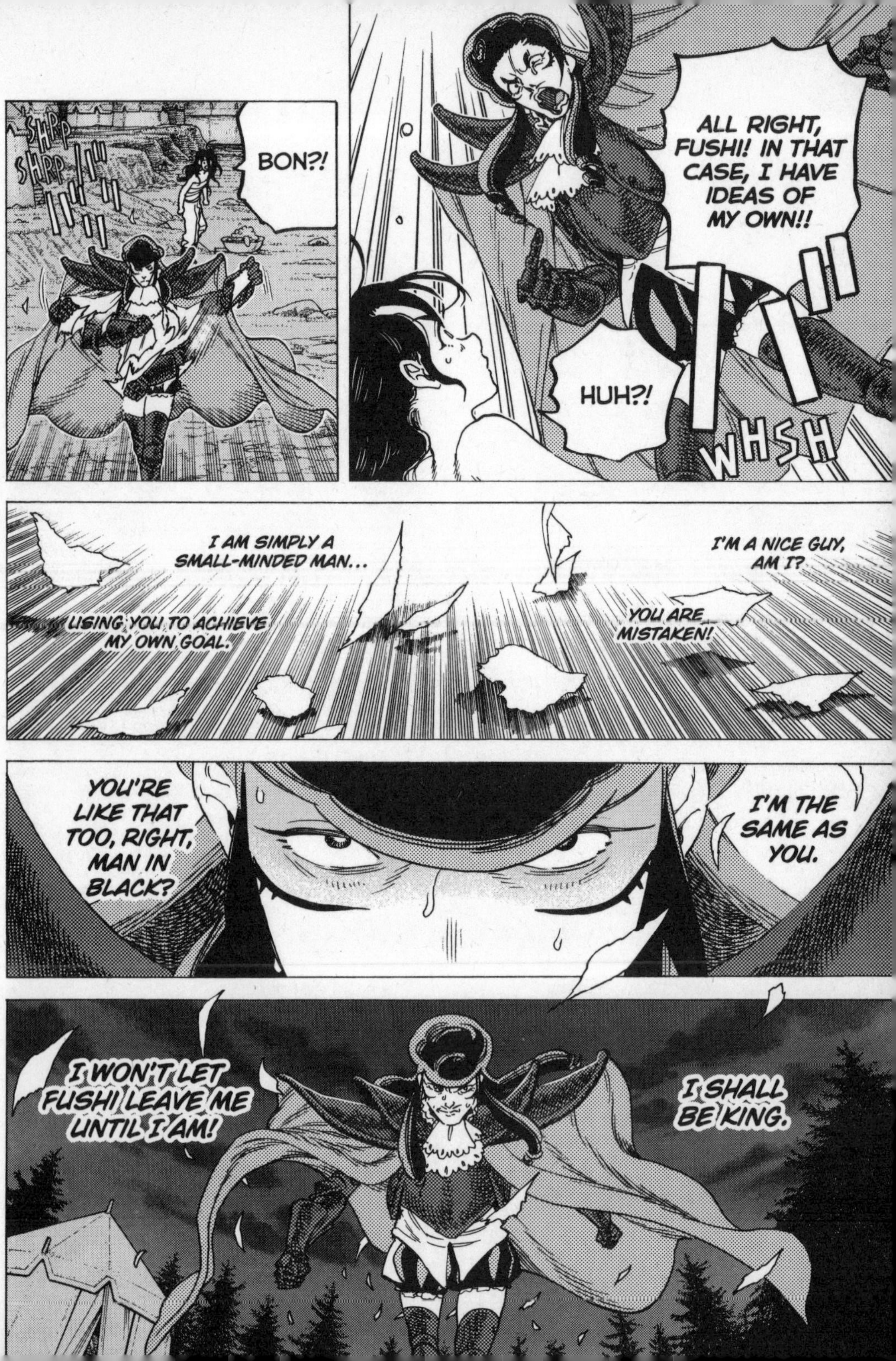
ALL RIGHT, FUSHI! IN THAT CASE, I HAVE IDEAS OF MY OWN!!
HUH?!
WHSH
SHRP
SHRP
BON?!
I'M A NICE GUY, AM I?
YOU ARE MISTAKEN!
I AM SIMPLY A SMALL-MINDED MAN...
USING YOU TO ACHIEVE MY OWN GOAL.
I'M THE SAME AS YOU.
YOU'RE LIKE THAT TOO, RIGHT, MAN IN BLACK?
I SHALL BE KING.
I WON'T LET FUSHI LEAVE ME UNTIL I AM!

TO YOUR ETERNITY

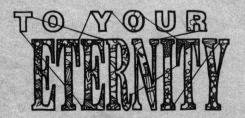

TO YOUR ETERNITY

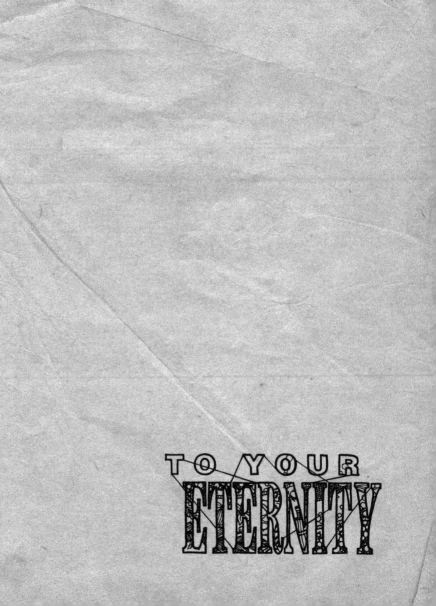

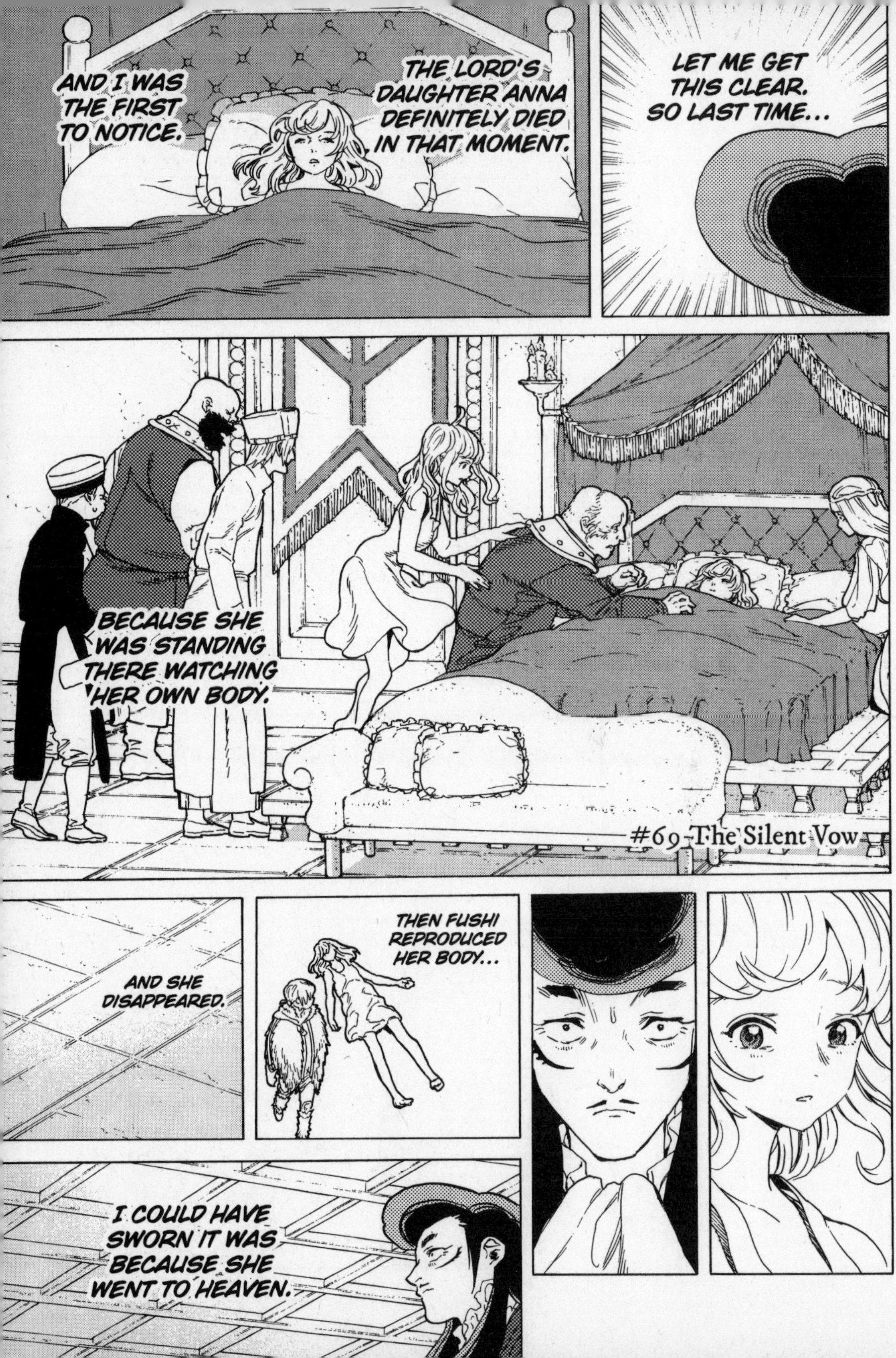
LET ME GET THIS CLEAR. SO LAST TIME...
THE LORD'S DAUGHTER ANNA DEFINITELY DIED IN THAT MOMENT.
AND I WAS THE FIRST TO NOTICE.
BECAUSE SHE WAS STANDING THERE WATCHING HER OWN BODY.
#69 The Silent Vow
THEN FUSHI REPRODUCED HER BODY...
AND SHE DISAPPEARED.
I COULD HAVE SWORN IT WAS BECAUSE SHE WENT TO HEAVEN.

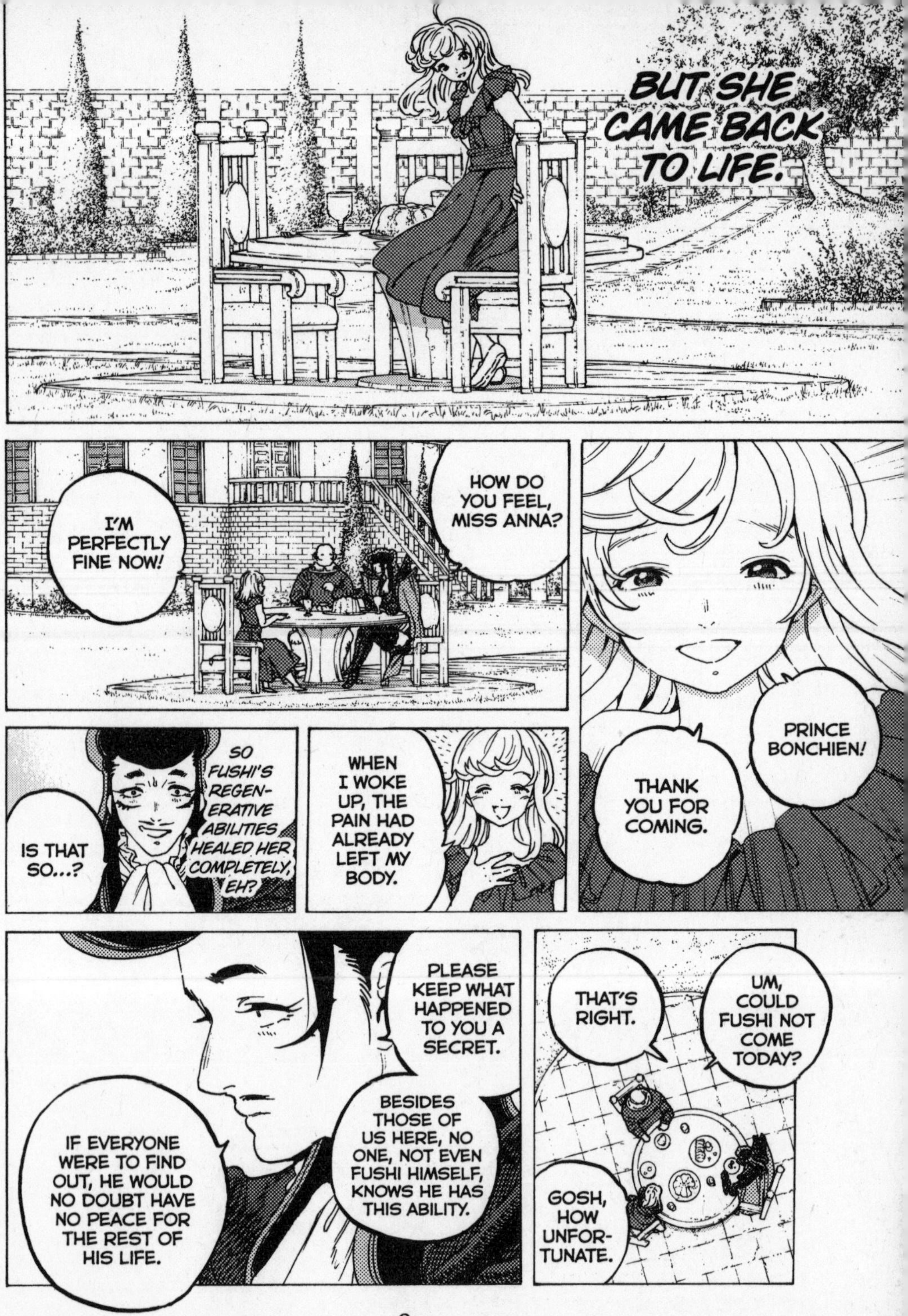
BUT SHE CAME BACK TO LIFE.
PRINCE BONCHIEN!
THANK YOU FOR COMING.
HOW DO YOU FEEL, MISS ANNA?
I'M PERFECTLY FINE NOW!
WHEN I WOKE UP, THE PAIN HAD ALREADY LEFT MY BODY.
SO FUSHI'S REGENERATIVE ABILITIES HEALED HER COMPLETELY, EH?
IS THAT SO...?
UM, COULD FUSHI NOT COME TODAY?
THAT'S RIGHT.
GOSH, HOW UNFORTUNATE.
PLEASE KEEP WHAT HAPPENED TO YOU A SECRET.
BESIDES THOSE OF US HERE, NO ONE, NOT EVEN FUSHI HIMSELF, KNOWS HE HAS THIS ABILITY.
IF EVERYONE WERE TO FIND OUT, HE WOULD NO DOUBT HAVE NO PEACE FOR THE REST OF HIS LIFE.

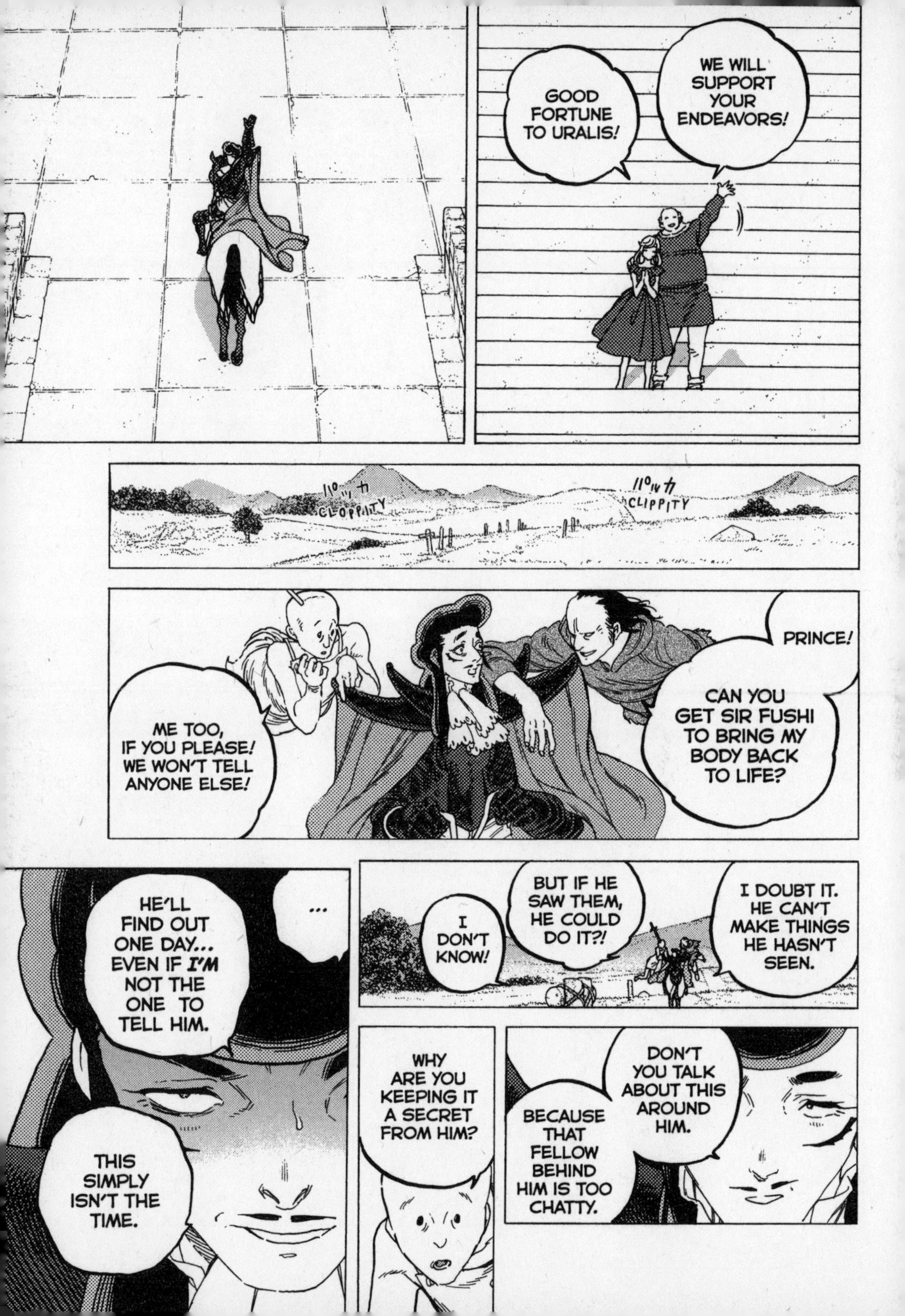
WE WILL SUPPORT YOUR ENDEAVORS!
GOOD FORTUNE TO URALIS!
CLIPPITY
CLOPPITY
PRINCE!
CAN YOU GET SIR FUSHI TO BRING MY BODY BACK TO LIFE?
ME TOO, IF YOU PLEASE! WE WON'T TELL ANYONE ELSE!
I DOUBT IT. HE CAN'T MAKE THINGS HE HASN'T SEEN.
BUT IF HE SAW THEM, HE COULD DO IT?!
I DON'T KNOW!
DON'T YOU TALK ABOUT THIS AROUND HIM.
WHY ARE YOU KEEPING IT A SECRET FROM HIM?
BECAUSE THAT FELLOW BEHIND HIM IS TOO CHATTY.
...
HE'LL FIND OUT ONE DAY... EVEN IF *I'M* NOT THE ONE TO TELL HIM.
THIS SIMPLY ISN'T THE TIME.

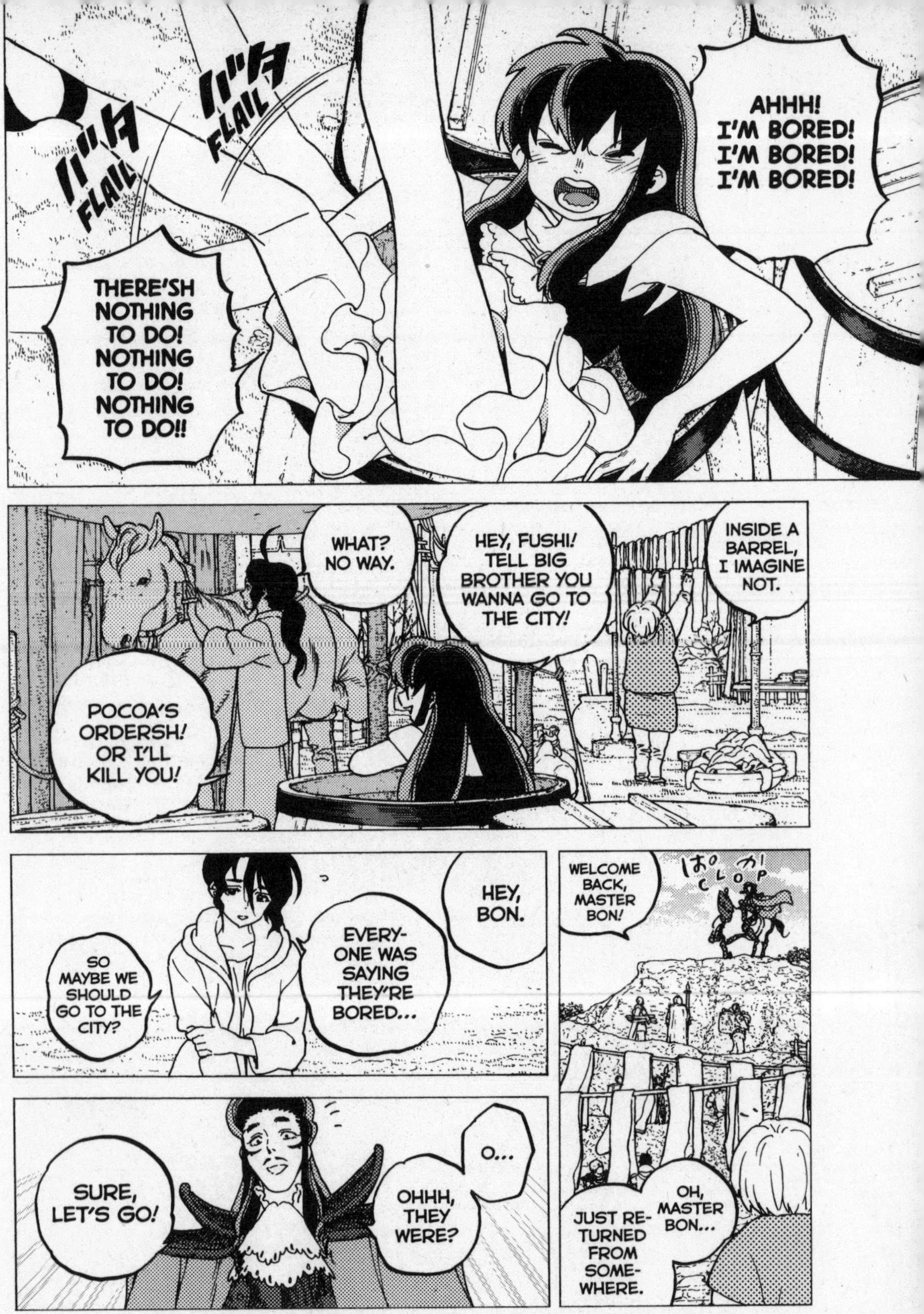
AHHH! I'M BORED! I'M BORED! I'M BORED!
FLAIL
FLAIL
THERE'SH NOTHING TO DO! NOTHING TO DO! NOTHING TO DO!!
INSIDE A BARREL, I IMAGINE NOT.
HEY, FUSHI! TELL BIG BROTHER YOU WANNA GO TO THE CITY!
WHAT? NO WAY.
POCOA'S ORDERSH! OR I'LL KILL YOU!
CLOP
WELCOME BACK, MASTER BON!
OH, MASTER BON...
JUST RETURNED FROM SOMEWHERE.
HEY, BON.
EVERYONE WAS SAYING THEY'RE BORED...
SO MAYBE WE SHOULD GO TO THE CITY?
O...
OHHH, THEY WERE?
SURE, LET'S GO!

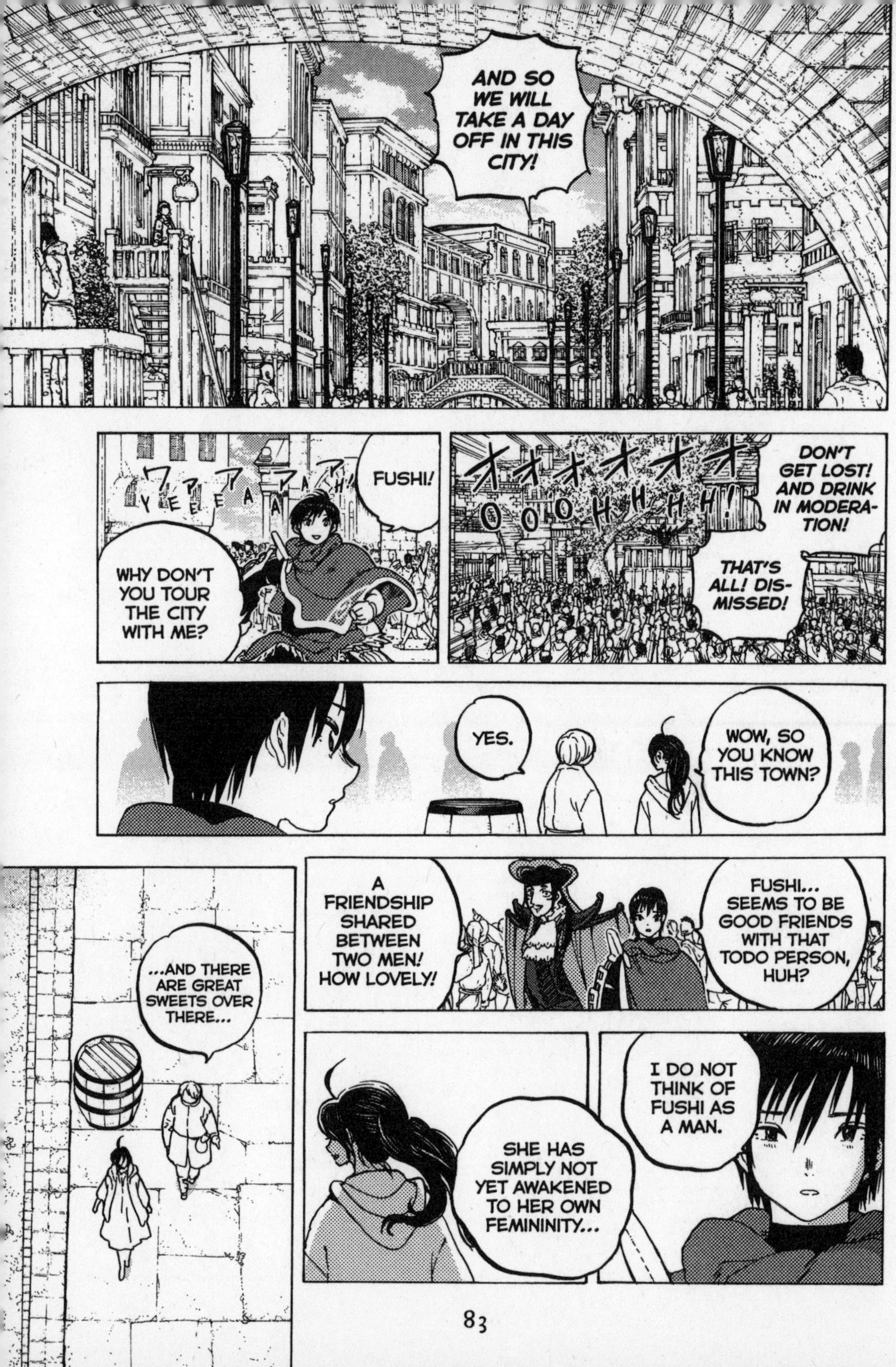
AND SO WE WILL TAKE A DAY OFF IN THIS CITY!
オオオオオオ
OOOHHHH!
DON'T GET LOST! AND DRINK IN MODERATION!
THAT'S ALL! DISMISSED!
FUSHI!
ワアアアア
YEEEAAAH!
WHY DON'T YOU TOUR THE CITY WITH ME?
WOW, SO YOU KNOW THIS TOWN?
YES.
FUSHI... SEEMS TO BE GOOD FRIENDS WITH THAT TODO PERSON, HUH?
A FRIENDSHIP SHARED BETWEEN TWO MEN! HOW LOVELY!
I DO NOT THINK OF FUSHI AS A MAN.
SHE HAS SIMPLY NOT YET AWAKENED TO HER OWN FEMININITY...
...AND THERE ARE GREAT SWEETS OVER THERE...

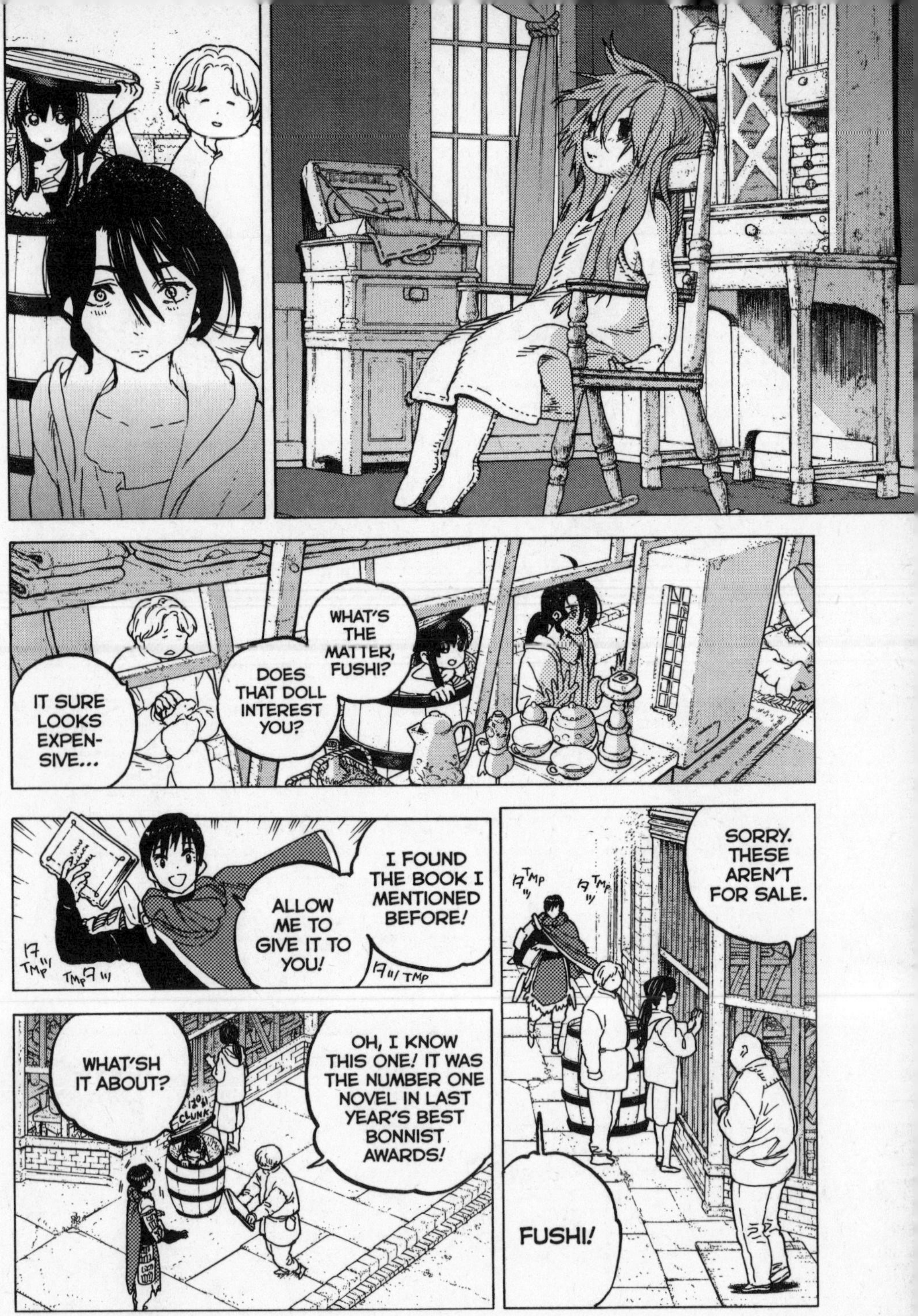
WHAT'S THE MATTER, FUSHI?
DOES THAT DOLL INTEREST YOU?
IT SURE LOOKS EXPENSIVE...
SORRY. THESE AREN'T FOR SALE.
TMP
TMP
FUSHI!
I FOUND THE BOOK I MENTIONED BEFORE!
ALLOW ME TO GIVE IT TO YOU!
TMP
TMP
TMP
OH, I KNOW THIS ONE! IT WAS THE NUMBER ONE NOVEL IN LAST YEAR'S BEST BONNIST AWARDS!
WHAT'SH IT ABOUT?
CLUNK

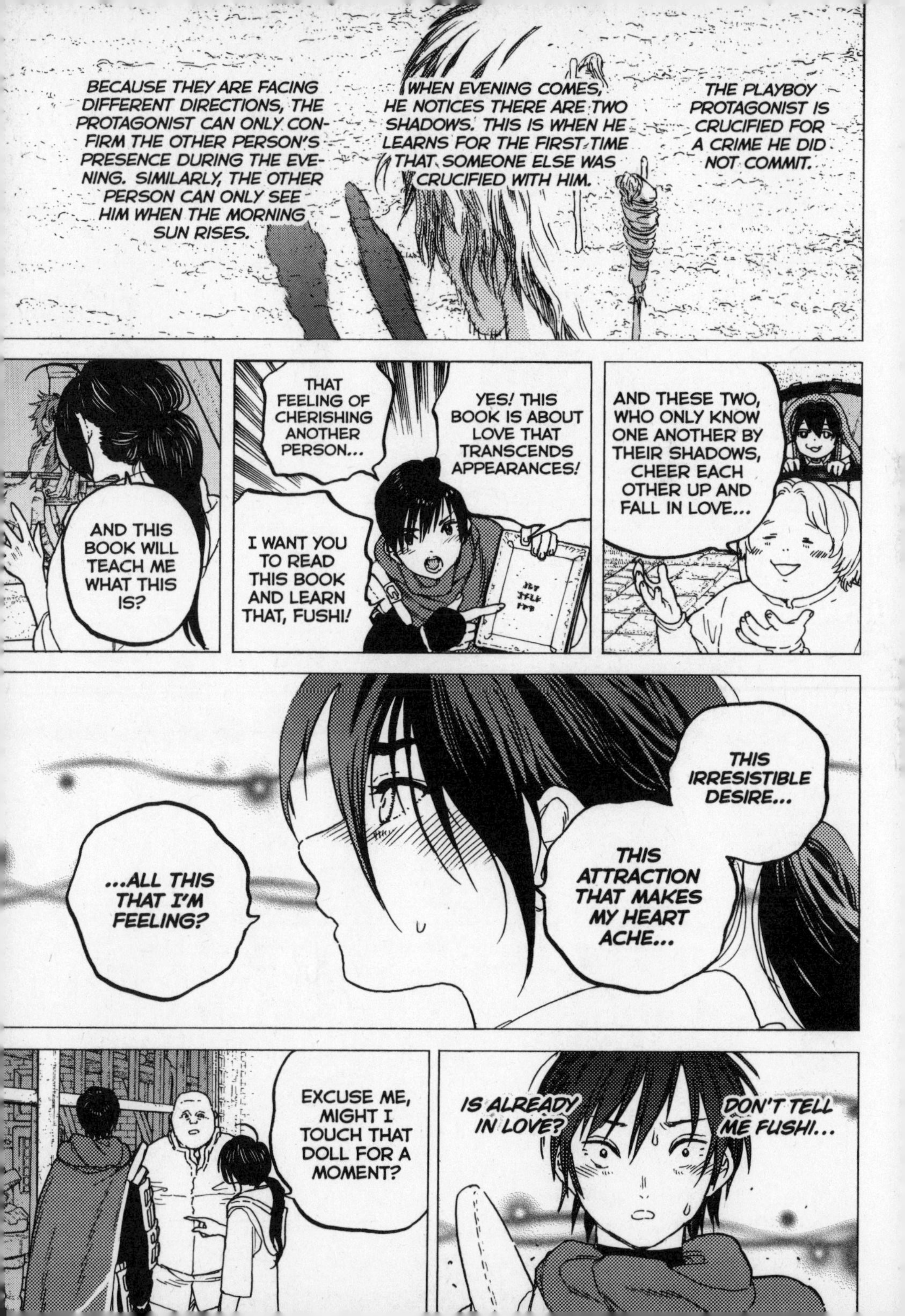
THE PLAYBOY PROTAGONIST IS CRUCIFIED FOR A CRIME HE DID NOT COMMIT.
WHEN EVENING COMES, HE NOTICES THERE ARE TWO SHADOWS. THIS IS WHEN HE LEARNS FOR THE FIRST TIME THAT SOMEONE ELSE WAS CRUCIFIED WITH HIM.
BECAUSE THEY ARE FACING DIFFERENT DIRECTIONS, THE PROTAGONIST CAN ONLY CONFIRM THE OTHER PERSON'S PRESENCE DURING THE EVENING. SIMILARLY, THE OTHER PERSON CAN ONLY SEE HIM WHEN THE MORNING SUN RISES.
AND THESE TWO, WHO ONLY KNOW ONE ANOTHER BY THEIR SHADOWS, CHEER EACH OTHER UP AND FALL IN LOVE...
THAT FEELING OF CHERISHING ANOTHER PERSON...
YES! THIS BOOK IS ABOUT LOVE THAT TRANSCENDS APPEARANCES!
I WANT YOU TO READ THIS BOOK AND LEARN THAT, FUSHI!
AND THIS BOOK WILL TEACH ME WHAT THIS IS?
THIS IRRESISTIBLE DESIRE...
THIS ATTRACTION THAT MAKES MY HEART ACHE...
...ALL THIS THAT I'M FEELING?
DON'T TELL ME FUSHI...
IS ALREADY IN LOVE?
EXCUSE ME, MIGHT I TOUCH THAT DOLL FOR A MOMENT?

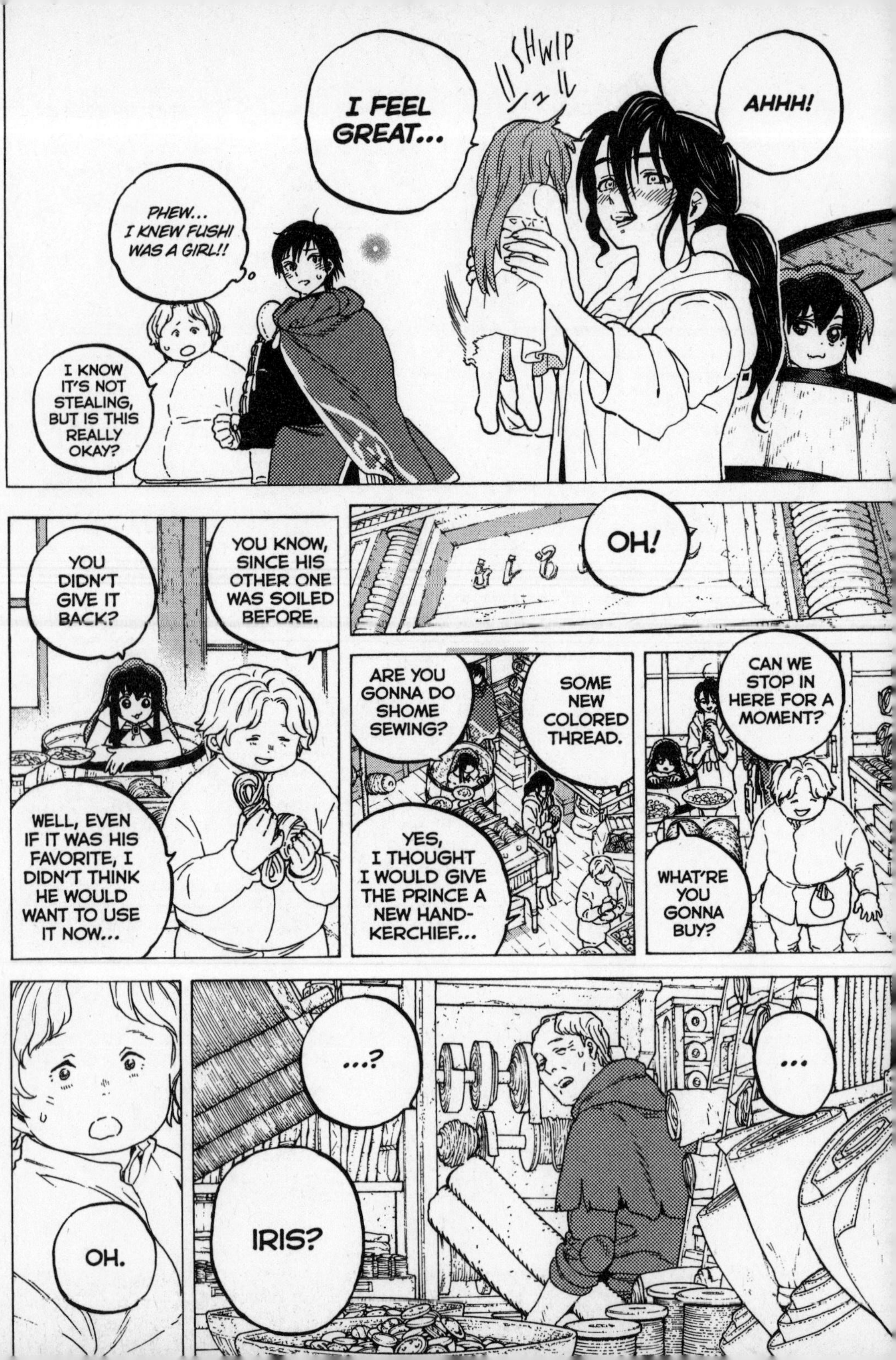
AHHH!
SHWIP
I FEEL GREAT...
PHEW... I KNEW FUSHI WAS A GIRL!!
I KNOW IT'S NOT STEALING, BUT IS THIS REALLY OKAY?
OH!
CAN WE STOP IN HERE FOR A MOMENT?
WHAT'RE YOU GONNA BUY?
SOME NEW COLORED THREAD.
ARE YOU GONNA DO SHOME SEWING?
YES, I THOUGHT I WOULD GIVE THE PRINCE A NEW HAND-KERCHIEF...
YOU KNOW, SINCE HIS OTHER ONE WAS SOILED BEFORE.
YOU DIDN'T GIVE IT BACK?
WELL, EVEN IF IT WAS HIS FAVORITE, I DIDN'T THINK HE WOULD WANT TO USE IT NOW...
...
...?
IRIS?
OH.

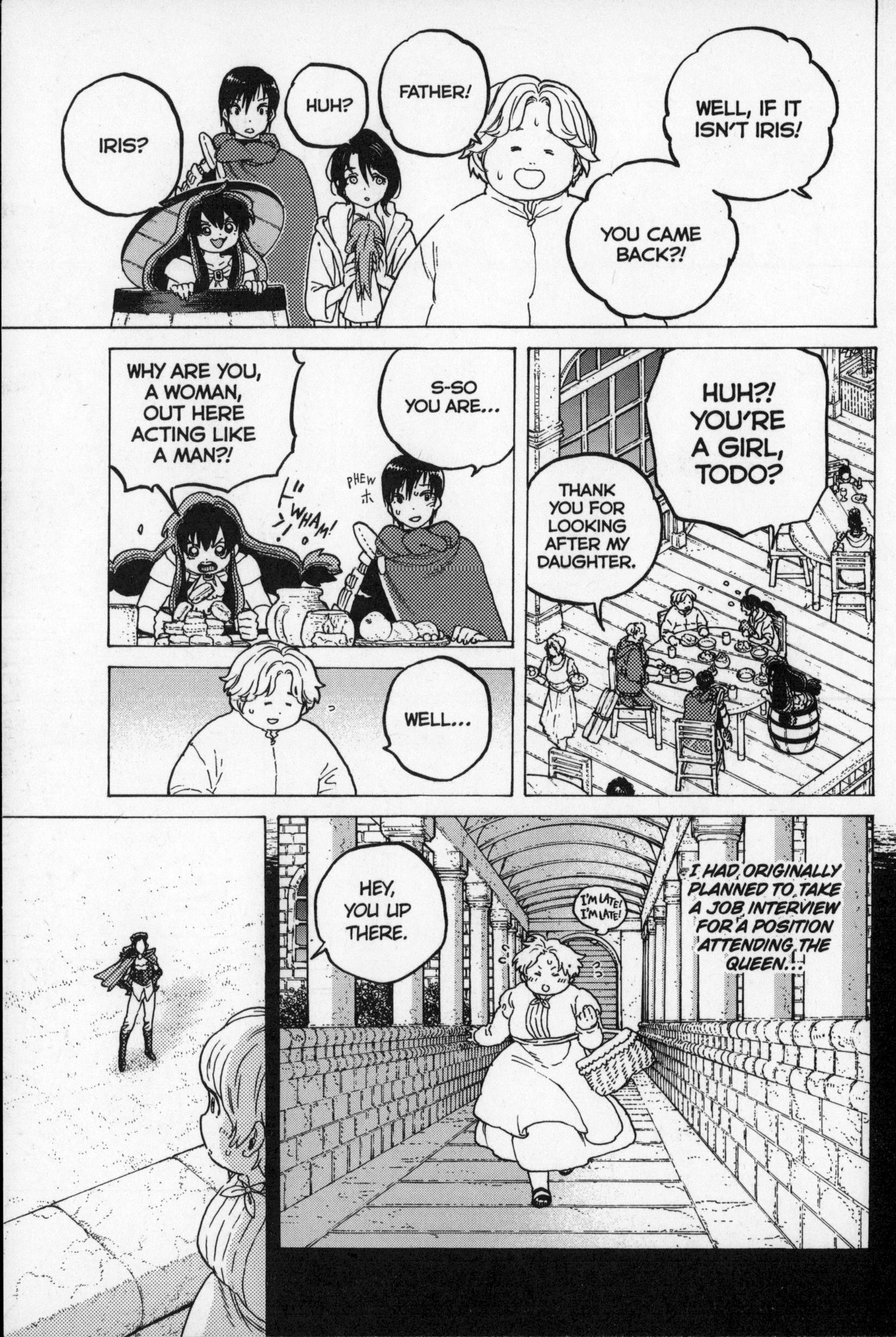
WELL, IF IT ISN'T IRIS!
YOU CAME BACK?!
FATHER!
HUH?
IRIS?
HUH?! YOU'RE A GIRL, TODO?
THANK YOU FOR LOOKING AFTER MY DAUGHTER.
S-SO YOU ARE...
PHEW
WHY ARE YOU, A WOMAN, OUT HERE ACTING LIKE A MAN?!
WHAM!
WELL...
I HAD ORIGINALLY PLANNED TO TAKE A JOB INTERVIEW FOR A POSITION ATTENDING THE QUEEN...
I'M LATE! I'M LATE!
HEY, YOU UP THERE.

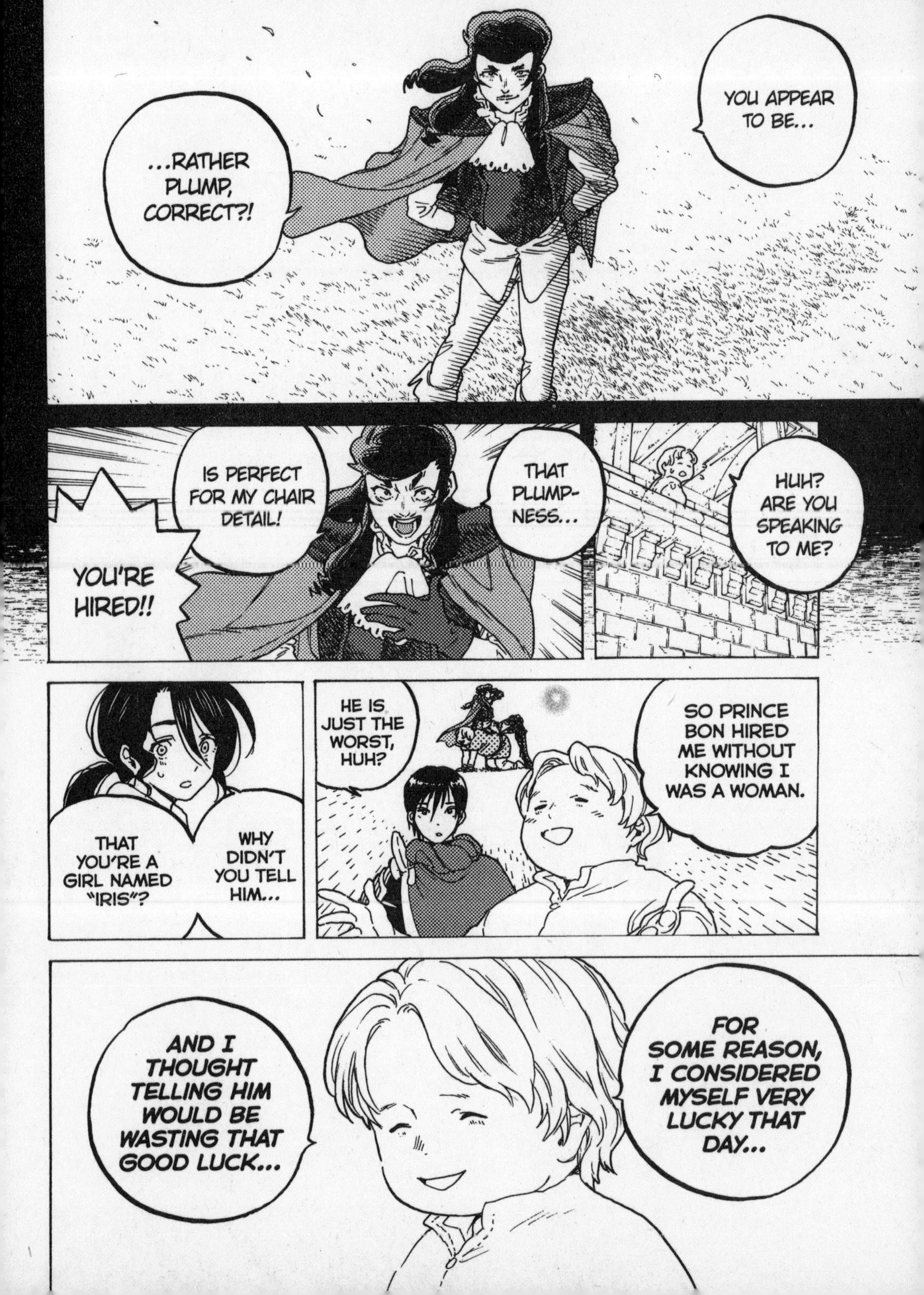
YOU APPEAR TO BE...
...RATHER PLUMP, CORRECT?!
HUH? ARE YOU SPEAKING TO ME?
THAT PLUMP-NESS...
IS PERFECT FOR MY CHAIR DETAIL!
YOU'RE HIRED!!
SO PRINCE BON HIRED ME WITHOUT KNOWING I WAS A WOMAN.
HE IS JUST THE WORST, HUH?
WHY DIDN'T YOU TELL HIM...
THAT YOU'RE A GIRL NAMED "IRIS"?
FOR SOME REASON, I CONSIDERED MYSELF VERY LUCKY THAT DAY...
AND I THOUGHT TELLING HIM WOULD BE WASTING THAT GOOD LUCK...

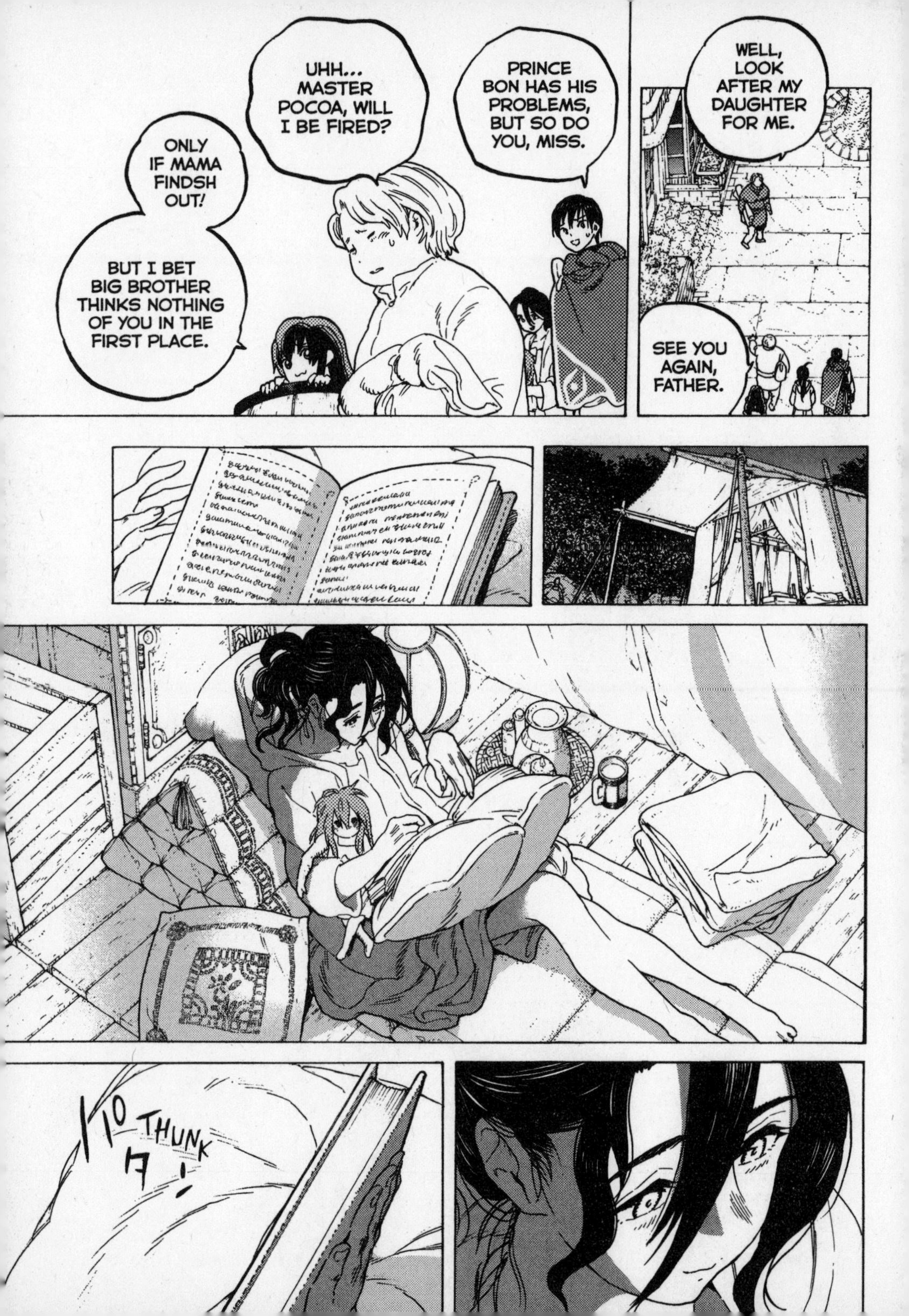
WELL, LOOK AFTER MY DAUGHTER FOR ME.
SEE YOU AGAIN, FATHER.
PRINCE BON HAS HIS PROBLEMS, BUT SO DO YOU, MISS.
UHH... MASTER POCOA, WILL I BE FIRED?
ONLY IF MAMA FINDSH OUT!
BUT I BET BIG BROTHER THINKS NOTHING OF YOU IN THE FIRST PLACE.
THUNK

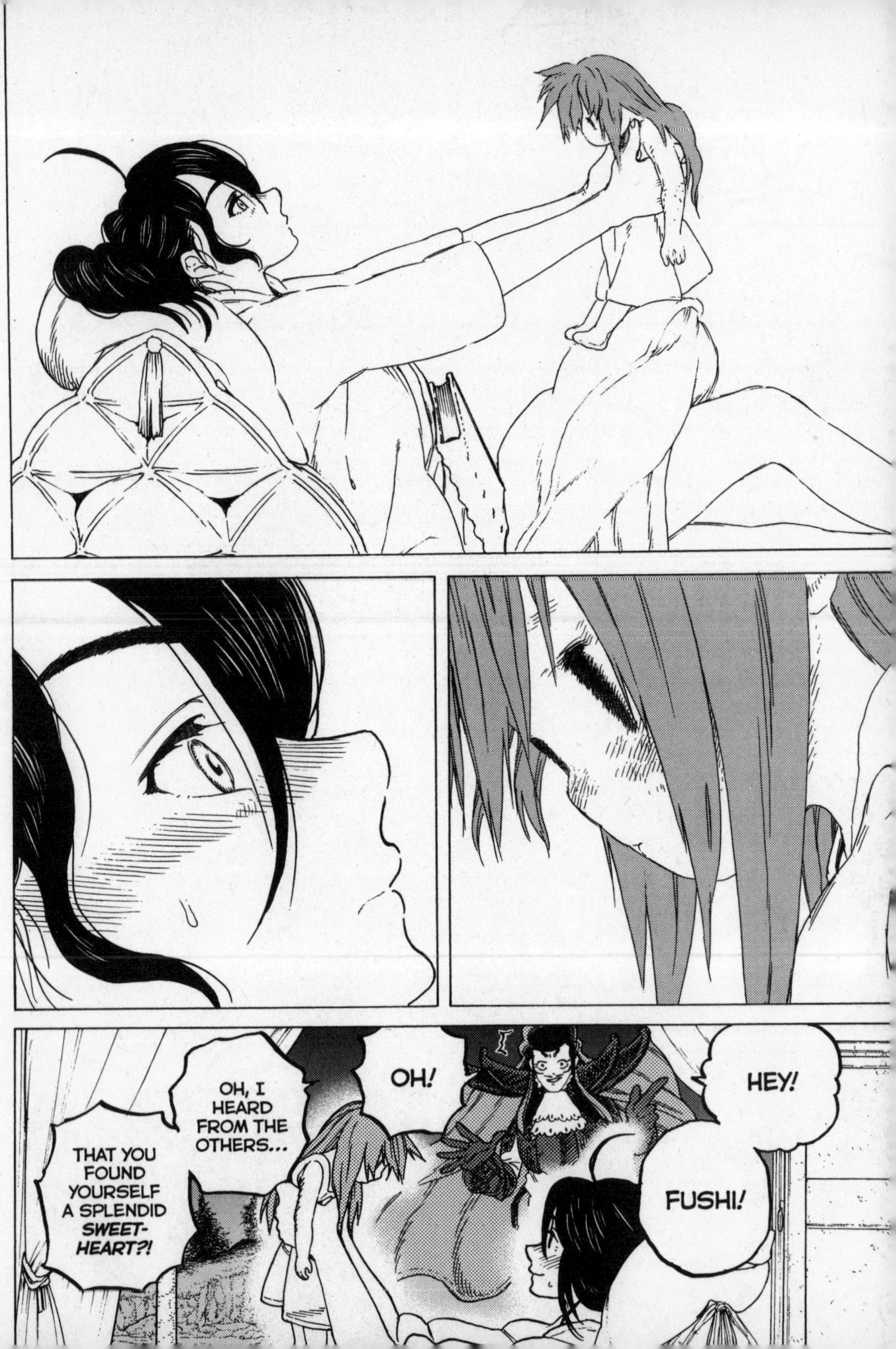
HEY!
FUSHI!
OH!
OH, I HEARD FROM THE OTHERS...
THAT YOU FOUND YOURSELF A SPLENDID *SWEET-HEART?!*

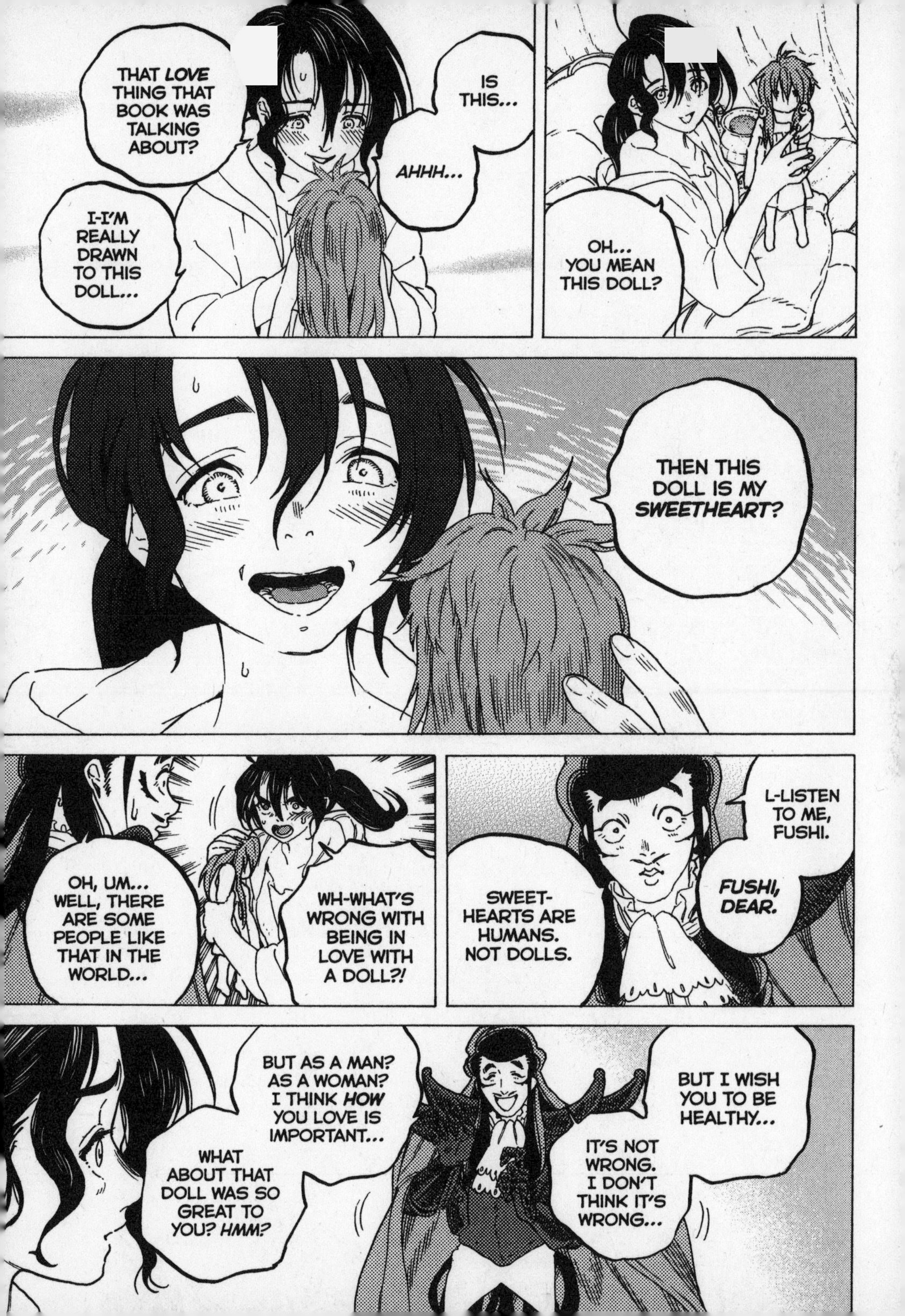
OH... YOU MEAN THIS DOLL?
IS THIS...
AHHH...
THAT LOVE THING THAT BOOK WAS TALKING ABOUT?
I-I'M REALLY DRAWN TO THIS DOLL...
THEN THIS DOLL IS MY SWEETHEART?
L-LISTEN TO ME, FUSHI.
FUSHI, DEAR.
SWEET-HEARTS ARE HUMANS. NOT DOLLS.
WH-WHAT'S WRONG WITH BEING IN LOVE WITH A DOLL?!
OH, UM... WELL, THERE ARE SOME PEOPLE LIKE THAT IN THE WORLD...
BUT I WISH YOU TO BE HEALTHY...
IT'S NOT WRONG. I DON'T THINK IT'S WRONG...
BUT AS A MAN? AS A WOMAN? I THINK HOW YOU LOVE IS IMPORTANT...
WHAT ABOUT THAT DOLL WAS SO GREAT TO YOU? HMM?

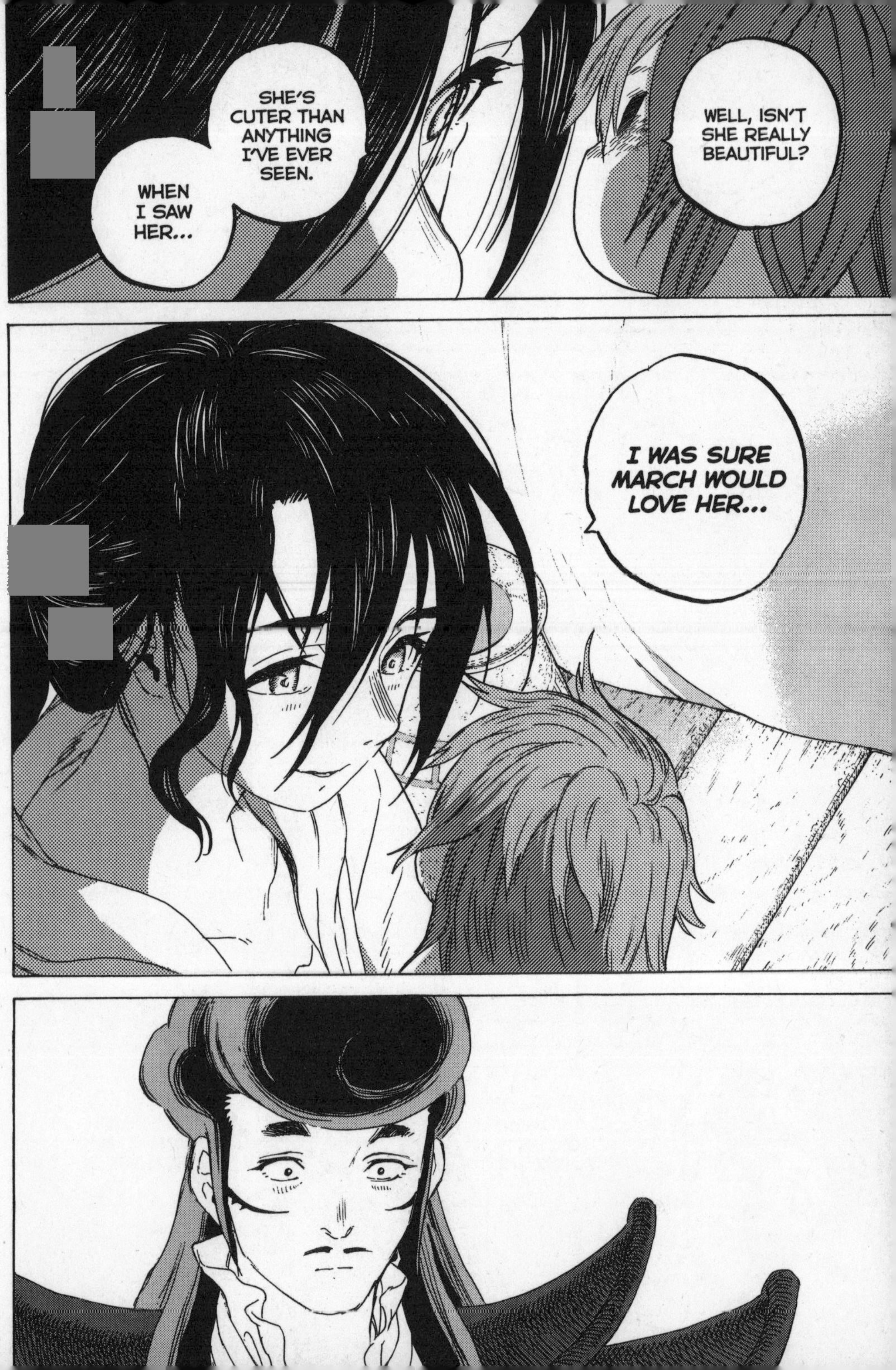
WELL, ISN'T SHE REALLY BEAUTIFUL?
SHE'S CUTER THAN ANYTHING I'VE EVER SEEN.
WHEN I SAW HER...
I WAS SURE MARCH WOULD LOVE HER...

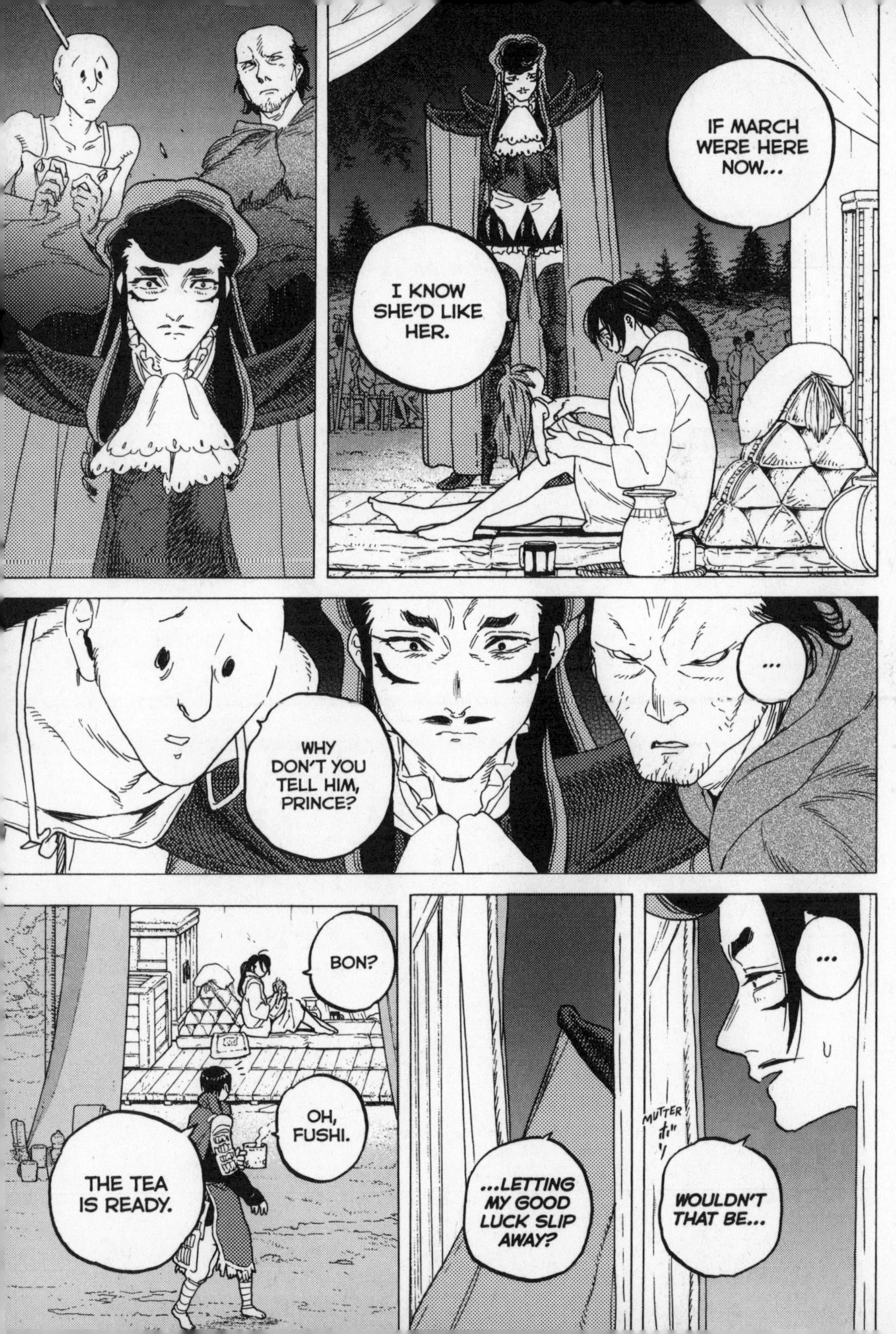
IF MARCH WERE HERE NOW...
I KNOW SHE'D LIKE HER.
...
WHY DON'T YOU TELL HIM, PRINCE?
...
MUTTER
WOULDN'T THAT BE...
...LETTING MY GOOD LUCK SLIP AWAY?
BON?
OH, FUSHI.
THE TEA IS READY.

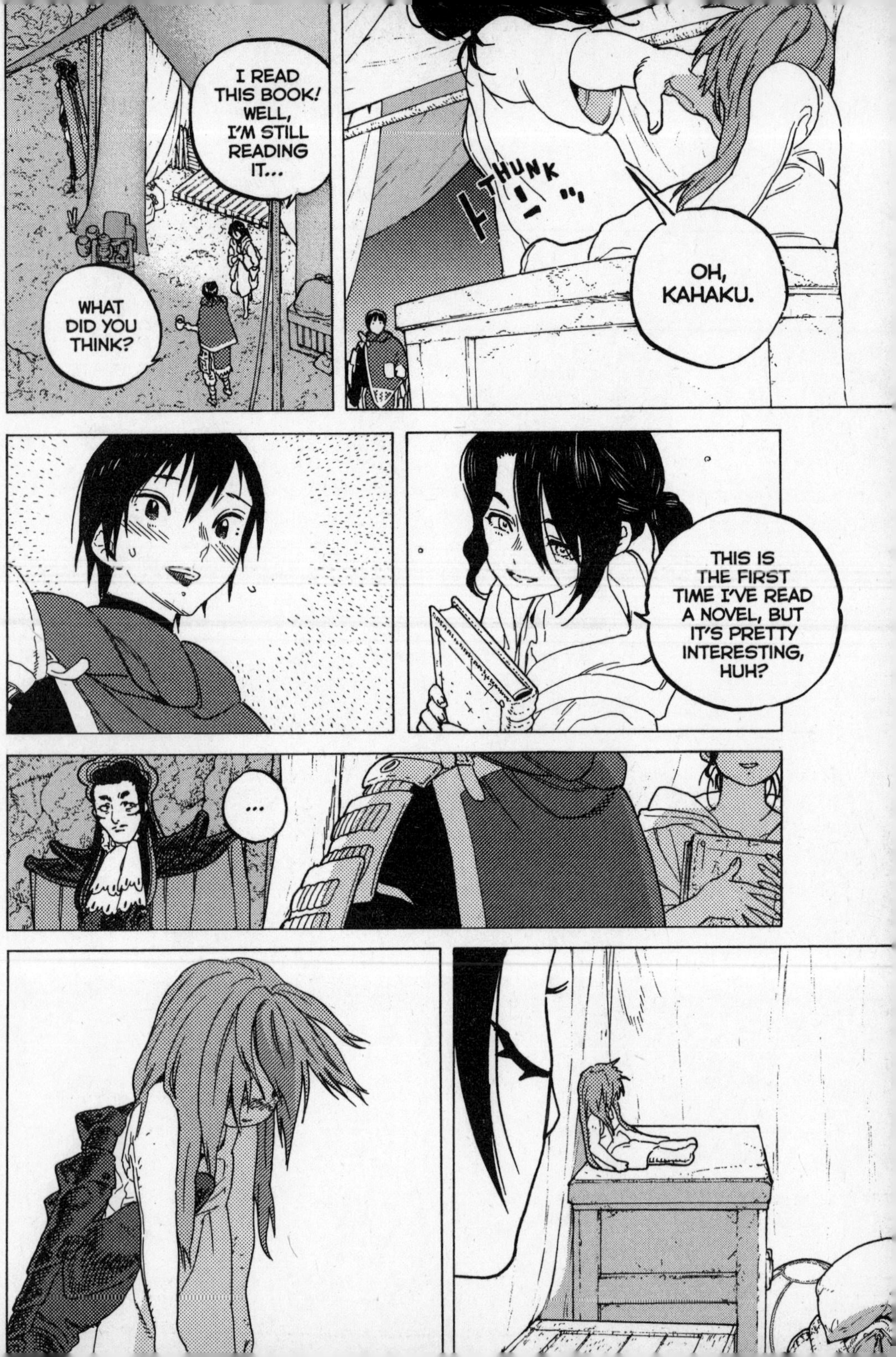
THUNK
OH, KAHAKU.
I READ THIS BOOK! WELL, I'M STILL READING IT...
WHAT DID YOU THINK?
THIS IS THE FIRST TIME I'VE READ A NOVEL, BUT IT'S PRETTY INTERESTING, HUH?
...

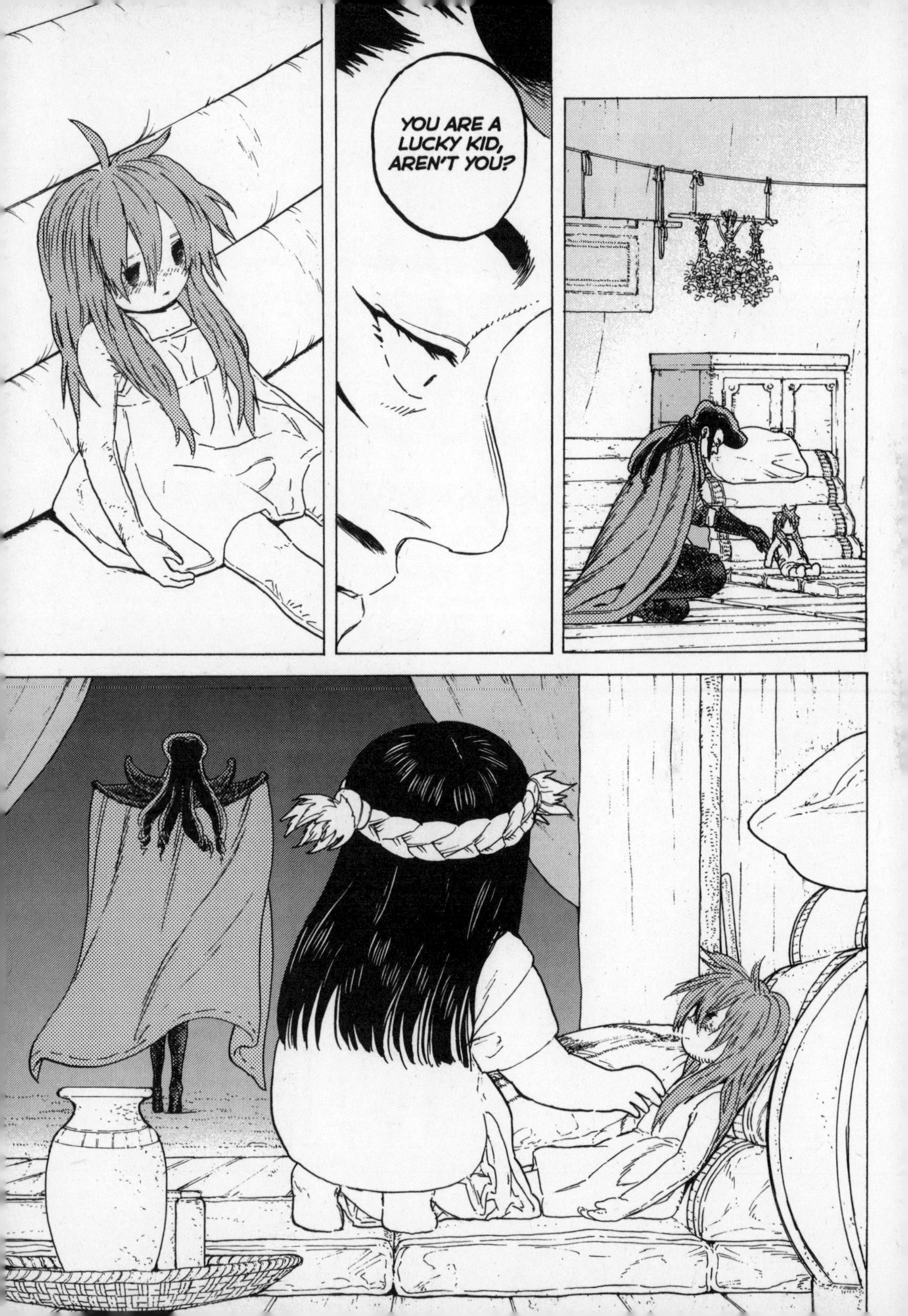
YOU ARE A LUCKY KID, AREN'T YOU?

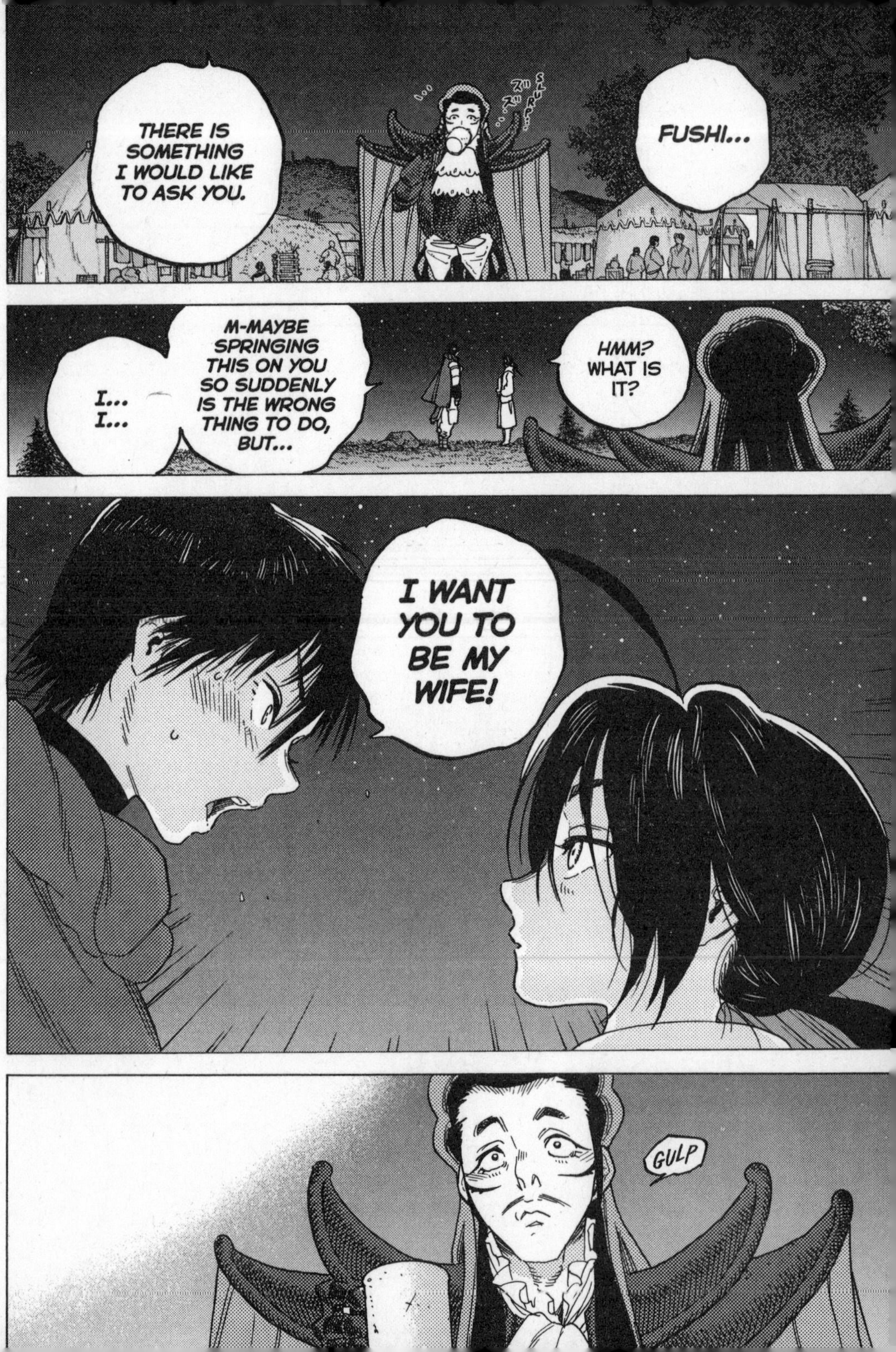
FUSHI...
SLURP...
THERE IS SOMETHING I WOULD LIKE TO ASK YOU.
HMM? WHAT IS IT?
M-MAYBE SPRINGING THIS ON YOU SO SUDDENLY IS THE WRONG THING TO DO, BUT...
I... I...
I WANT YOU TO BE MY WIFE!
GULP

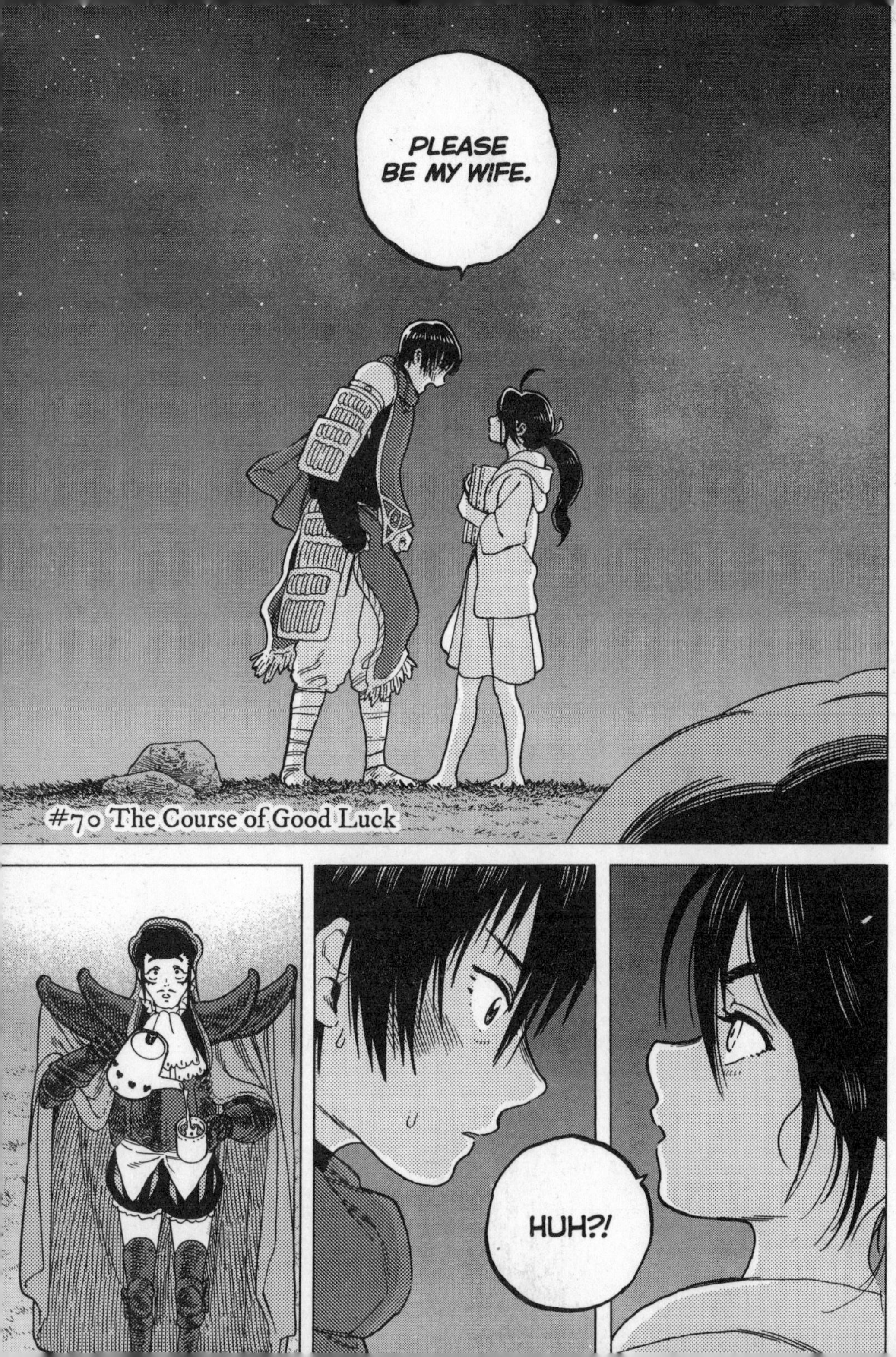
PLEASE BE MY WIFE.
#70 The Course of Good Luck
HUH?!

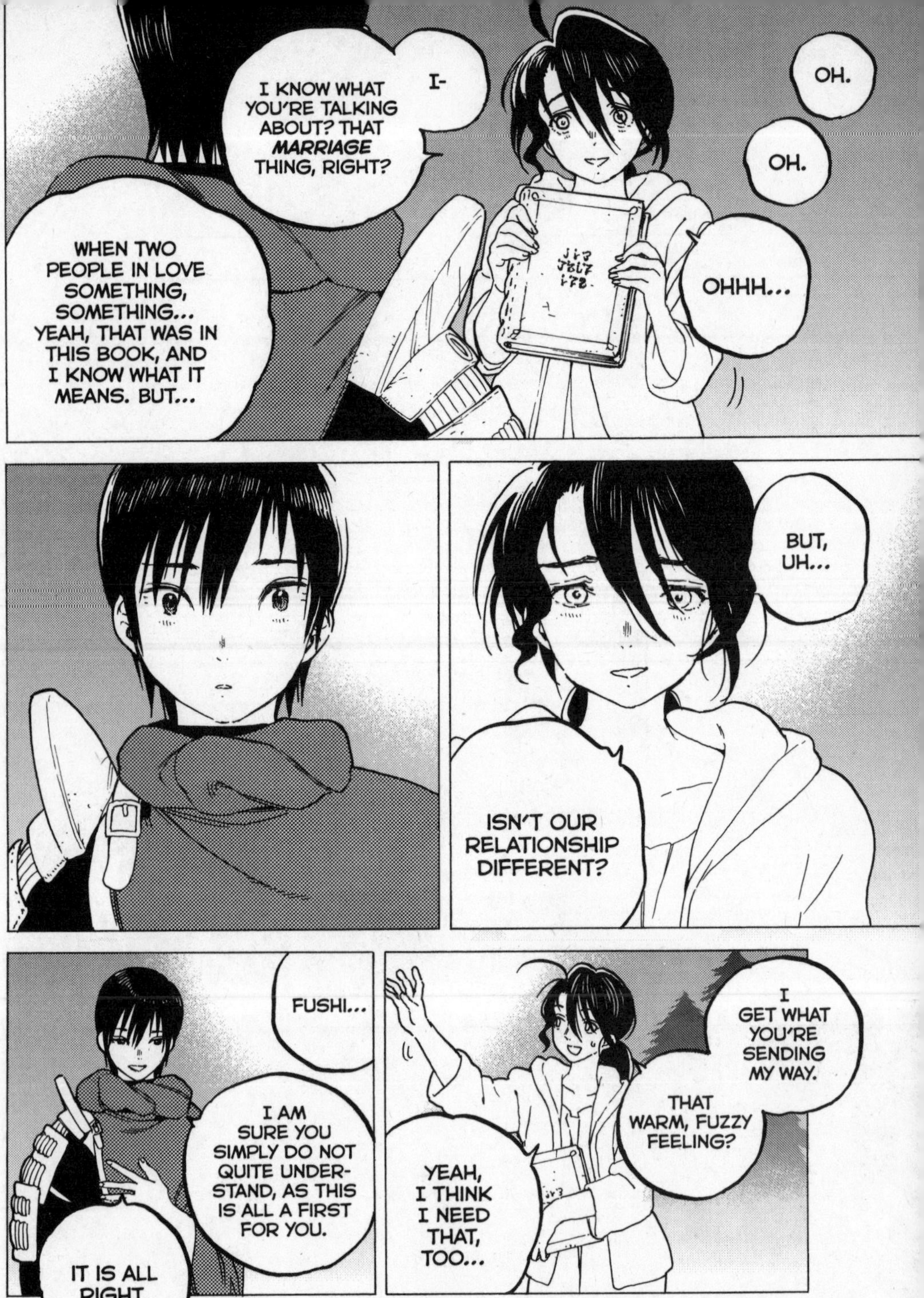
OH.
OH.
OHHH...
I-
I KNOW WHAT YOU'RE TALKING ABOUT? THAT *MARRIAGE* THING, RIGHT?
WHEN TWO PEOPLE IN LOVE SOMETHING, SOMETHING... YEAH, THAT WAS IN THIS BOOK, AND I KNOW WHAT IT MEANS. BUT...
BUT, UH...
ISN'T OUR RELATIONSHIP DIFFERENT?
I GET WHAT YOU'RE SENDING MY WAY.
THAT WARM, FUZZY FEELING?
YEAH, I THINK I NEED THAT, TOO...
FUSHI...
I AM SURE YOU SIMPLY DO NOT QUITE UNDER-STAND, AS THIS IS ALL A FIRST FOR YOU.
IT IS ALL RIGHT.

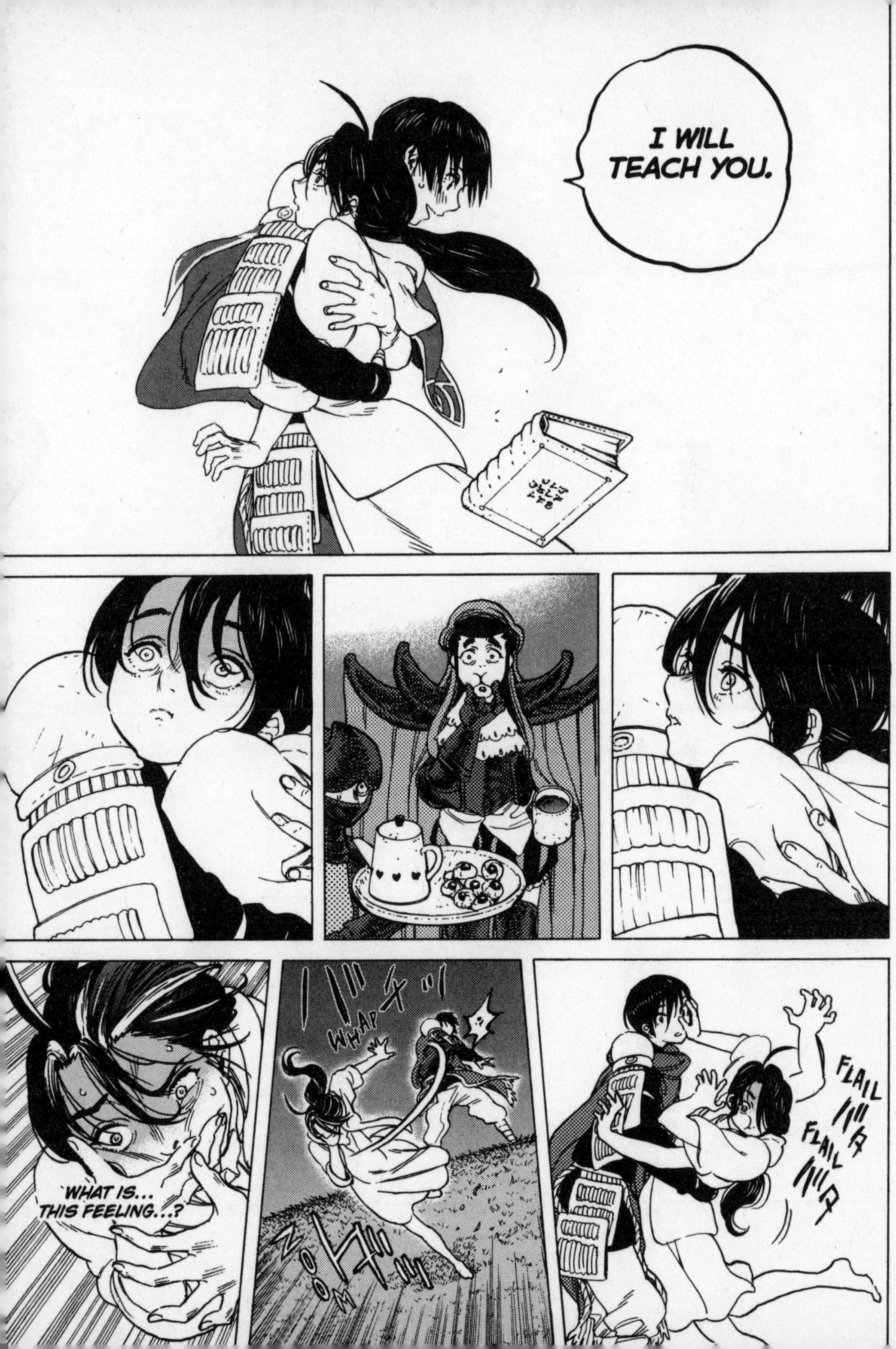
I WILL TEACH YOU.
FLAIL
FLAIL
WHAP
ZOOM
WHAT IS... THIS FEELING...?

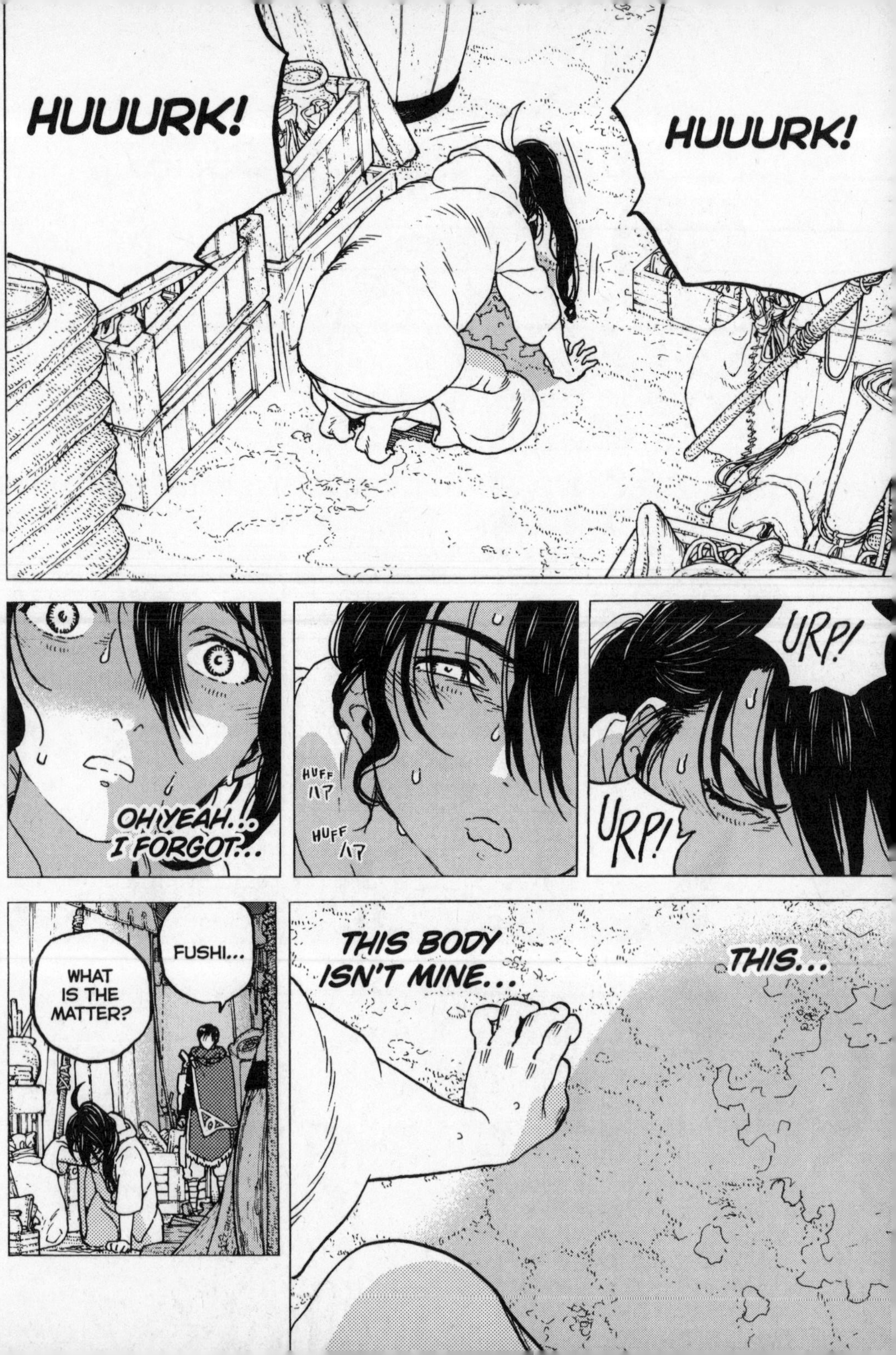
HUUURK!
HUUURK!
URP!
URP!
HUFF ハア
HUFF ハア
OH YEAH... I FORGOT...
THIS BODY ISN'T MINE...
THIS...
FUSHI...
WHAT IS THE MATTER?

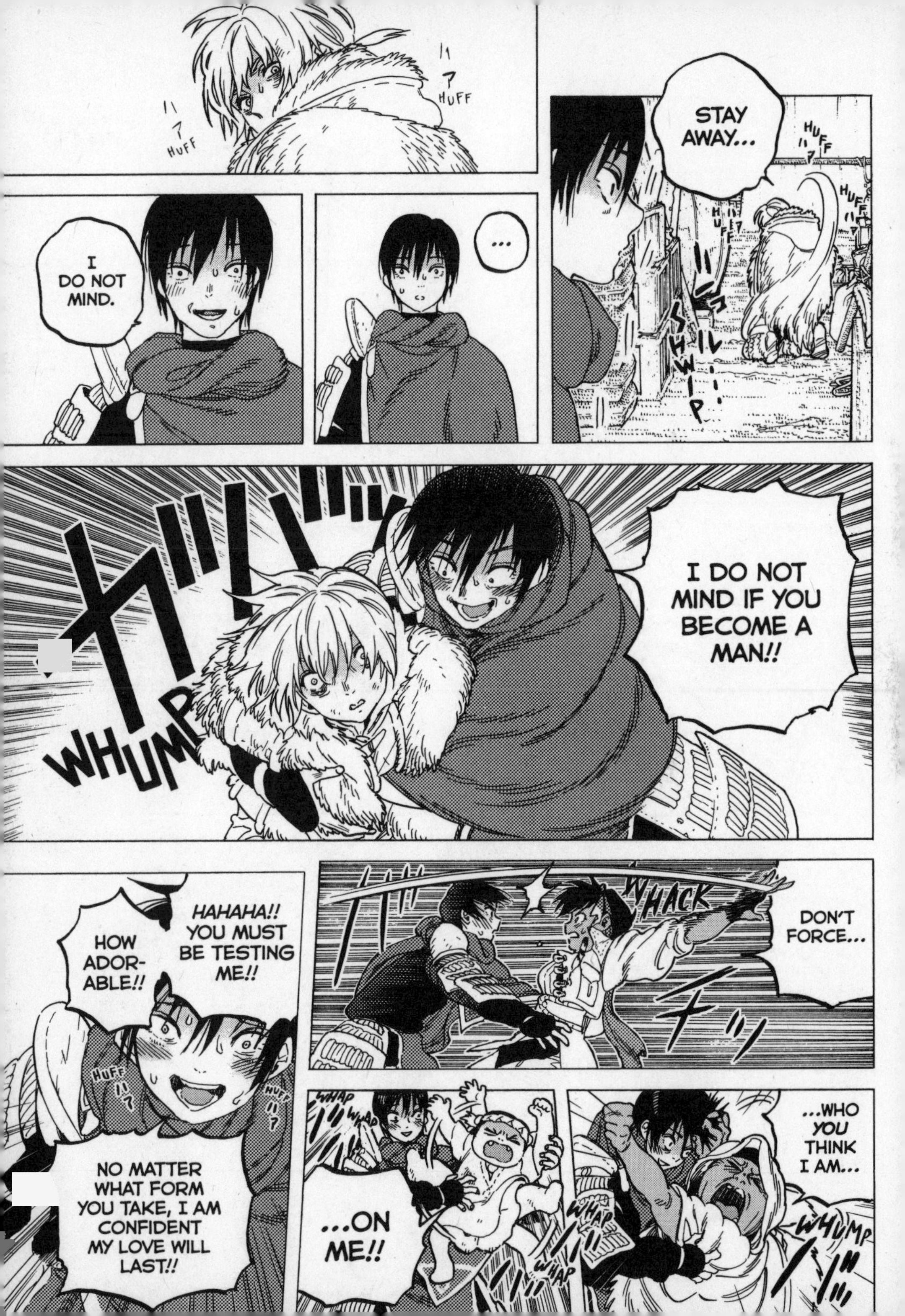
STAY AWAY...
HUFF
HUFF
SHWIP
HUFF
HUFF
HUFF
...
I DO NOT MIND.
I DO NOT MIND IF YOU BECOME A MAN!!
WHUMP
DON'T FORCE...
WHACK
...WHO YOU THINK I AM...
WHUMP
WHAP
WHAP
WHAP
WHAP
...ON ME!!
HAHAHA!! YOU MUST BE TESTING ME!!
HOW ADORABLE!!
HUFF
HUFF
NO MATTER WHAT FORM YOU TAKE, I AM CONFIDENT MY LOVE WILL LAST!!

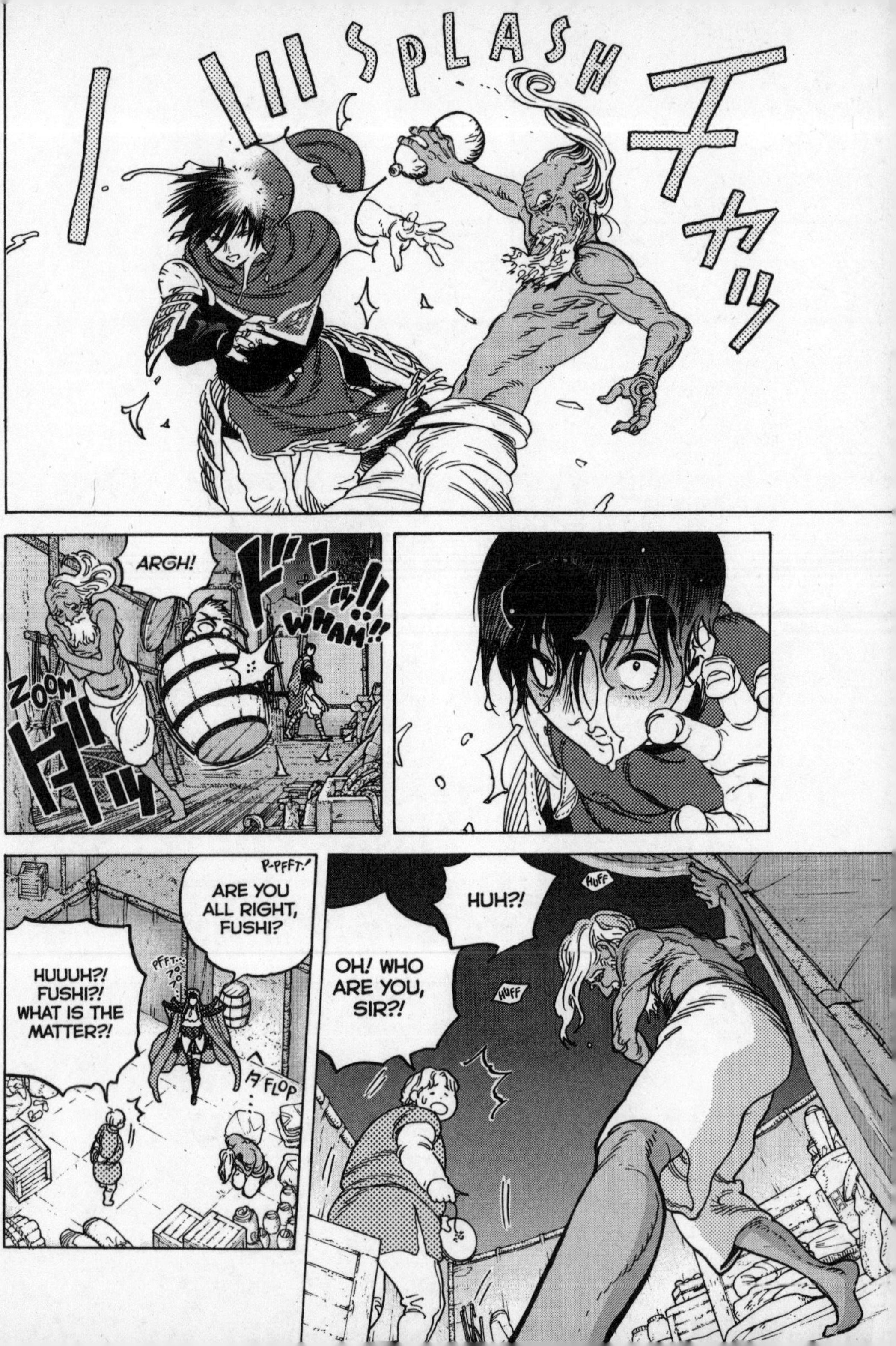
SPLASH
WHAM!!
ARGH!
ZOOM
HUFF
HUH?!
HUFF
OH! WHO ARE YOU, SIR?!
P-PFFT!
ARE YOU ALL RIGHT, FUSHI?
PFFT...
HUUUH?! FUSHI?! WHAT IS THE MATTER?!
FLOP

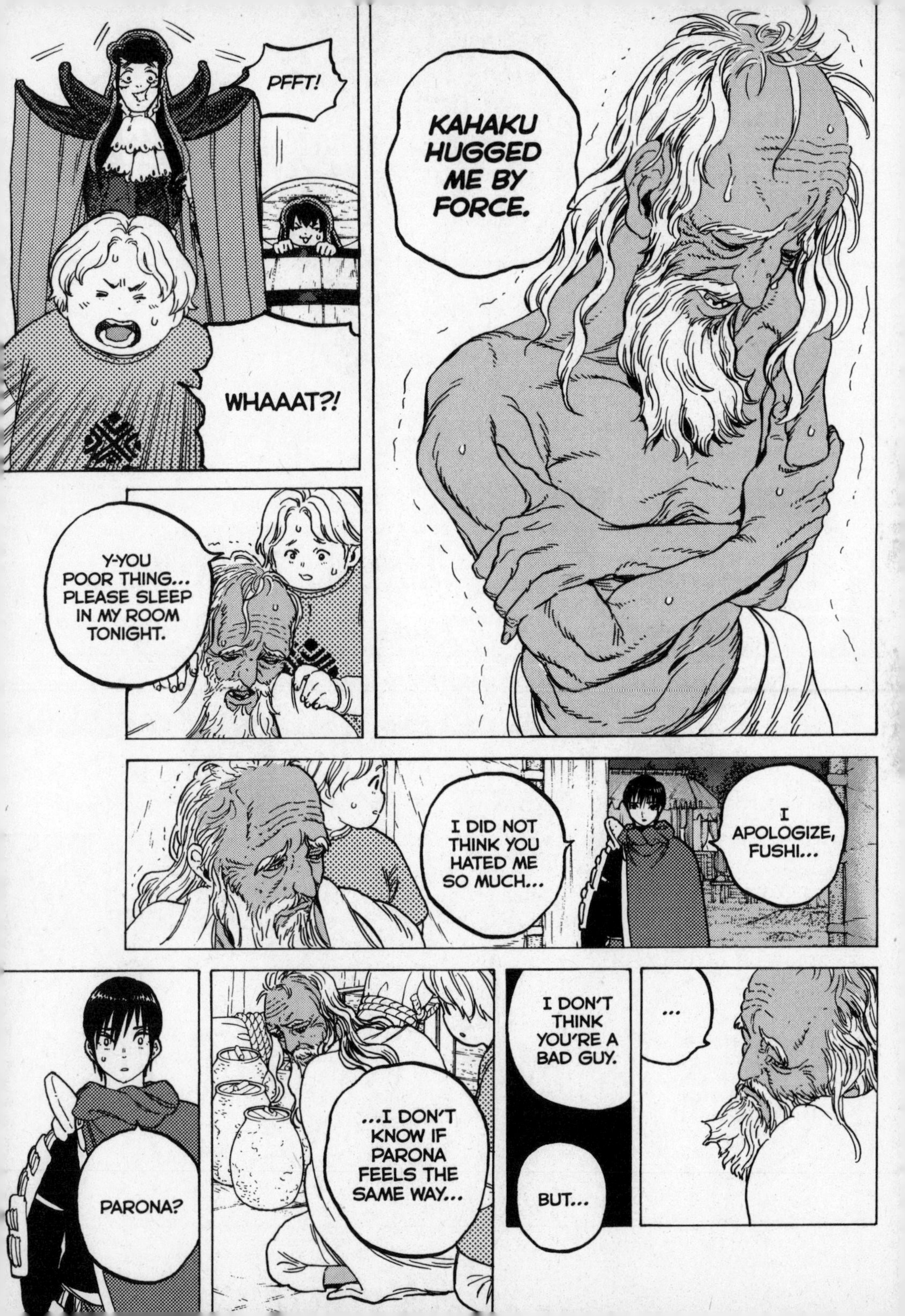
KAHAKU HUGGED ME BY FORCE.
PFFT!
WHAAAT?!
Y-YOU POOR THING... PLEASE SLEEP IN MY ROOM TONIGHT.
I APOLOGIZE, FUSHI...
I DID NOT THINK YOU HATED ME SO MUCH...
...
I DON'T THINK YOU'RE A BAD GUY.
BUT...
...I DON'T KNOW IF PARONA FEELS THE SAME WAY...
PARONA?

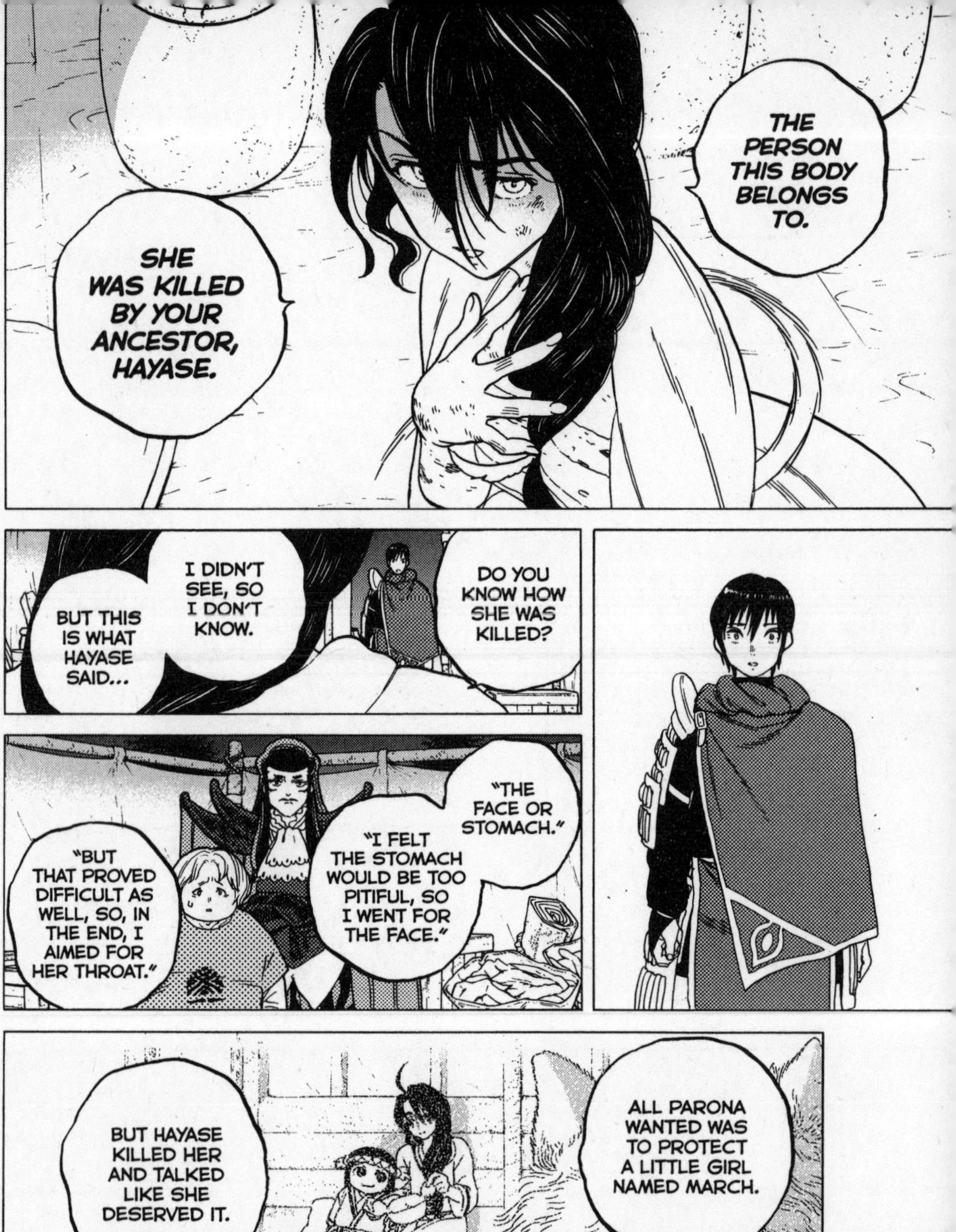
THE PERSON THIS BODY BELONGS TO.
SHE WAS KILLED BY YOUR ANCESTOR, HAYASE.
DO YOU KNOW HOW SHE WAS KILLED?
I DIDN'T SEE, SO I DON'T KNOW.
BUT THIS IS WHAT HAYASE SAID...
"THE FACE OR STOMACH."
"I FELT THE STOMACH WOULD BE TOO PITIFUL, SO I WENT FOR THE FACE."
"BUT THAT PROVED DIFFICULT AS WELL, SO, IN THE END, I AIMED FOR HER THROAT."
ALL PARONA WANTED WAS TO PROTECT A LITTLE GIRL NAMED MARCH.
BUT HAYASE KILLED HER AND TALKED LIKE SHE DESERVED IT.

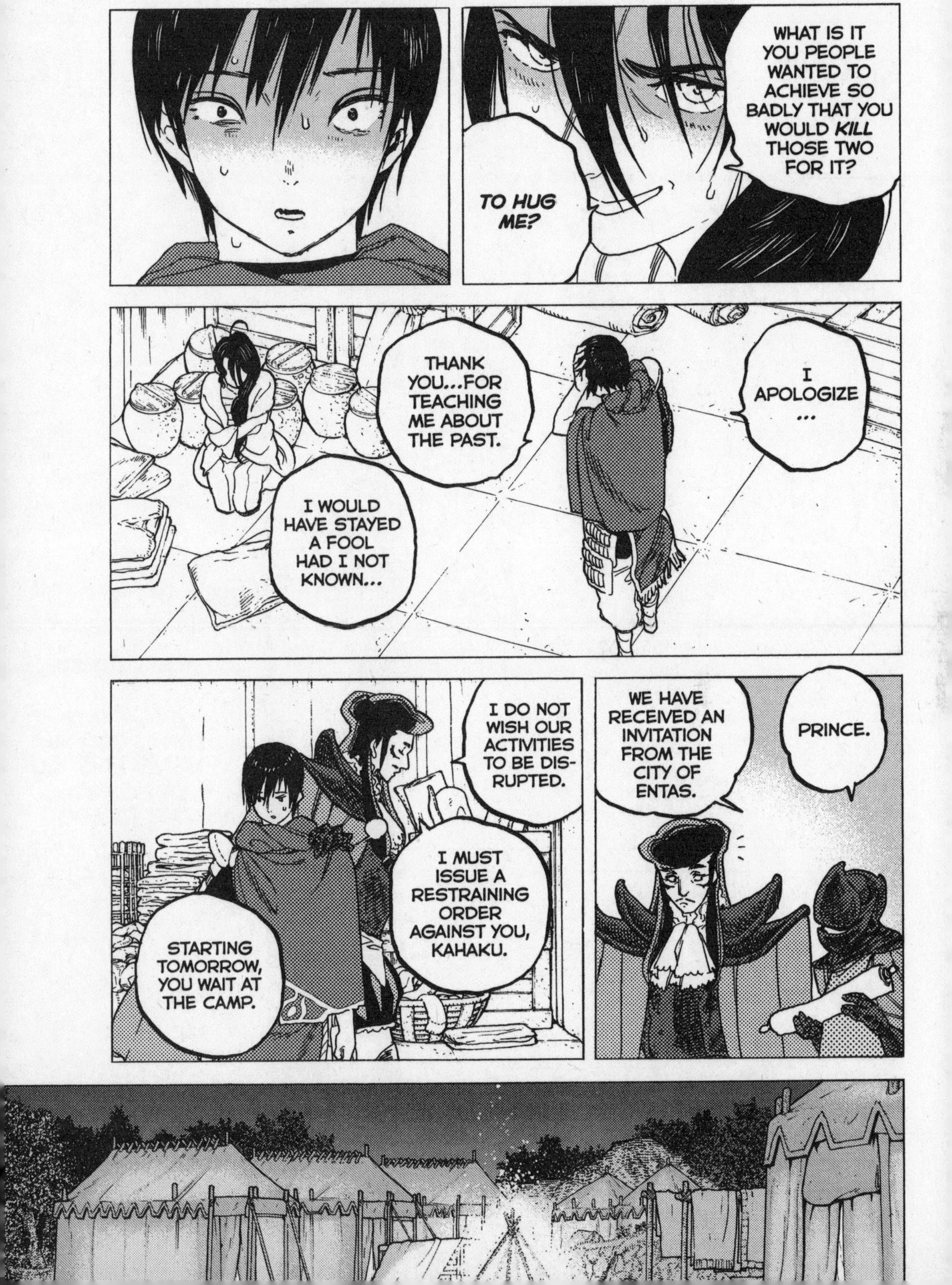
WHAT IS IT YOU PEOPLE WANTED TO ACHIEVE SO BADLY THAT YOU WOULD *KILL* THOSE TWO FOR IT?
TO HUG ME?
I APOLOGIZE ...
THANK YOU...FOR TEACHING ME ABOUT THE PAST.
I WOULD HAVE STAYED A FOOL HAD I NOT KNOWN...
PRINCE.
WE HAVE RECEIVED AN INVITATION FROM THE CITY OF ENTAS.
I DO NOT WISH OUR ACTIVITIES TO BE DIS-RUPTED.
I MUST ISSUE A RESTRAINING ORDER AGAINST YOU, KAHAKU.
STARTING TOMORROW, YOU WAIT AT THE CAMP.

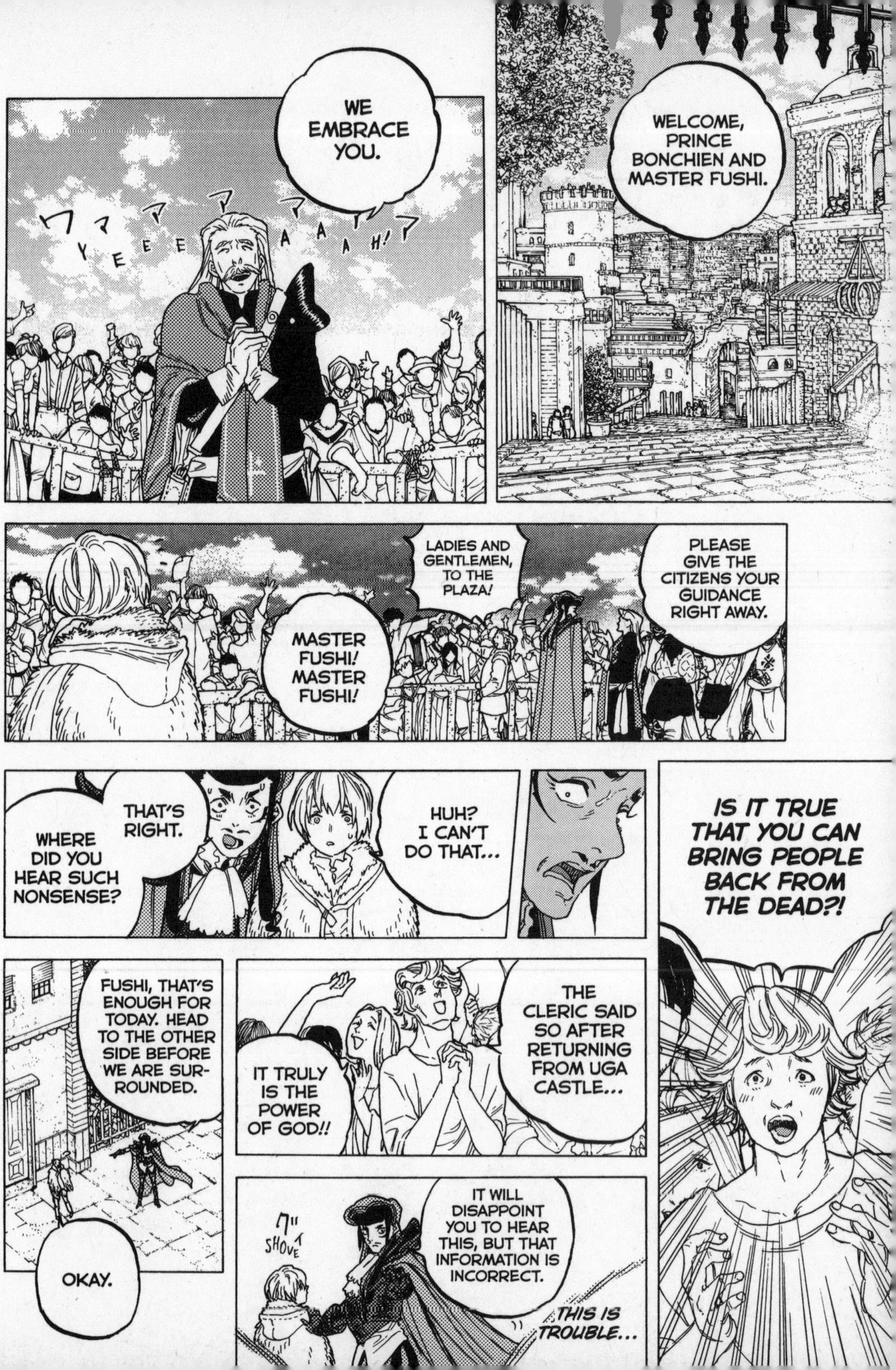
WELCOME, PRINCE BONCHIEN AND MASTER FUSHI.
WE EMBRACE YOU.
ワァァァ
YEEEAAAH!
PLEASE GIVE THE CITIZENS YOUR GUIDANCE RIGHT AWAY.
LADIES AND GENTLEMEN, TO THE PLAZA!
MASTER FUSHI! MASTER FUSHI!
IS IT TRUE THAT YOU CAN BRING PEOPLE BACK FROM THE DEAD?!
HUH? I CAN'T DO THAT...
THAT'S RIGHT.
WHERE DID YOU HEAR SUCH NONSENSE?
THE CLERIC SAID SO AFTER RETURNING FROM UGA CASTLE...
IT TRULY IS THE POWER OF GOD!!
IT WILL DISAPPOINT YOU TO HEAR THIS, BUT THAT INFORMATION IS INCORRECT.
グイ
SHOVE
THIS IS TROUBLE...
FUSHI, THAT'S ENOUGH FOR TODAY. HEAD TO THE OTHER SIDE BEFORE WE ARE SUR-ROUNDED.
OKAY.

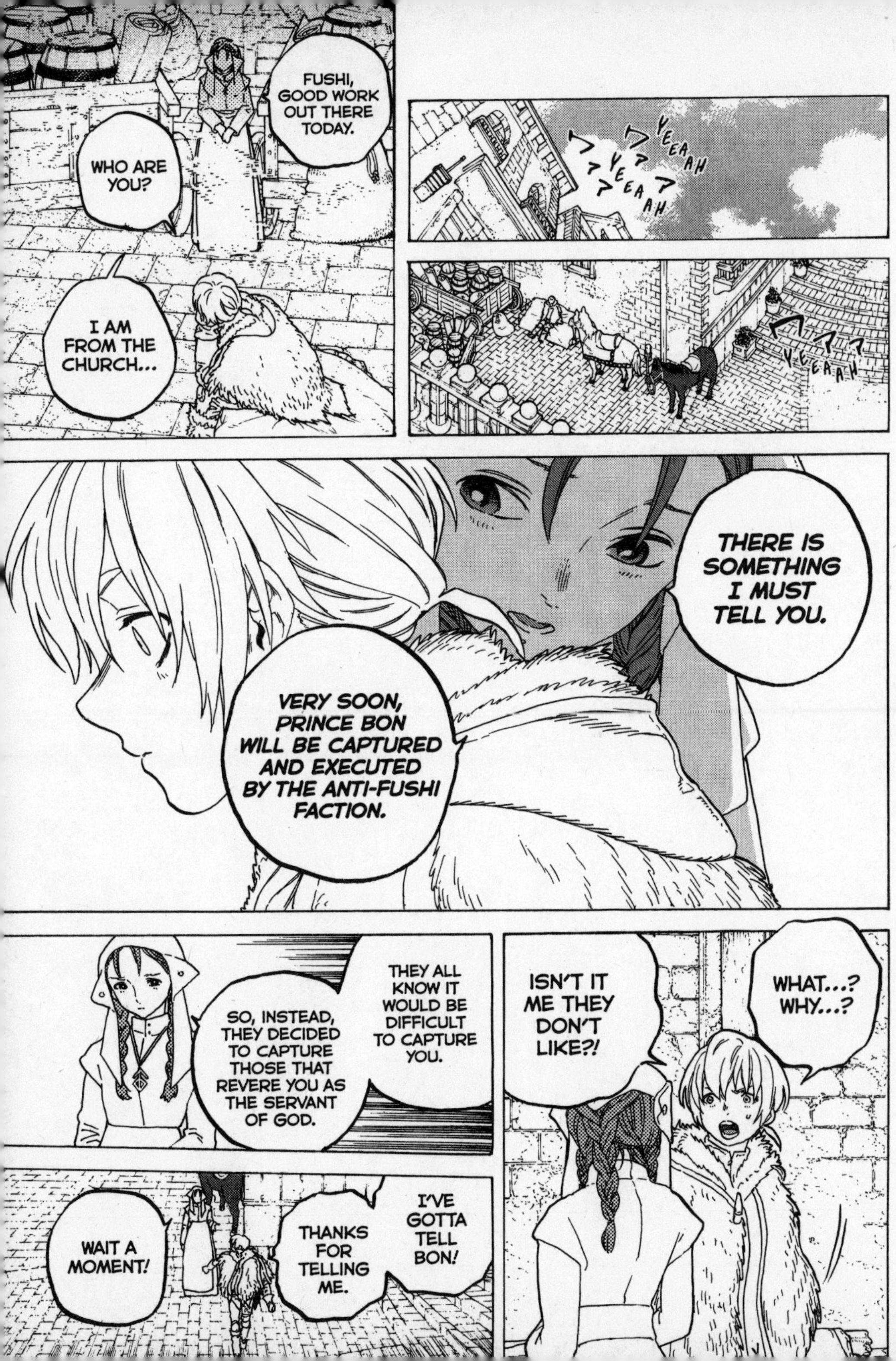
YEEAAH
YEEAAH
YEEAAH
FUSHI, GOOD WORK OUT THERE TODAY.
WHO ARE YOU?
I AM FROM THE CHURCH...
THERE IS SOMETHING I MUST TELL YOU.
VERY SOON, PRINCE BON WILL BE CAPTURED AND EXECUTED BY THE ANTI-FUSHI FACTION.
WHAT...? WHY...?
ISN'T IT ME THEY DON'T LIKE?!
THEY ALL KNOW IT WOULD BE DIFFICULT TO CAPTURE YOU.
SO, INSTEAD, THEY DECIDED TO CAPTURE THOSE THAT REVERE YOU AS THE SERVANT OF GOD.
I'VE GOTTA TELL BON!
THANKS FOR TELLING ME.
WAIT A MOMENT!

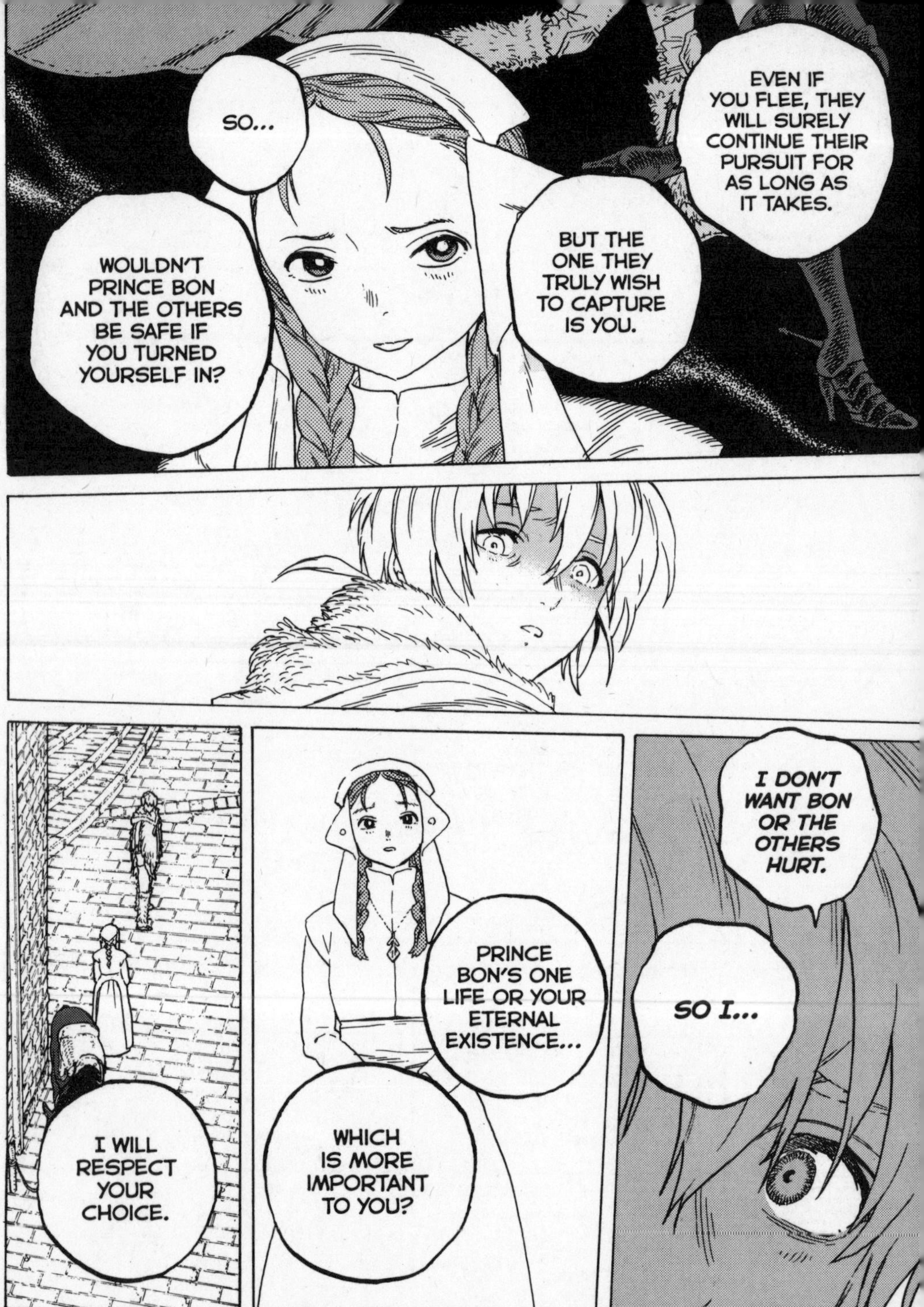
EVEN IF YOU FLEE, THEY WILL SURELY CONTINUE THEIR PURSUIT FOR AS LONG AS IT TAKES.
BUT THE ONE THEY TRULY WISH TO CAPTURE IS YOU.
SO...
WOULDN'T PRINCE BON AND THE OTHERS BE SAFE IF YOU TURNED YOURSELF IN?
I DON'T WANT BON OR THE OTHERS HURT.
SO I...
PRINCE BON'S ONE LIFE OR YOUR ETERNAL EXISTENCE...
WHICH IS MORE IMPORTANT TO YOU?
I WILL RESPECT YOUR CHOICE.

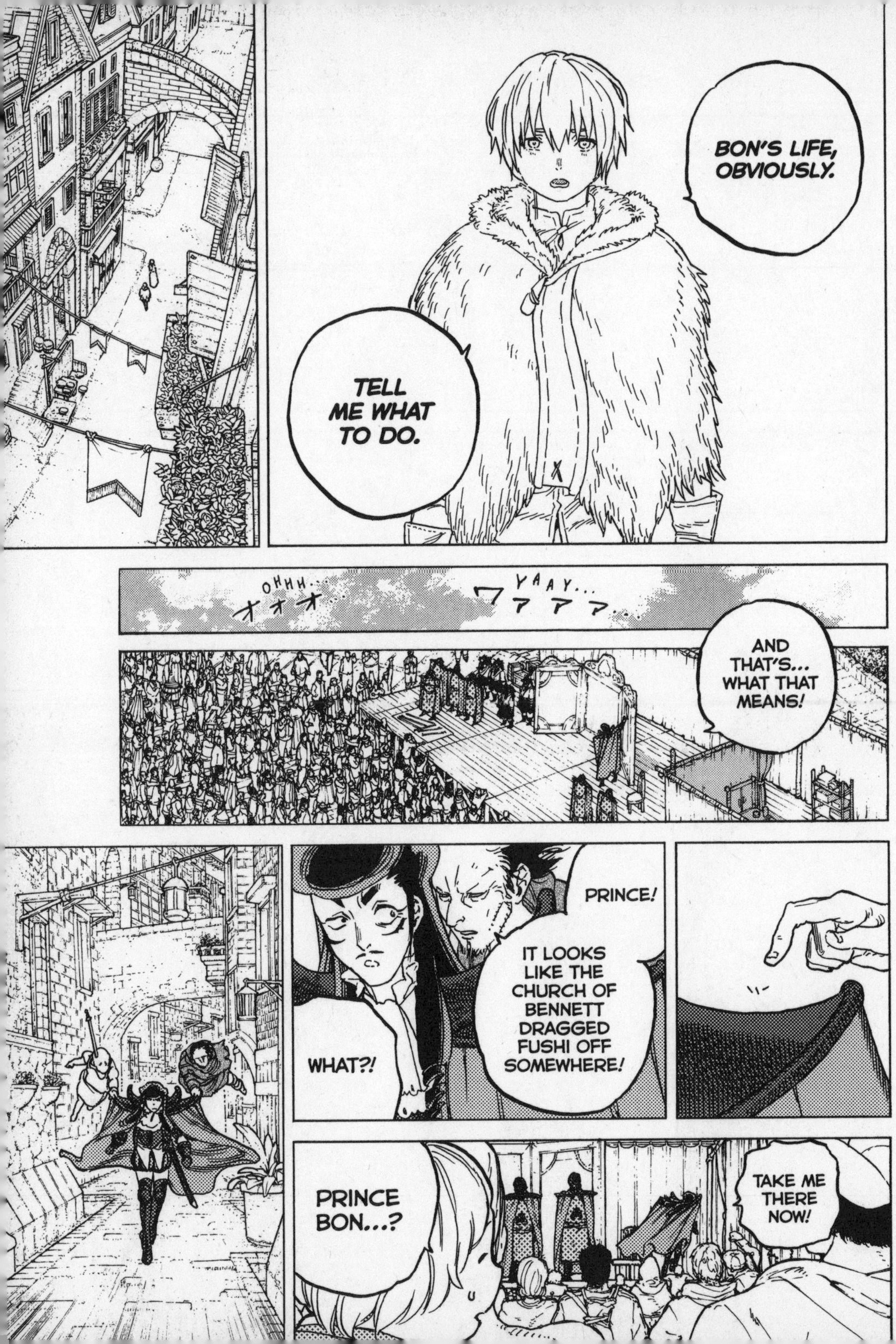
BON'S LIFE, OBVIOUSLY.
TELL ME WHAT TO DO.
YAAY...
ワァァァ...
OHHH...
オオオ...
AND THAT'S... WHAT THAT MEANS!
PRINCE!
IT LOOKS LIKE THE CHURCH OF BENNETT DRAGGED FUSHI OFF SOMEWHERE!
WHAT?!
TAKE ME THERE NOW!
PRINCE BON...?

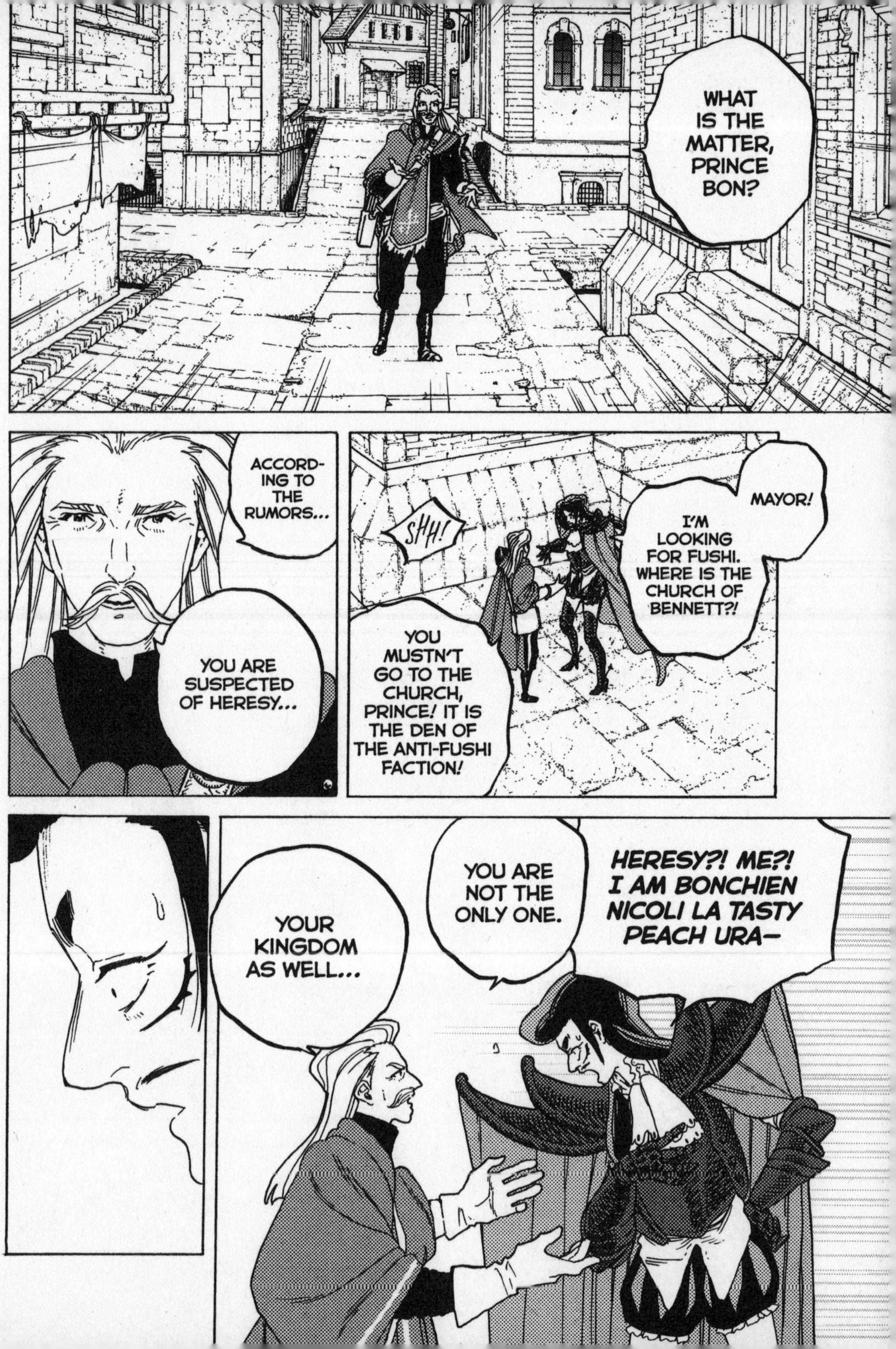
WHAT IS THE MATTER, PRINCE BON?
MAYOR!
I'M LOOKING FOR FUSHI. WHERE IS THE CHURCH OF BENNETT?!
SHH!
YOU MUSTN'T GO TO THE CHURCH, PRINCE! IT IS THE DEN OF THE ANTI-FUSHI FACTION!
ACCORD-ING TO THE RUMORS...
YOU ARE SUSPECTED OF HERESY...
HERESY?! ME?! I AM BONCHIEN NICOLI LA TASTY PEACH URA—
YOU ARE NOT THE ONLY ONE.
YOUR KINGDOM AS WELL...

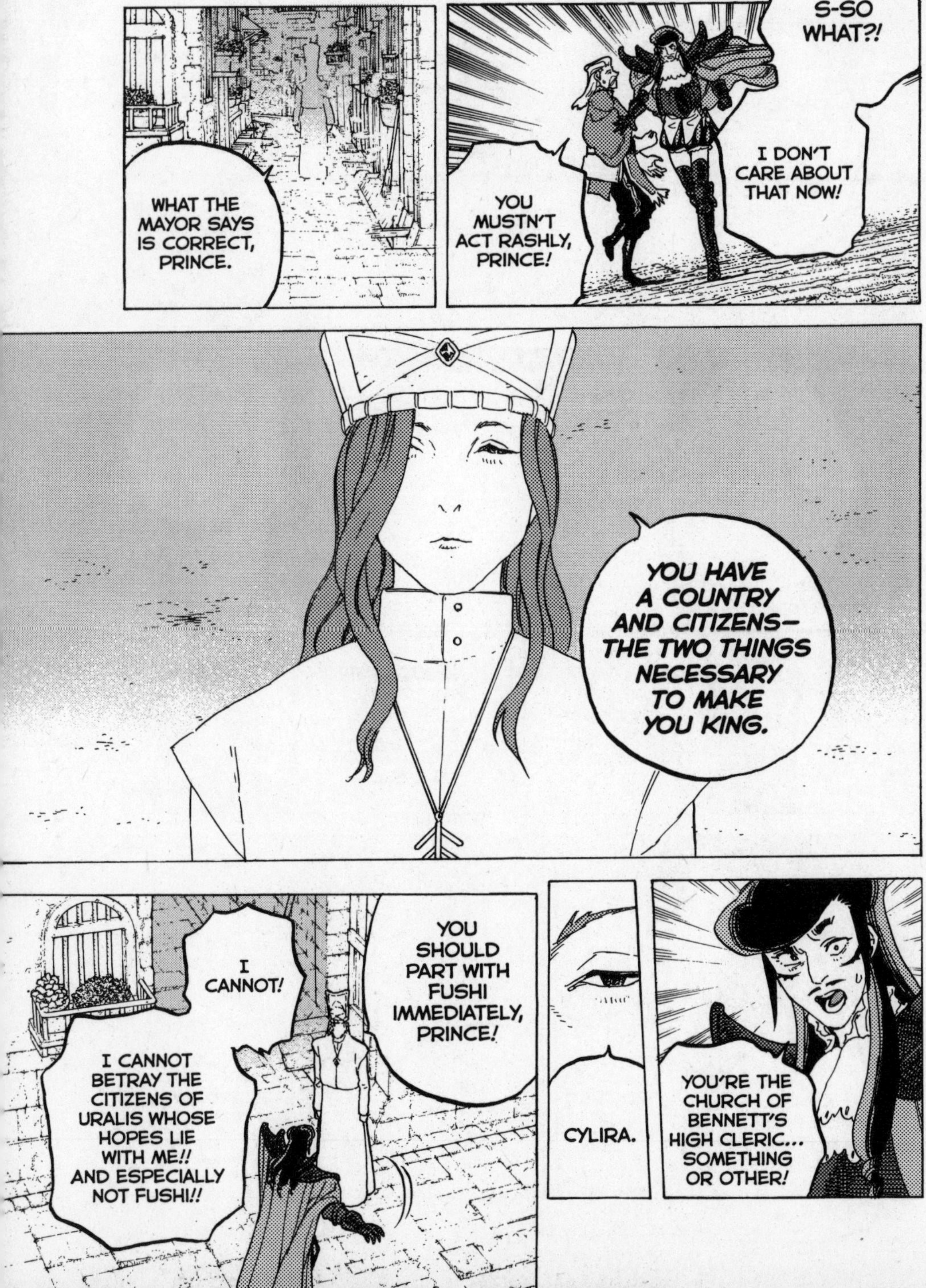
S-SO WHAT?!
I DON'T CARE ABOUT THAT NOW!
YOU MUSTN'T ACT RASHLY, PRINCE!
WHAT THE MAYOR SAYS IS CORRECT, PRINCE.
YOU HAVE A COUNTRY AND CITIZENS— THE TWO THINGS NECESSARY TO MAKE YOU KING.
YOU'RE THE CHURCH OF BENNETT'S HIGH CLERIC... SOMETHING OR OTHER!
CYLIRA.
YOU SHOULD PART WITH FUSHI IMMEDIATELY, PRINCE!
I CANNOT!
I CANNOT BETRAY THE CITIZENS OF URALIS WHOSE HOPES LIE WITH ME!! AND ESPECIALLY NOT FUSHI!!

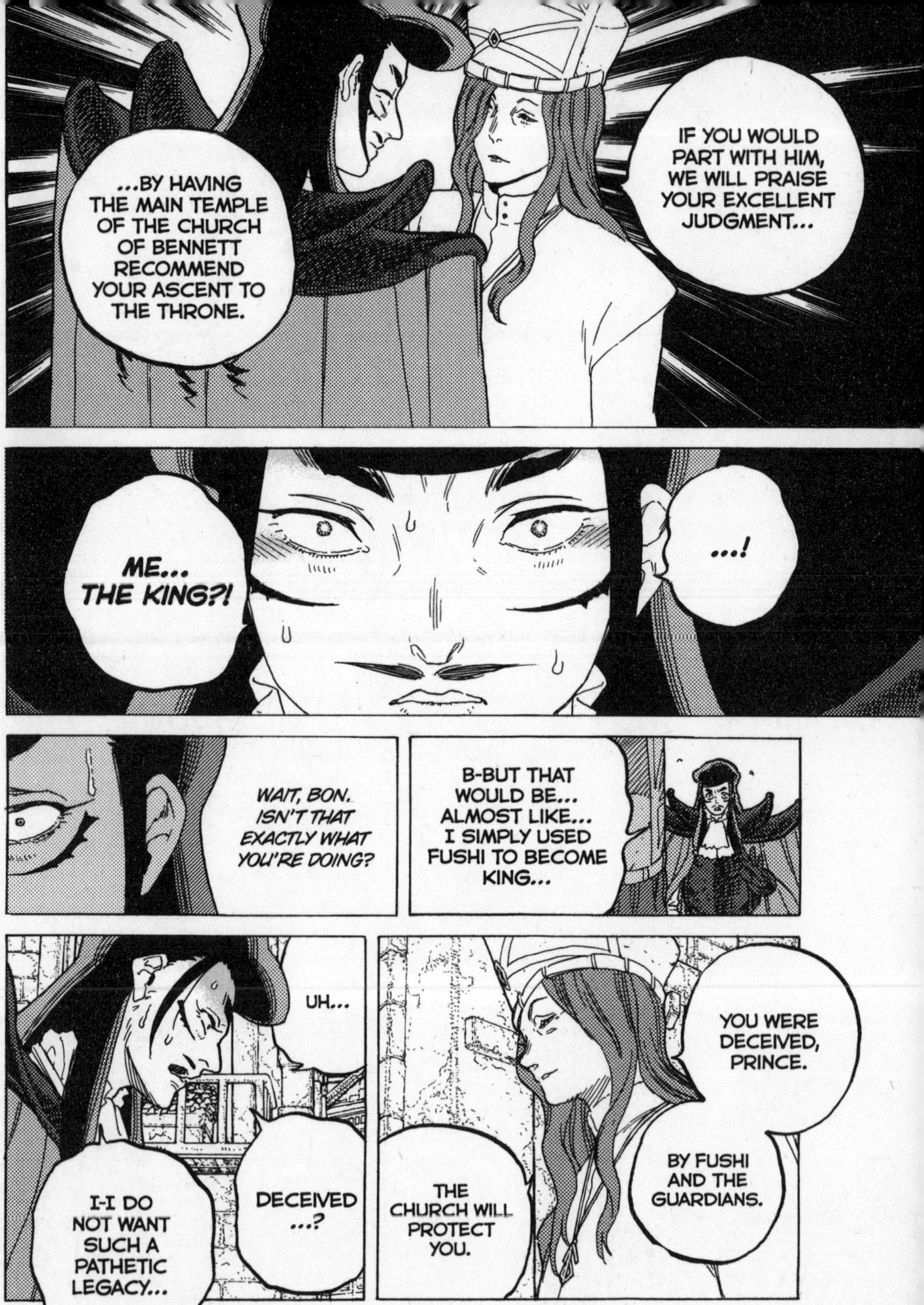
IF YOU WOULD PART WITH HIM, WE WILL PRAISE YOUR EXCELLENT JUDGMENT...
...BY HAVING THE MAIN TEMPLE OF THE CHURCH OF BENNETT RECOMMEND YOUR ASCENT TO THE THRONE.
...!
ME... THE KING?!
B-BUT THAT WOULD BE... ALMOST LIKE... I SIMPLY USED FUSHI TO BECOME KING...
WAIT, BON. ISN'T THAT EXACTLY WHAT YOU'RE DOING?
YOU WERE DECEIVED, PRINCE.
BY FUSHI AND THE GUARDIANS.
THE CHURCH WILL PROTECT YOU.
UH...
DECEIVED ...?
I-I DO NOT WANT SUCH A PATHETIC LEGACY...

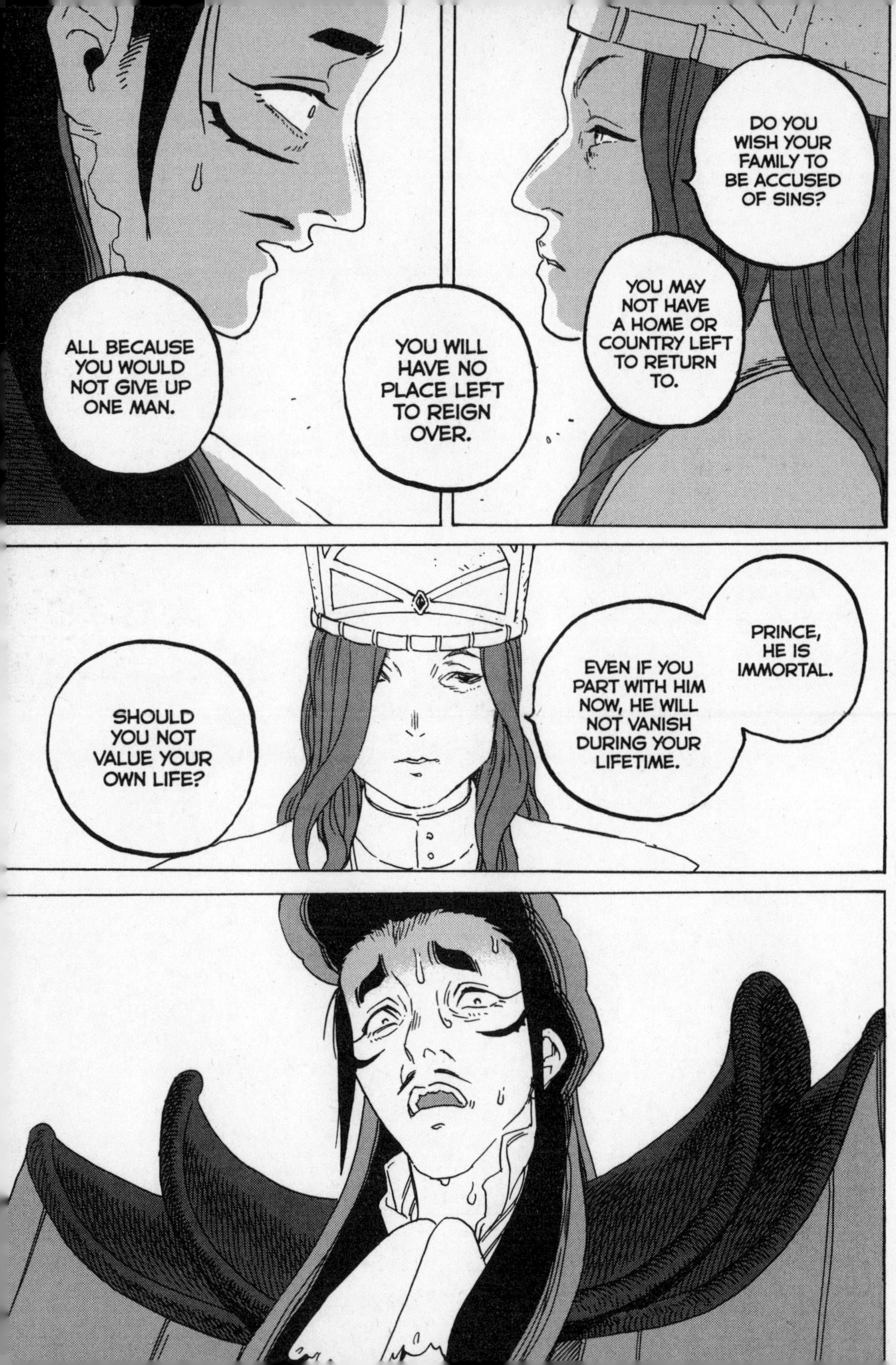
DO YOU WISH YOUR FAMILY TO BE ACCUSED OF SINS?
YOU MAY NOT HAVE A HOME OR COUNTRY LEFT TO RETURN TO.
YOU WILL HAVE NO PLACE LEFT TO REIGN OVER.
ALL BECAUSE YOU WOULD NOT GIVE UP ONE MAN.
PRINCE, HE IS IMMORTAL.
EVEN IF YOU PART WITH HIM NOW, HE WILL NOT VANISH DURING YOUR LIFETIME.
SHOULD YOU NOT VALUE YOUR OWN LIFE?

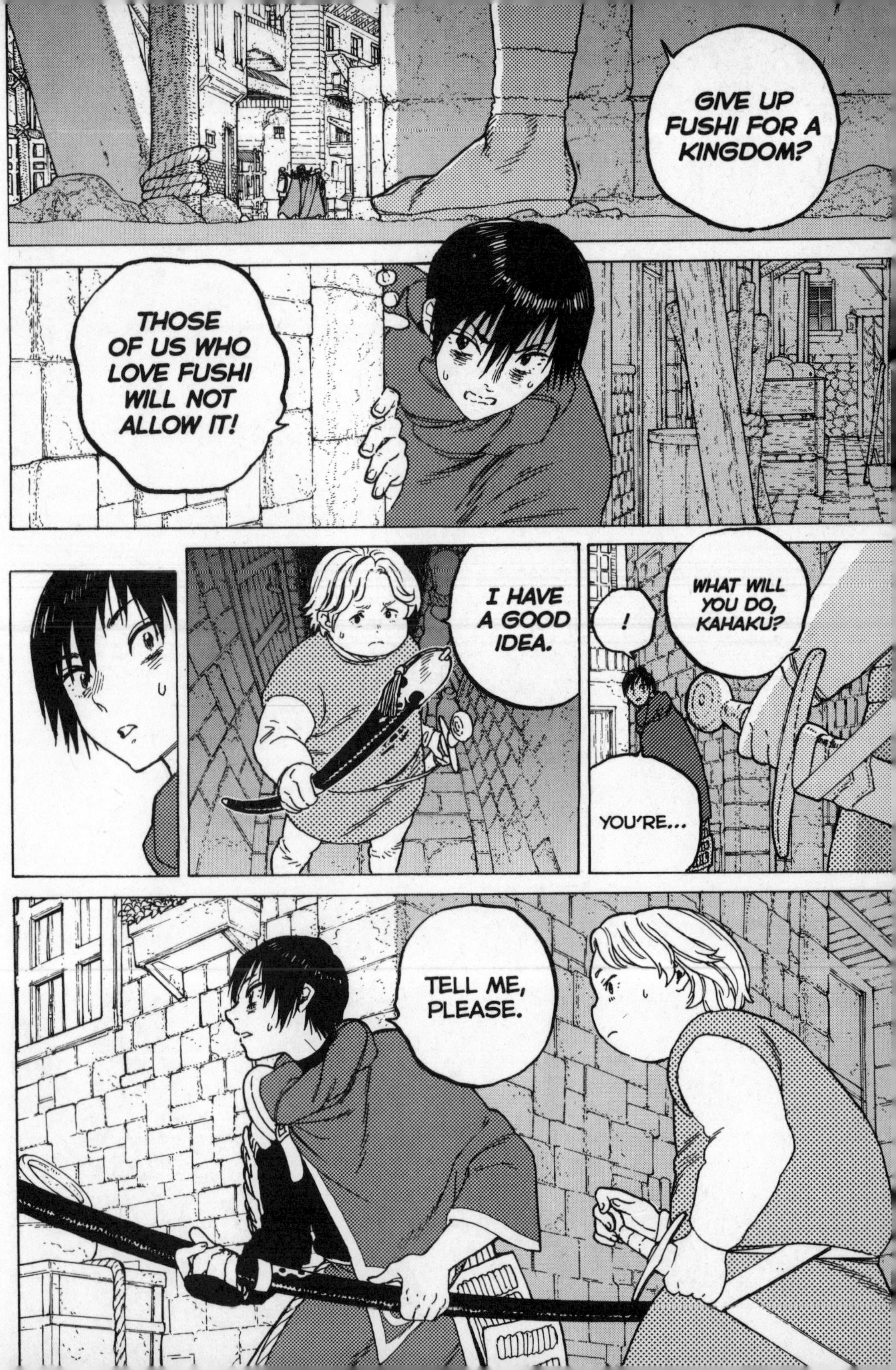
GIVE UP FUSHI FOR A KINGDOM?
THOSE OF US WHO LOVE FUSHI WILL NOT ALLOW IT!
WHAT WILL YOU DO, KAHAKU?
!
YOU'RE...
I HAVE A GOOD IDEA.
TELL ME, PLEASE.

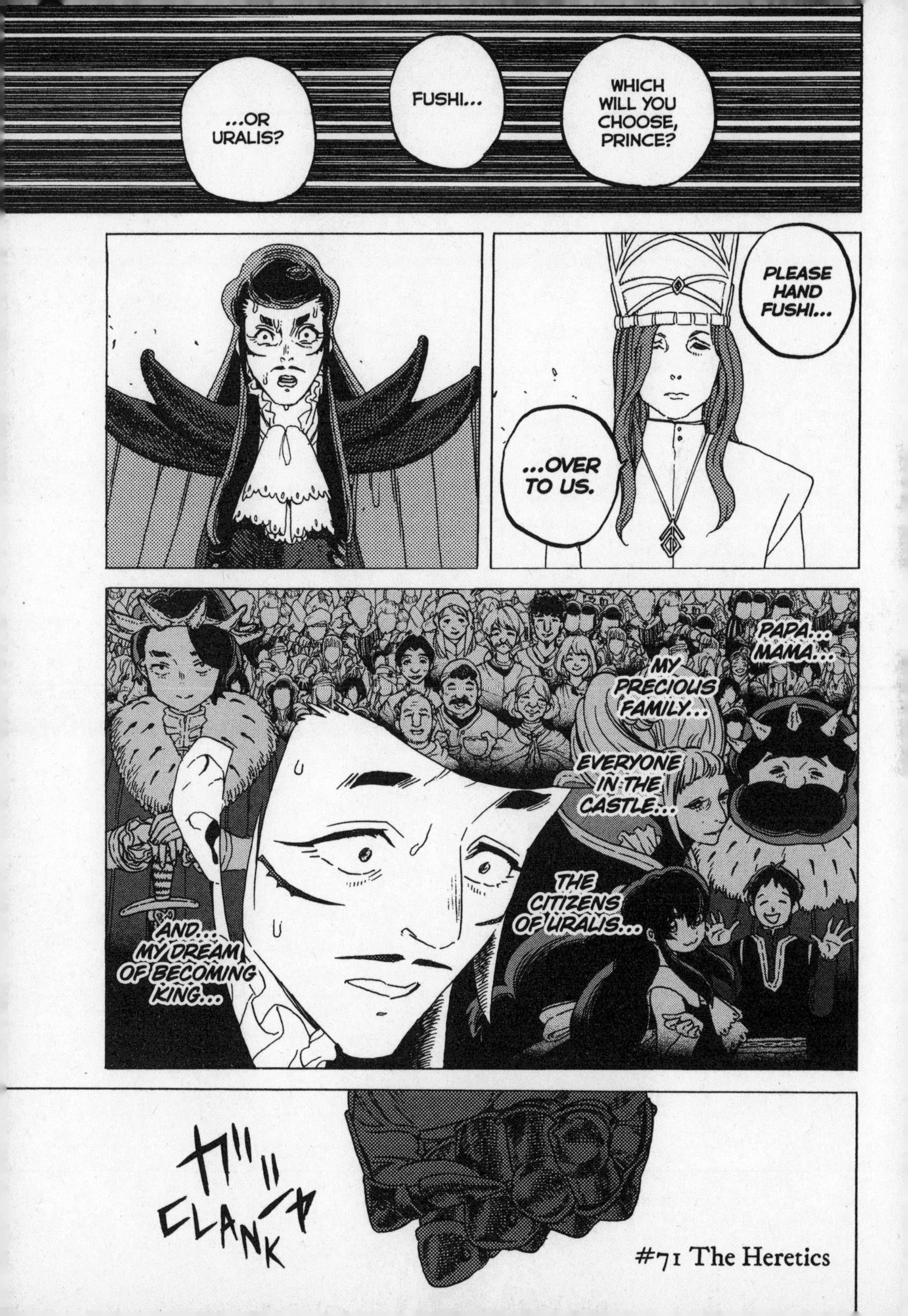
WHICH WILL YOU CHOOSE, PRINCE?
FUSHI...
...OR URALIS?
PLEASE HAND FUSHI...
...OVER TO US.
PAPA... MAMA...
MY PRECIOUS FAMILY...
EVERYONE IN THE CASTLE...
THE CITIZENS OF URALIS...
AND... MY DREAM OF BECOMING KING...
CLANK
#71 The Heretics

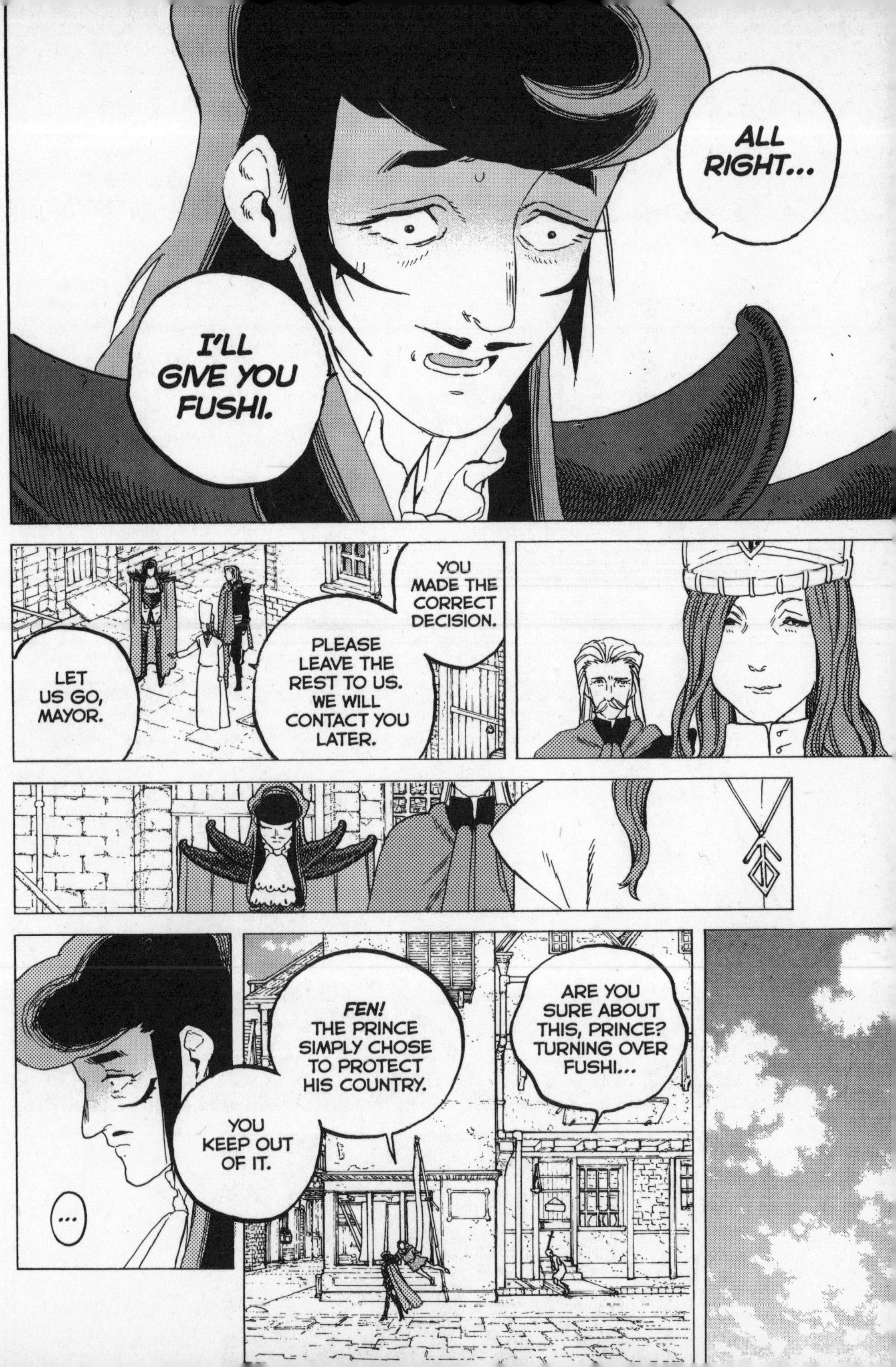
ALL RIGHT...
I'LL GIVE YOU FUSHI.
YOU MADE THE CORRECT DECISION.
PLEASE LEAVE THE REST TO US. WE WILL CONTACT YOU LATER.
LET US GO, MAYOR.
ARE YOU SURE ABOUT THIS, PRINCE? TURNING OVER FUSHI...
FEN! THE PRINCE SIMPLY CHOSE TO PROTECT HIS COUNTRY.
YOU KEEP OUT OF IT.
...

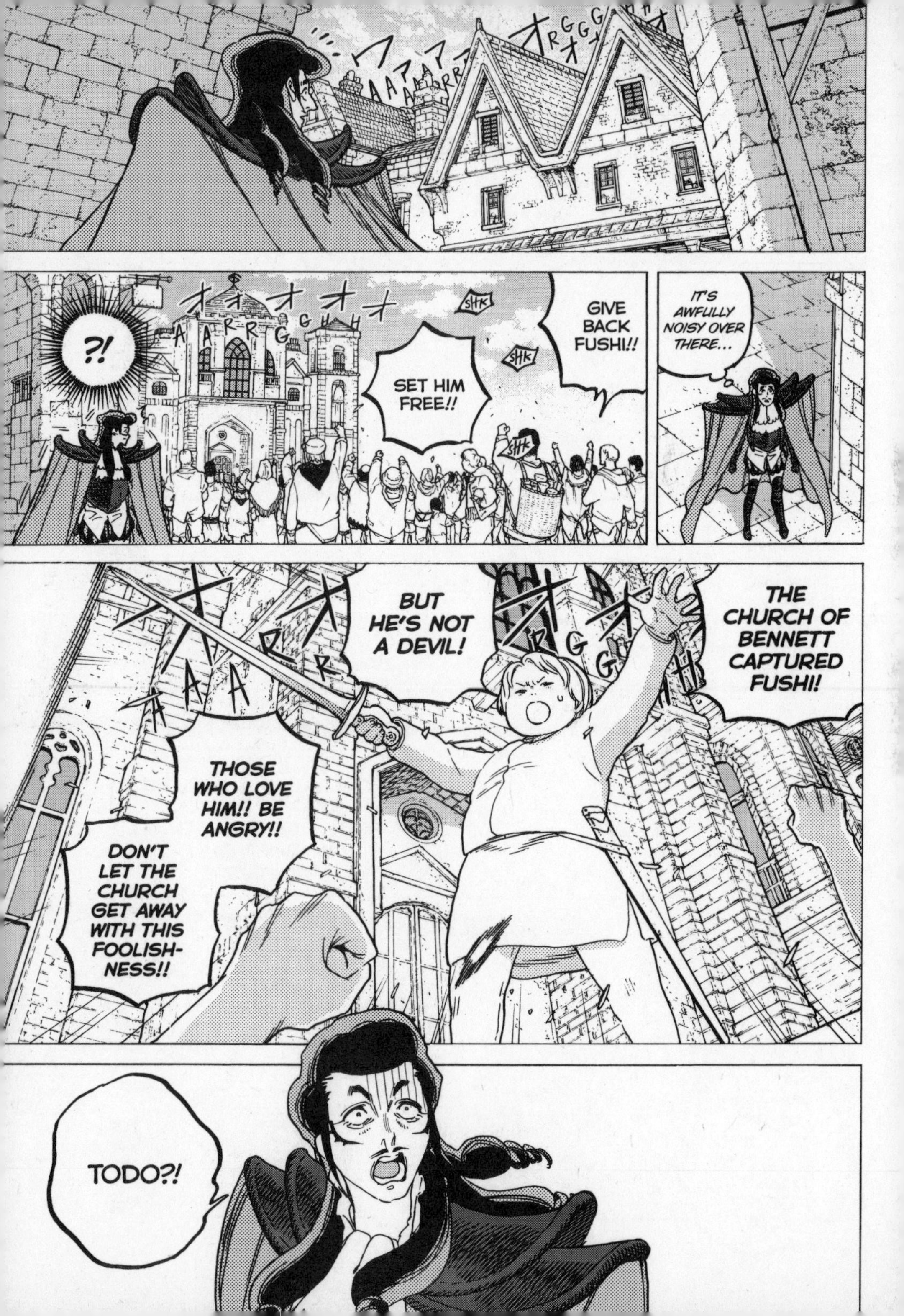
RGGG
IT'S AWFULLY NOISY OVER THERE...
GIVE BACK FUSHI!!
SHK
SET HIM FREE!!
SHK
AARRGGHH
?!
THE CHURCH OF BENNETT CAPTURED FUSHI!
BUT HE'S NOT A DEVIL!
THOSE WHO LOVE HIM!! BE ANGRY!!
DON'T LET THE CHURCH GET AWAY WITH THIS FOOLISH-NESS!!
TODO?!

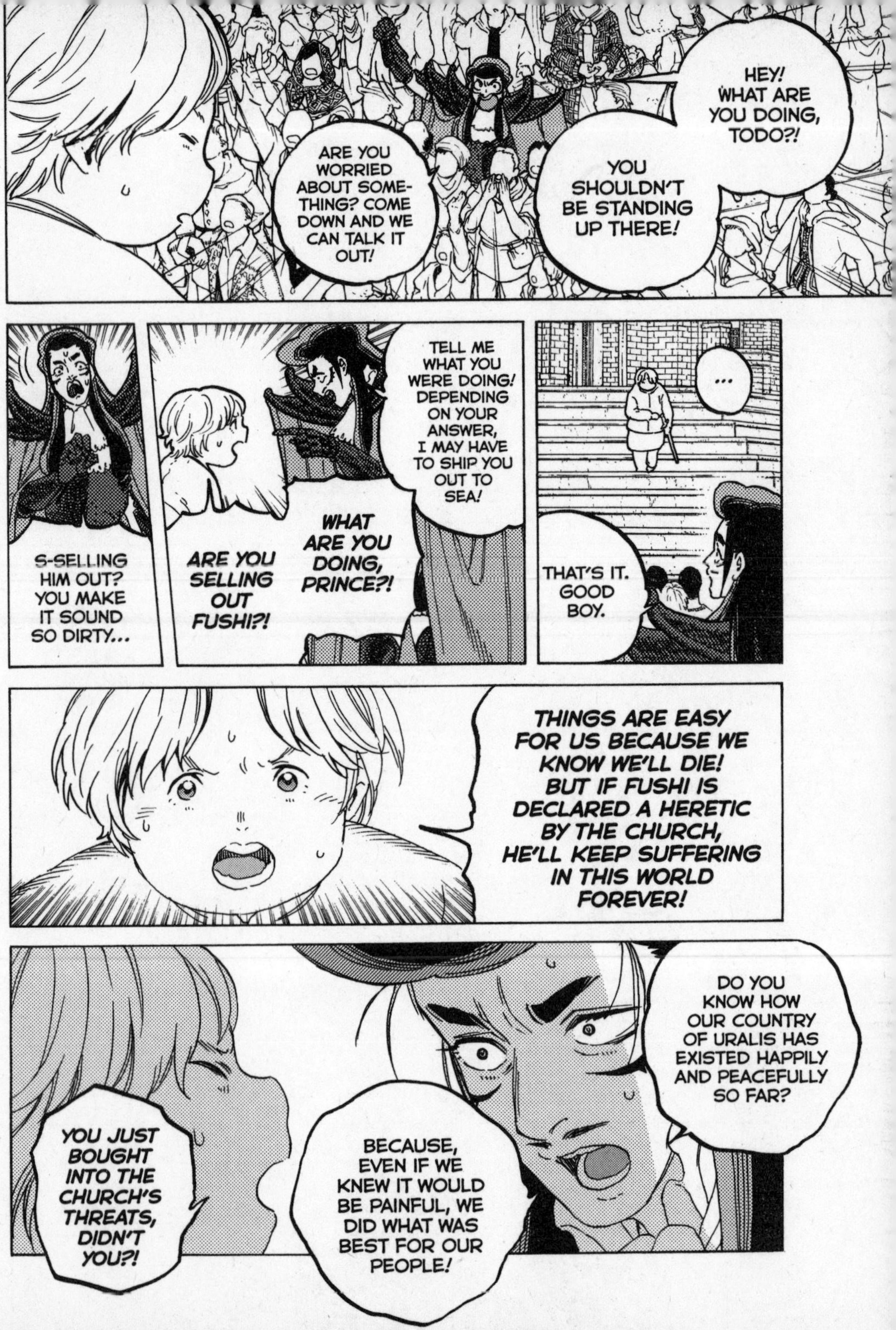
HEY! WHAT ARE YOU DOING, TODO?!
YOU SHOULDN'T BE STANDING UP THERE!
ARE YOU WORRIED ABOUT SOME-THING? COME DOWN AND WE CAN TALK IT OUT!
...
THAT'S IT. GOOD BOY.
TELL ME WHAT YOU WERE DOING! DEPENDING ON YOUR ANSWER, I MAY HAVE TO SHIP YOU OUT TO SEA!
WHAT ARE YOU DOING, PRINCE?!
ARE YOU SELLING OUT FUSHI?!
S-SELLING HIM OUT? YOU MAKE IT SOUND SO DIRTY...
THINGS ARE EASY FOR US BECAUSE WE KNOW WE'LL DIE! BUT IF FUSHI IS DECLARED A HERETIC BY THE CHURCH, HE'LL KEEP SUFFERING IN THIS WORLD FOREVER!
DO YOU KNOW HOW OUR COUNTRY OF URALIS HAS EXISTED HAPPILY AND PEACEFULLY SO FAR?
BECAUSE, EVEN IF WE KNEW IT WOULD BE PAINFUL, WE DID WHAT WAS BEST FOR OUR PEOPLE!
YOU JUST BOUGHT INTO THE CHURCH'S THREATS, DIDN'T YOU?!

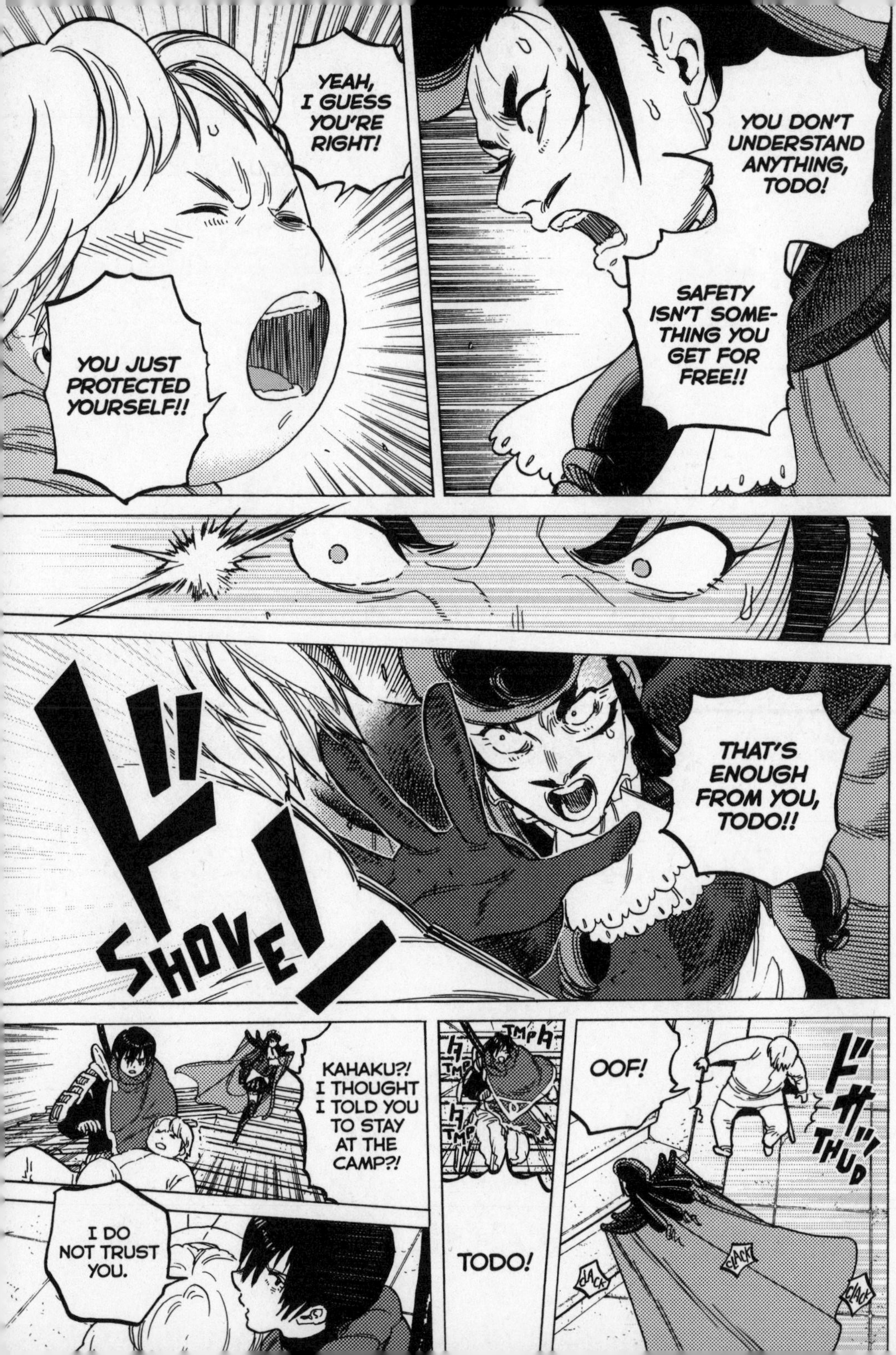
YOU DON'T UNDERSTAND ANYTHING, TODO!
SAFETY ISN'T SOME-THING YOU GET FOR FREE!!
YEAH, I GUESS YOU'RE RIGHT!
YOU JUST PROTECTED YOURSELF!!
THAT'S ENOUGH FROM YOU, TODO!!
SHOVE
OOF!
THUD
CLACK
CLACK
CLACK
TMP
TMP
TMP
TODO!
KAHAKU?! I THOUGHT I TOLD YOU TO STAY AT THE CAMP?!
I DO NOT TRUST YOU.

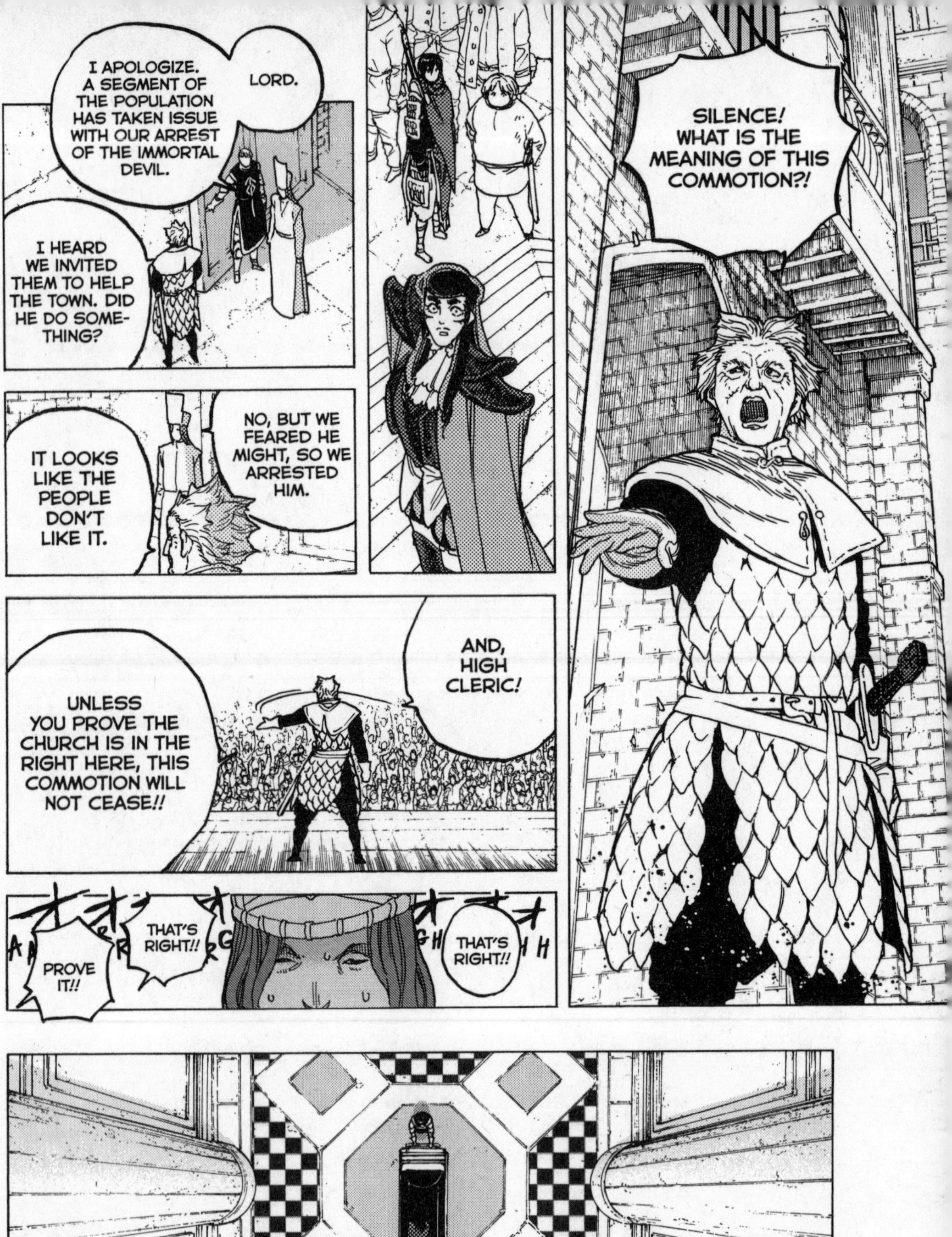
SILENCE! WHAT IS THE MEANING OF THIS COMMOTION?!
LORD.
I APOLOGIZE. A SEGMENT OF THE POPULATION HAS TAKEN ISSUE WITH OUR ARREST OF THE IMMORTAL DEVIL.
I HEARD WE INVITED THEM TO HELP THE TOWN. DID HE DO SOME-THING?
NO, BUT WE FEARED HE MIGHT, SO WE ARRESTED HIM.
IT LOOKS LIKE THE PEOPLE DON'T LIKE IT.
AND, HIGH CLERIC!
UNLESS YOU PROVE THE CHURCH IS IN THE RIGHT HERE, THIS COMMOTION WILL NOT CEASE!!
THAT'S RIGHT!!
THAT'S RIGHT!!
PROVE IT!!

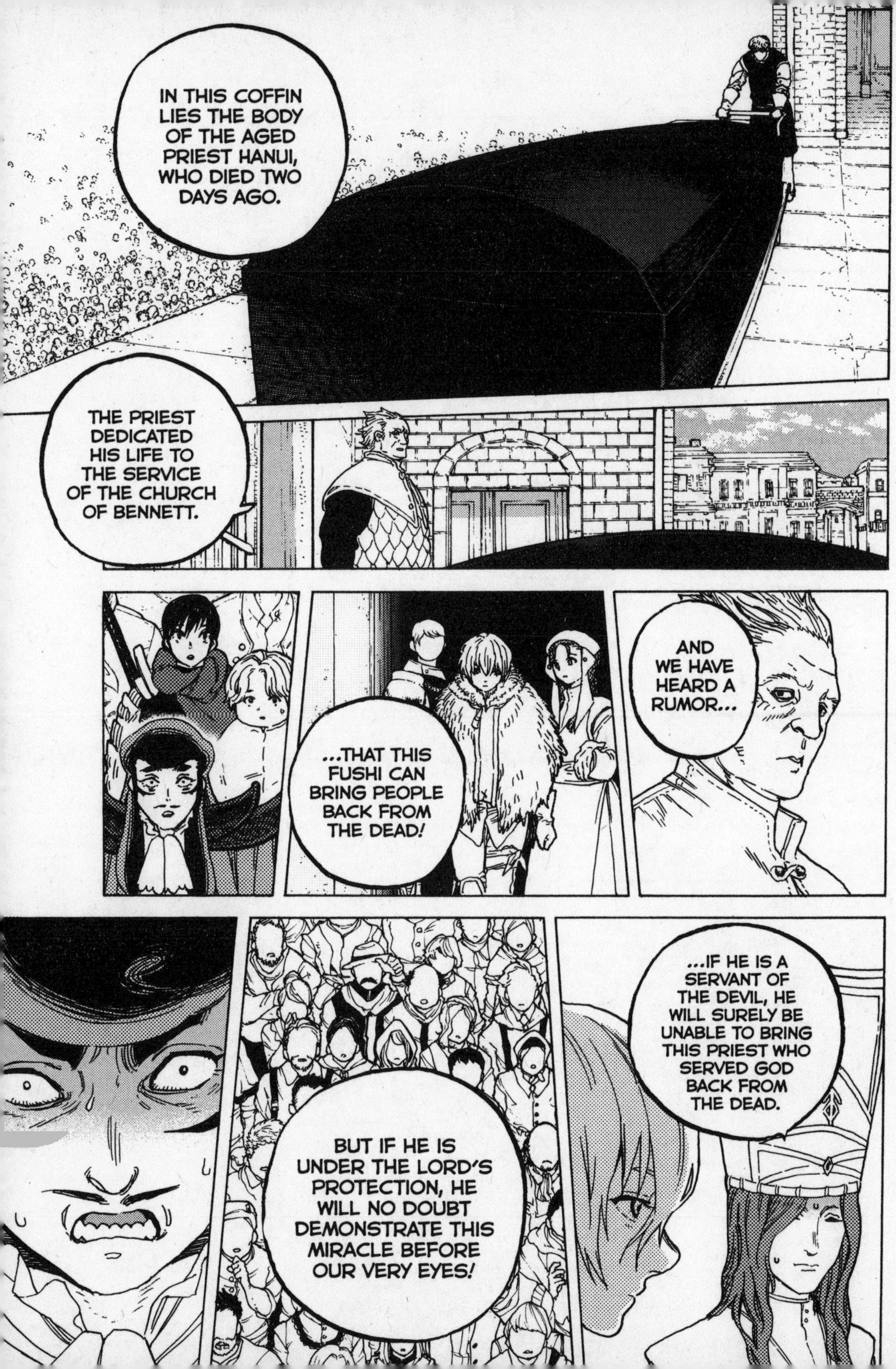
IN THIS COFFIN LIES THE BODY OF THE AGED PRIEST HANUI, WHO DIED TWO DAYS AGO.
THE PRIEST DEDICATED HIS LIFE TO THE SERVICE OF THE CHURCH OF BENNETT.
AND WE HAVE HEARD A RUMOR...
...THAT THIS FUSHI CAN BRING PEOPLE BACK FROM THE DEAD!
...IF HE IS A SERVANT OF THE DEVIL, HE WILL SURELY BE UNABLE TO BRING THIS PRIEST WHO SERVED GOD BACK FROM THE DEAD.
BUT IF HE IS UNDER THE LORD'S PROTECTION, HE WILL NO DOUBT DEMONSTRATE THIS MIRACLE BEFORE OUR VERY EYES!

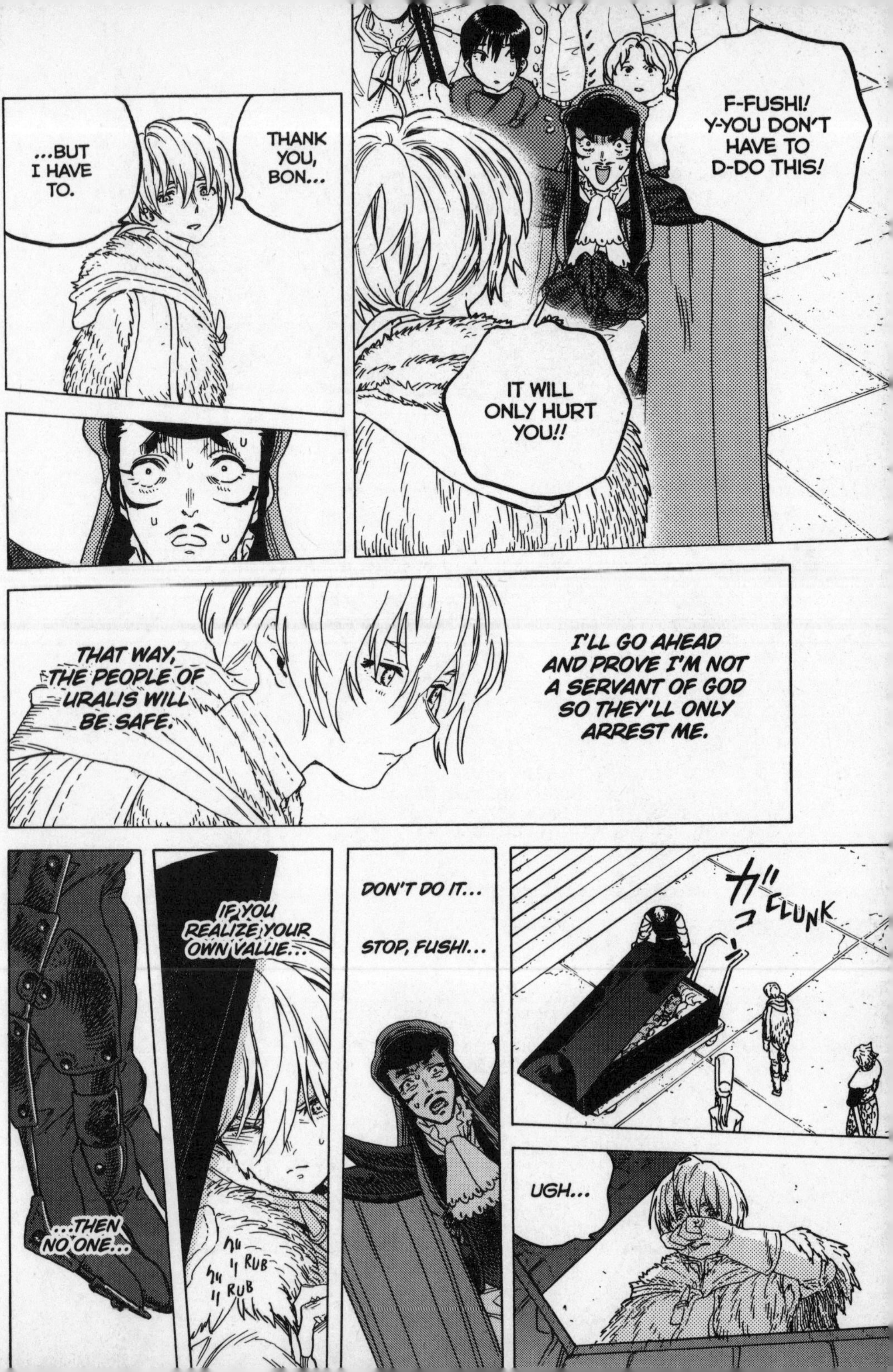
F-FUSHI! Y-YOU DON'T HAVE TO D-DO THIS!
IT WILL ONLY HURT YOU!!
THANK YOU, BON...
...BUT I HAVE TO.
I'LL GO AHEAD AND PROVE I'M NOT A SERVANT OF GOD SO THEY'LL ONLY ARREST ME.
THAT WAY, THE PEOPLE OF URALIS WILL BE SAFE.
CLUNK
UGH...
DON'T DO IT...
STOP, FUSHI...
IF YOU REALIZE YOUR OWN VALUE...
RUB
RUB
...THEN NO ONE...

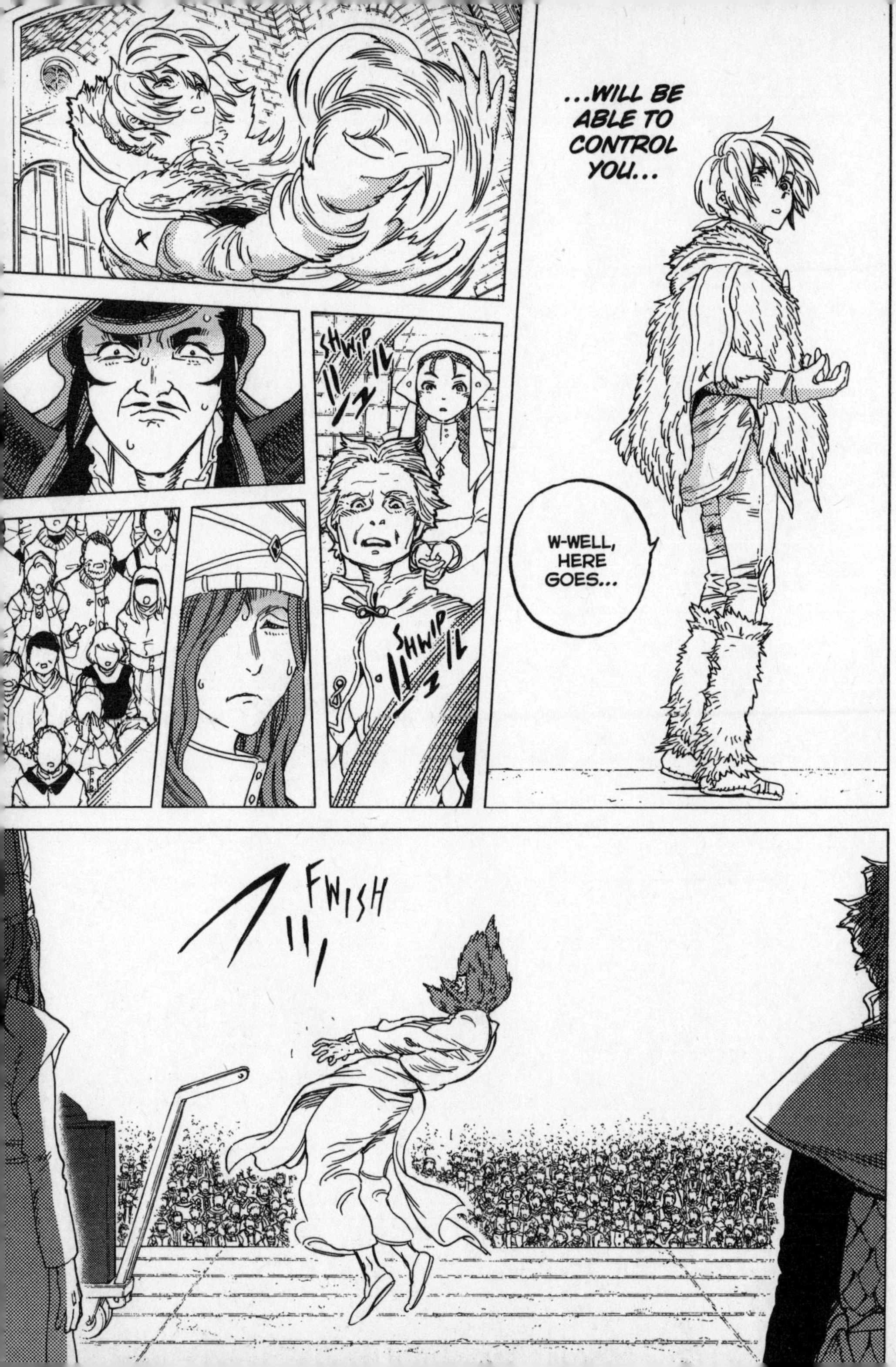
...WILL BE ABLE TO CONTROL YOU...
W-WELL, HERE GOES...
SHWIP
SHWIP
FWISH

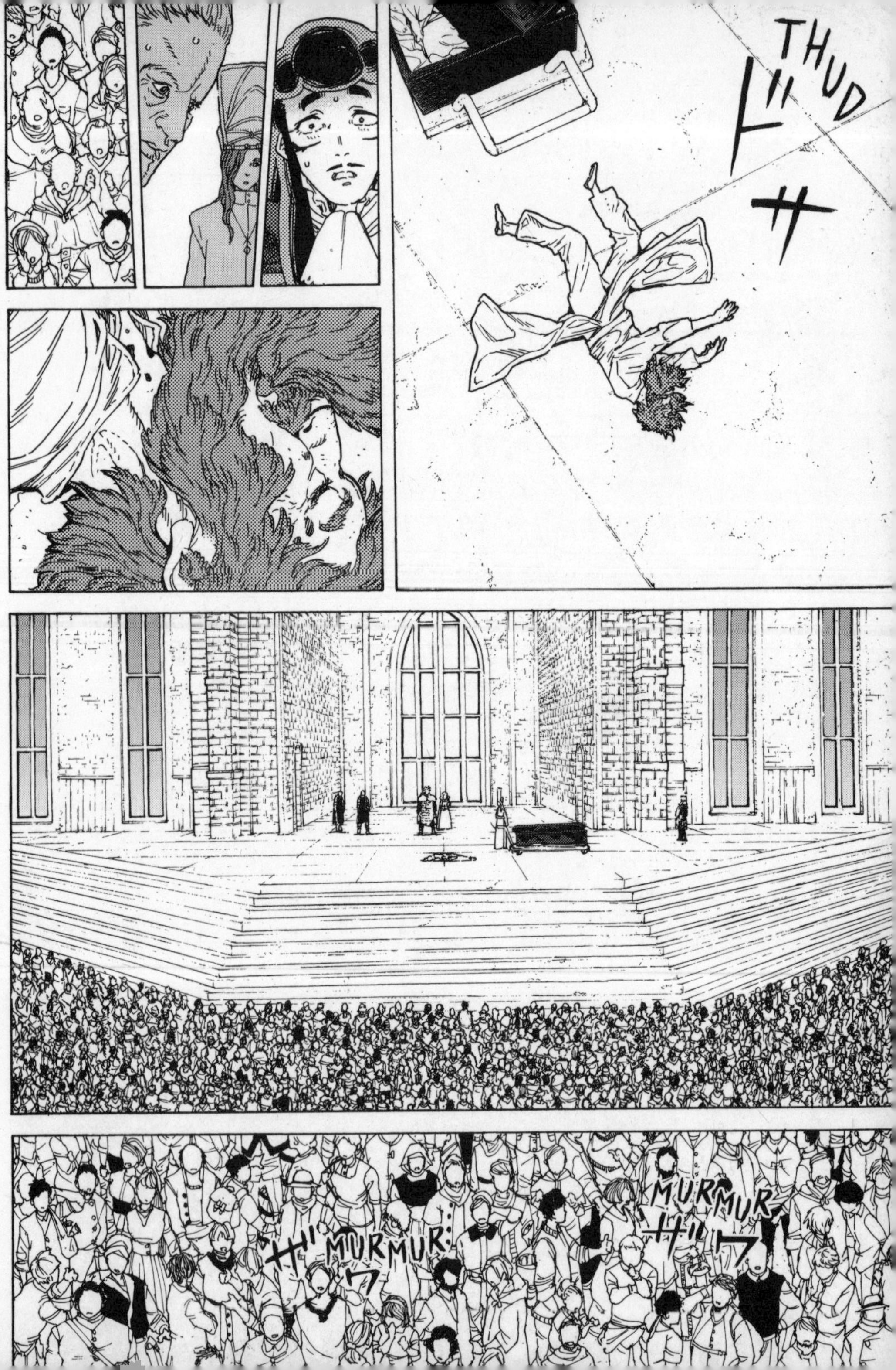
THUD
ドサ
MURMUR
ザワ
MURMUR
ザワ

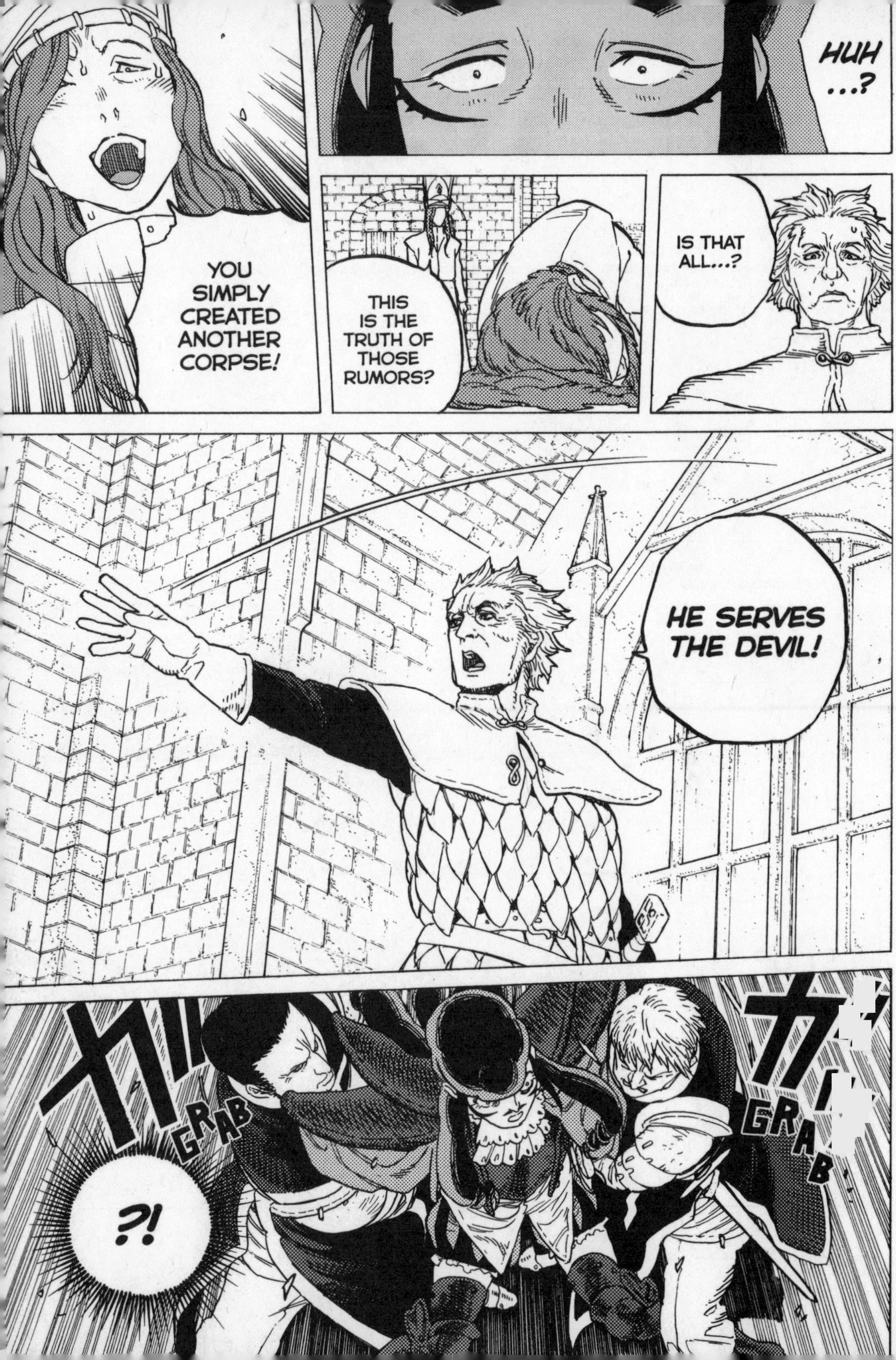
HUH ...?
IS THAT ALL...?
THIS IS THE TRUTH OF THOSE RUMORS?
YOU SIMPLY CREATED ANOTHER CORPSE!
HE SERVES THE DEVIL!
GRAB
GRAB
?!

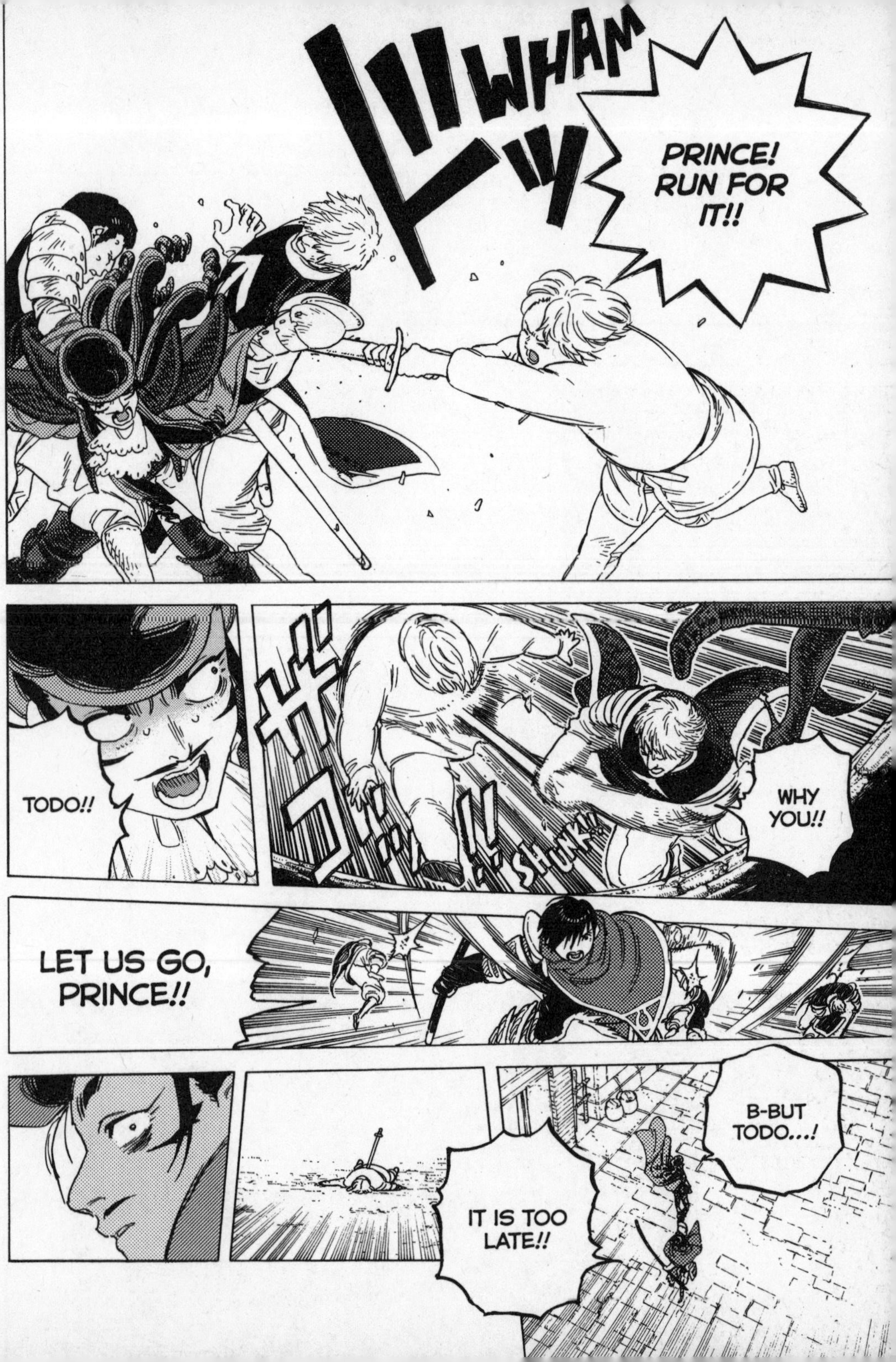
WHAM
PRINCE! RUN FOR IT!!
WHY YOU!!
SHUNK!!
TODO!!
LET US GO, PRINCE!!
B-BUT TODO...!
IT IS TOO LATE!!

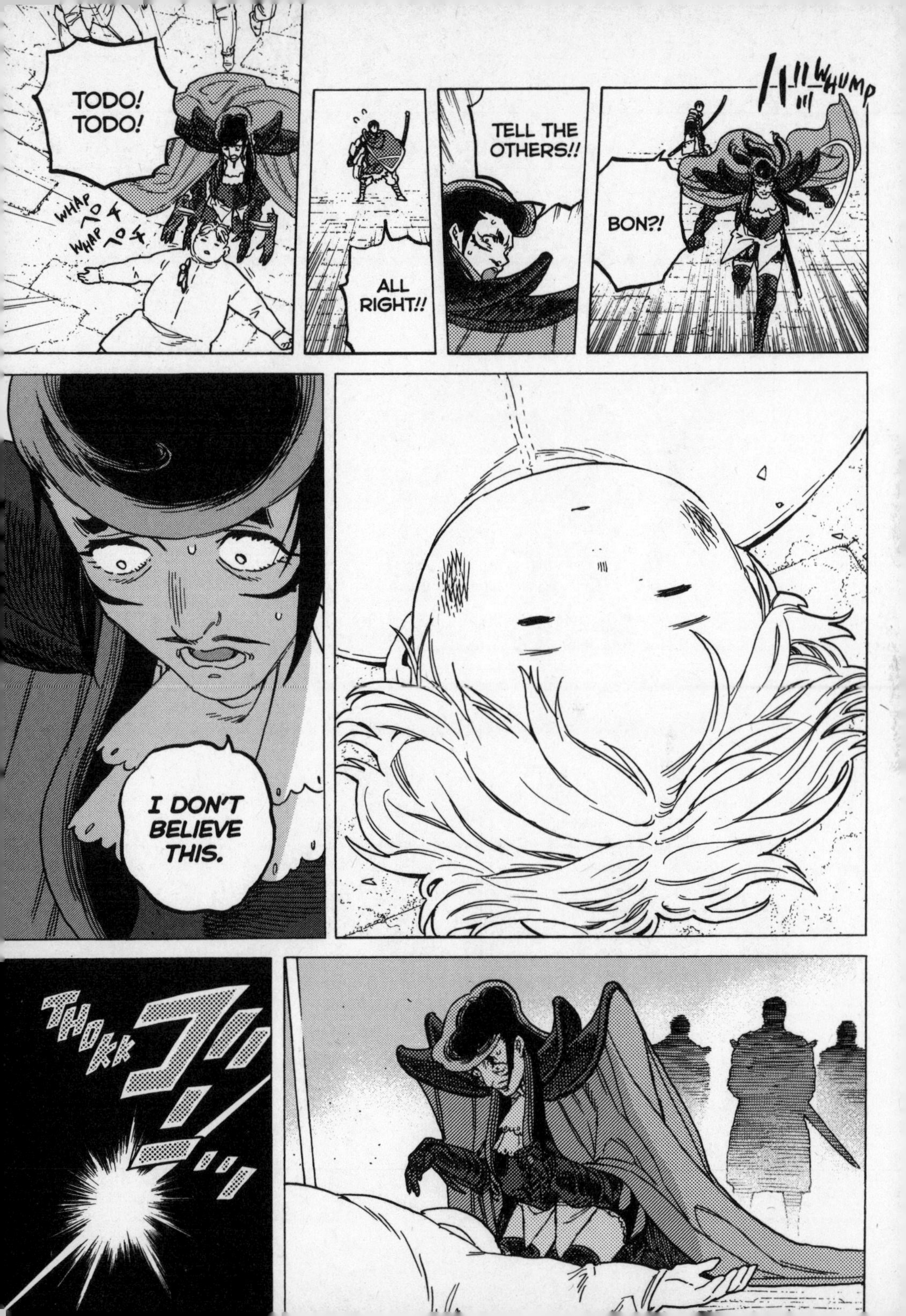
WHUMP
BON?!
TELL THE OTHERS!!
ALL RIGHT!!
TODO! TODO!
WHAP
WHAP
I DON'T BELIEVE THIS.
THOKK

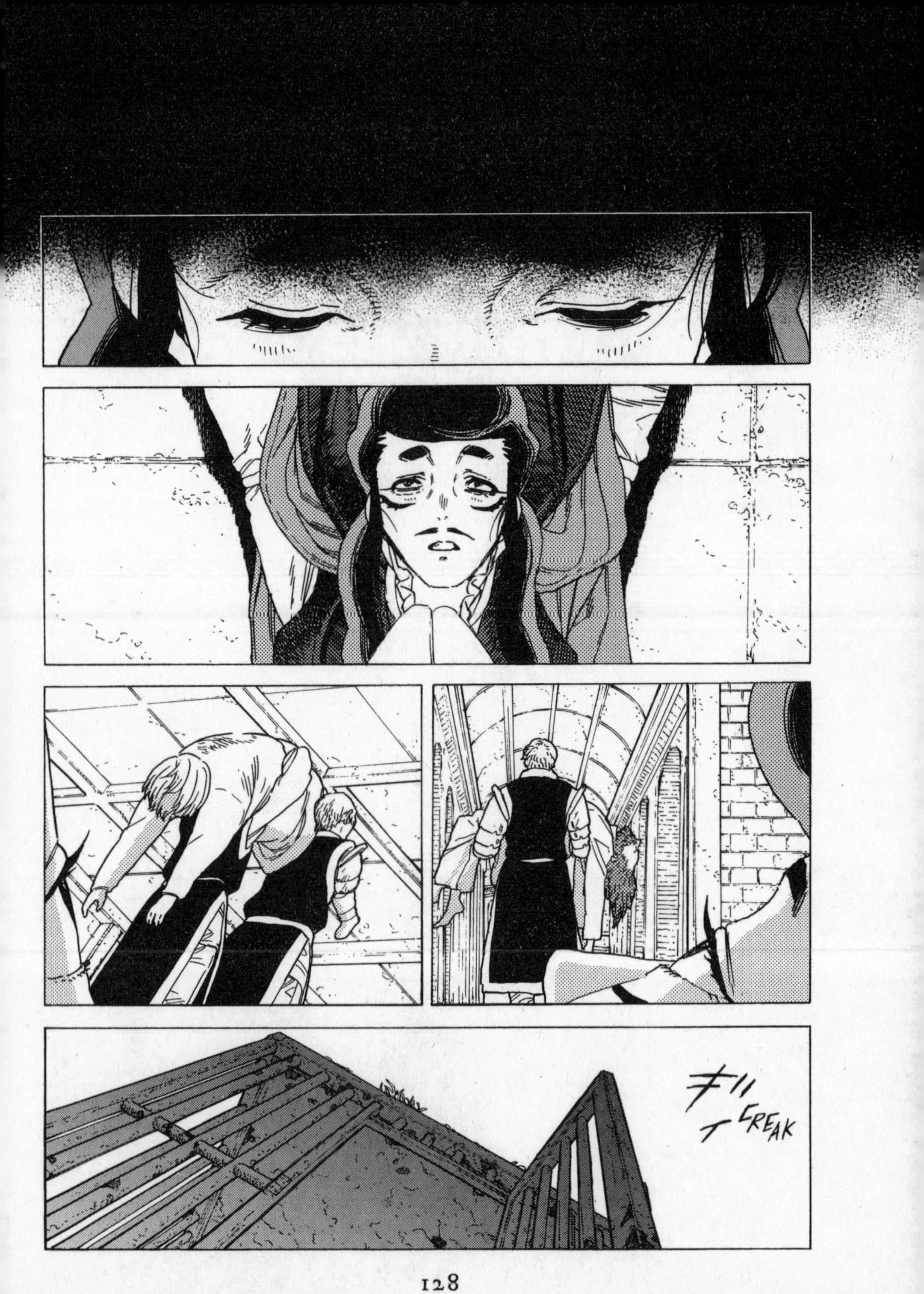
ギイ
CREAK

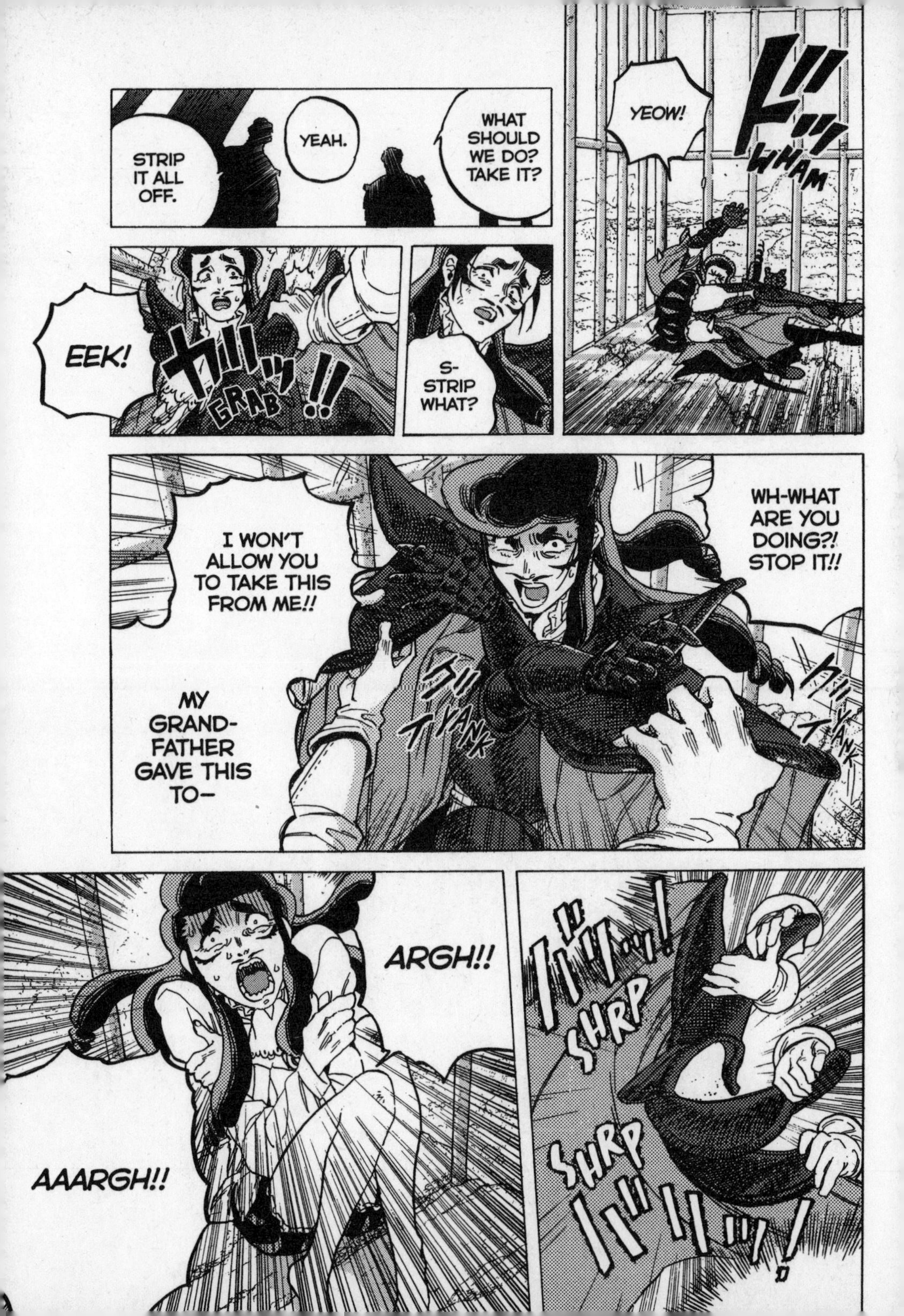

YEOW!
WHAM
WHAT SHOULD WE DO? TAKE IT?
YEAH.
STRIP IT ALL OFF.
S-STRIP WHAT?
EEK!
GRAB!!
WH-WHAT ARE YOU DOING?! STOP IT!!
YANK
YANK
I WON'T ALLOW YOU TO TAKE THIS FROM ME!!
MY GRAND-FATHER GAVE THIS TO–
SHRP
SHRP
ARGH!!
AAARGH!!

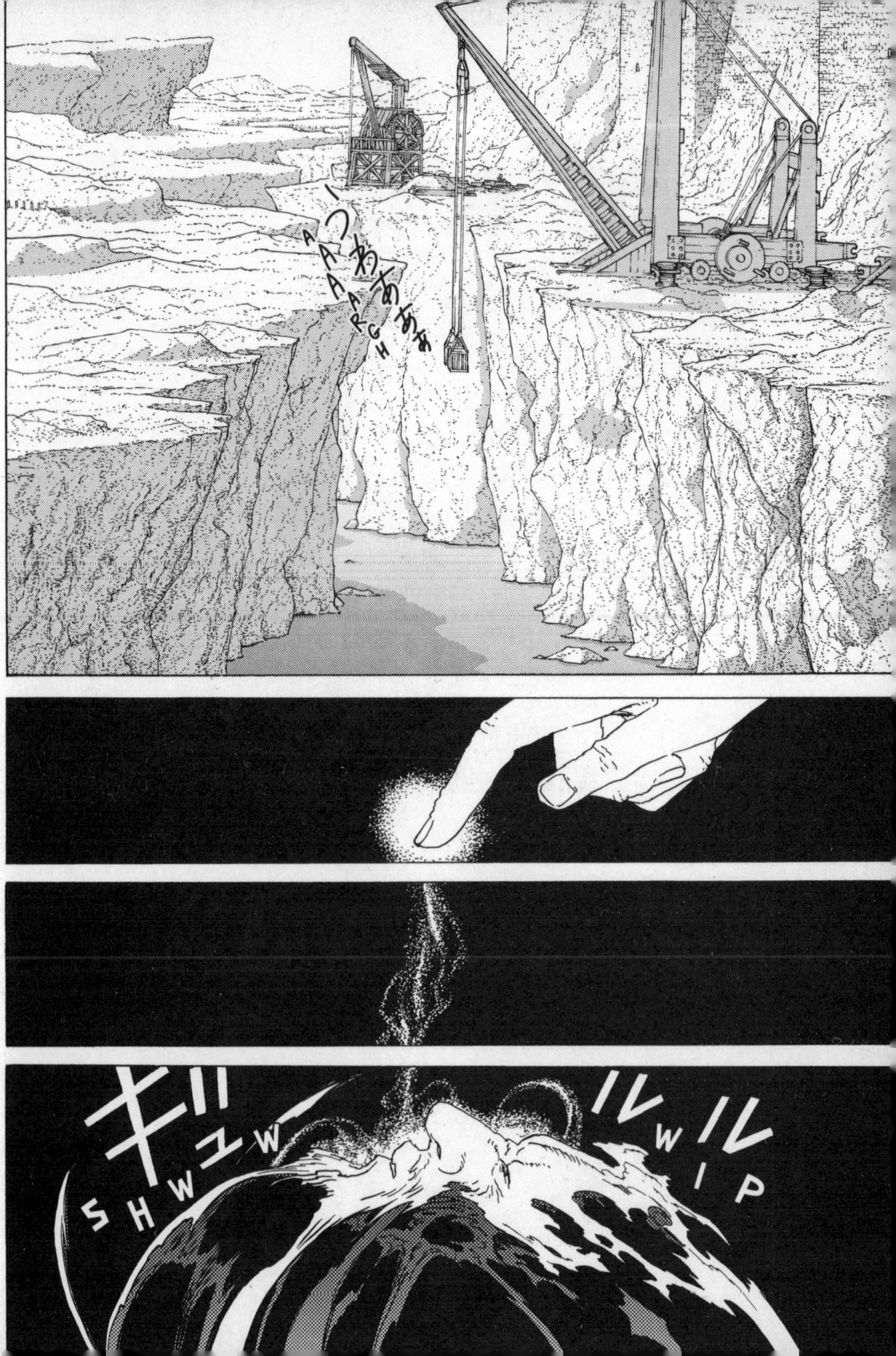
ーっあ゛あああ
AAAARGH
ギュルル
SHWWIP

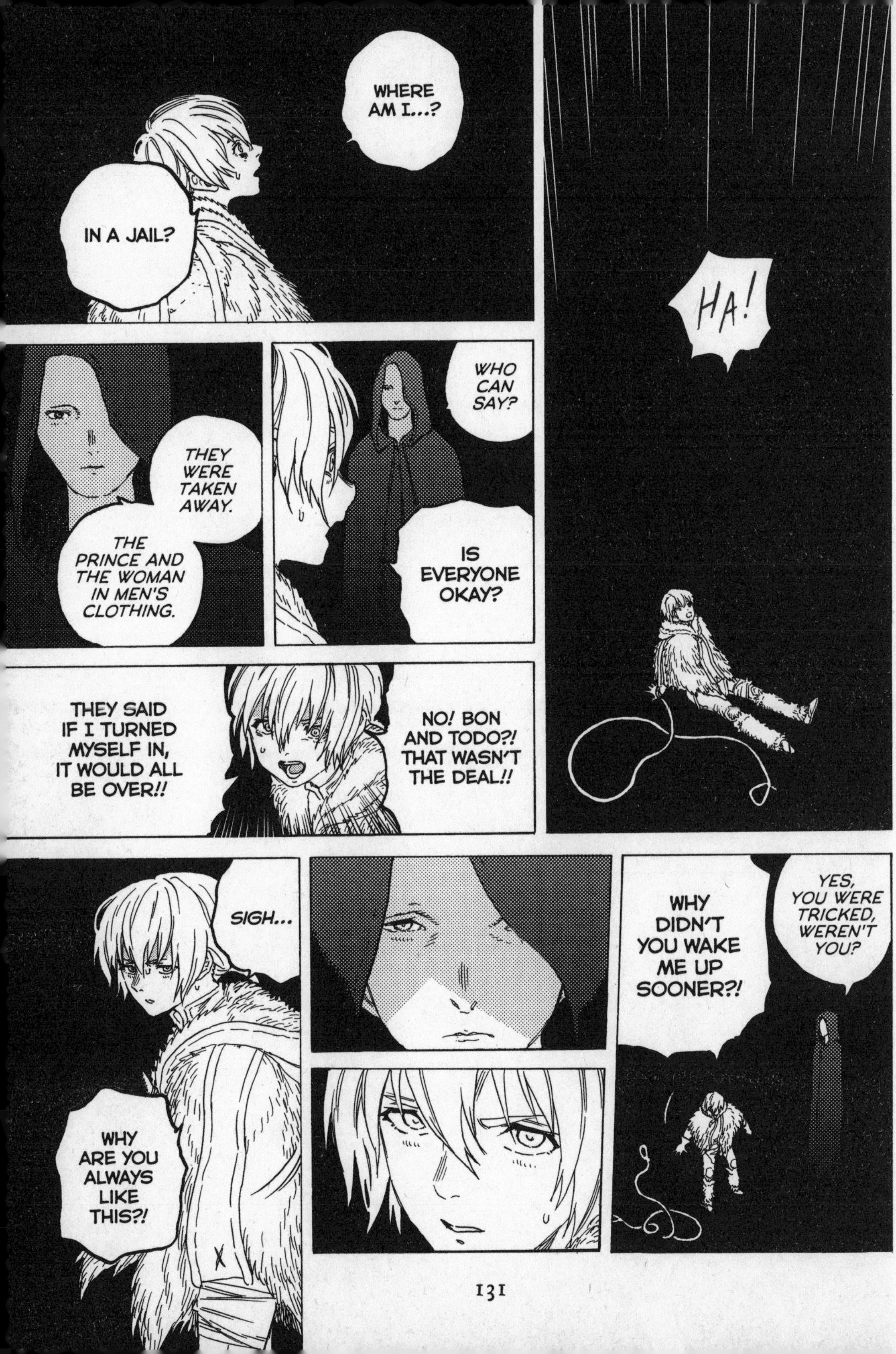
HA!
WHERE AM I...?
IN A JAIL?
WHO CAN SAY?
IS EVERYONE OKAY?
THEY WERE TAKEN AWAY.
THE PRINCE AND THE WOMAN IN MEN'S CLOTHING.
NO! BON AND TODO?! THAT WASN'T THE DEAL!!
THEY SAID IF I TURNED MYSELF IN, IT WOULD ALL BE OVER!!
YES, YOU WERE TRICKED, WEREN'T YOU?
WHY DIDN'T YOU WAKE ME UP SOONER?!
SIGH...
WHY ARE YOU ALWAYS LIKE THIS?!

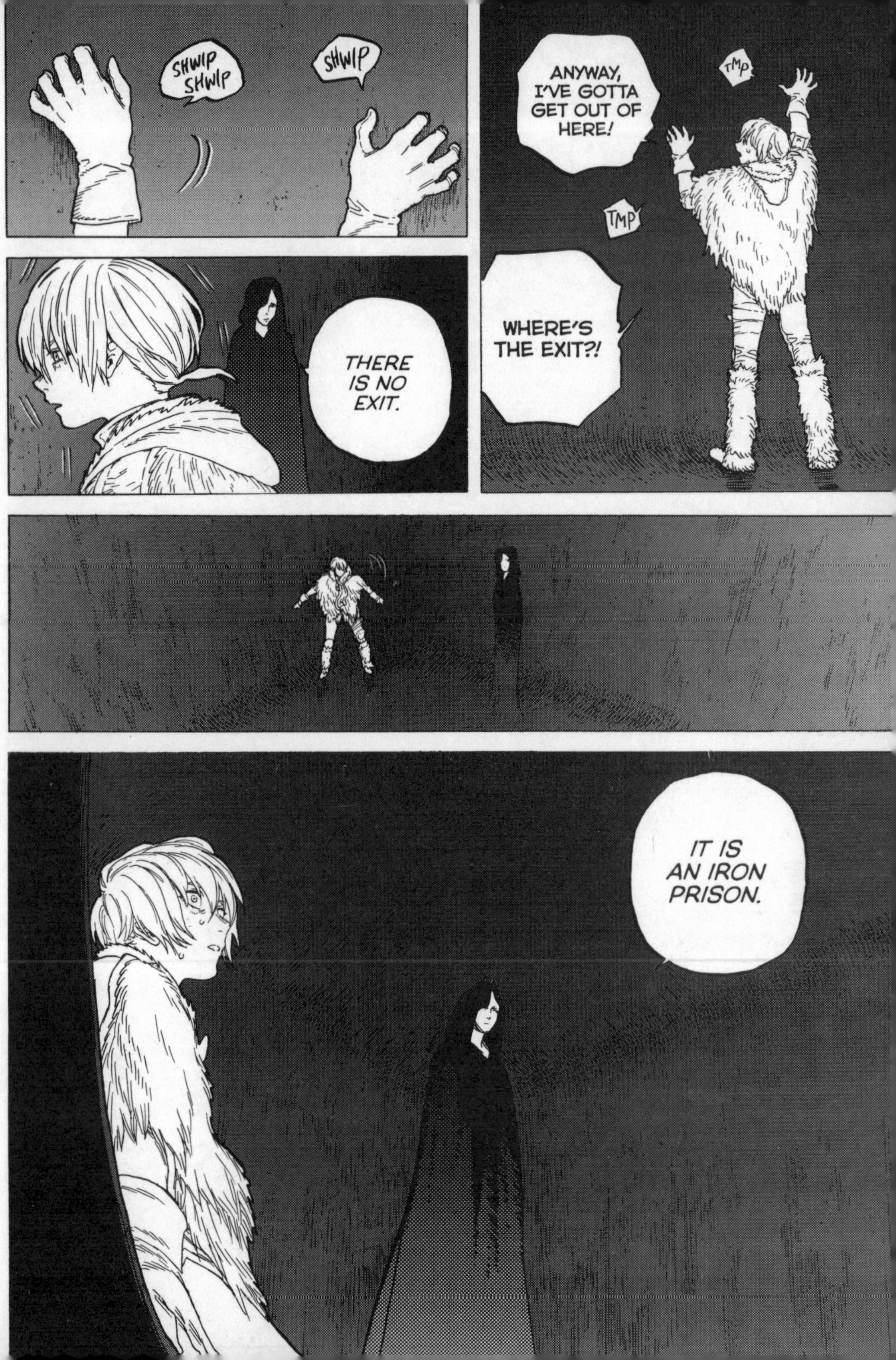
TMP
ANYWAY, I'VE GOTTA GET OUT OF HERE!
TMP
WHERE'S THE EXIT?!
SHWIP
SHWIP SHWIP
THERE IS NO EXIT.
IT IS AN IRON PRISON.

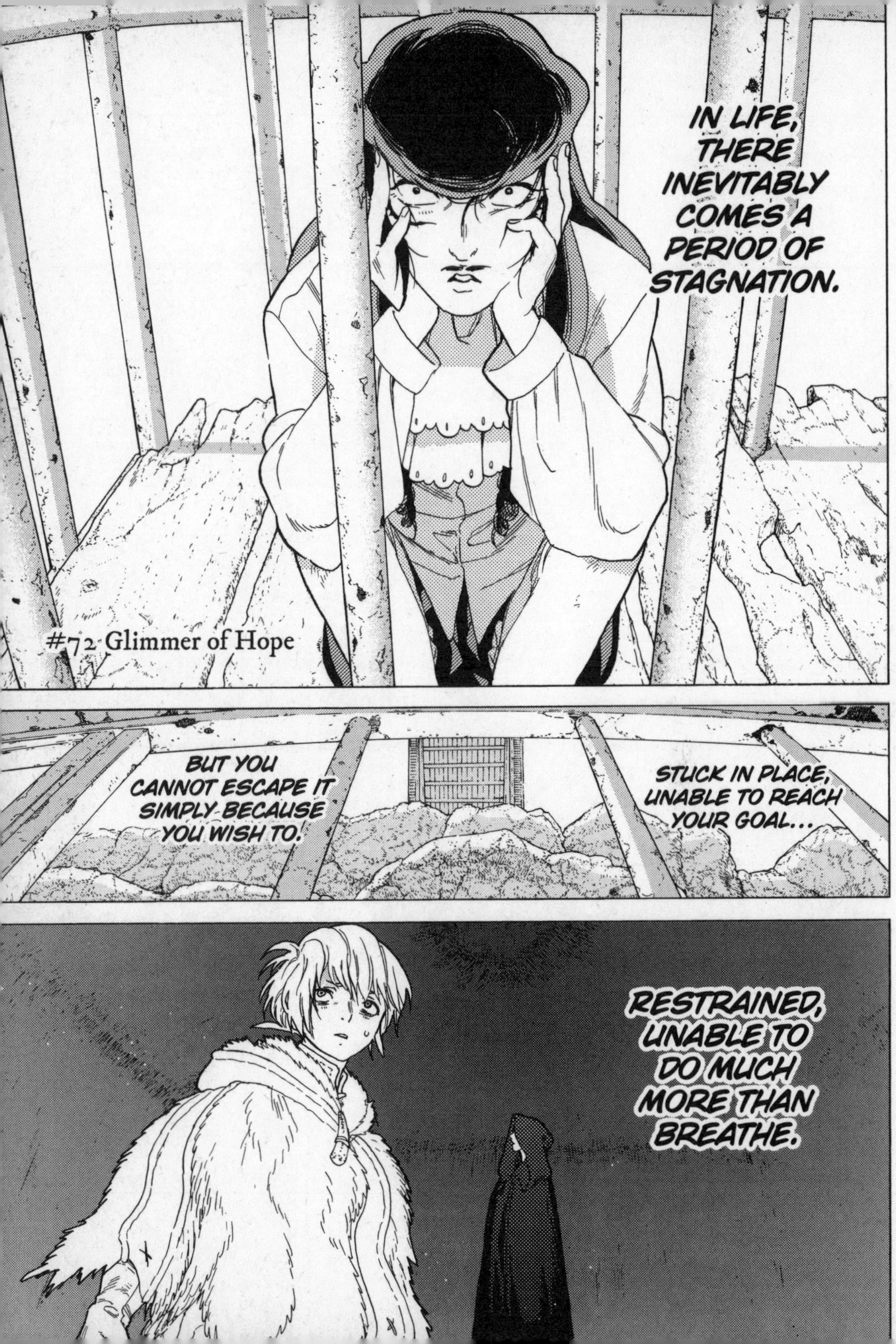
IN LIFE, THERE INEVITABLY COMES A PERIOD OF STAGNATION.
#72 Glimmer of Hope
STUCK IN PLACE, UNABLE TO REACH YOUR GOAL...
BUT YOU CANNOT ESCAPE IT SIMPLY BECAUSE YOU WISH TO.
RESTRAINED, UNABLE TO DO MUCH MORE THAN BREATHE.

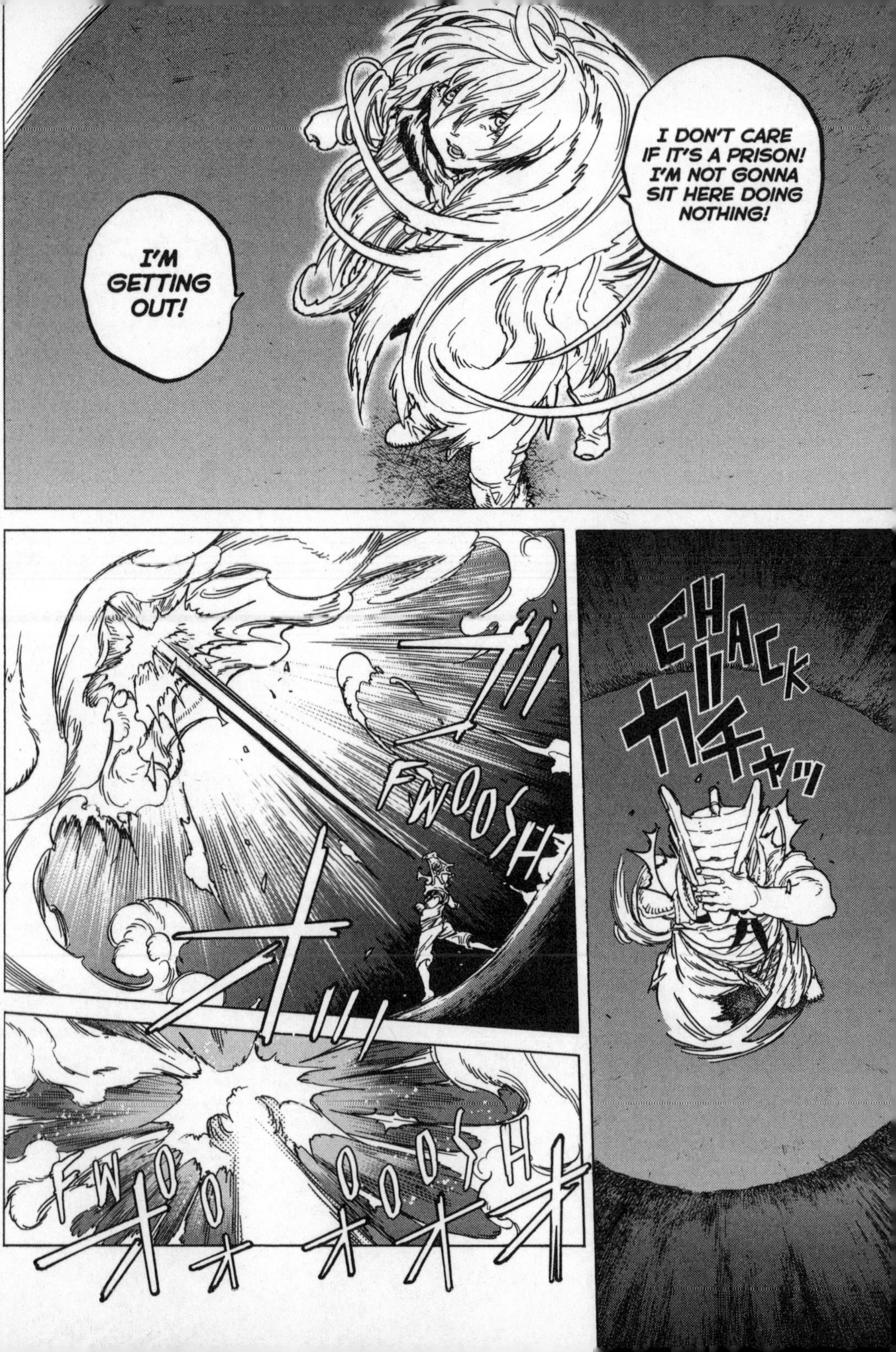
I DON'T CARE IF IT'S A PRISON! I'M NOT GONNA SIT HERE DOING NOTHING!
I'M GETTING OUT!
CHACK
カチャッ
FWOOSH
FWOOOOOSH

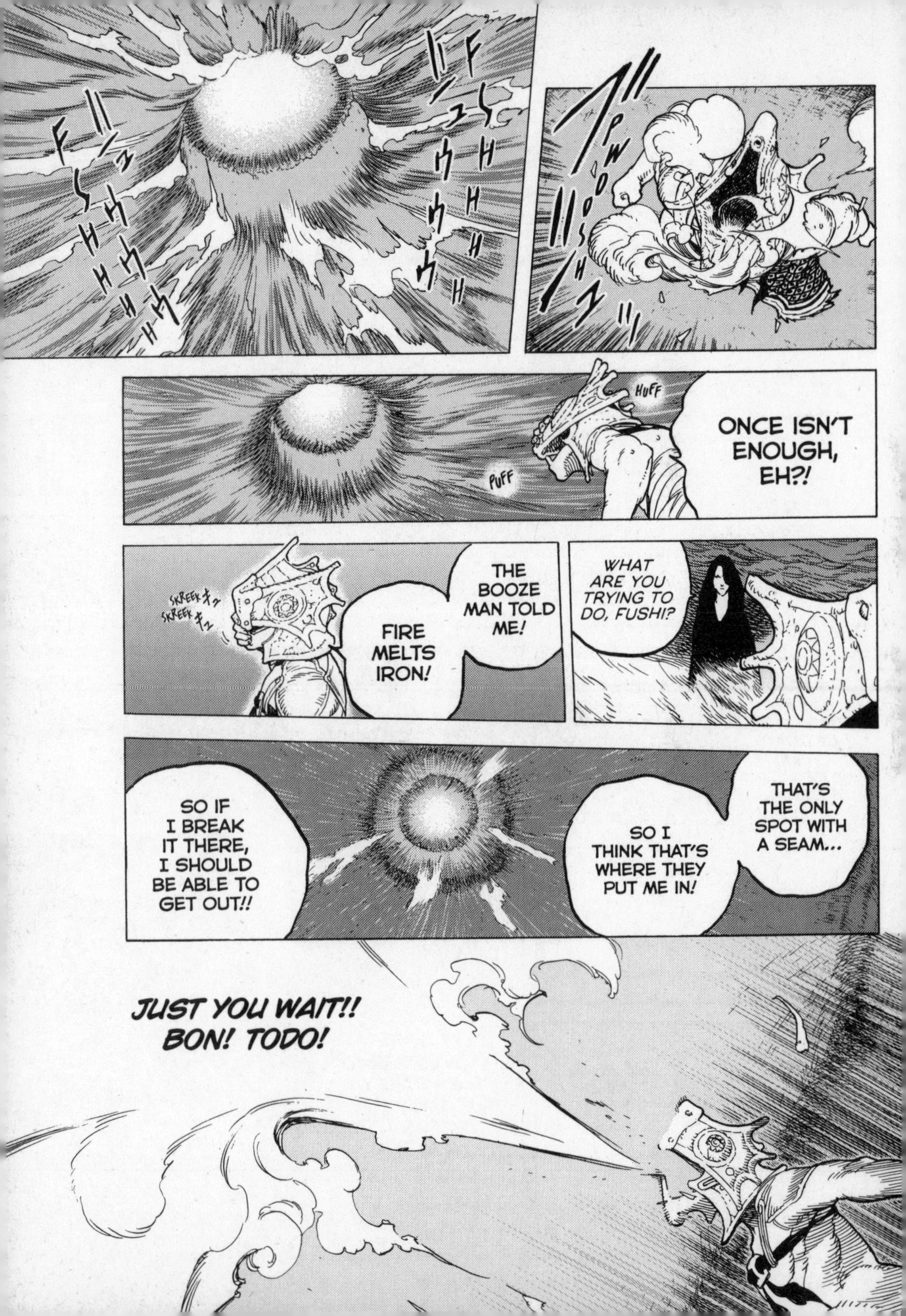
PWOOSH
FSHHHH
FSHHHH
HUFF
PUFF
ONCE ISN'T ENOUGH, EH?!
WHAT ARE YOU TRYING TO DO, FUSHI?
THE BOOZE MAN TOLD ME!
FIRE MELTS IRON!
SKREEK
SKREEK
THAT'S THE ONLY SPOT WITH A SEAM...
SO I THINK THAT'S WHERE THEY PUT ME IN!
SO IF I BREAK IT THERE, I SHOULD BE ABLE TO GET OUT!!
JUST YOU WAIT!! BON! TODO!

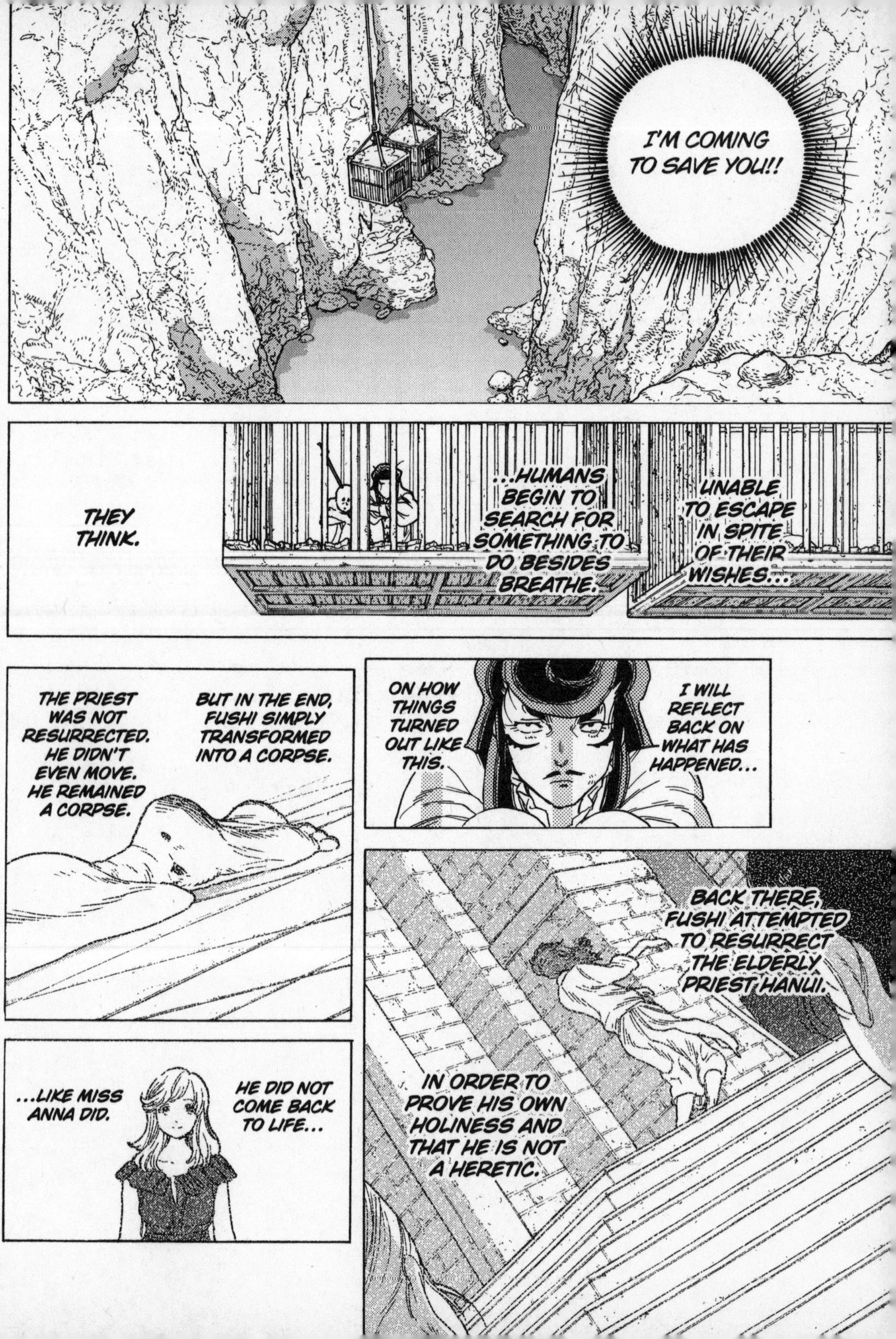

I'M COMING TO SAVE YOU!!
UNABLE TO ESCAPE IN SPITE OF THEIR WISHES...
...HUMANS BEGIN TO SEARCH FOR SOMETHING TO DO BESIDES BREATHE.
THEY THINK.
I WILL REFLECT BACK ON WHAT HAS HAPPENED...
ON HOW THINGS TURNED OUT LIKE THIS.
BACK THERE, FUSHI ATTEMPTED TO RESURRECT THE ELDERLY PRIEST HANUI.
IN ORDER TO PROVE HIS OWN HOLINESS AND THAT HE IS NOT A HERETIC.
BUT IN THE END, FUSHI SIMPLY TRANSFORMED INTO A CORPSE.
THE PRIEST WAS NOT RESURRECTED. HE DIDN'T EVEN MOVE. HE REMAINED A CORPSE.
HE DID NOT COME BACK TO LIFE...
...LIKE MISS ANNA DID.

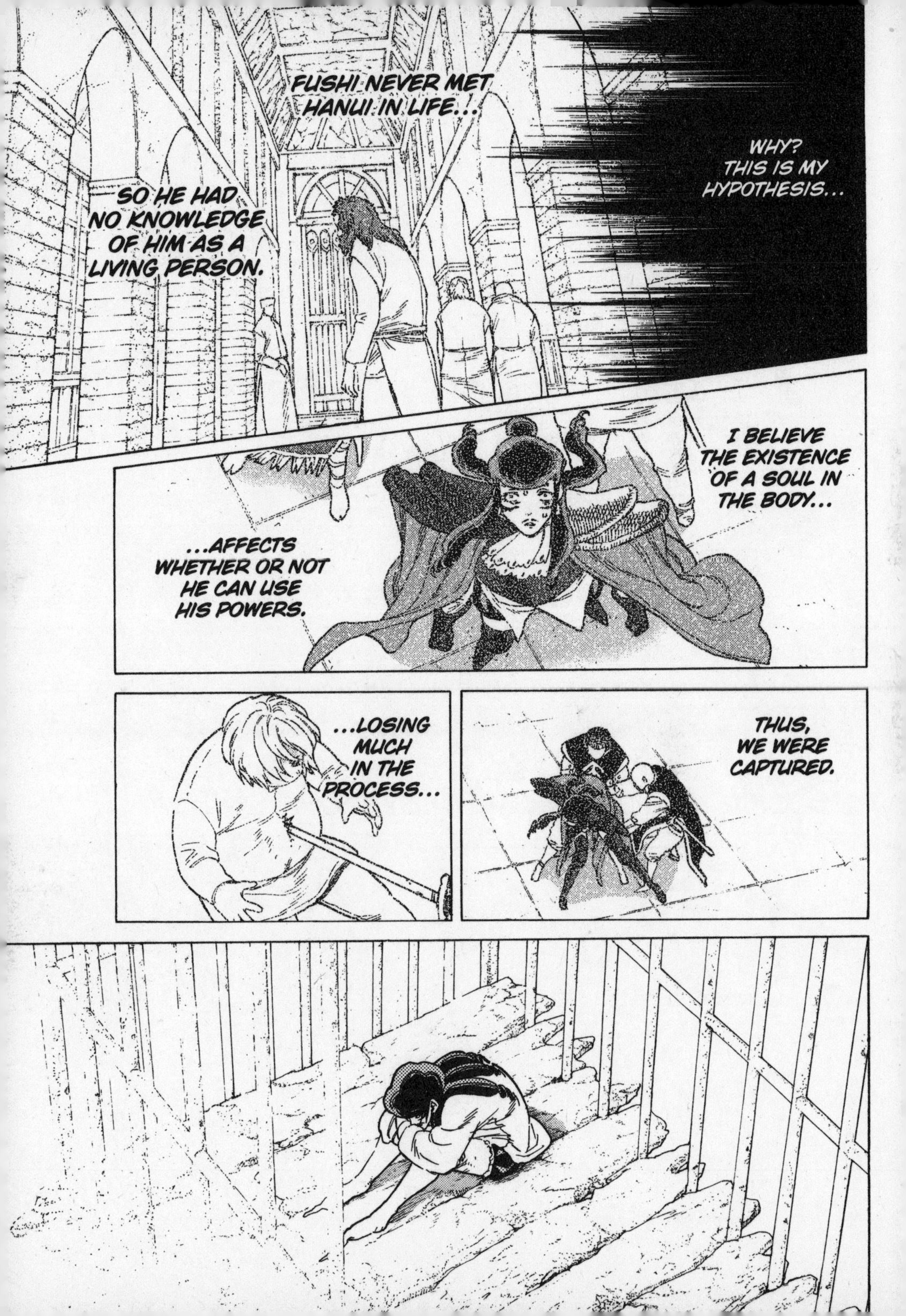
FUSHI NEVER MET HANUI IN LIFE...
SO HE HAD NO KNOWLEDGE OF HIM AS A LIVING PERSON.
WHY? THIS IS MY HYPOTHESIS...
I BELIEVE THE EXISTENCE OF A SOUL IN THE BODY...
...AFFECTS WHETHER OR NOT HE CAN USE HIS POWERS.
THUS, WE WERE CAPTURED.
...LOSING MUCH IN THE PROCESS...

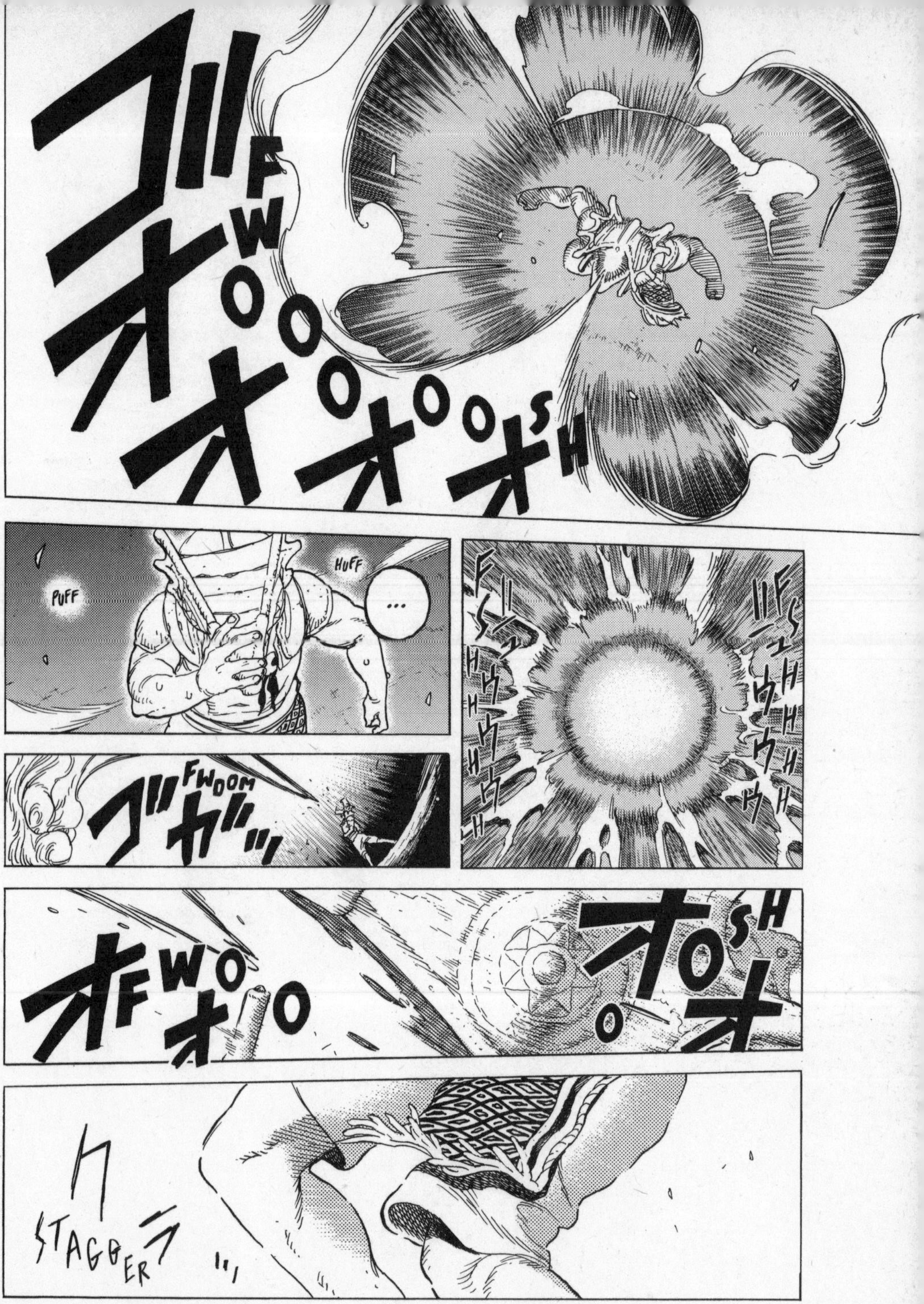
FWOOOOSH
FSHHHH
FSHHHHH
HUFF
PUFF
...
FWOOM
FWOOOOSH
STAGGER

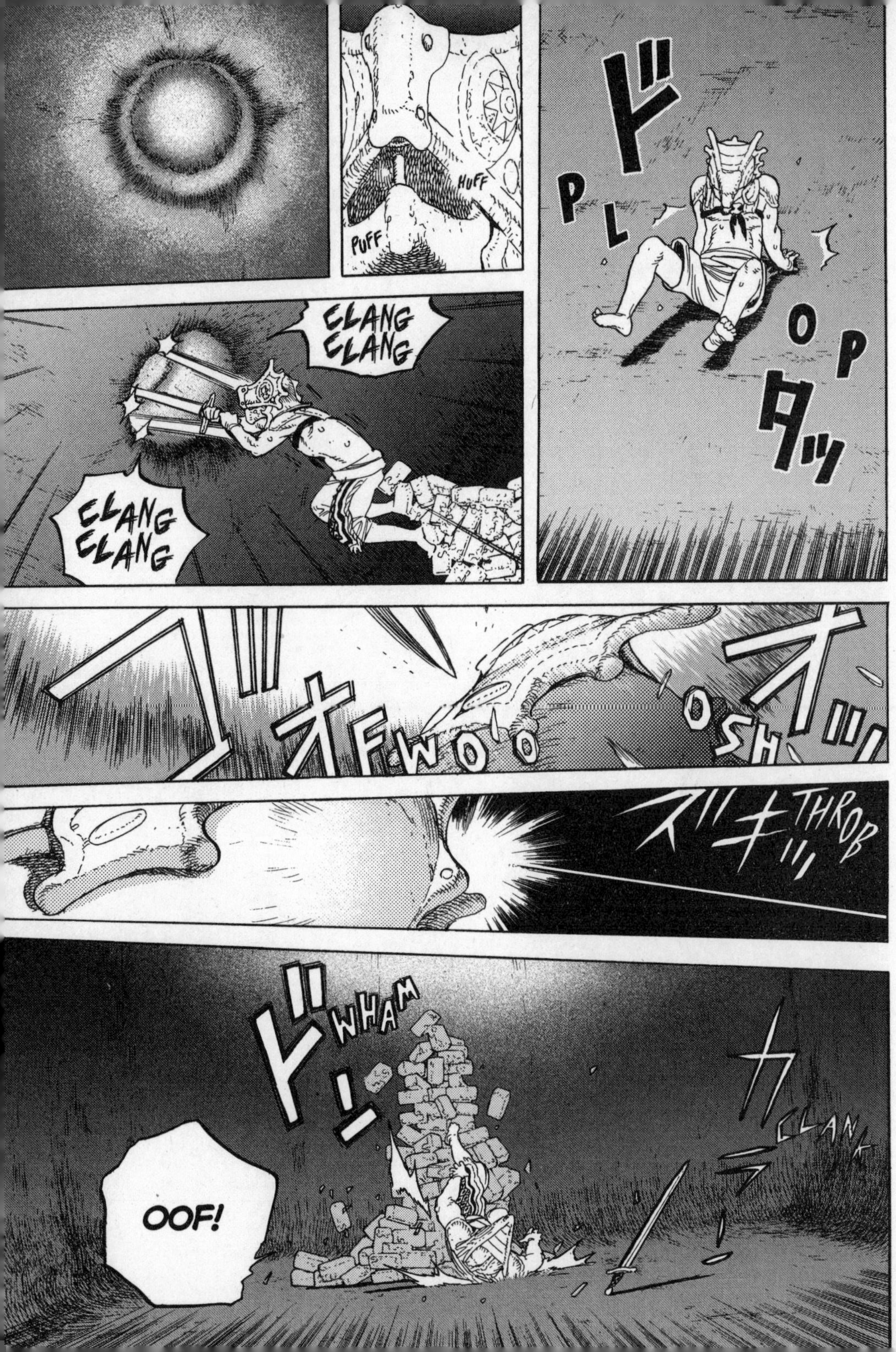
ド
PLOP
ダッ
HUFF
PUFF
CLANG CLANG
CLANG CLANG
ゴオオッ
FWOOOSH
ズキッ
THROB
ドン
WHAM
カラ
CLANK
OOF!

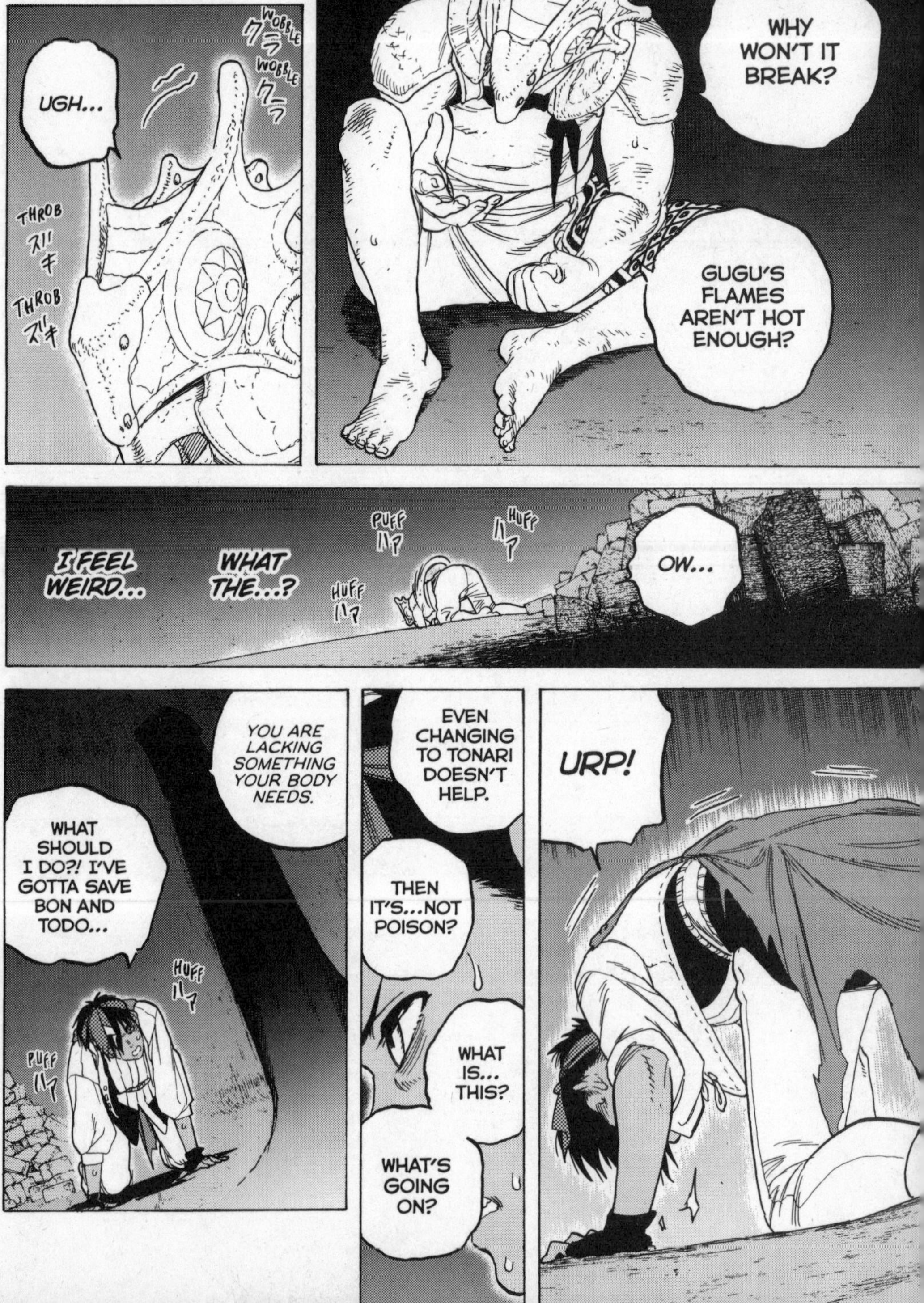
WHY WON'T IT BREAK?
GUGU'S FLAMES AREN'T HOT ENOUGH?
WOBBLE クラ
WOBBLE クラ
UGH...
THROB ズキ
THROB ズキ
OW...
HUFF ハア
PUFF ハア
HUFF ハア
WHAT THE...?
I FEEL WEIRD...
URP!
EVEN CHANGING TO TONARI DOESN'T HELP.
THEN IT'S...NOT POISON?
WHAT IS... THIS?
WHAT'S GOING ON?
YOU ARE LACKING SOMETHING YOUR BODY NEEDS.
WHAT SHOULD I DO?! I'VE GOTTA SAVE BON AND TODO...
HUFF ハア
PUFF ハア

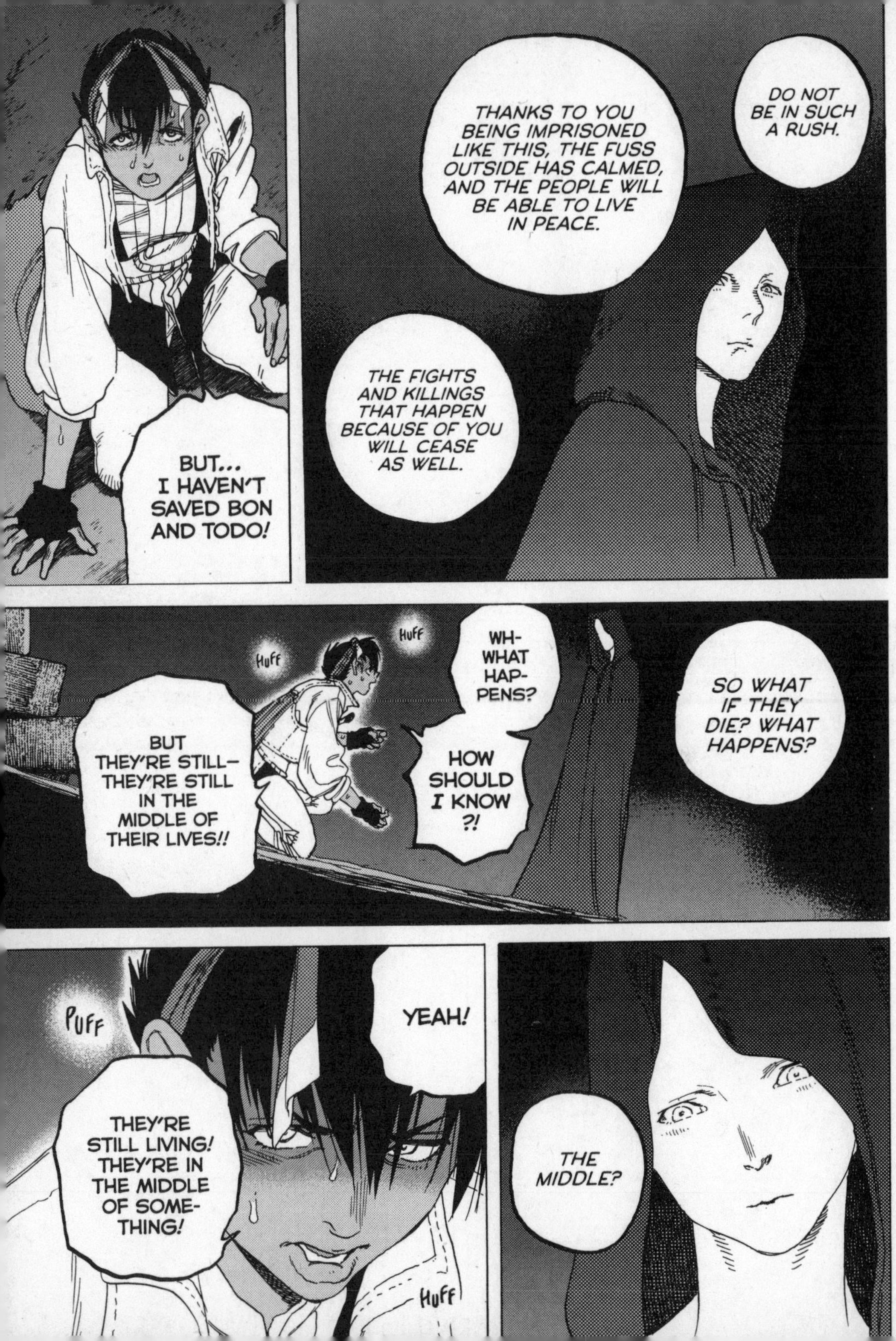
DO NOT BE IN SUCH A RUSH.
THANKS TO YOU BEING IMPRISONED LIKE THIS, THE FUSS OUTSIDE HAS CALMED, AND THE PEOPLE WILL BE ABLE TO LIVE IN PEACE.
THE FIGHTS AND KILLINGS THAT HAPPEN BECAUSE OF YOU WILL CEASE AS WELL.
BUT... I HAVEN'T SAVED BON AND TODO!
SO WHAT IF THEY DIE? WHAT HAPPENS?
WH- WHAT HAP- PENS?
HOW SHOULD I KNOW ?!
HUFF
HUFF
BUT THEY'RE STILL— THEY'RE STILL IN THE MIDDLE OF THEIR LIVES!!
THE MIDDLE?
YEAH!
PUFF
THEY'RE STILL LIVING! THEY'RE IN THE MIDDLE OF SOME- THING!
HUFF

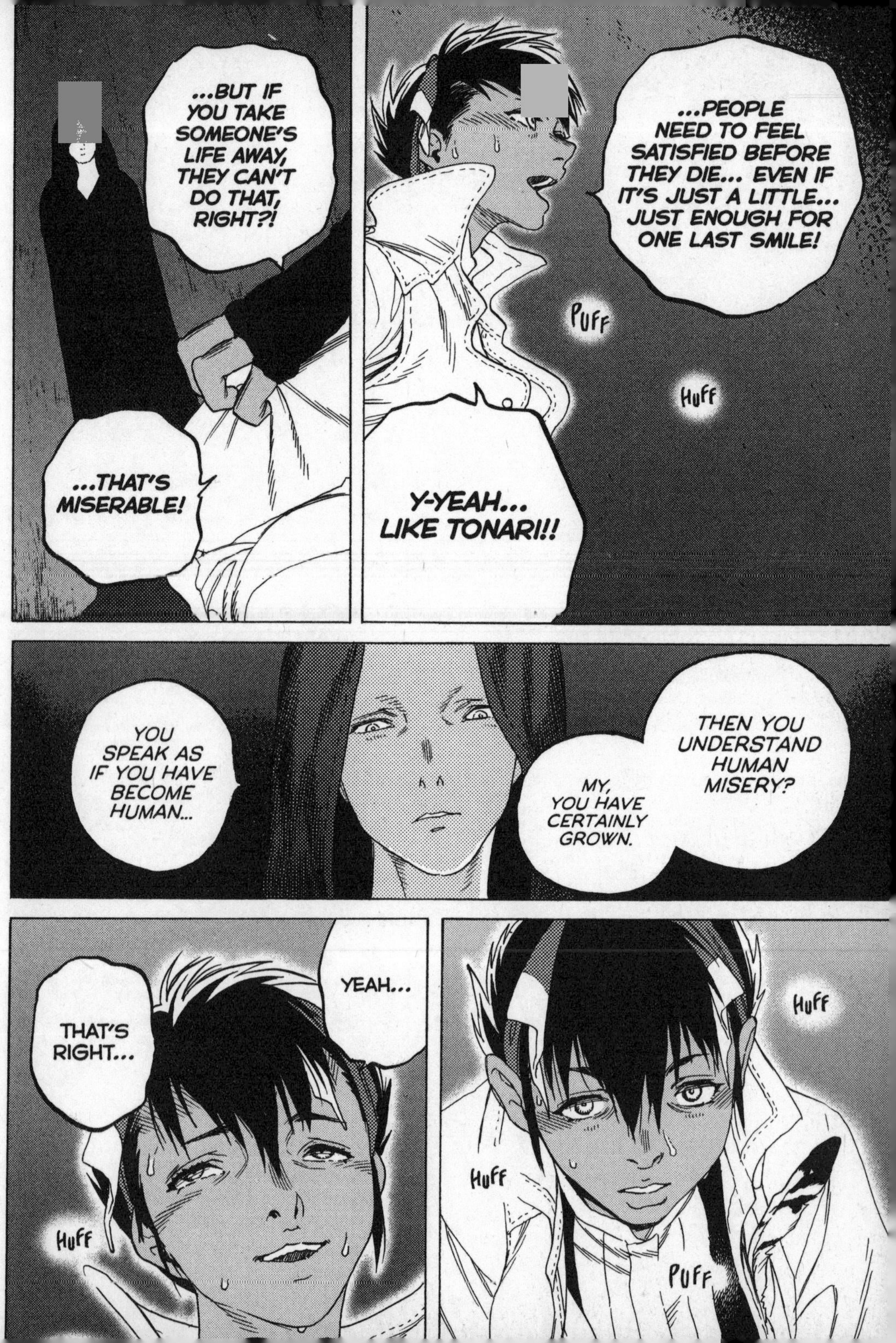
...PEOPLE NEED TO FEEL SATISFIED BEFORE THEY DIE... EVEN IF IT'S JUST A LITTLE... JUST ENOUGH FOR ONE LAST SMILE!
PUFF
HUFF
Y-YEAH... LIKE TONARI!!
...BUT IF YOU TAKE SOMEONE'S LIFE AWAY, THEY CAN'T DO THAT, RIGHT?!
...THAT'S MISERABLE!
THEN YOU UNDERSTAND HUMAN MISERY?
MY, YOU HAVE CERTAINLY GROWN.
YOU SPEAK AS IF YOU HAVE BECOME HUMAN...
HUFF
HUFF
PUFF
YEAH...
THAT'S RIGHT...
HUFF

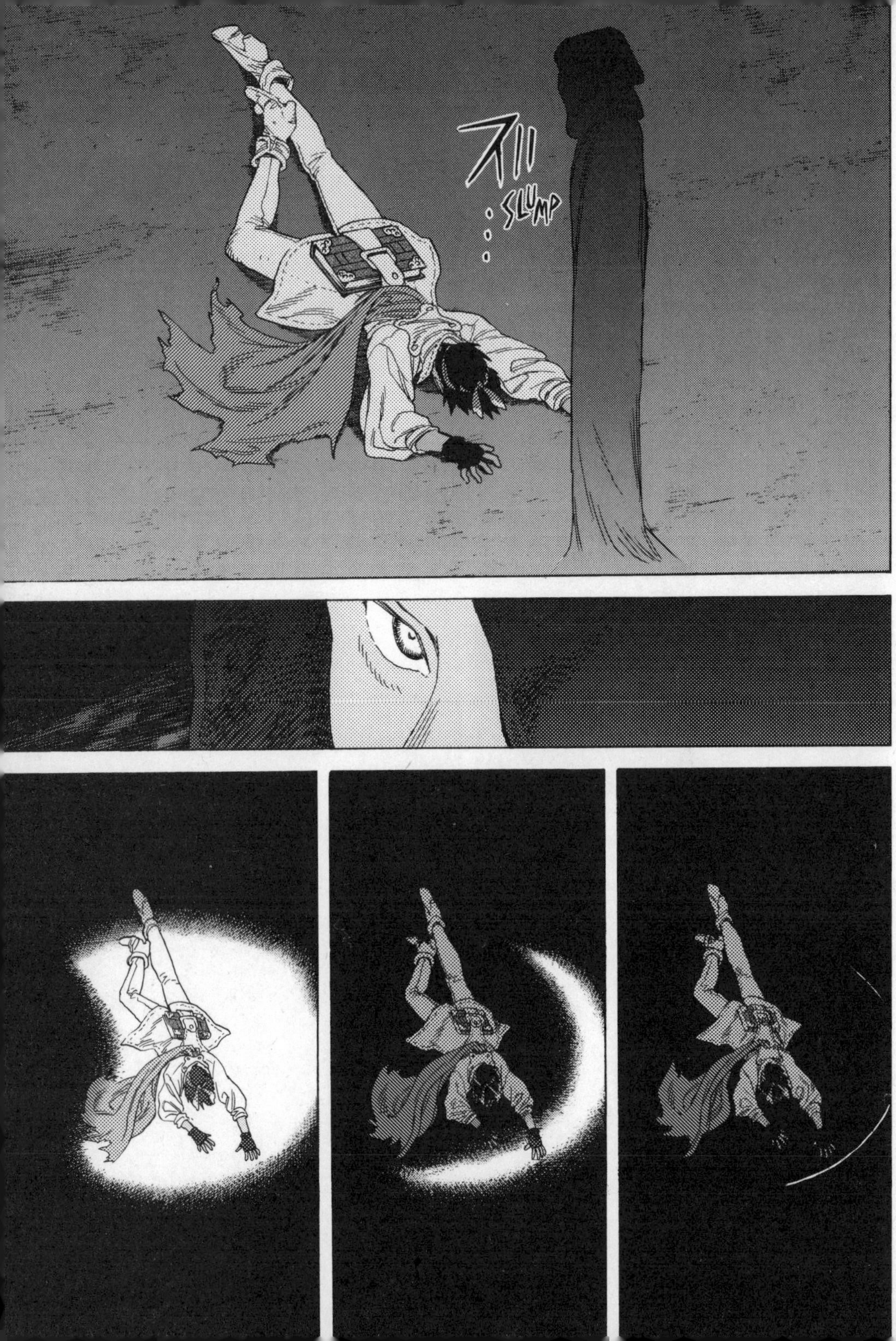
ズ…
SLUMP

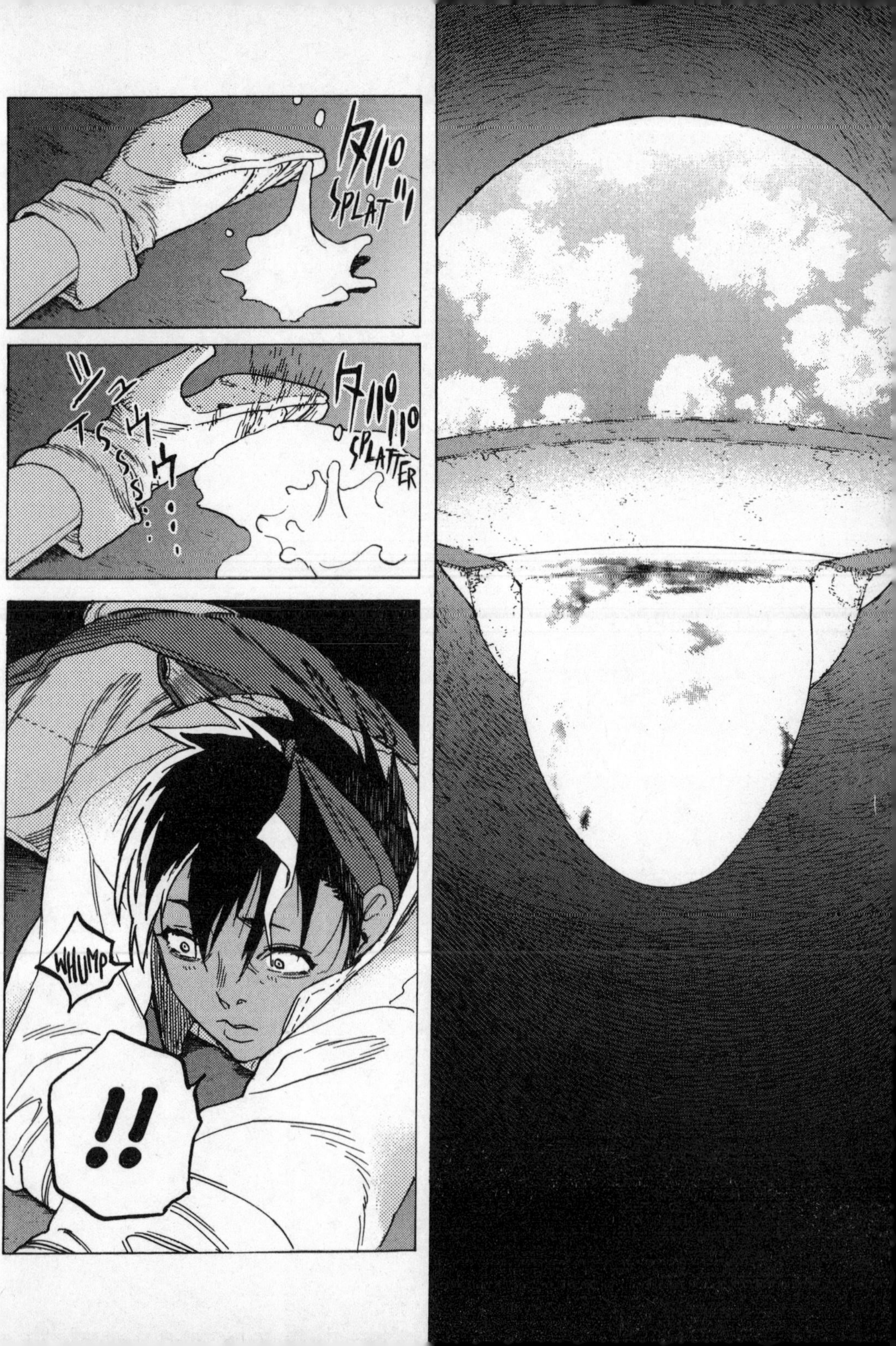
SPLAT
SPLATTER
TSSSS
WHUMP
!!

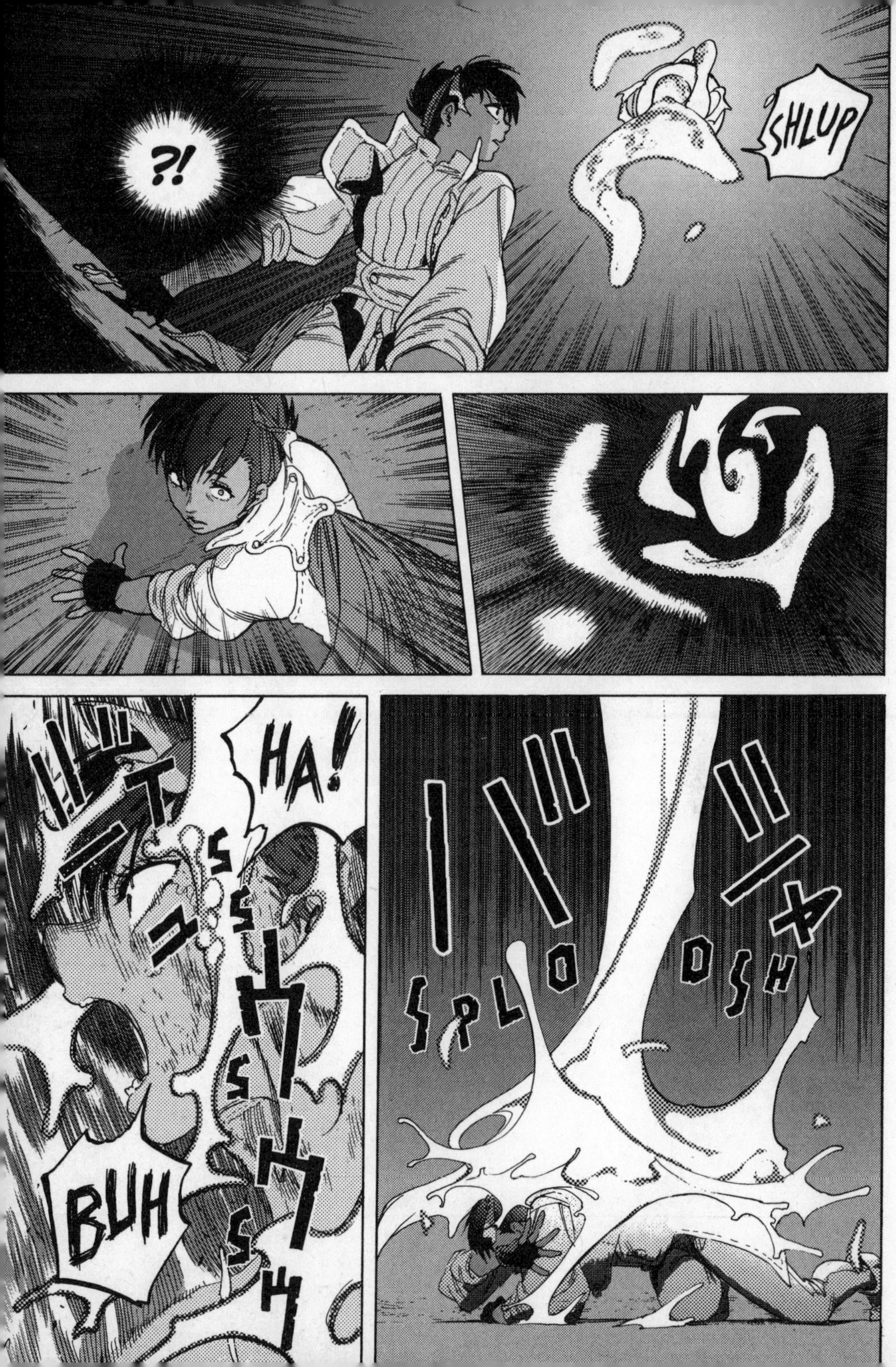
SHLUP
?!
SPLOOSH
HA!
SSSSSH
BUH

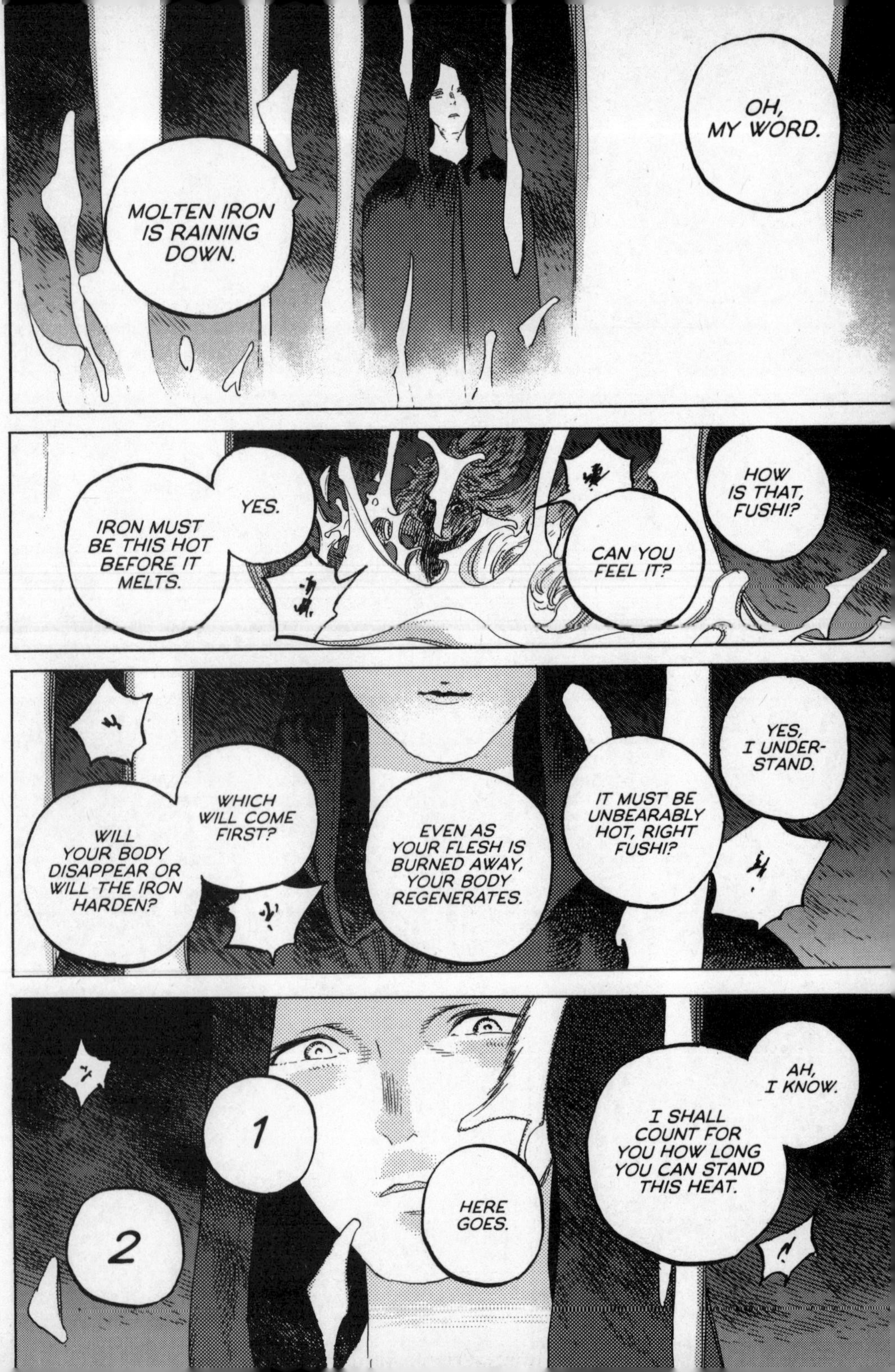
OH, MY WORD.
MOLTEN IRON IS RAINING DOWN.
HOW IS THAT, FUSHI?
CAN YOU FEEL IT?
YES.
IRON MUST BE THIS HOT BEFORE IT MELTS.
YES, I UNDERSTAND.
IT MUST BE UNBEARABLY HOT, RIGHT FUSHI?
EVEN AS YOUR FLESH IS BURNED AWAY, YOUR BODY REGENERATES.
WHICH WILL COME FIRST?
WILL YOUR BODY DISAPPEAR OR WILL THE IRON HARDEN?
AH, I KNOW.
I SHALL COUNT FOR YOU HOW LONG YOU CAN STAND THIS HEAT.
HERE GOES.
1
2

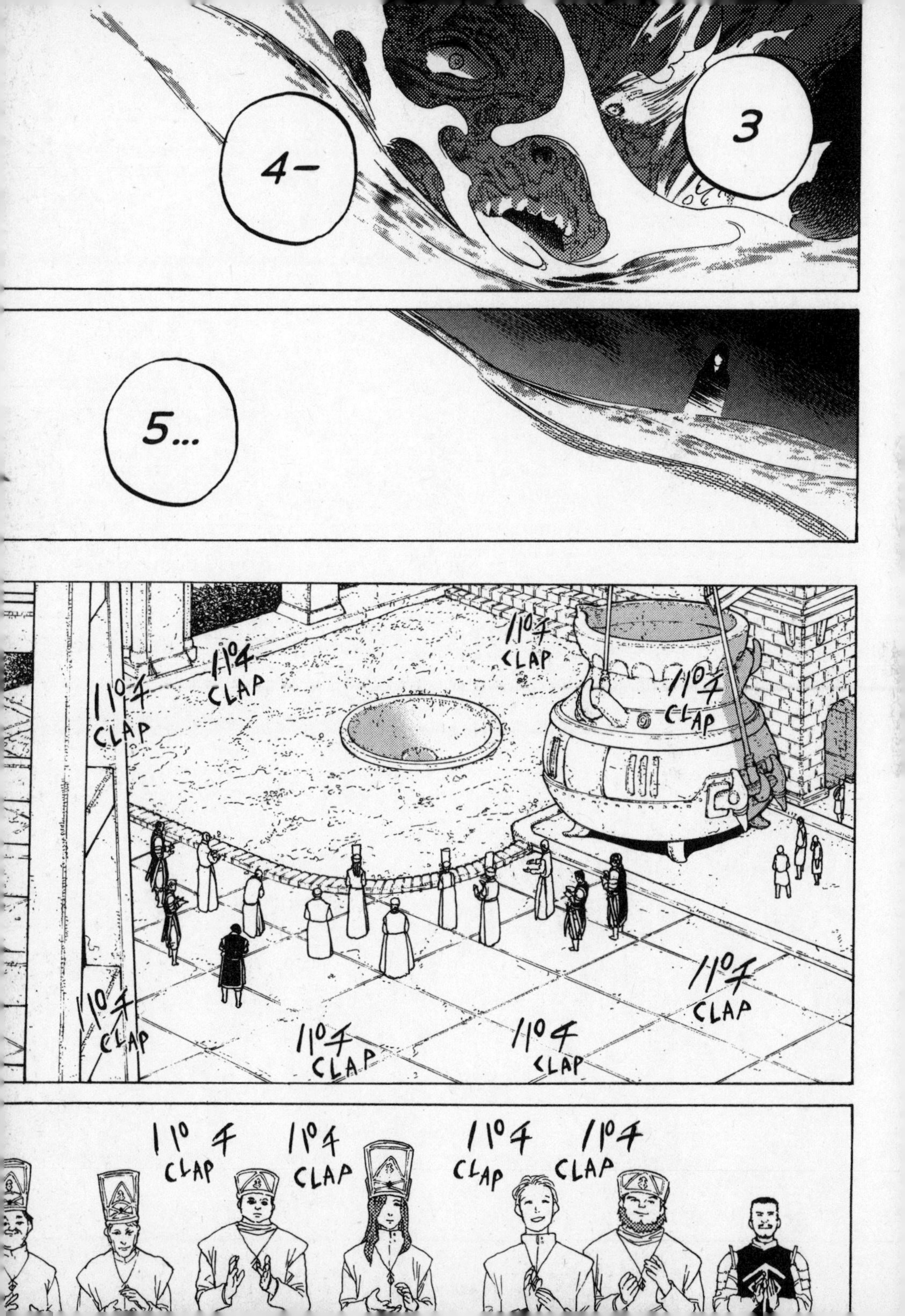
3
4–
5...
パチ CLAP
パチ CLAP
パチ CLAP
パチ CLAP
パチ CLAP
パチ CLAP
パチ CLAP
パチ CLAP
パチ CLAP
パチ CLAP
パチ CLAP
パチ CLAP

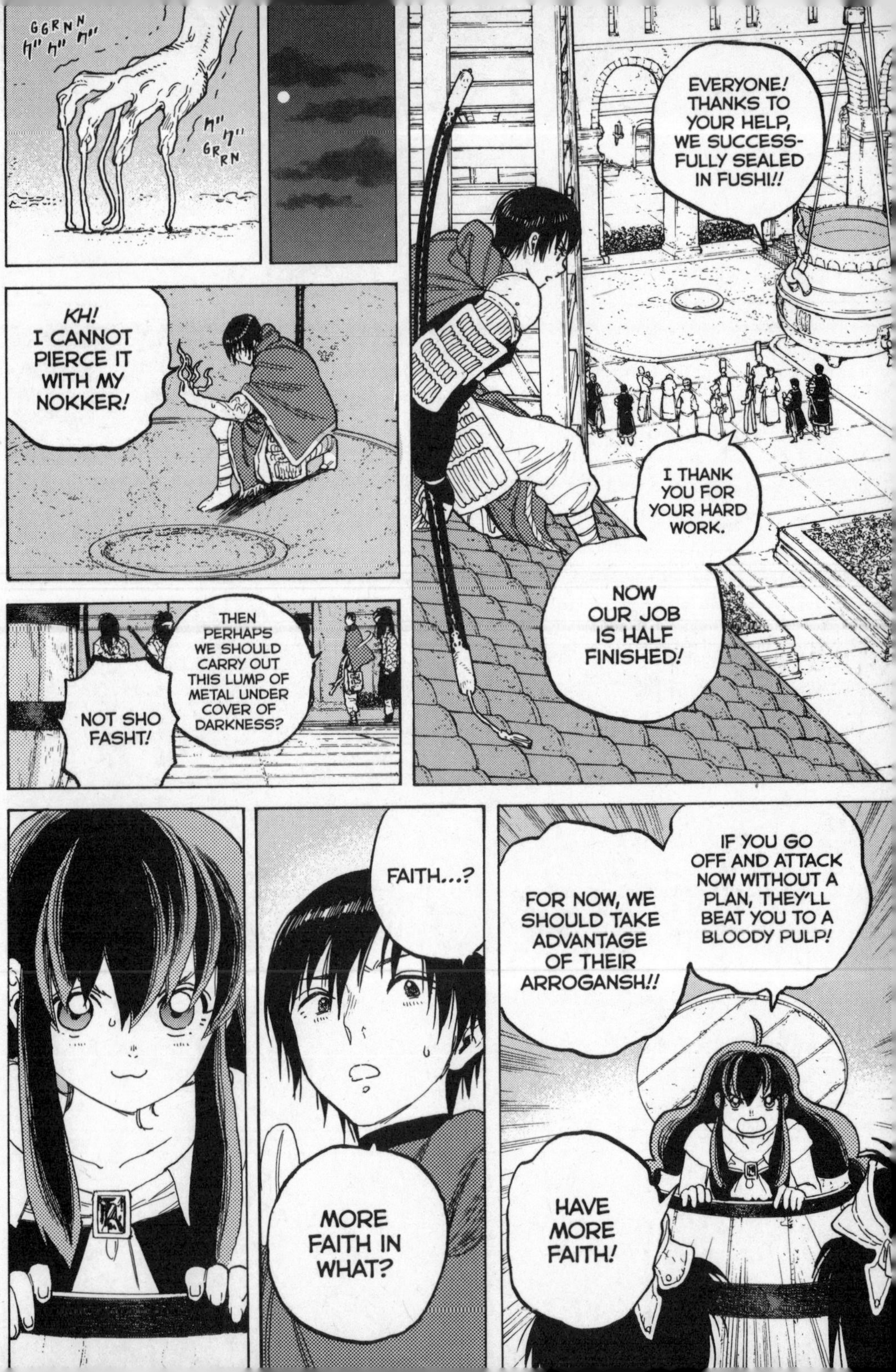
EVERYONE! THANKS TO YOUR HELP, WE SUCCESS-FULLY SEALED IN FUSHI!!
I THANK YOU FOR YOUR HARD WORK.
NOW OUR JOB IS HALF FINISHED!
GGRNN
GRRN
KH! I CANNOT PIERCE IT WITH MY NOKKER!
THEN PERHAPS WE SHOULD CARRY OUT THIS LUMP OF METAL UNDER COVER OF DARKNESS?
NOT SHO FASHT!
IF YOU GO OFF AND ATTACK NOW WITHOUT A PLAN, THEY'LL BEAT YOU TO A BLOODY PULP!
FOR NOW, WE SHOULD TAKE ADVANTAGE OF THEIR ARROGANSH!!
HAVE MORE FAITH!
FAITH...?
MORE FAITH IN WHAT?

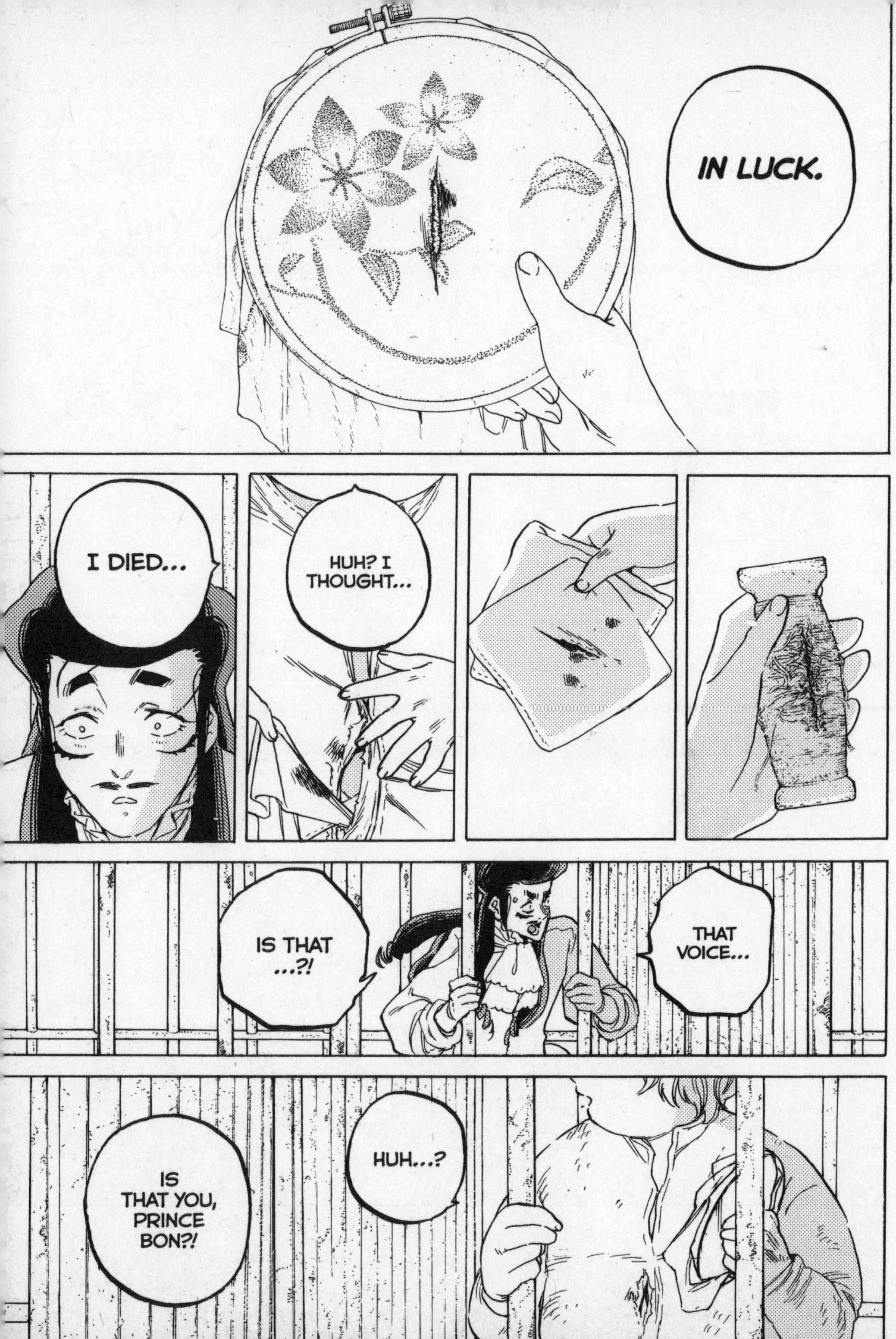
IN LUCK.
HUH? I THOUGHT...
I DIED...
THAT VOICE...
IS THAT ...?!
HUH...?
IS THAT YOU, PRINCE BON?!

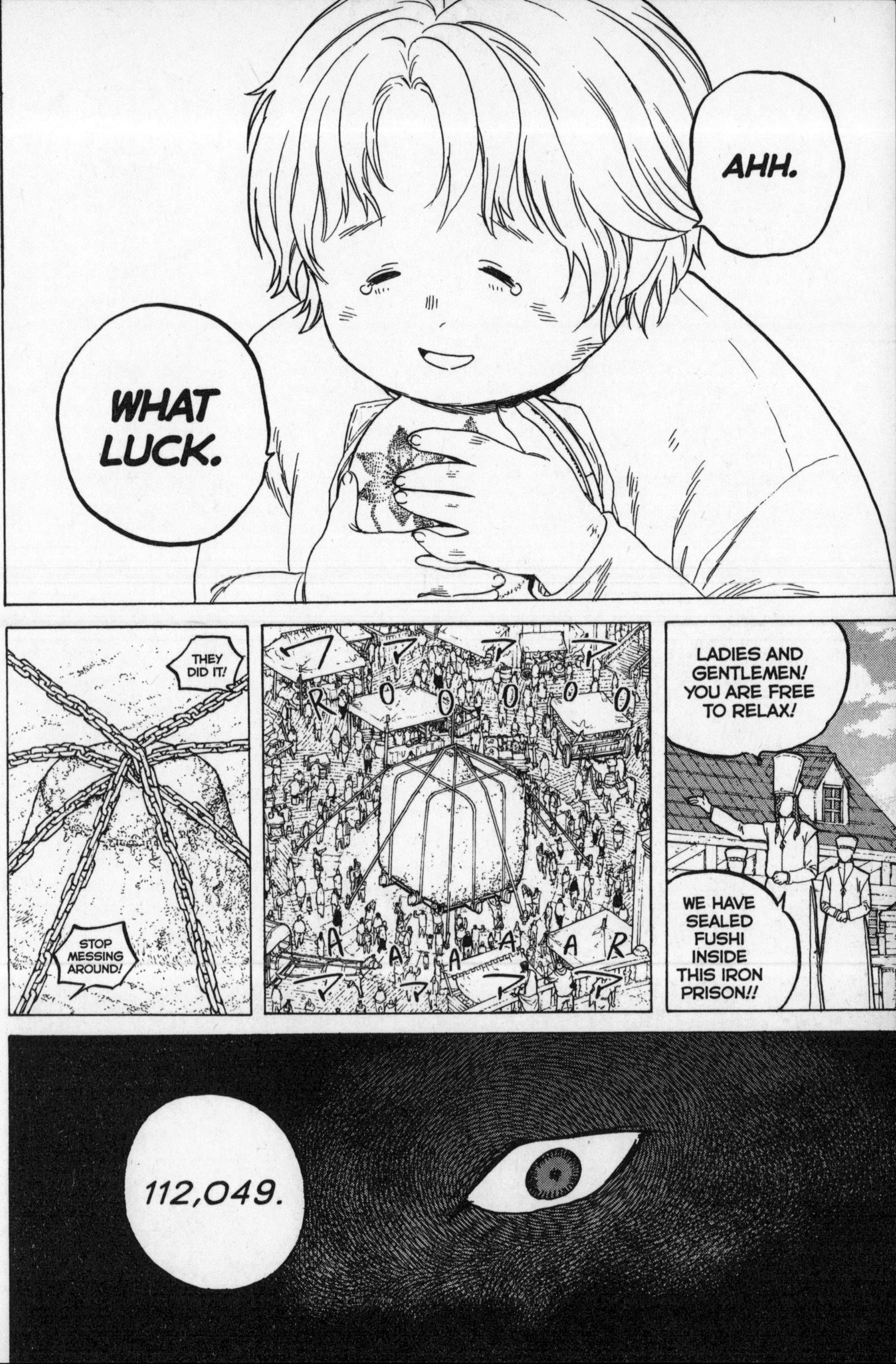
AHH.
WHAT LUCK.
LADIES AND GENTLEMEN! YOU ARE FREE TO RELAX!
WE HAVE SEALED FUSHI INSIDE THIS IRON PRISON!!
ROOOO
AAAAR
THEY DID IT!
STOP MESSING AROUND!
112,049.

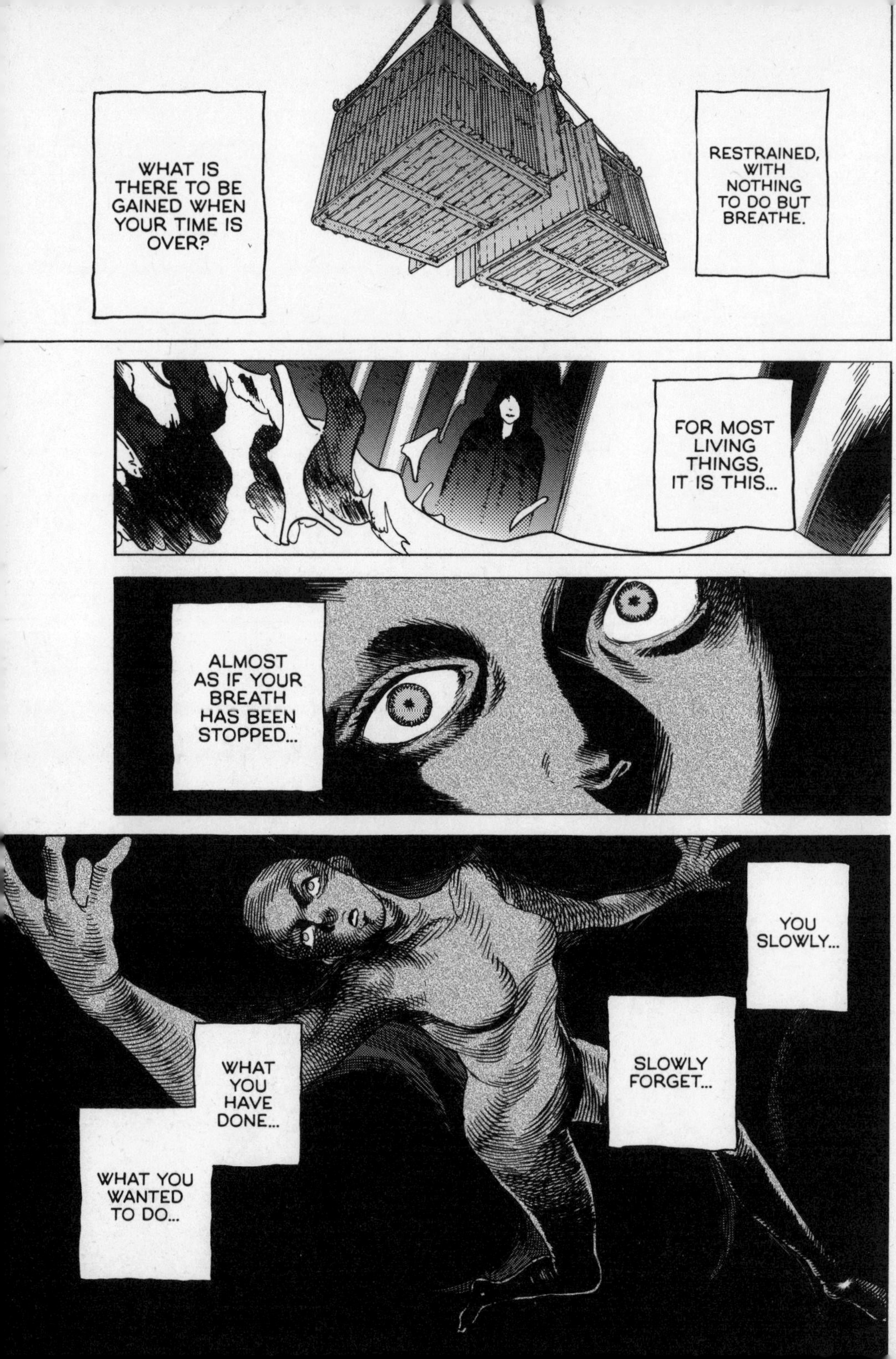
RESTRAINED, WITH NOTHING TO DO BUT BREATHE.
WHAT IS THERE TO BE GAINED WHEN YOUR TIME IS OVER?
FOR MOST LIVING THINGS, IT IS THIS...
ALMOST AS IF YOUR BREATH HAS BEEN STOPPED...
YOU SLOWLY...
SLOWLY FORGET...
WHAT YOU HAVE DONE...
WHAT YOU WANTED TO DO...

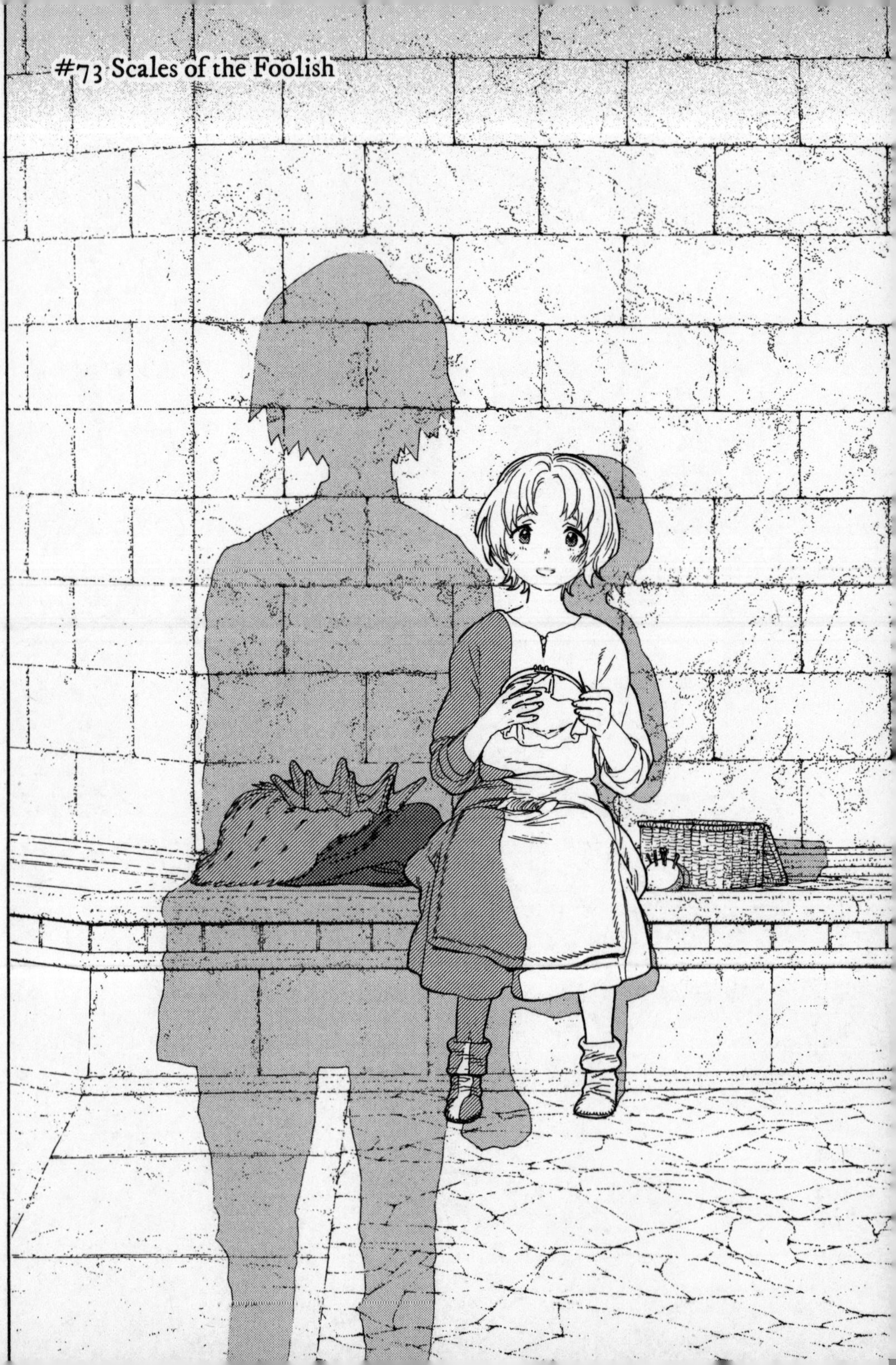
#73 Scales of the Foolish

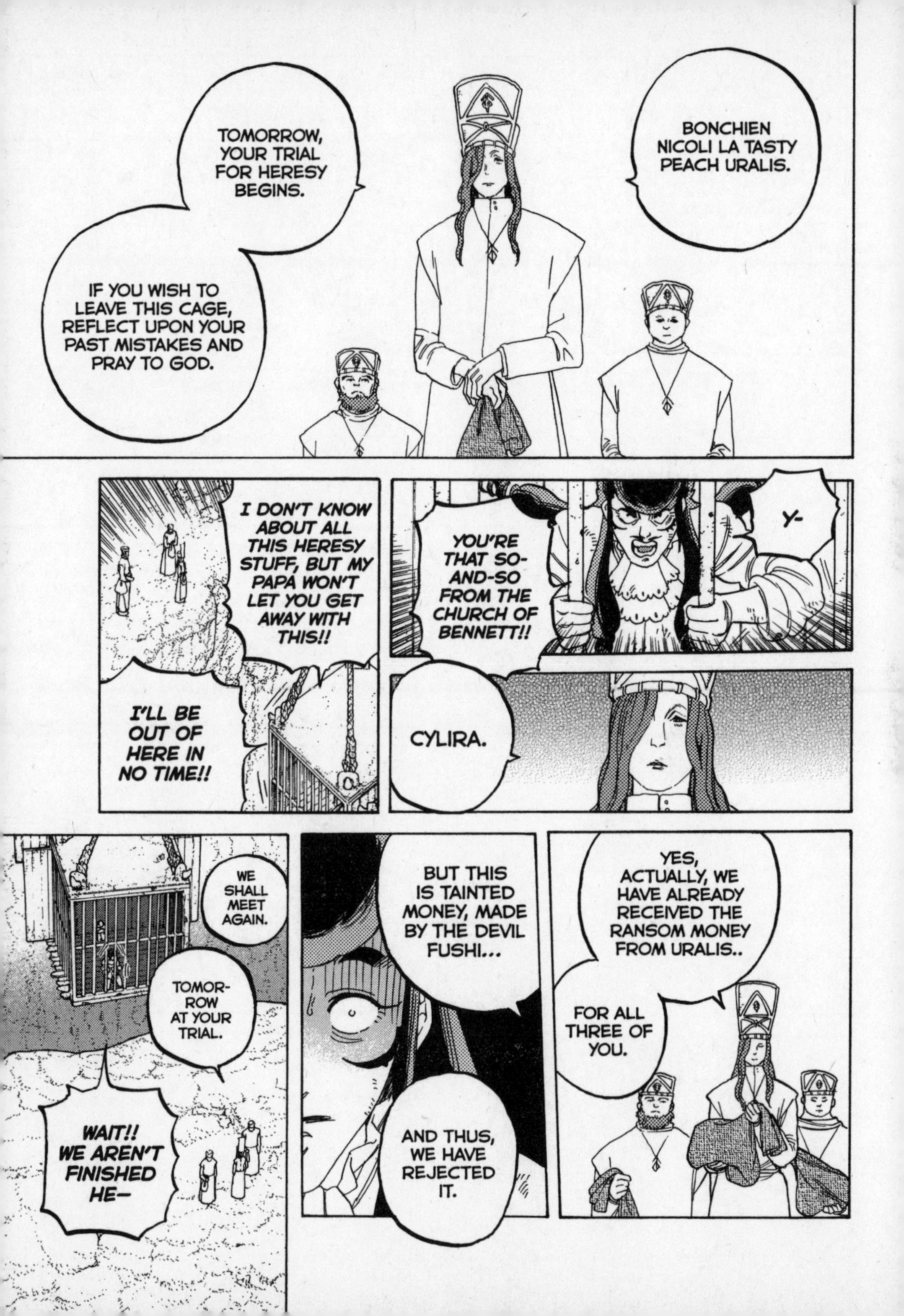
BONCHIEN NICOLI LA TASTY PEACH URALIS.
TOMORROW, YOUR TRIAL FOR HERESY BEGINS.
IF YOU WISH TO LEAVE THIS CAGE, REFLECT UPON YOUR PAST MISTAKES AND PRAY TO GOD.
Y-
YOU'RE THAT SO-AND-SO FROM THE CHURCH OF BENNETT!!
CYLIRA.
I DON'T KNOW ABOUT ALL THIS HERESY STUFF, BUT MY PAPA WON'T LET YOU GET AWAY WITH THIS!!
I'LL BE OUT OF HERE IN NO TIME!!
YES, ACTUALLY, WE HAVE ALREADY RECEIVED THE RANSOM MONEY FROM URALIS..
FOR ALL THREE OF YOU.
BUT THIS IS TAINTED MONEY, MADE BY THE DEVIL FUSHI...
AND THUS, WE HAVE REJECTED IT.
WE SHALL MEET AGAIN.
TOMOR-ROW AT YOUR TRIAL.
WAIT!! WE AREN'T FINISHED HE–

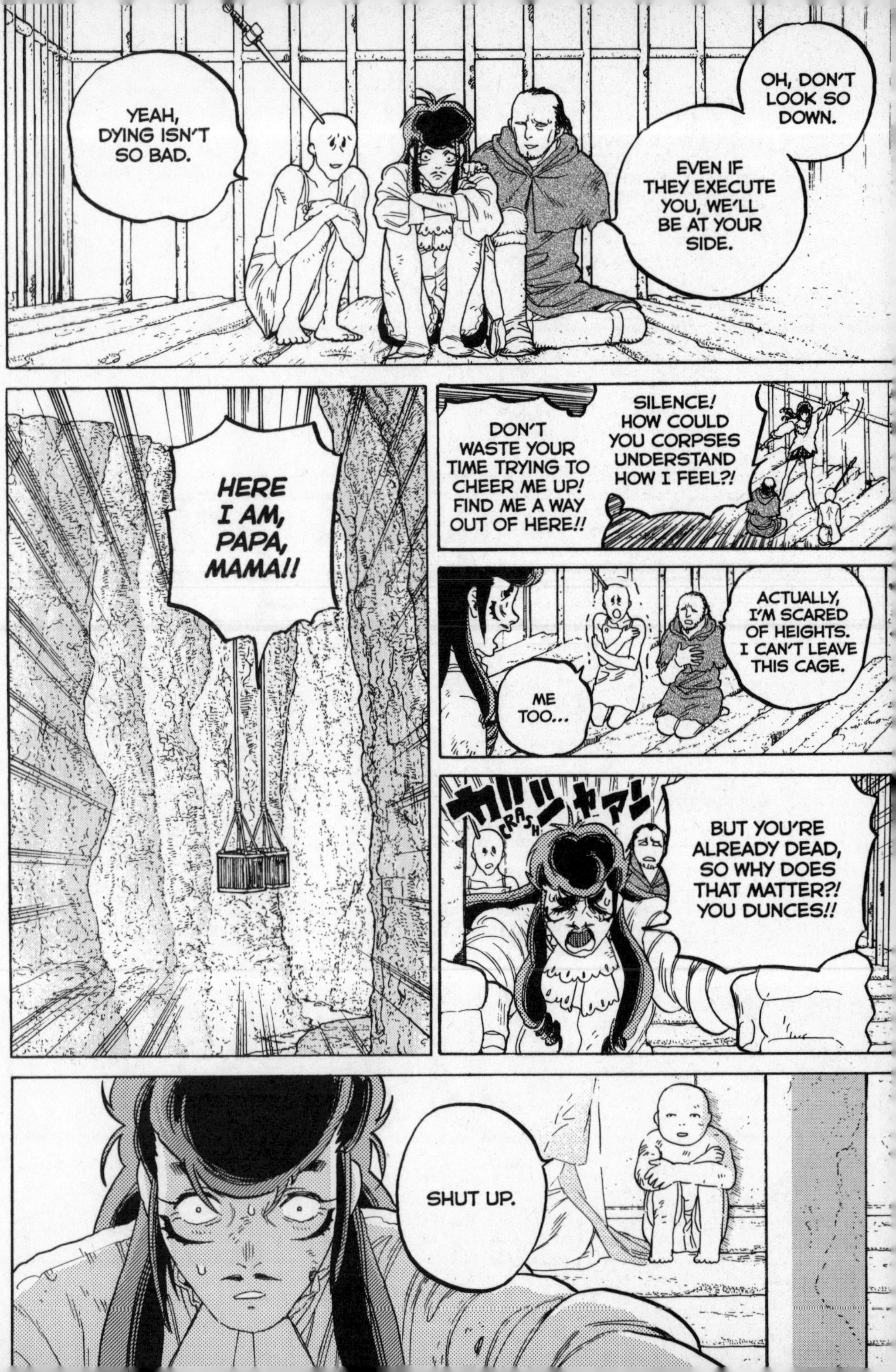
OH, DON'T LOOK SO DOWN.
EVEN IF THEY EXECUTE YOU, WE'LL BE AT YOUR SIDE.
YEAH, DYING ISN'T SO BAD.
SILENCE! HOW COULD YOU CORPSES UNDERSTAND HOW I FEEL?!
DON'T WASTE YOUR TIME TRYING TO CHEER ME UP! FIND ME A WAY OUT OF HERE!!
ACTUALLY, I'M SCARED OF HEIGHTS. I CAN'T LEAVE THIS CAGE.
ME TOO...
CRASH
BUT YOU'RE ALREADY DEAD, SO WHY DOES THAT MATTER?! YOU DUNCES!!
HERE I AM, PAPA, MAMA!!
SHUT UP.

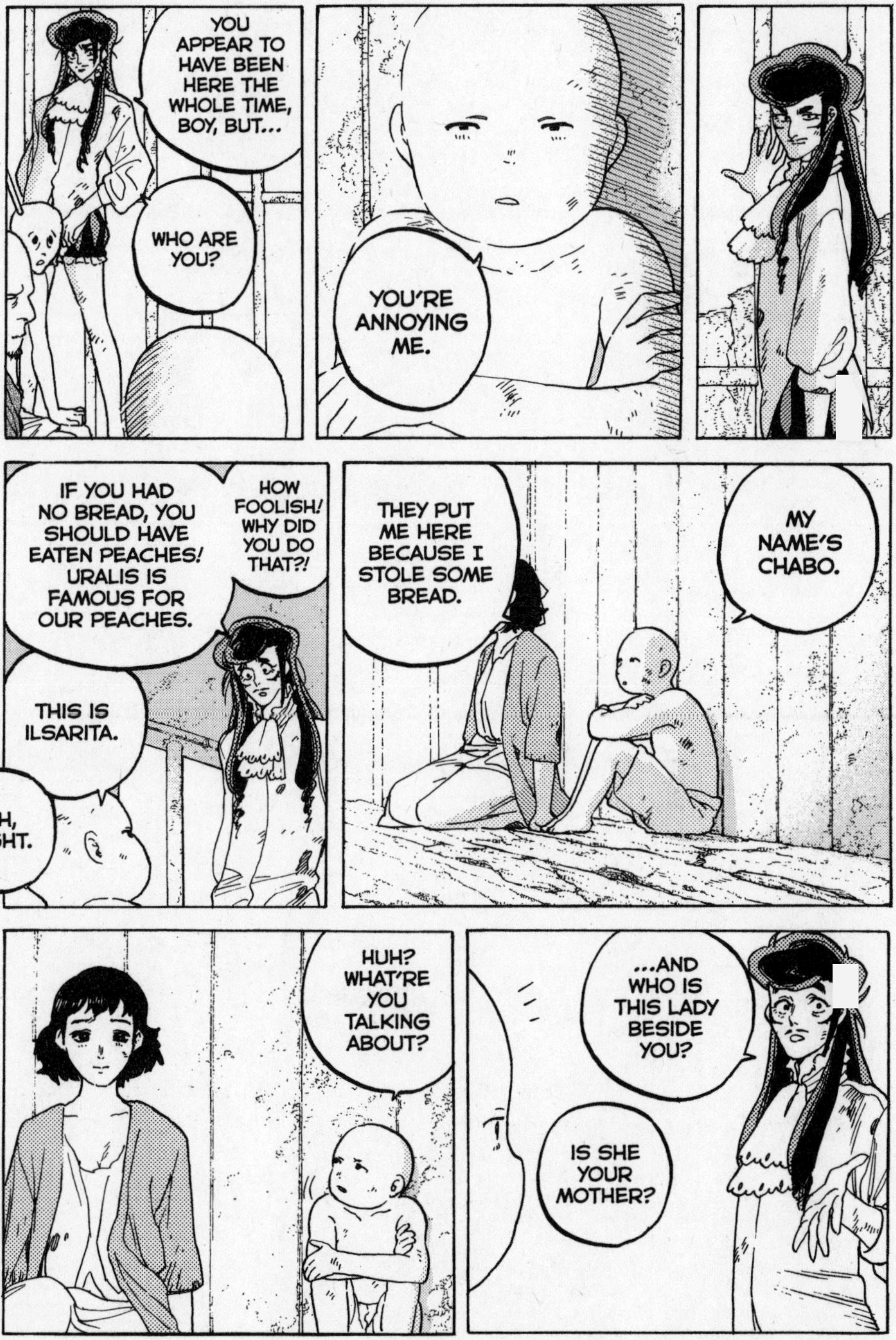
YOU'RE ANNOYING ME.
YOU APPEAR TO HAVE BEEN HERE THE WHOLE TIME, BOY, BUT...
WHO ARE YOU?
MY NAME'S CHABO.
THEY PUT ME HERE BECAUSE I STOLE SOME BREAD.
HOW FOOLISH! WHY DID YOU DO THAT?!
IF YOU HAD NO BREAD, YOU SHOULD HAVE EATEN PEACHES! URALIS IS FAMOUS FOR OUR PEACHES.
THIS IS ILSARITA.
OH, RIGHT.
...AND WHO IS THIS LADY BESIDE YOU?
IS SHE YOUR MOTHER?
HUH? WHAT'RE YOU TALKING ABOUT?

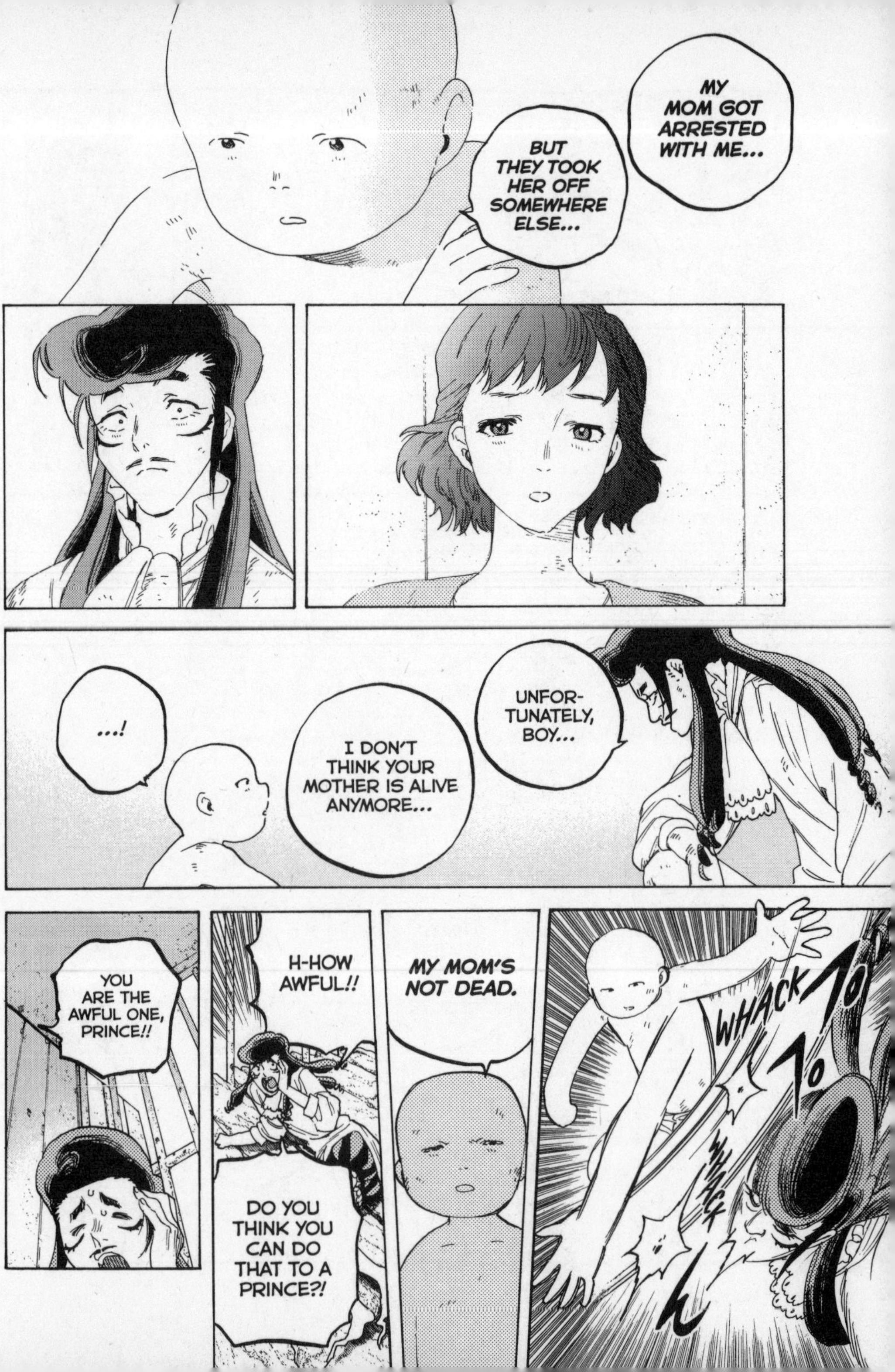
MY MOM GOT ARRESTED WITH ME...
BUT THEY TOOK HER OFF SOMEWHERE ELSE...
UNFOR-TUNATELY, BOY...
I DON'T THINK YOUR MOTHER IS ALIVE ANYMORE...
...!
WHACK
WHACK
MY MOM'S NOT DEAD.
H-HOW AWFUL!!
DO YOU THINK YOU CAN DO THAT TO A PRINCE?!
YOU ARE THE AWFUL ONE, PRINCE!!

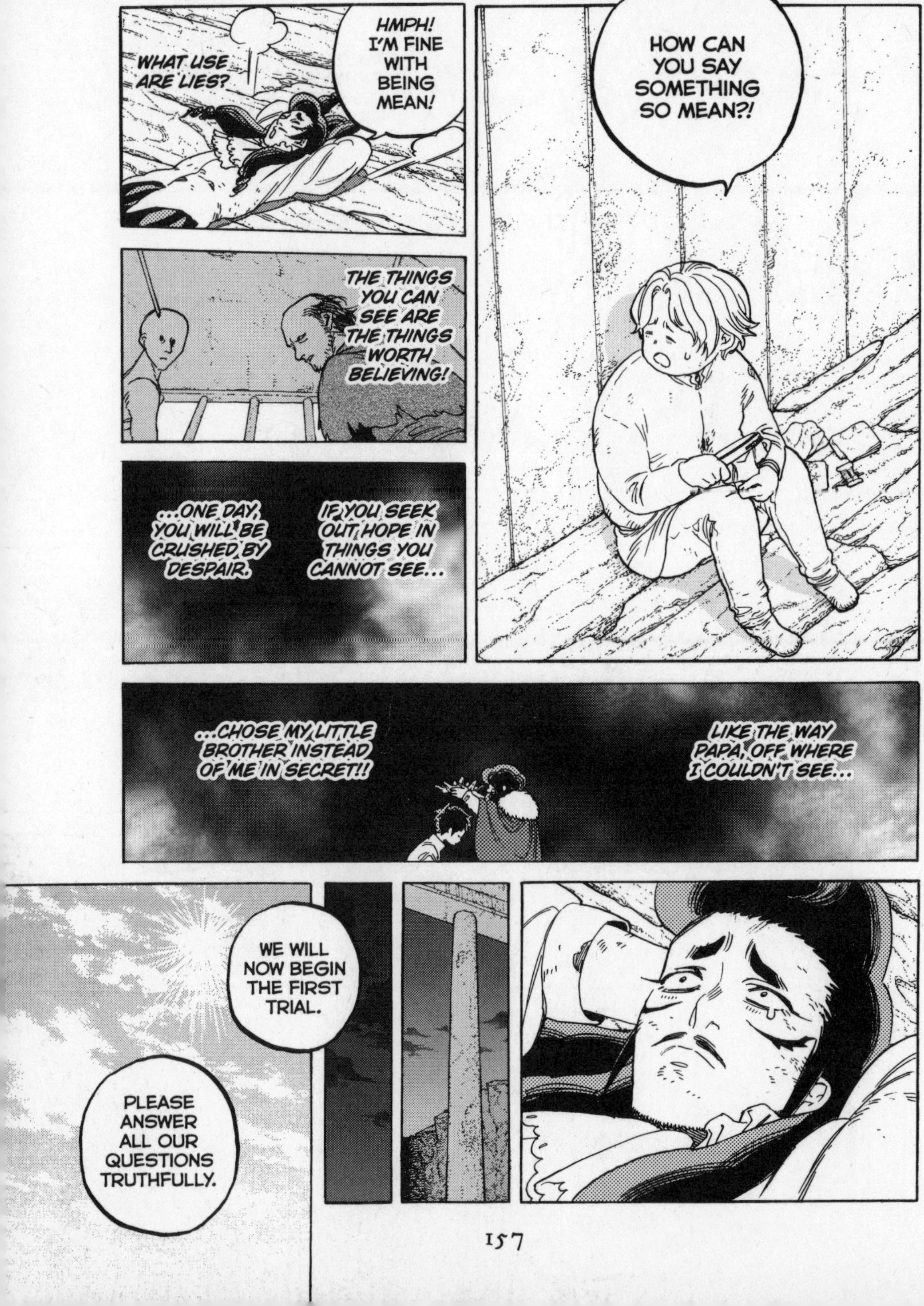
HOW CAN YOU SAY SOMETHING SO MEAN?!
HMPH! I'M FINE WITH BEING MEAN!
WHAT USE ARE LIES?
THE THINGS YOU CAN SEE ARE THE THINGS WORTH BELIEVING!
IF YOU SEEK OUT HOPE IN THINGS YOU CANNOT SEE...
...ONE DAY, YOU WILL BE CRUSHED BY DESPAIR.
LIKE THE WAY PAPA, OFF WHERE I COULDN'T SEE...
...CHOSE MY LITTLE BROTHER INSTEAD OF ME IN SECRET!!
WE WILL NOW BEGIN THE FIRST TRIAL.
PLEASE ANSWER ALL OUR QUESTIONS TRUTHFULLY.

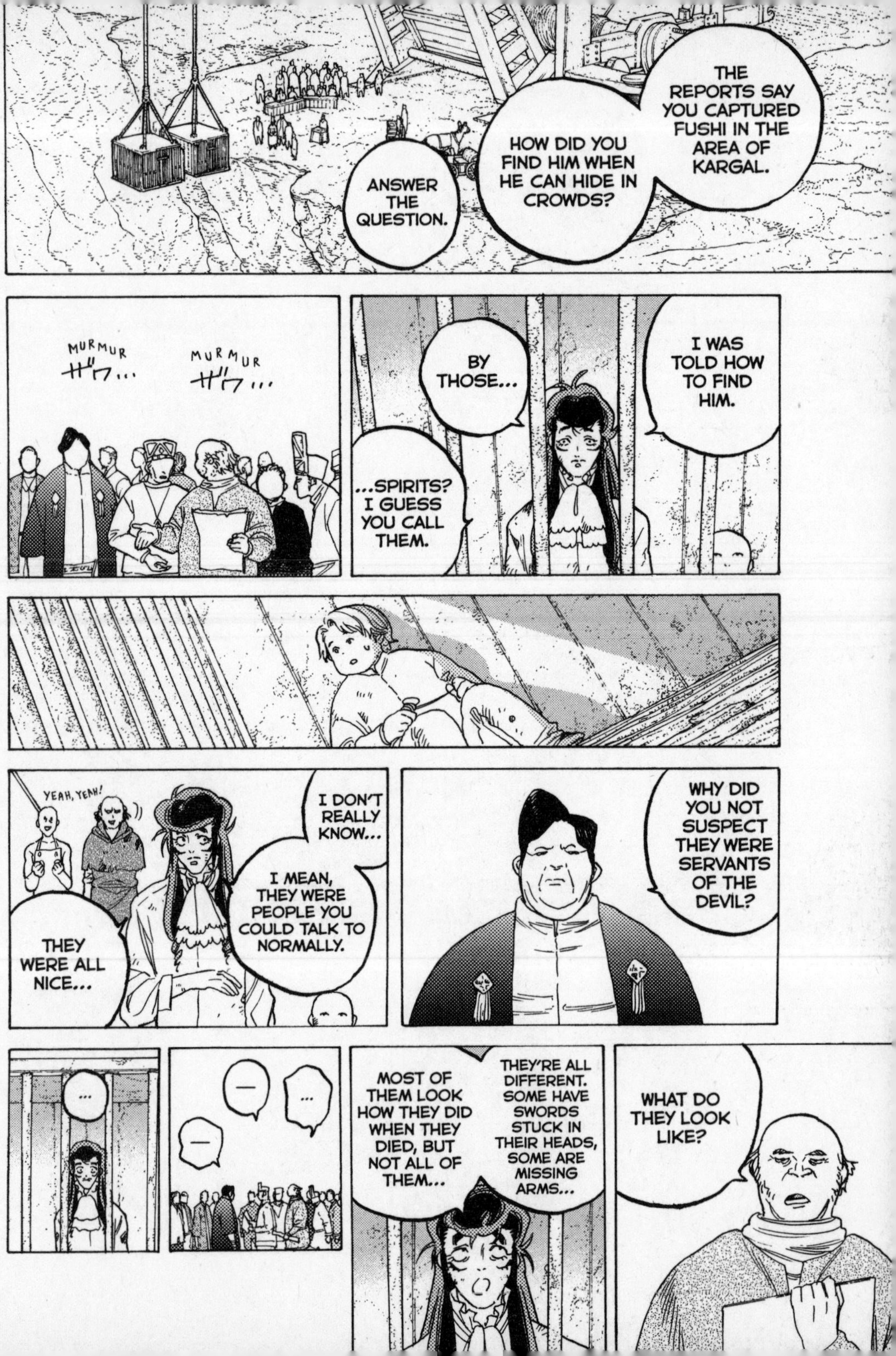
THE REPORTS SAY YOU CAPTURED FUSHI IN THE AREA OF KARGAL.
HOW DID YOU FIND HIM WHEN HE CAN HIDE IN CROWDS?
ANSWER THE QUESTION.
I WAS TOLD HOW TO FIND HIM.
BY THOSE...
...SPIRITS? I GUESS YOU CALL THEM.
MURMUR ザワ...
MURMUR ザワ...
WHY DID YOU NOT SUSPECT THEY WERE SERVANTS OF THE DEVIL?
I DON'T REALLY KNOW...
I MEAN, THEY WERE PEOPLE YOU COULD TALK TO NORMALLY.
YEAH, YEAH!
THEY WERE ALL NICE...
WHAT DO THEY LOOK LIKE?
THEY'RE ALL DIFFERENT. SOME HAVE SWORDS STUCK IN THEIR HEADS, SOME ARE MISSING ARMS...
MOST OF THEM LOOK HOW THEY DID WHEN THEY DIED, BUT NOT ALL OF THEM...
...
—
...
—
...

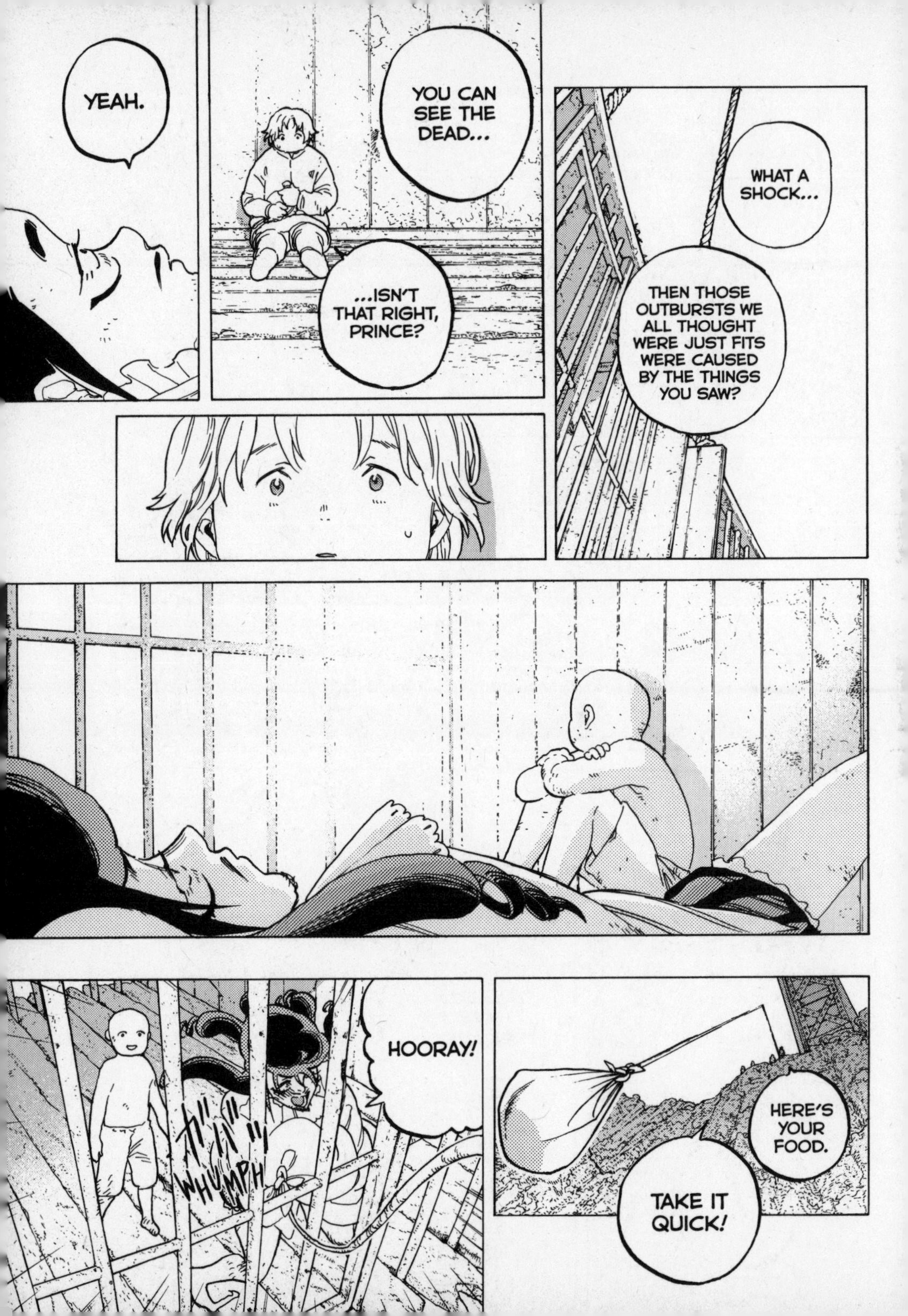
WHAT A SHOCK...
THEN THOSE OUTBURSTS WE ALL THOUGHT WERE JUST FITS WERE CAUSED BY THE THINGS YOU SAW?
YOU CAN SEE THE DEAD...
...ISN'T THAT RIGHT, PRINCE?
YEAH.
HERE'S YOUR FOOD.
TAKE IT QUICK!
HOORAY!
WHUMPH

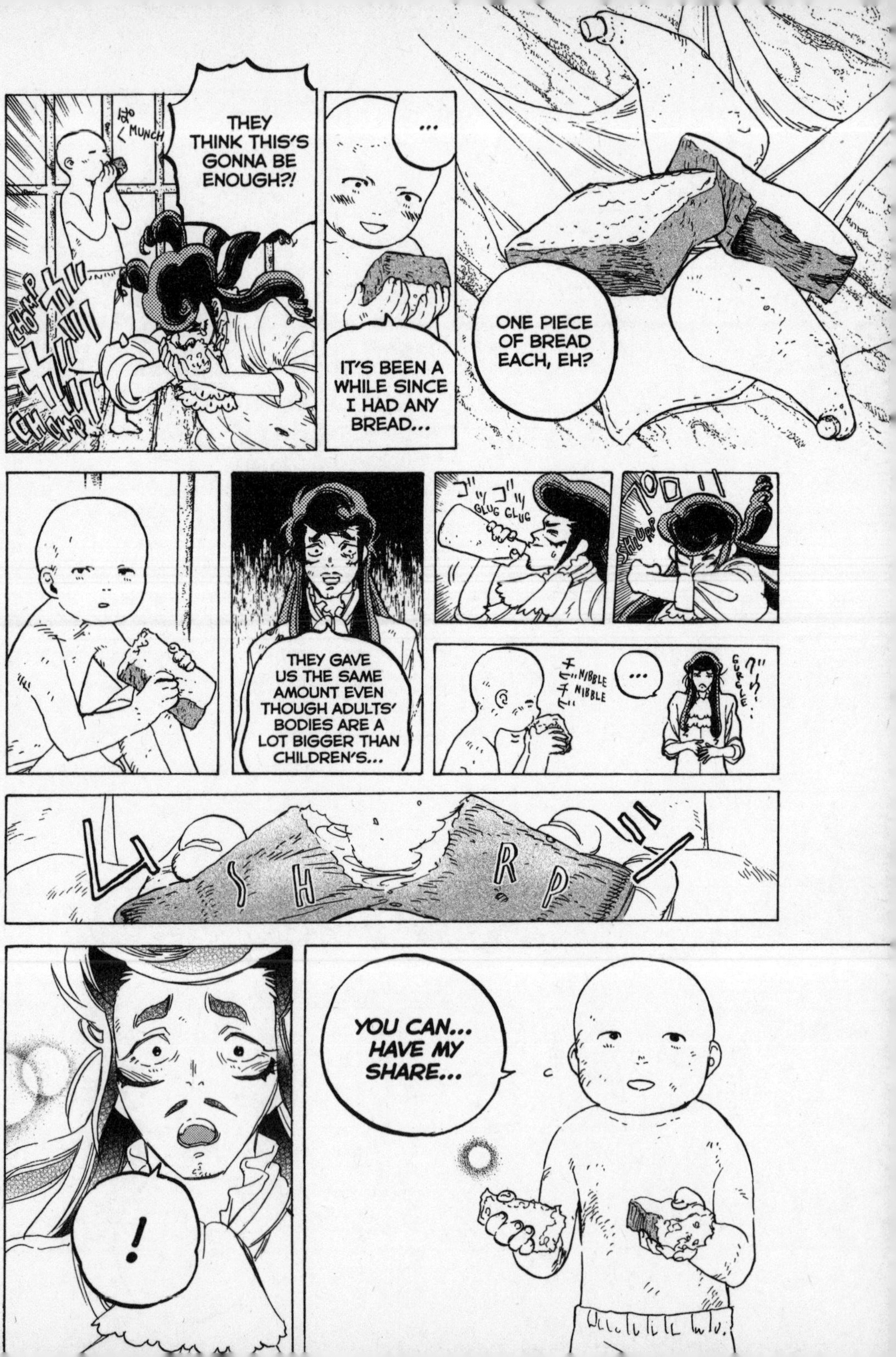
ONE PIECE OF BREAD EACH, EH?
...
IT'S BEEN A WHILE SINCE I HAD ANY BREAD...
THEY THINK THIS'S GONNA BE ENOUGH?!
MUNCH
CHOMP
CHOMP
SHLURP
GLUG GLUG
NIBBLE NIBBLE
...
GURGLE
THEY GAVE US THE SAME AMOUNT EVEN THOUGH ADULTS' BODIES ARE A LOT BIGGER THAN CHILDREN'S...
LSHRP
YOU CAN... HAVE MY SHARE...
!

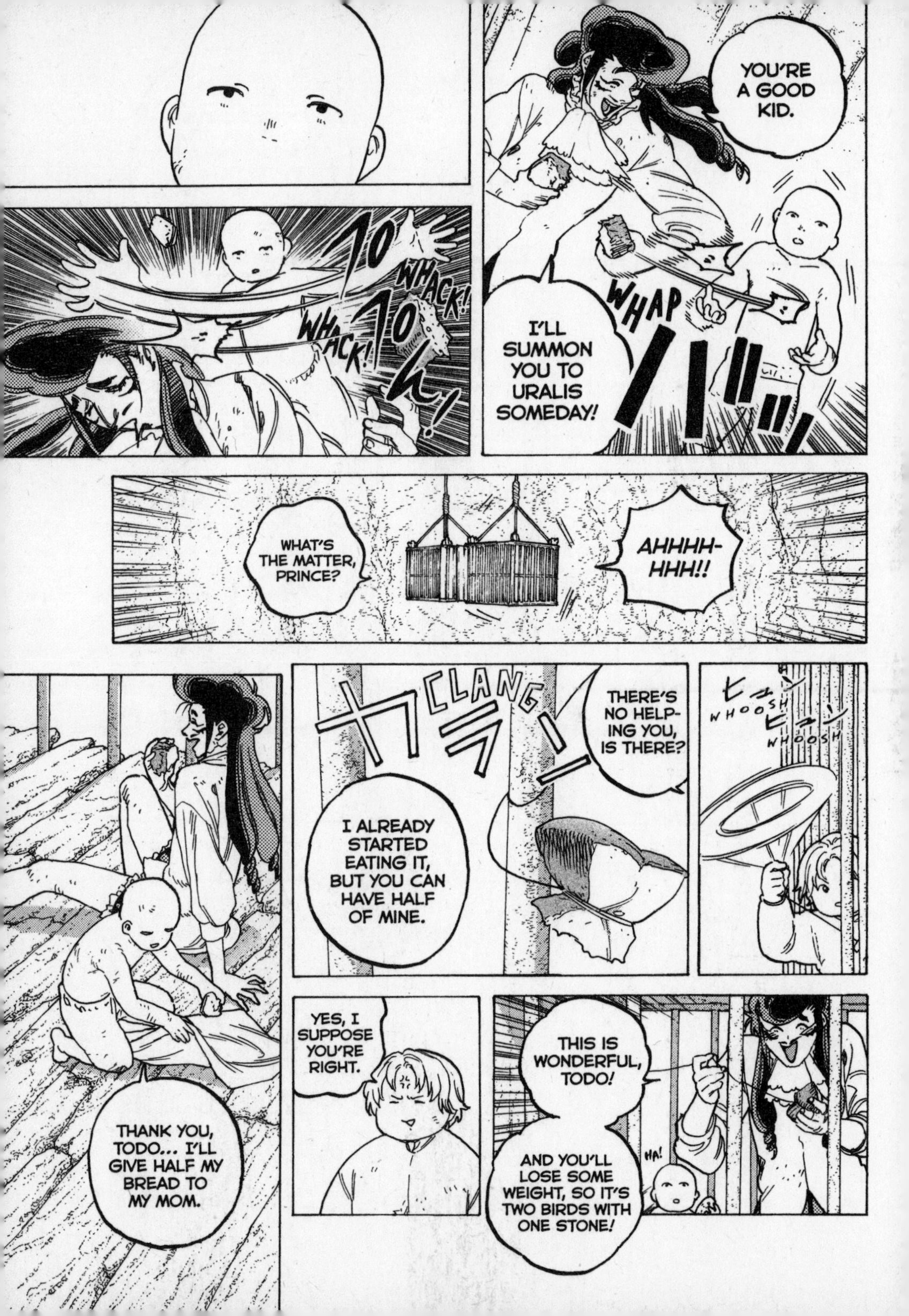
YOU'RE A GOOD KID.
WHAP
I'LL SUMMON YOU TO URALIS SOMEDAY!
WHACK!
WHACK!
AHHHH-HHH!!
WHAT'S THE MATTER, PRINCE?
WHOOSH
WHOOSH
THERE'S NO HELPING YOU, IS THERE?
CLANG
I ALREADY STARTED EATING IT, BUT YOU CAN HAVE HALF OF MINE.
THIS IS WONDERFUL, TODO!
HA!
AND YOU'LL LOSE SOME WEIGHT, SO IT'S TWO BIRDS WITH ONE STONE!
YES, I SUPPOSE YOU'RE RIGHT.
THANK YOU, TODO... I'LL GIVE HALF MY BREAD TO MY MOM.

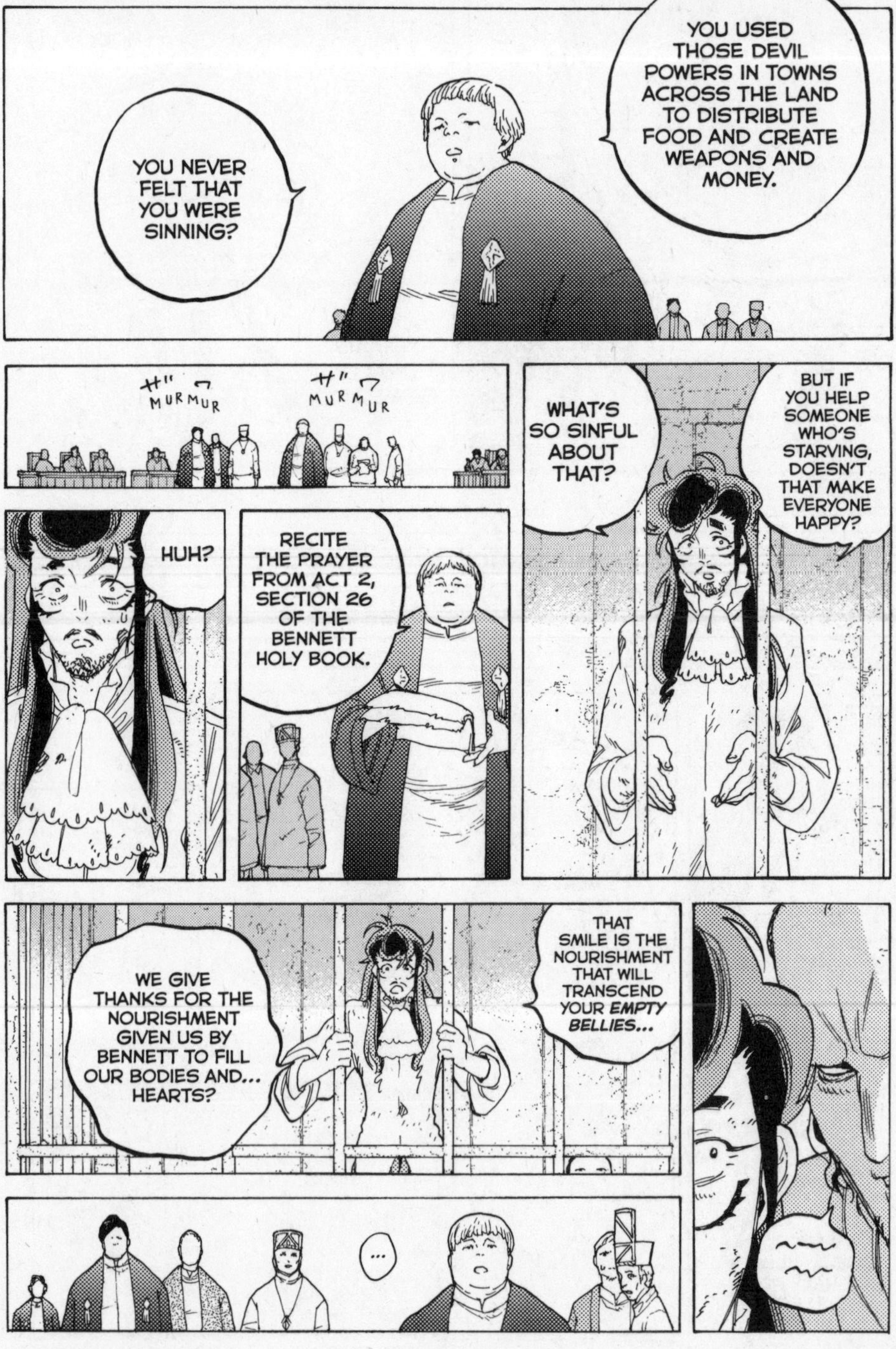
YOU USED THOSE DEVIL POWERS IN TOWNS ACROSS THE LAND TO DISTRIBUTE FOOD AND CREATE WEAPONS AND MONEY.
YOU NEVER FELT THAT YOU WERE SINNING?
BUT IF YOU HELP SOMEONE WHO'S STARVING, DOESN'T THAT MAKE EVERYONE HAPPY?
WHAT'S SO SINFUL ABOUT THAT?
MURMUR
MURMUR
RECITE THE PRAYER FROM ACT 2, SECTION 26 OF THE BENNETT HOLY BOOK.
HUH?
THAT SMILE IS THE NOURISHMENT THAT WILL TRANSCEND YOUR *EMPTY BELLIES*...
WE GIVE THANKS FOR THE NOURISHMENT GIVEN US BY BENNETT TO FILL OUR BODIES AND... HEARTS?
...

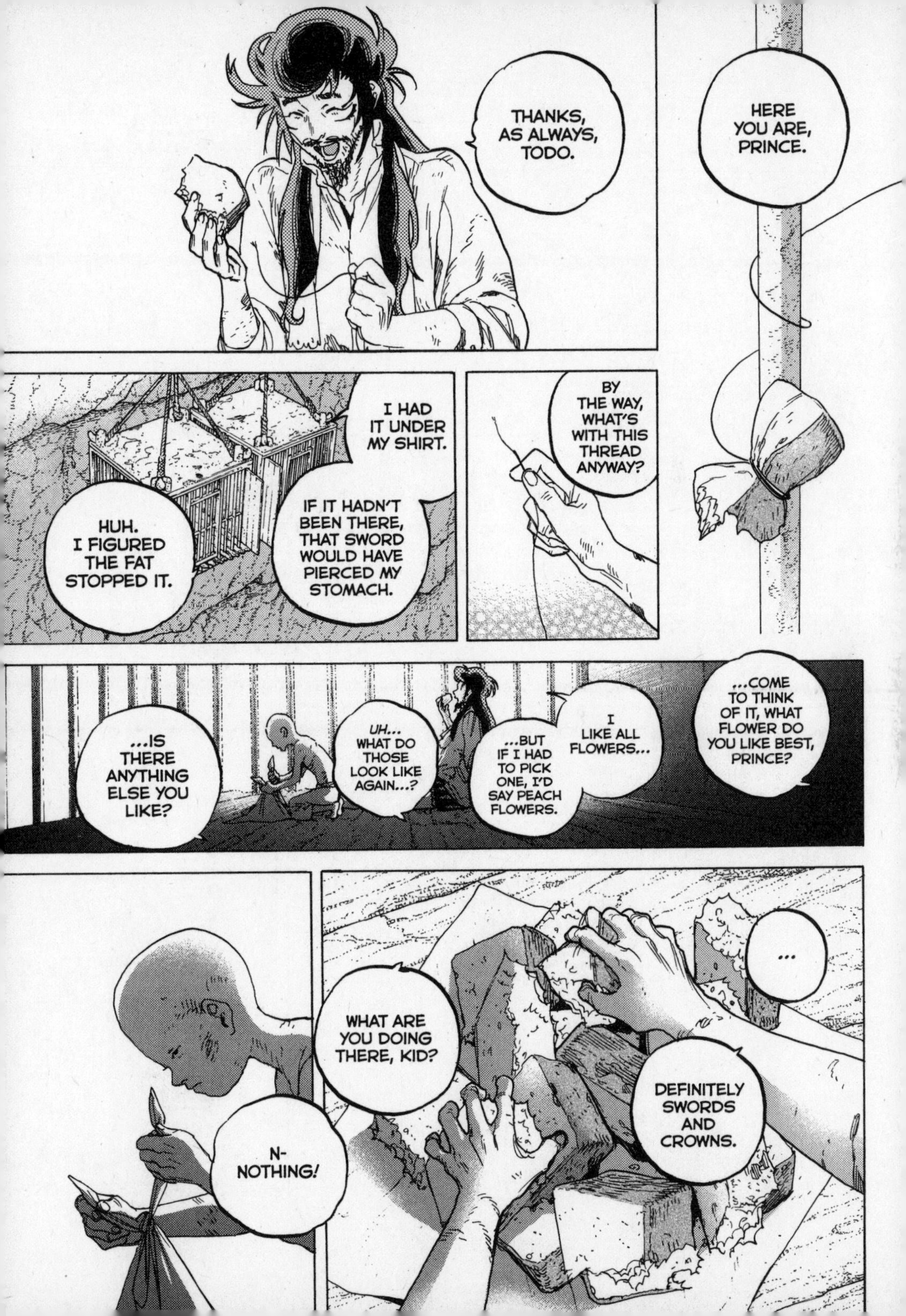
HERE YOU ARE, PRINCE.
THANKS, AS ALWAYS, TODO.
BY THE WAY, WHAT'S WITH THIS THREAD ANYWAY?
I HAD IT UNDER MY SHIRT.
IF IT HADN'T BEEN THERE, THAT SWORD WOULD HAVE PIERCED MY STOMACH.
HUH. I FIGURED THE FAT STOPPED IT.
...COME TO THINK OF IT, WHAT FLOWER DO YOU LIKE BEST, PRINCE?
I LIKE ALL FLOWERS...
...BUT IF I HAD TO PICK ONE, I'D SAY PEACH FLOWERS.
UH... WHAT DO THOSE LOOK LIKE AGAIN...?
...IS THERE ANYTHING ELSE YOU LIKE?
...
DEFINITELY SWORDS AND CROWNS.
WHAT ARE YOU DOING THERE, KID?
N- NOTHING!

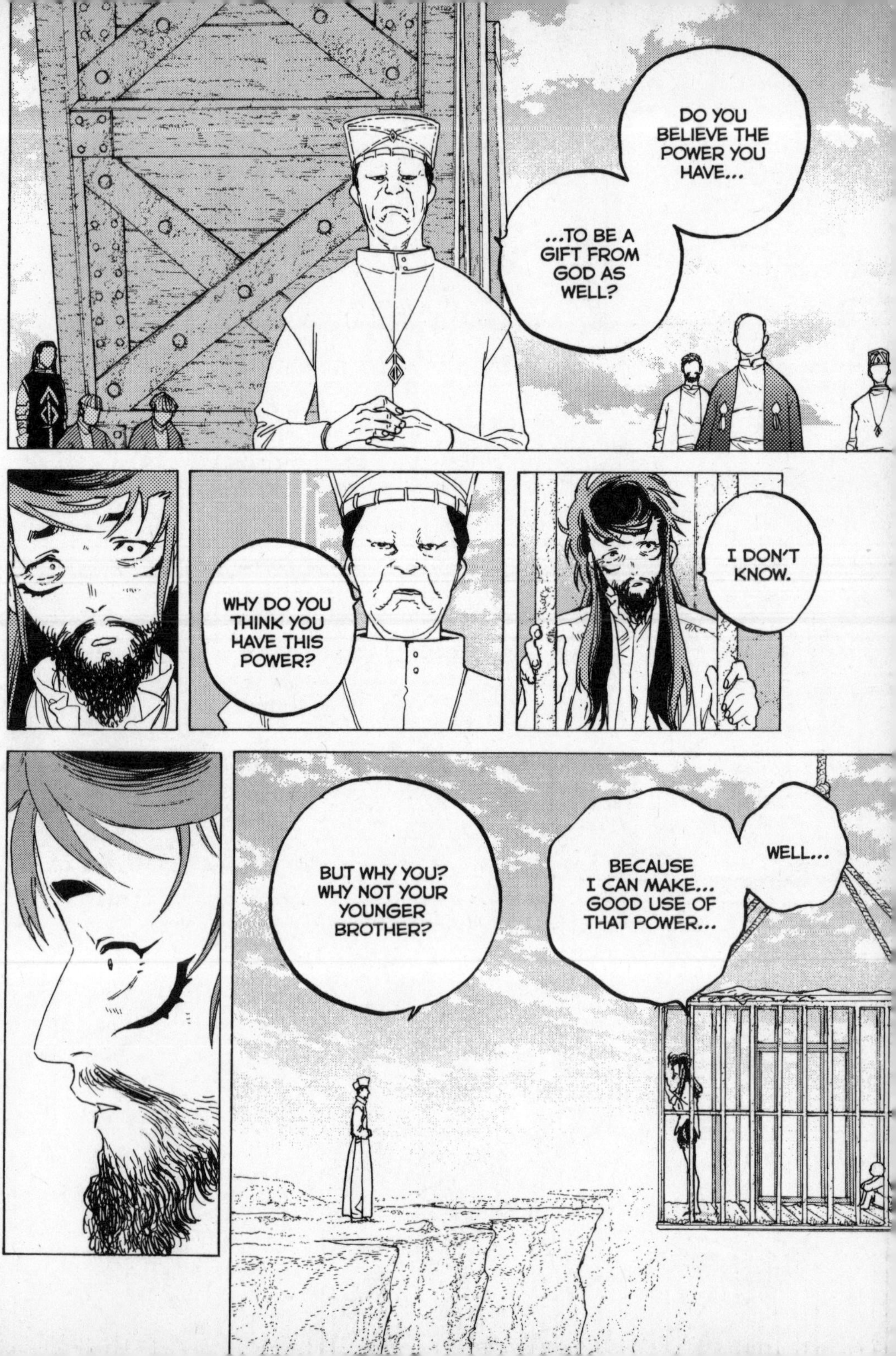
DO YOU BELIEVE THE POWER YOU HAVE...
...TO BE A GIFT FROM GOD AS WELL?
I DON'T KNOW.
WHY DO YOU THINK YOU HAVE THIS POWER?
WELL...
BECAUSE I CAN MAKE... GOOD USE OF THAT POWER...
BUT WHY YOU? WHY NOT YOUR YOUNGER BROTHER?

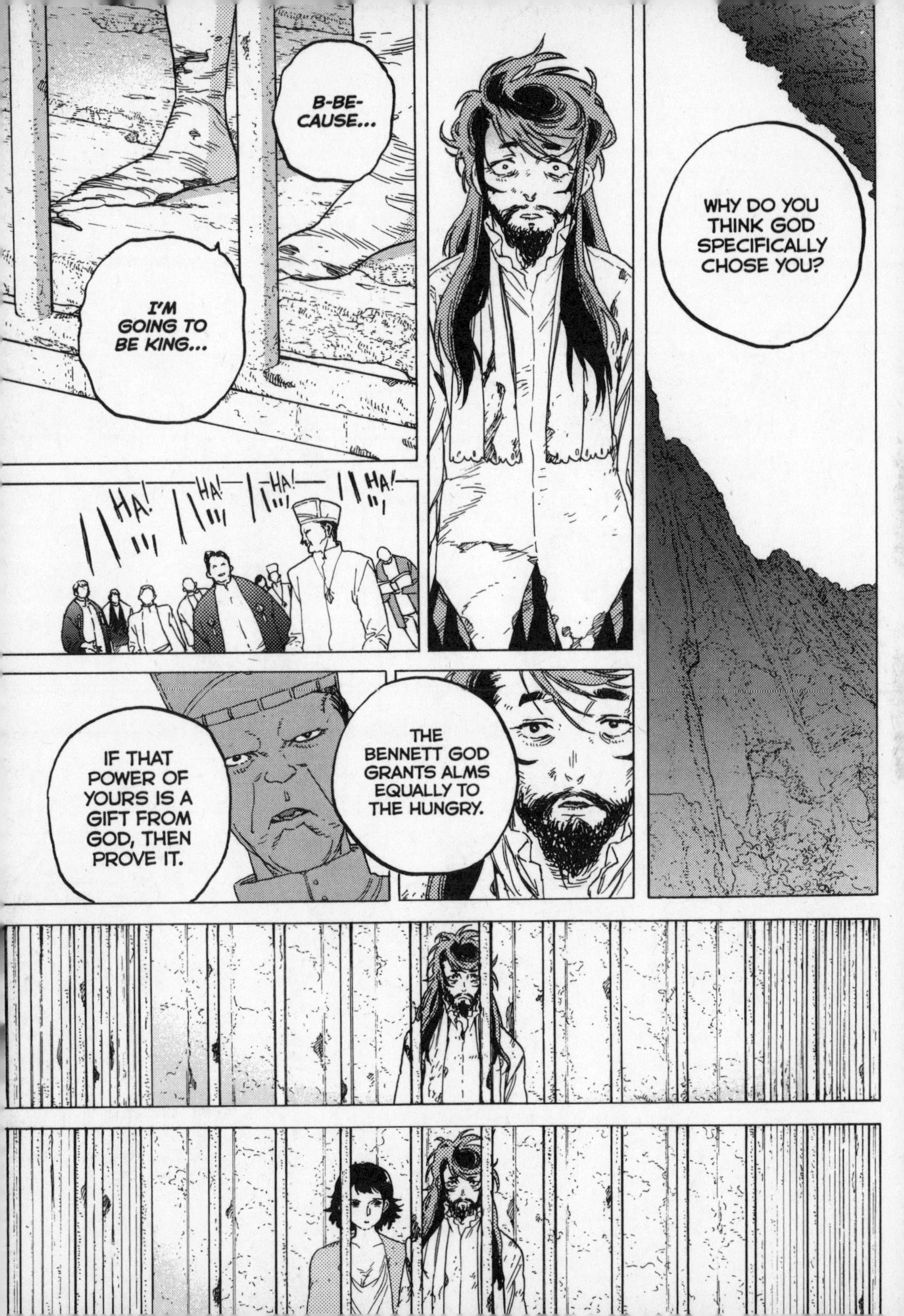
WHY DO YOU THINK GOD SPECIFICALLY CHOSE YOU?
B-BE-CAUSE...
I'M GOING TO BE KING...
HA! HA! HA! HA!
THE BENNETT GOD GRANTS ALMS EQUALLY TO THE HUNGRY.
IF THAT POWER OF YOURS IS A GIFT FROM GOD, THEN PROVE IT.

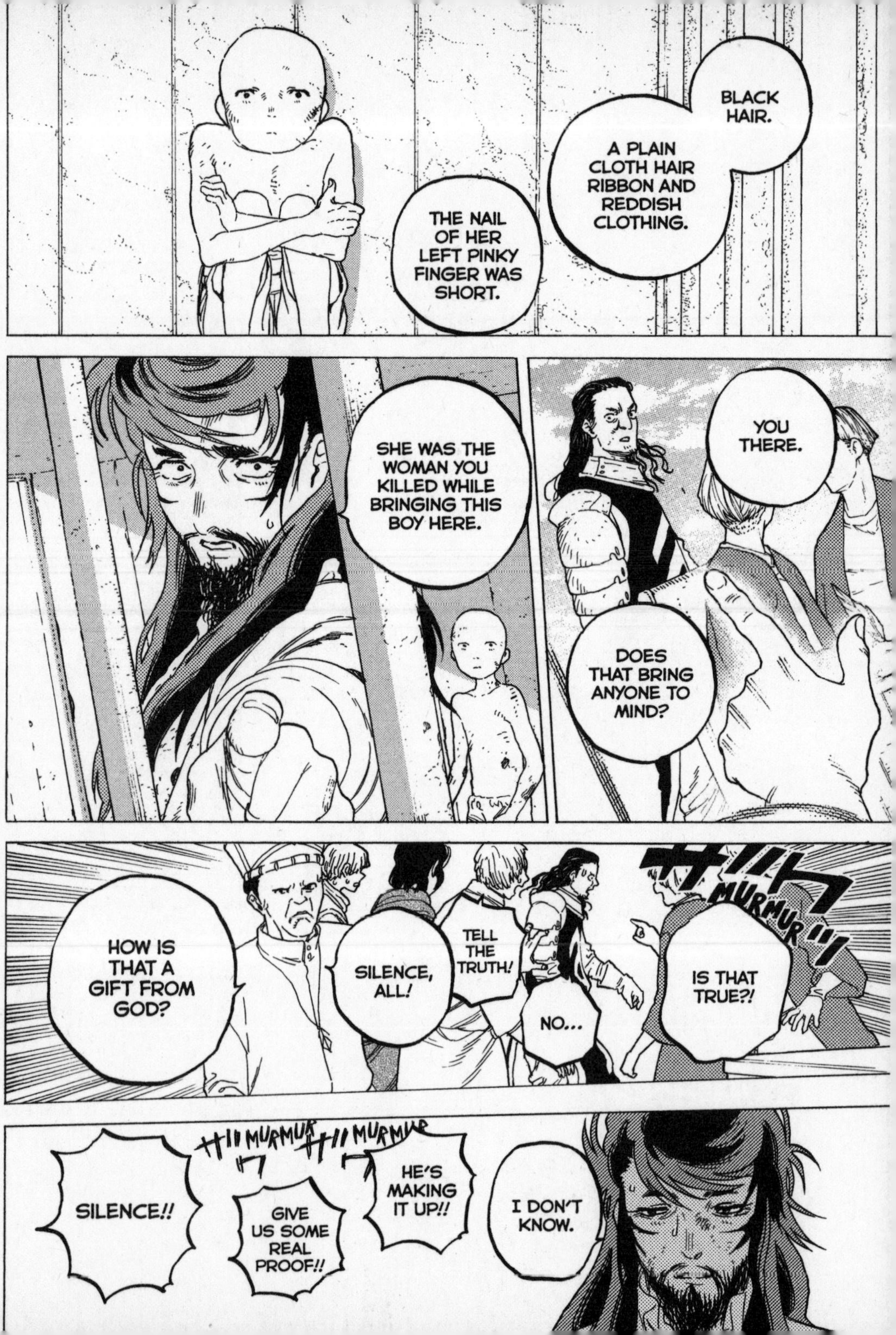
BLACK HAIR.
A PLAIN CLOTH HAIR RIBBON AND REDDISH CLOTHING.
THE NAIL OF HER LEFT PINKY FINGER WAS SHORT.
YOU THERE.
DOES THAT BRING ANYONE TO MIND?
SHE WAS THE WOMAN YOU KILLED WHILE BRINGING THIS BOY HERE.
MURMUR
IS THAT TRUE?!
NO...
TELL THE TRUTH!
SILENCE, ALL!
HOW IS THAT A GIFT FROM GOD?
I DON'T KNOW.
HE'S MAKING IT UP!!
MURMUR
MURMUR
GIVE US SOME REAL PROOF!!
SILENCE!!

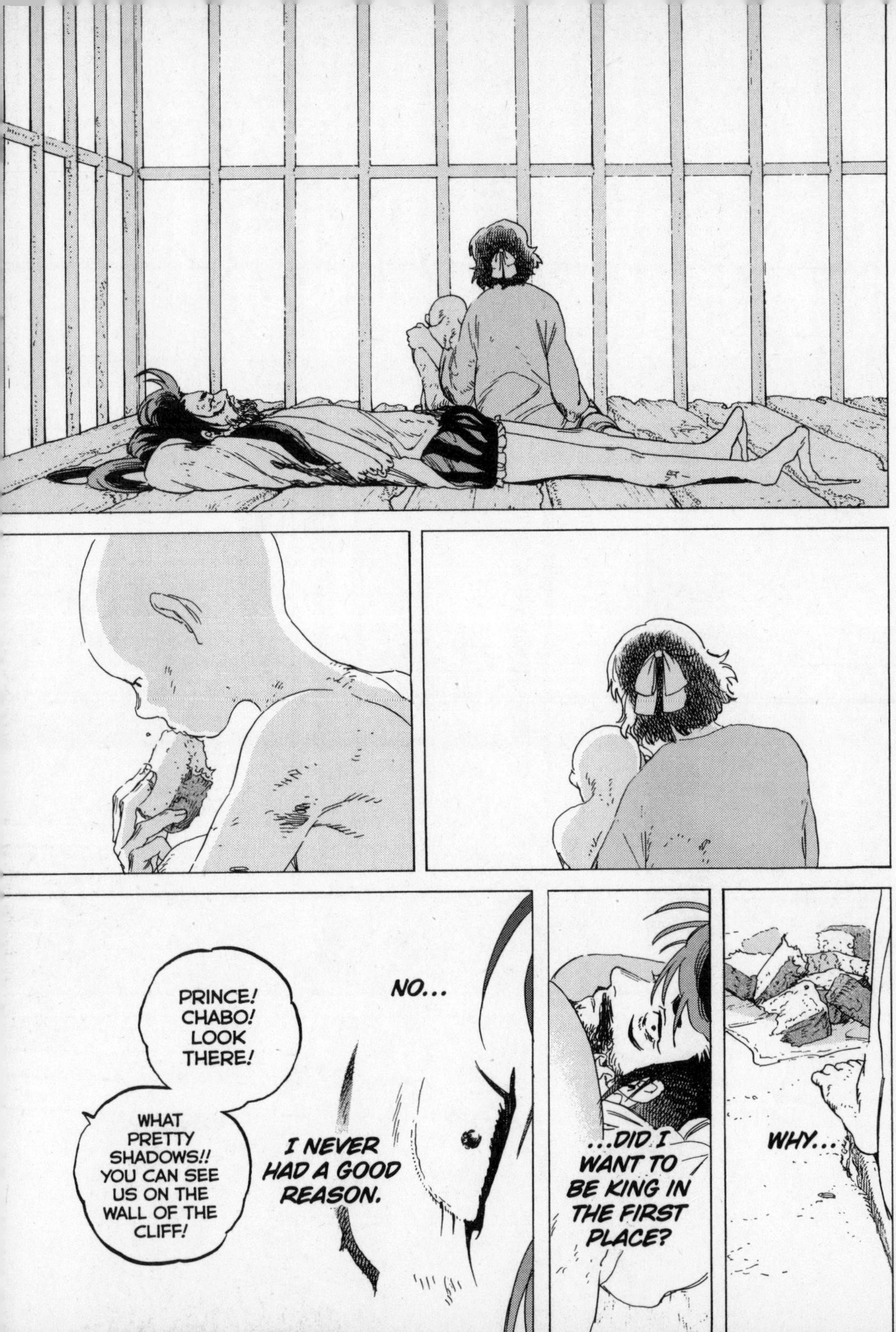
WHY...
...DID I WANT TO BE KING IN THE FIRST PLACE?
NO...
PRINCE! CHABO! LOOK THERE!
I NEVER HAD A GOOD REASON.
WHAT PRETTY SHADOWS!! YOU CAN SEE US ON THE WALL OF THE CLIFF!

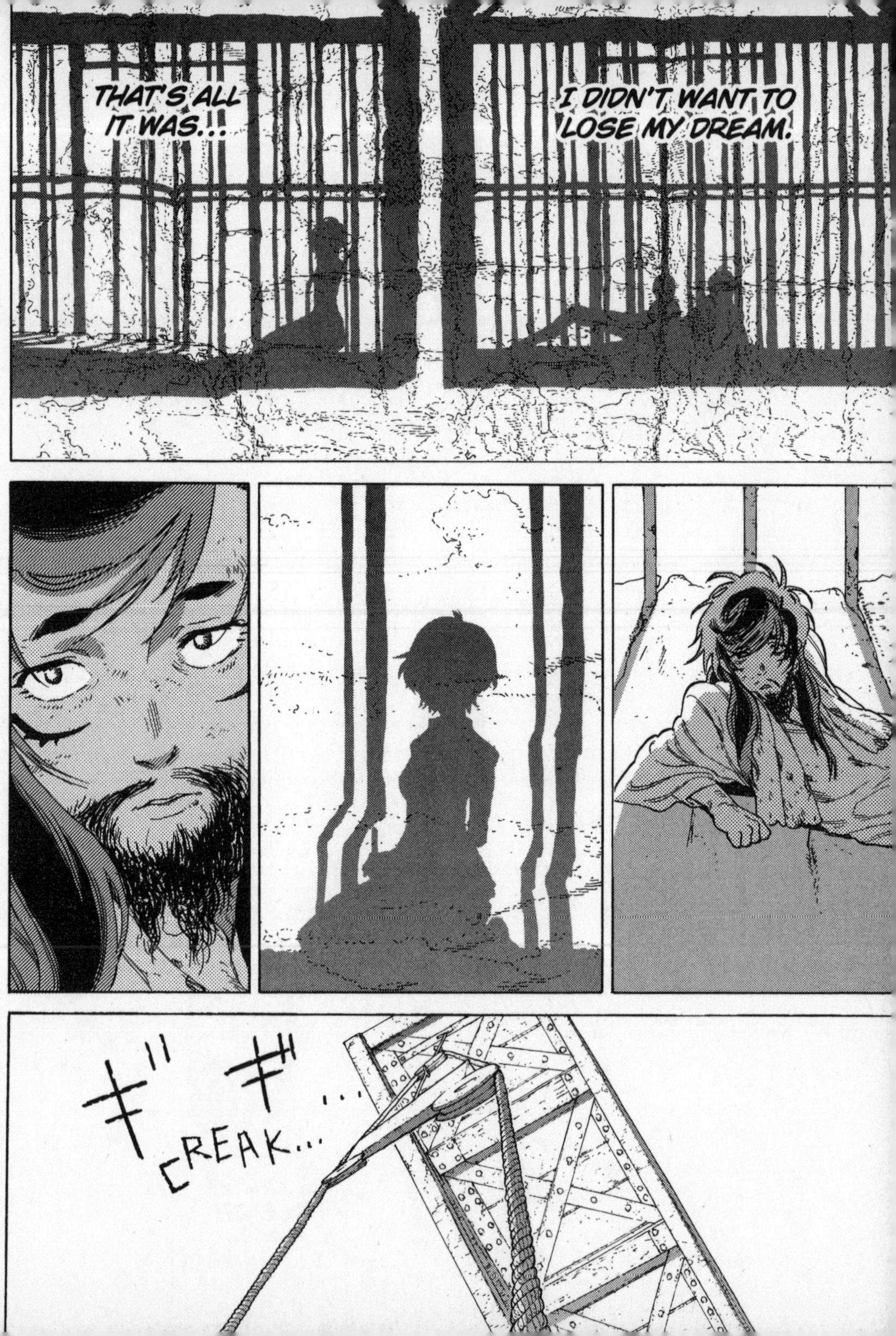
I DIDN'T WANT TO LOSE MY DREAM.
THAT'S ALL IT WAS...
ギギ...
CREAK...

"#12"

Two days had passed since she stopped talking.
Surely, this was the influence of that popular philosopher Kaijagam.
But that was no excuse to ignore me.
I questioned her all day.
"You don't like the fact that I was a marriage scammer?
I'm sorry, but this isn't how I pictured my life either.
But you can't be too clean either if you're crucified here. Am I right?"
Cordelia didn't speak that day either.

The next day, Cordelia's shadow was gone. She must have been rescued.
I thought back on the last words she said to me.
"I hope we can see each other the next time we meet."
In that case, don't leave without me. How am I supposed to find you?

There are birds flying over my head.
If I'm saved, I'll quit my swindling on the spot and take her hand in mine.
She's looking at me with a smile on her face. What kind of face am I making?
No, I guess it doesn't matter.
Oh? I hear someone calling me. She came to get me.
Then, my body slipped free of the ropes, and I was free.

LOVE LIVES IN THE IMAGINATION –END–

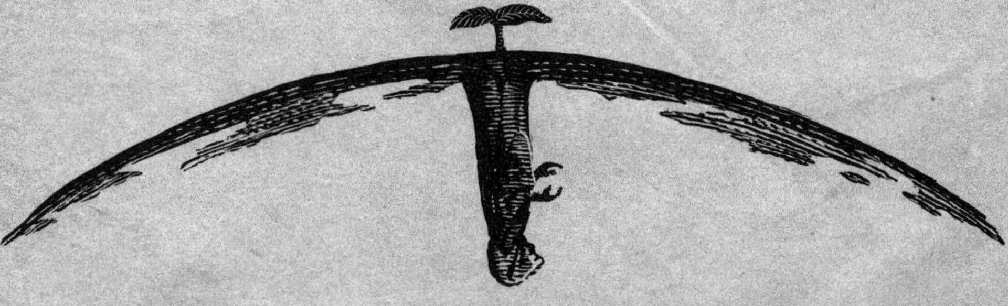

May 10th	In the city of Entas, where he had traveled on his expedition, Prince Bonchien is captured by the Church of Bennett High Cleric Cylira and accused of heresy. He is imprisoned with Fushi and the servant Todo.
May 11th	The metal prison in which Fushi is trapped is filled with molten iron.
May 12th	Through the cooperation of the Guardians and the Lord of Uga Castle, the ransom of 3,000 pieces of gold is paid.
May 14th	Word reaches the kingdom via messenger pigeon that Prince Bon has been arrested.
May 15th	Assistance in negotiations with the main church is requested at the Church of Bennett branch inside the Uralis Kingdom, but negotiations break down.
Same Day	The King himself raises 3,000 of his personal guards and horsemen and leaves Uralis to negotiate personally.
May 16th	The Church declares that they will not release Bonchien until the trial is over. Another group of 3,000, including the jurist Radwan, depart Uralis to go demonstrate how unjust Bonchien's imprisonment is.
May 17th	Protests against the Church of Bennett begin in the country. In addition to those supporters of Fushi, an anti-Fushi faction that believes he led Bon to this predicament also comes out of the woodwork.
May 18th	A petition demanding the release of Prince Bon and the signatures of 7,821 residents of Uralis are submitted to the Church.
May 19th	The King and his personal guards arrive at Entas, but the King is not admitted to the trial.
May 20th	The Guardians gather Ilsarita's pro-Fushi faction in order to forcibly free Prince Bon, creating a liberation army.
May 22nd	The liberation army marches, but its conflicts with the Bennett guard divisions cause many casualties. The situation reaches a stalemate.
May 27th	Prince Bon's trial continues.

URALIS KINGDOM BUTLERY RECORD

#74 Will of the Flesh

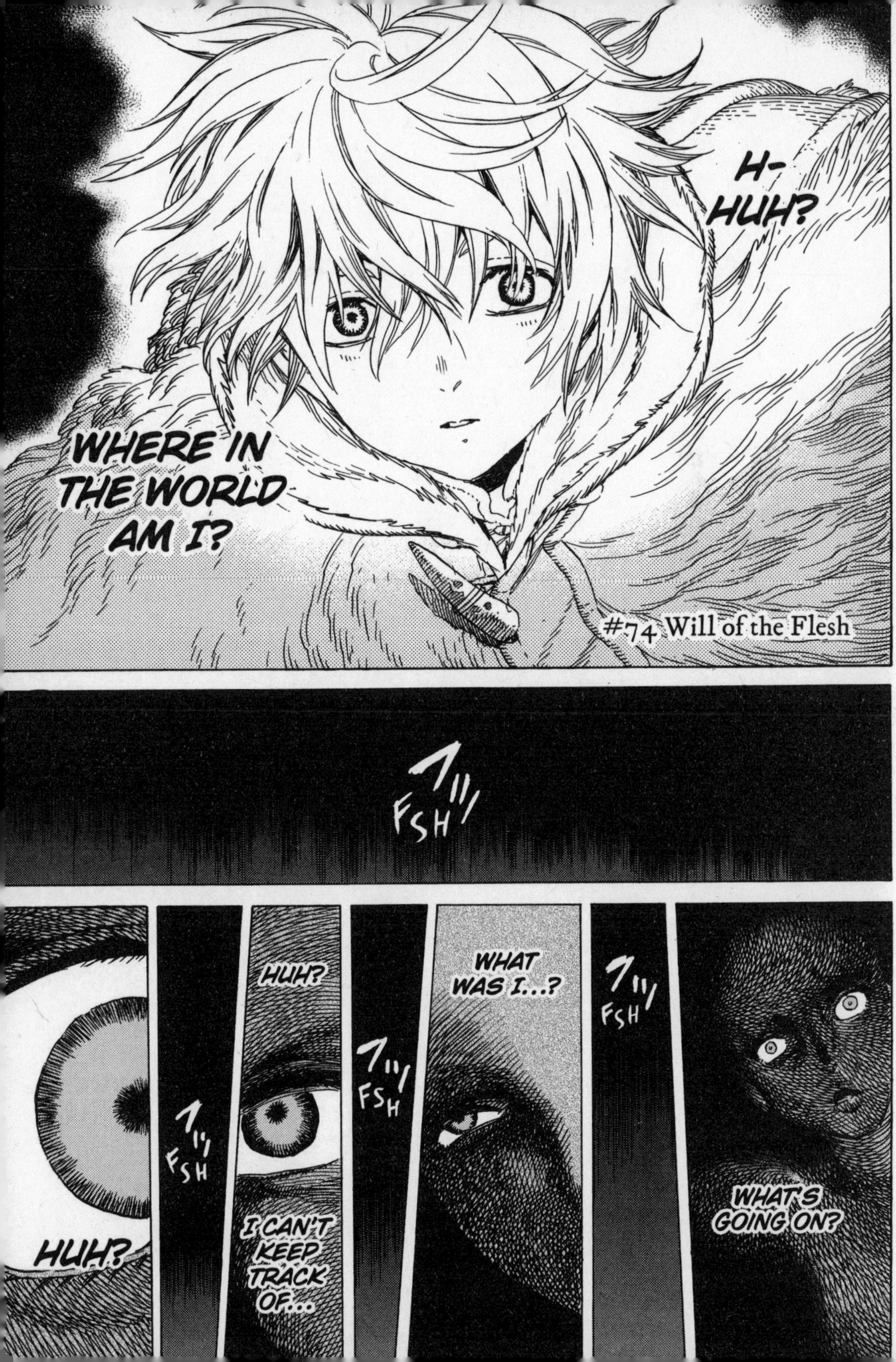
H-HUH?
WHERE IN THE WORLD AM I?
FSH
WHAT'S GOING ON?
FSH
WHAT WAS I...?
FSH
HUH?
I CAN'T KEEP TRACK OF...
FSH
HUH?

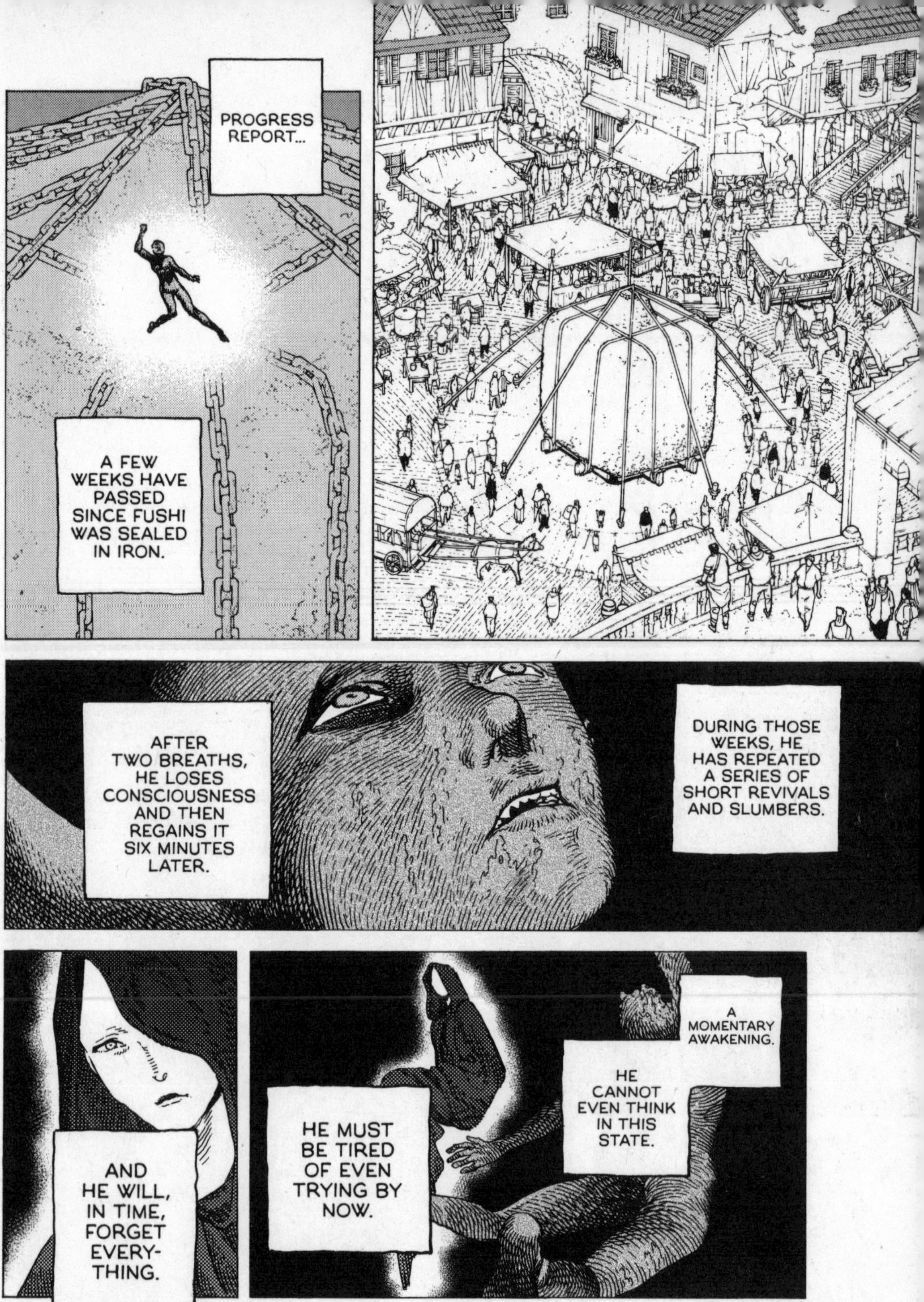
PROGRESS REPORT...
A FEW WEEKS HAVE PASSED SINCE FUSHI WAS SEALED IN IRON.
DURING THOSE WEEKS, HE HAS REPEATED A SERIES OF SHORT REVIVALS AND SLUMBERS.
AFTER TWO BREATHS, HE LOSES CONSCIOUSNESS AND THEN REGAINS IT SIX MINUTES LATER.
A MOMENTARY AWAKENING.
HE CANNOT EVEN THINK IN THIS STATE.
HE MUST BE TIRED OF EVEN TRYING BY NOW.
AND HE WILL, IN TIME, FORGET EVERY-THING.

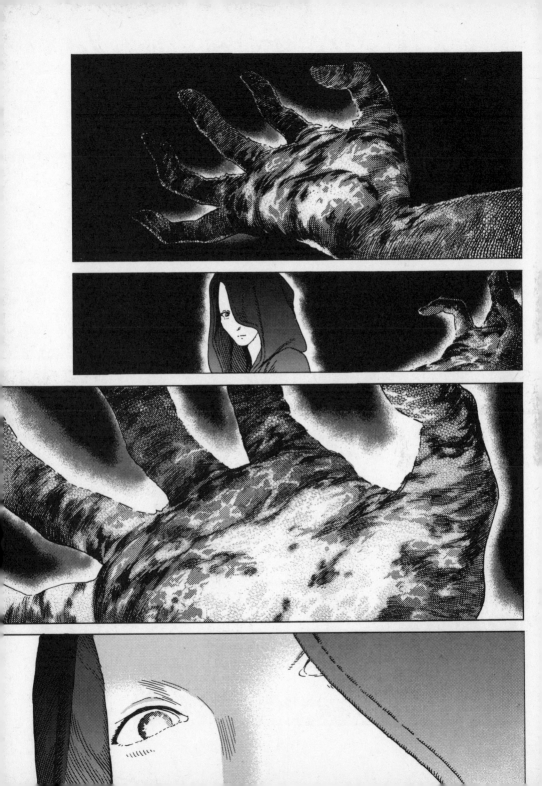

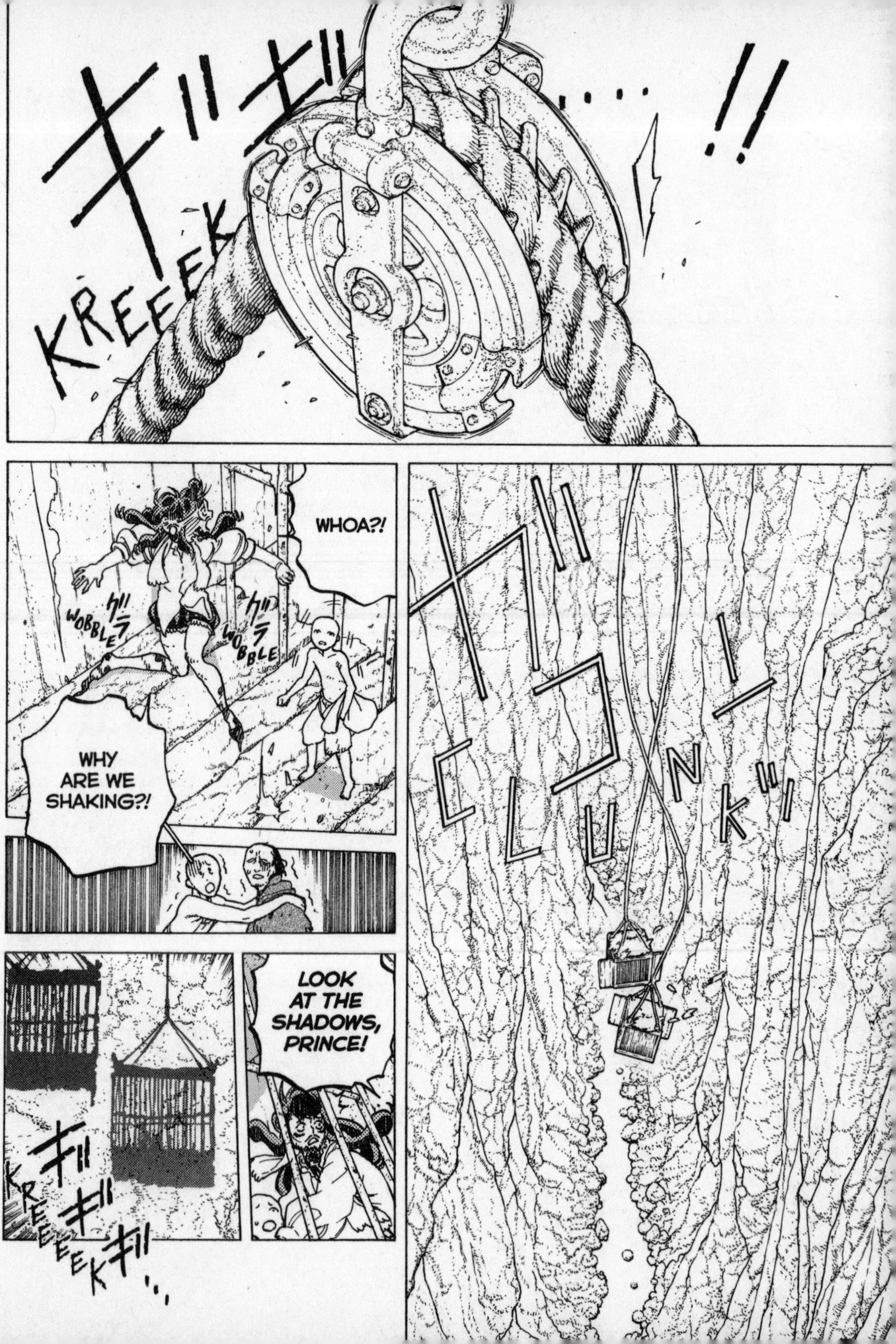

ギリギリ
KREEEK
.....!!
CLUNK
WHOA?!
WOBBLE
WOBBLE
WHY ARE WE SHAKING?!
LOOK AT THE SHADOWS, PRINCE!
KREEEEK...

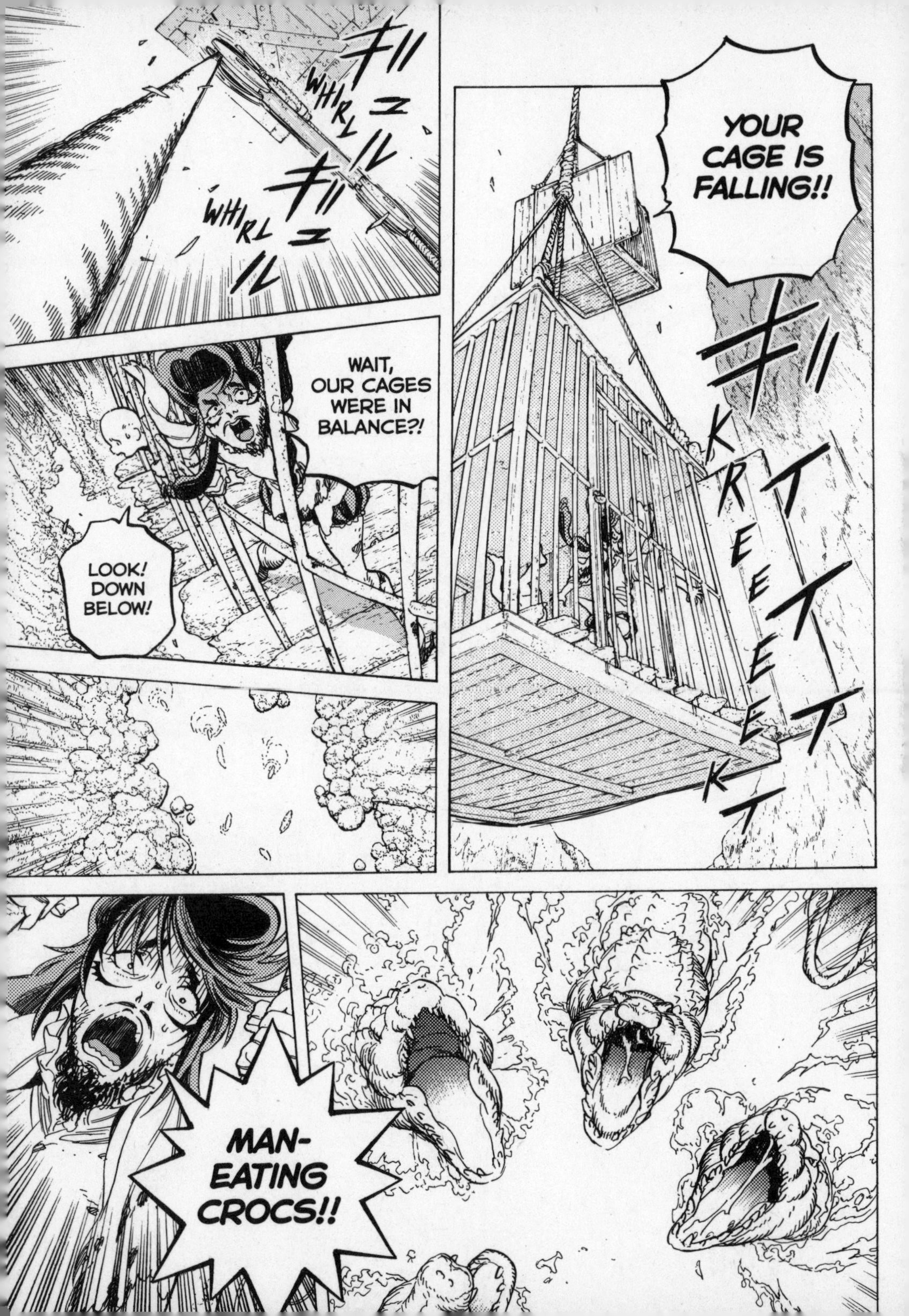
YOUR CAGE IS FALLING!!
KREEEEK
WHIRL
WHIRL
WAIT, OUR CAGES WERE IN BALANCE?!
LOOK! DOWN BELOW!
MAN-EATING CROCS!!

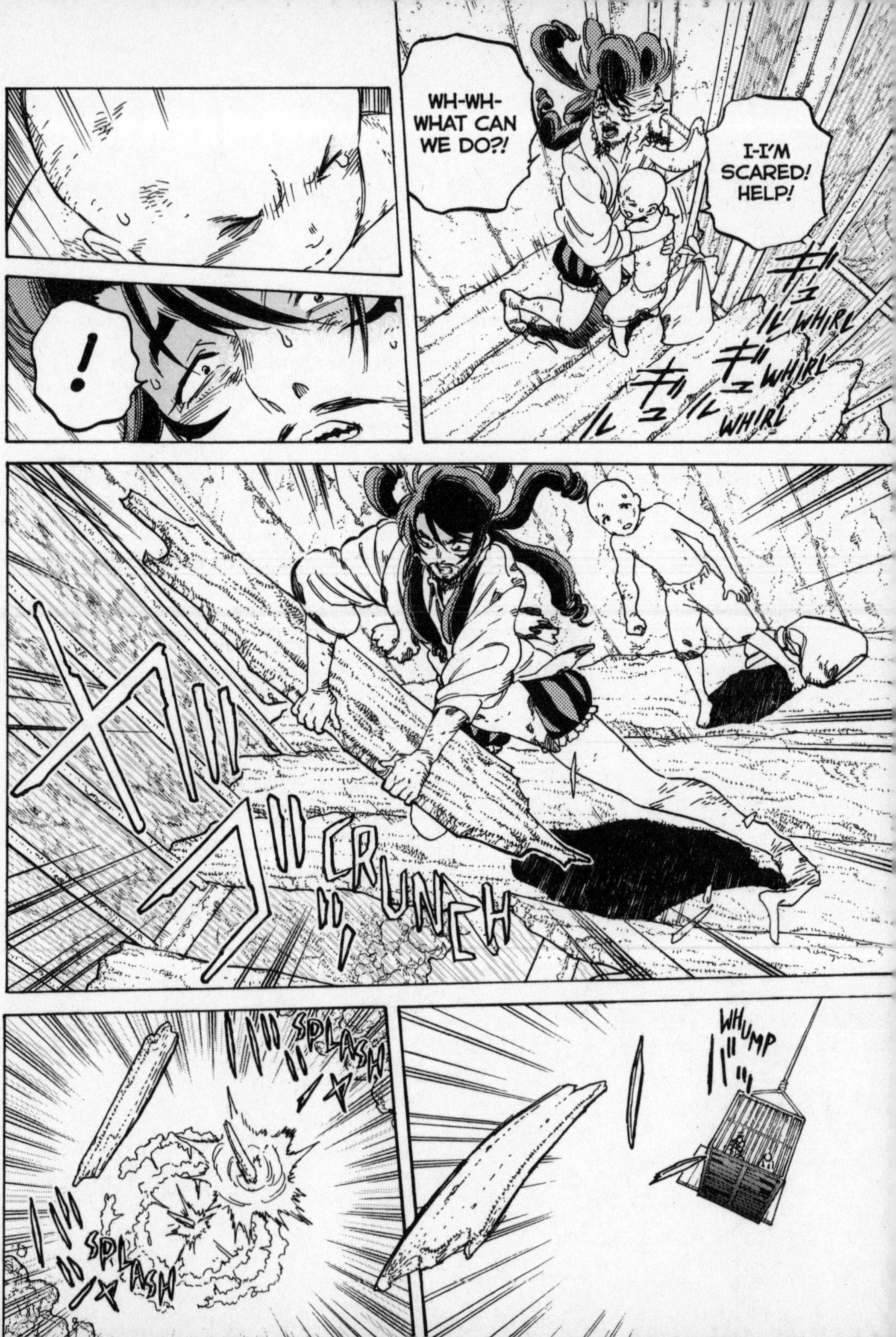
I-I'M SCARED! HELP!
WH-WH-WHAT CAN WE DO?!
WHIRL
WHIRL
WHIRL
!
CRUNCH
WHUMP
SPLASH
SPLASH

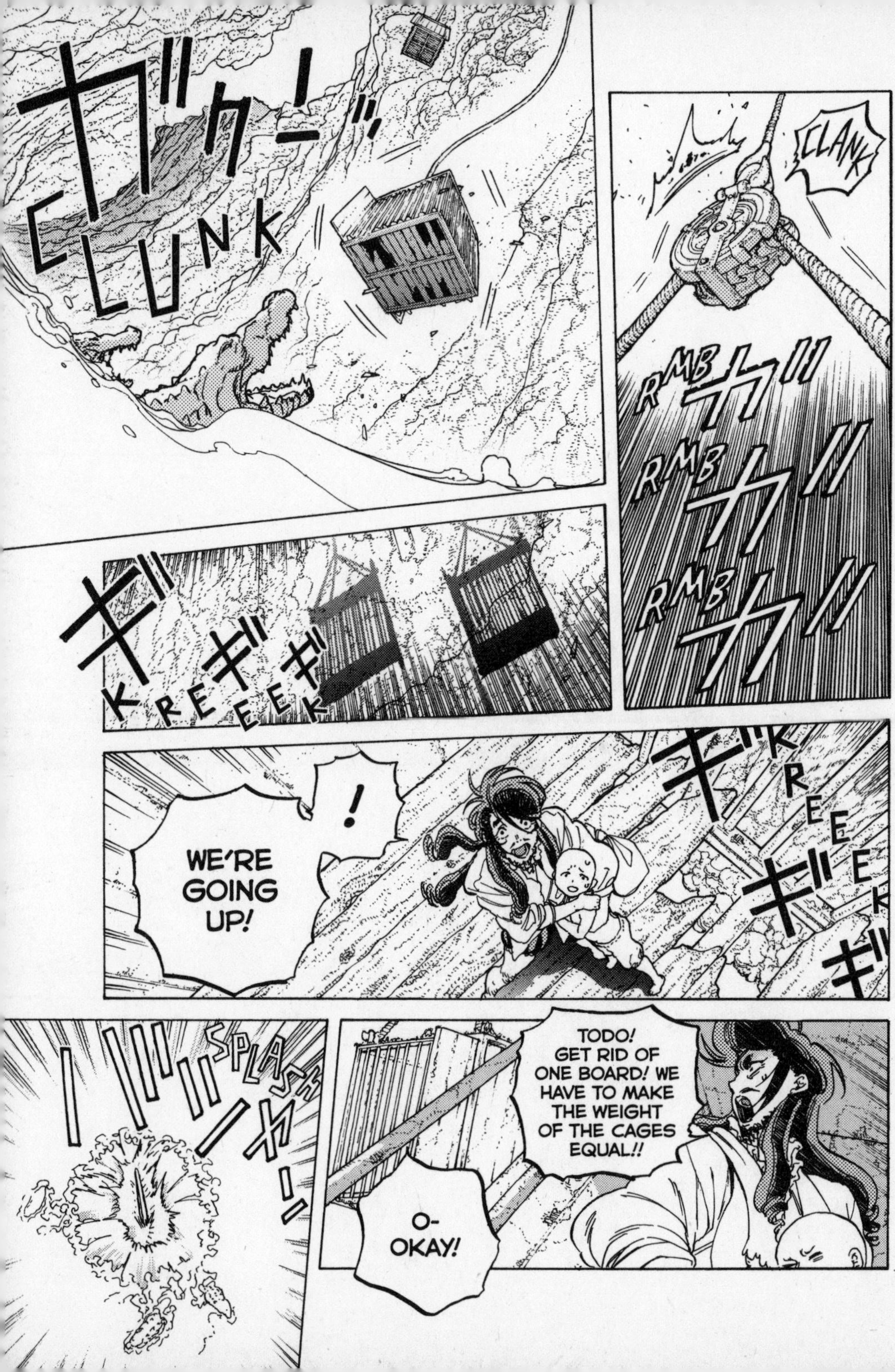
CLANK
RMB
RMB
RMB
CLUNK
KREEEK
KREEEK
!
WE'RE GOING UP!
TODO! GET RID OF ONE BOARD! WE HAVE TO MAKE THE WEIGHT OF THE CAGES EQUAL!!
O-OKAY!
SPLASH

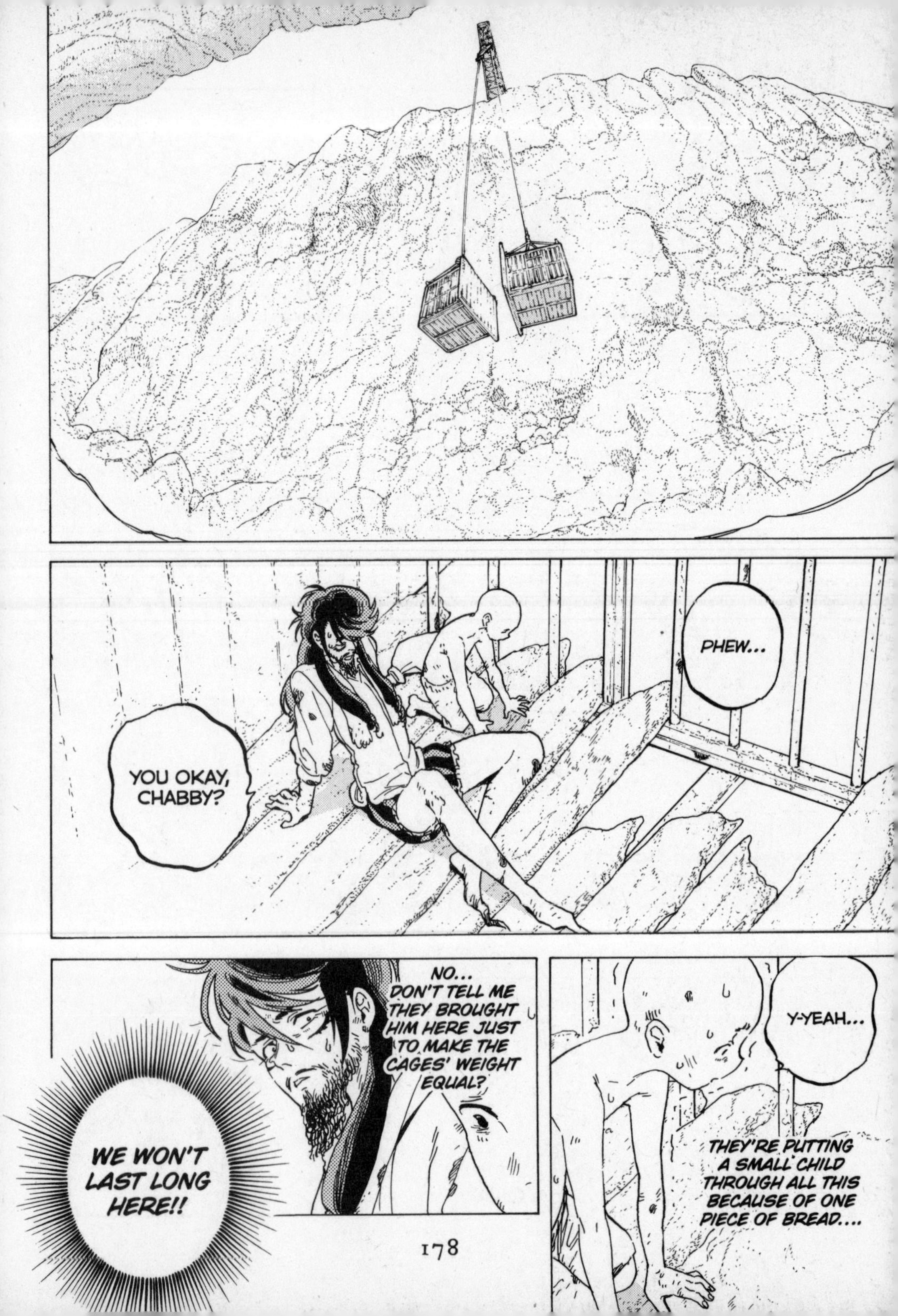
PHEW...
YOU OKAY, CHABBY?
Y-YEAH...
THEY'RE PUTTING A SMALL CHILD THROUGH ALL THIS BECAUSE OF ONE PIECE OF BREAD....
NO... DON'T TELL ME THEY BROUGHT HIM HERE JUST TO MAKE THE CAGES' WEIGHT EQUAL?
WE WON'T LAST LONG HERE!!

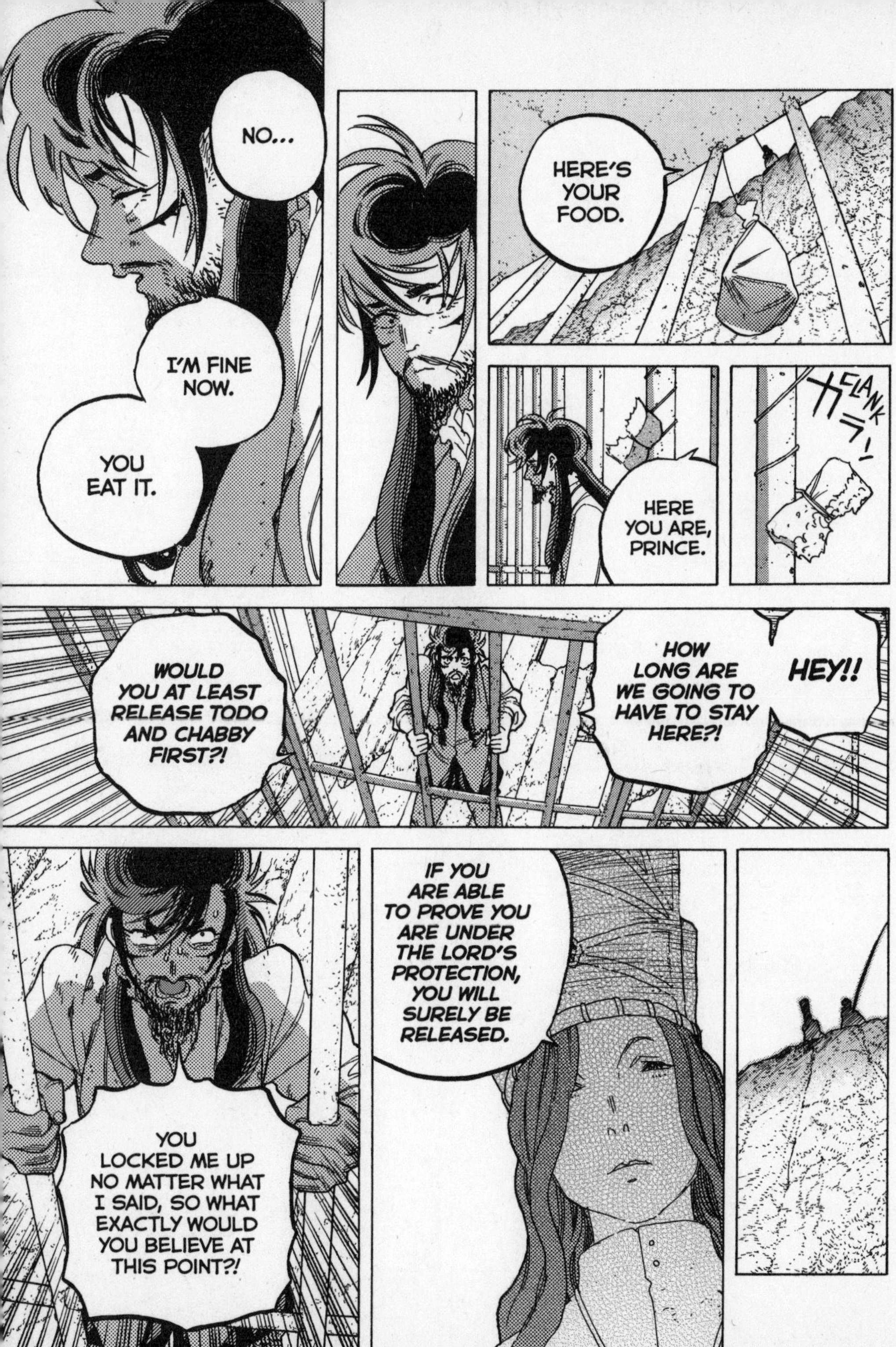
HERE'S YOUR FOOD.
CLANK
HERE YOU ARE, PRINCE.
NO...
I'M FINE NOW.
YOU EAT IT.
HEY!!
HOW LONG ARE WE GOING TO HAVE TO STAY HERE?!
WOULD YOU AT LEAST RELEASE TODO AND CHABBY FIRST?!
IF YOU ARE ABLE TO PROVE YOU ARE UNDER THE LORD'S PROTECTION, YOU WILL SURELY BE RELEASED.
YOU LOCKED ME UP NO MATTER WHAT I SAID, SO WHAT EXACTLY WOULD YOU BELIEVE AT THIS POINT?!

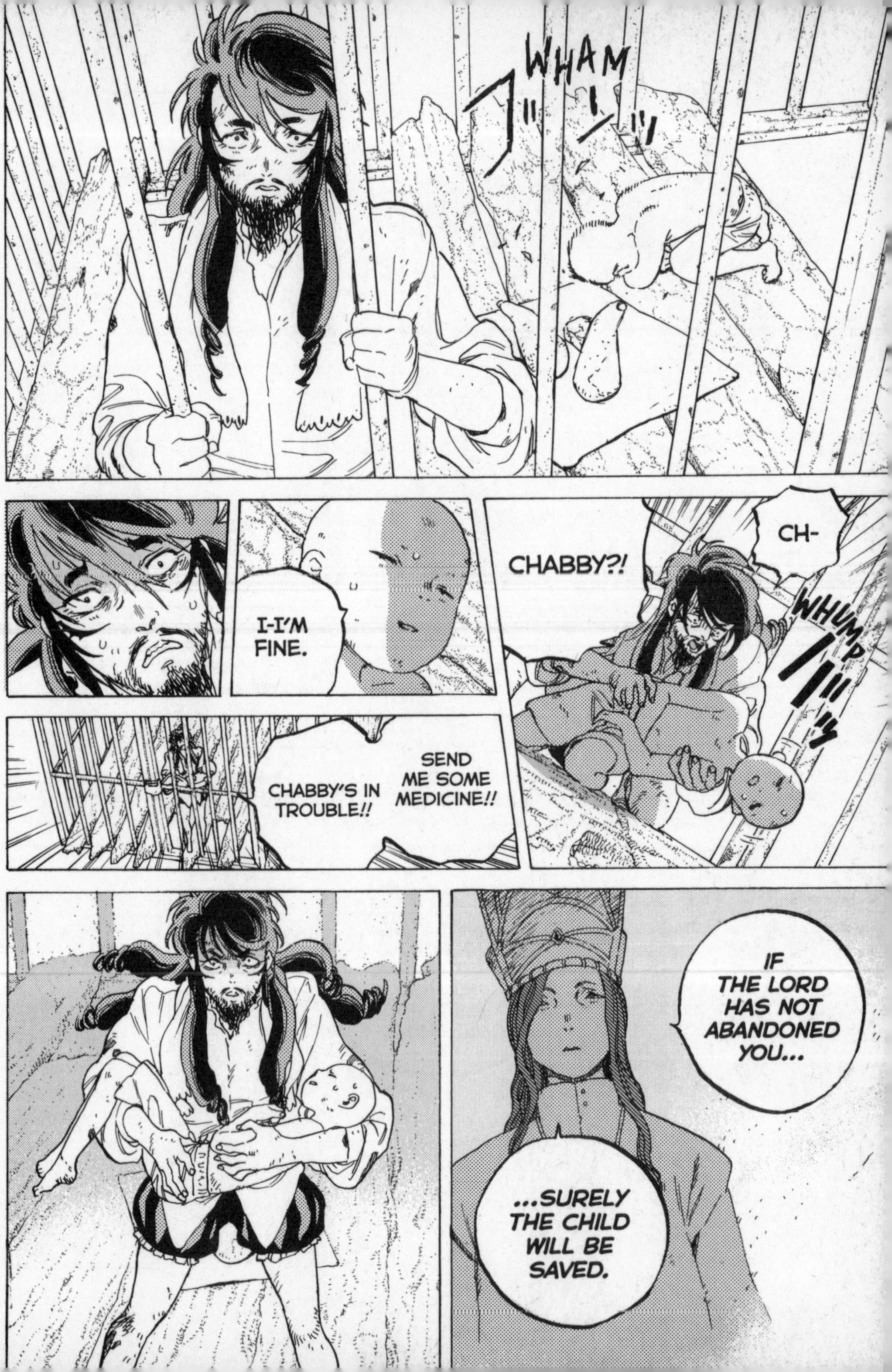
WHAM
CH-
CHABBY?!
WHUMP
I-I'M FINE.
SEND ME SOME MEDICINE!!
CHABBY'S IN TROUBLE!!
IF THE LORD HAS NOT ABANDONED YOU...
...SURELY THE CHILD WILL BE SAVED.

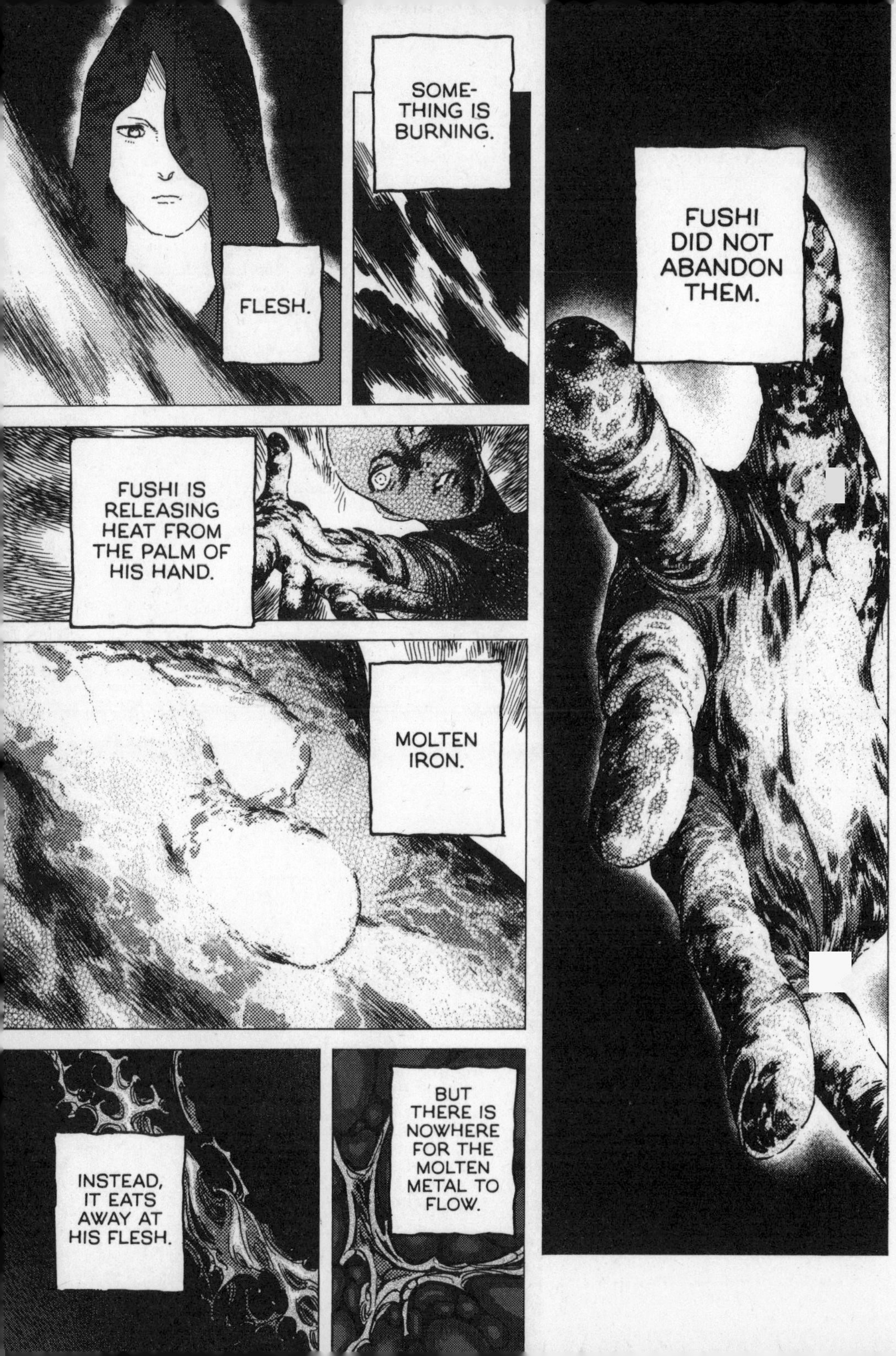
FUSHI DID NOT ABANDON THEM.
SOME-THING IS BURNING.
FLESH.
FUSHI IS RELEASING HEAT FROM THE PALM OF HIS HAND.
MOLTEN IRON.
BUT THERE IS NOWHERE FOR THE MOLTEN METAL TO FLOW.
INSTEAD, IT EATS AWAY AT HIS FLESH.

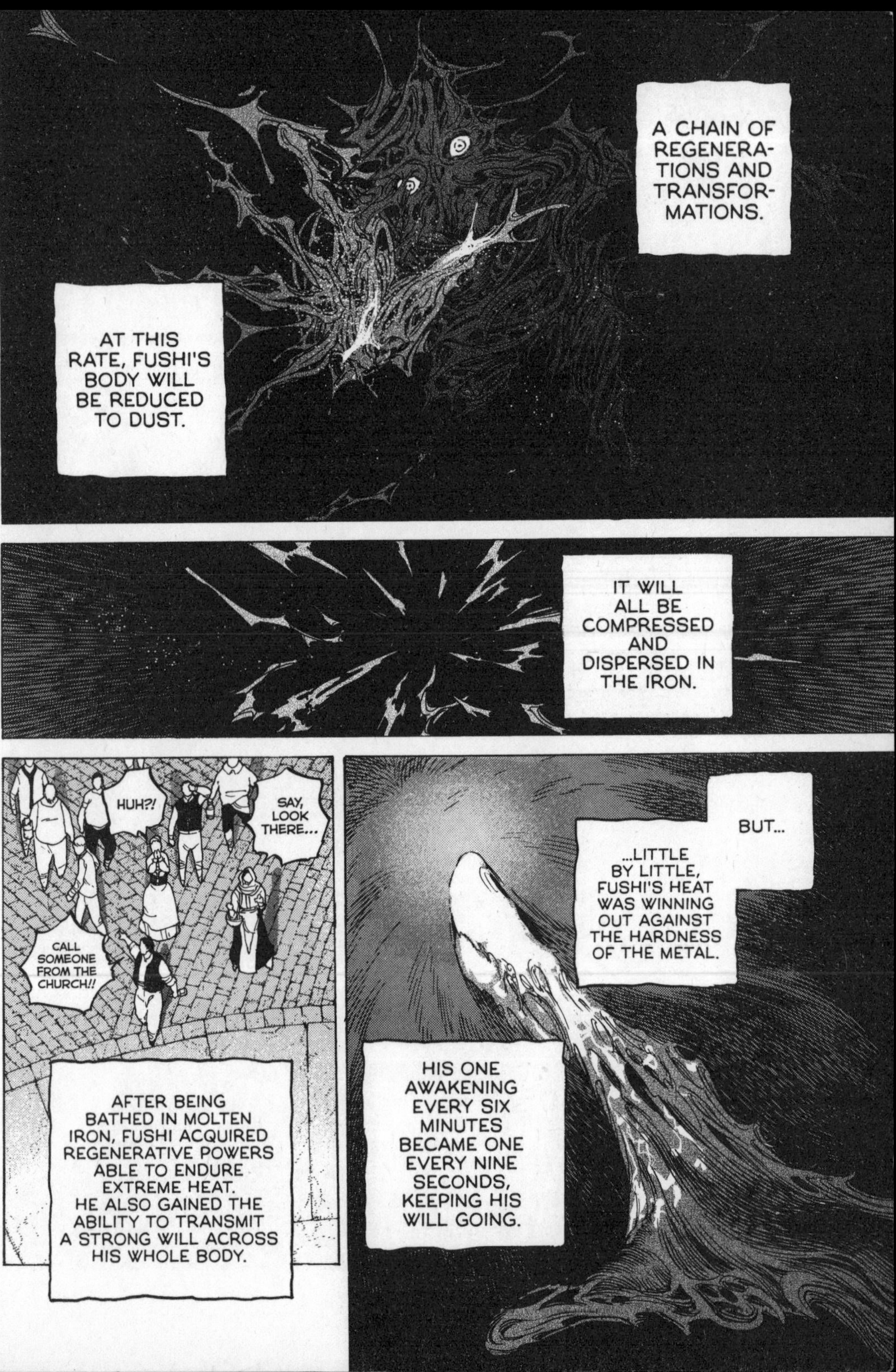
A CHAIN OF REGENERATIONS AND TRANSFORMATIONS.
AT THIS RATE, FUSHI'S BODY WILL BE REDUCED TO DUST.
IT WILL ALL BE COMPRESSED AND DISPERSED IN THE IRON.
BUT...
...LITTLE BY LITTLE, FUSHI'S HEAT WAS WINNING OUT AGAINST THE HARDNESS OF THE METAL.
HIS ONE AWAKENING EVERY SIX MINUTES BECAME ONE EVERY NINE SECONDS, KEEPING HIS WILL GOING.
SAY, LOOK THERE...
HUH?!
CALL SOMEONE FROM THE CHURCH!!
AFTER BEING BATHED IN MOLTEN IRON, FUSHI ACQUIRED REGENERATIVE POWERS ABLE TO ENDURE EXTREME HEAT. HE ALSO GAINED THE ABILITY TO TRANSMIT A STRONG WILL ACROSS HIS WHOLE BODY.

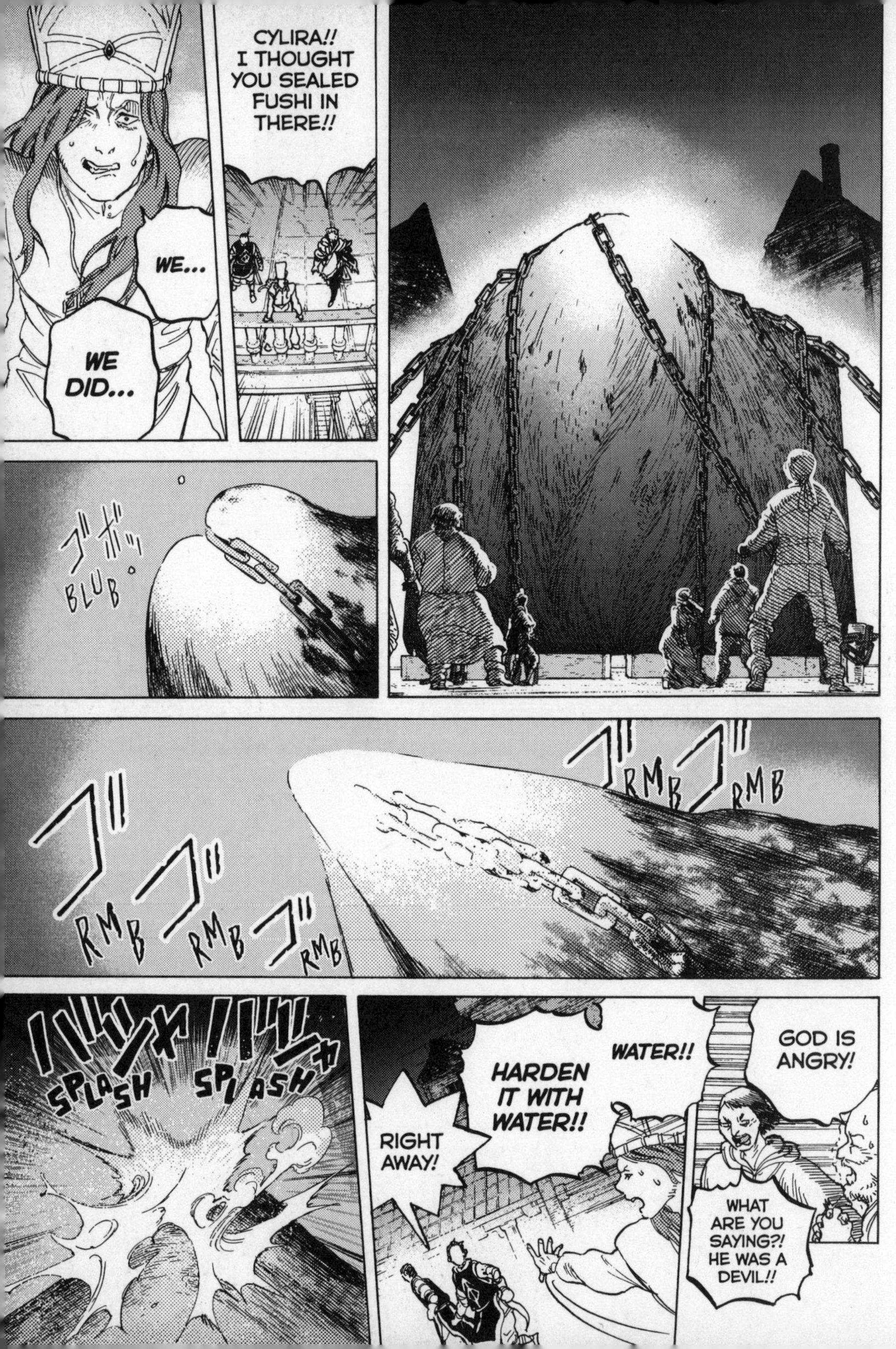

CYLIRA!! I THOUGHT YOU SEALED FUSHI IN THERE!!
WE...
WE DID...
ゴボッ BLUB
ゴゴ RMB ゴゴ RMB
ゴゴ RMB ゴゴ RMB ゴゴ RMB
GOD IS ANGRY!
WATER!!
HARDEN IT WITH WATER!!
WHAT ARE YOU SAYING?! HE WAS A DEVIL!!
RIGHT AWAY!
バシャ SPLASH バシャ SPLASH

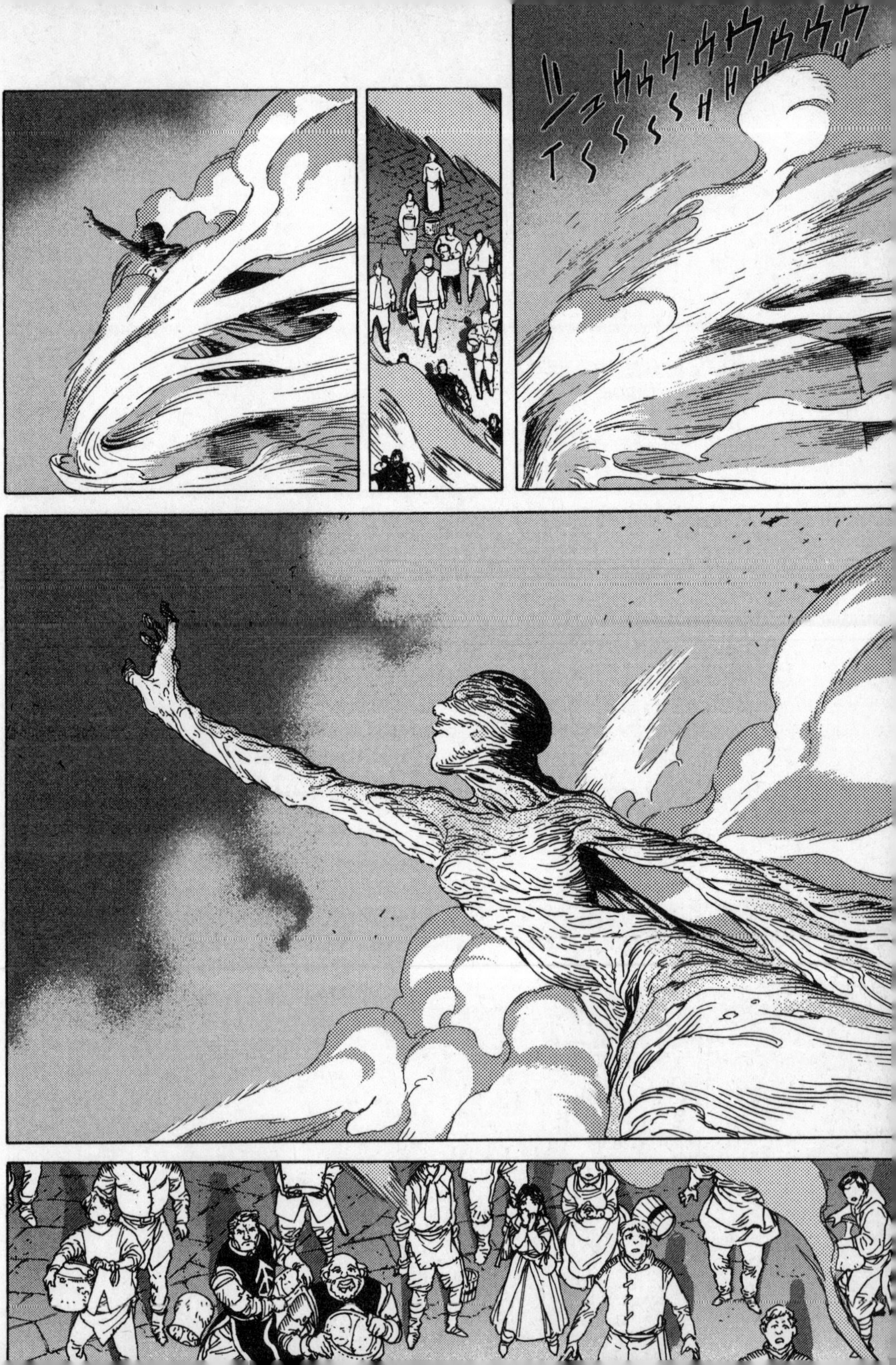
シュウウウウウウウウウ
TSSSSHHHHHH

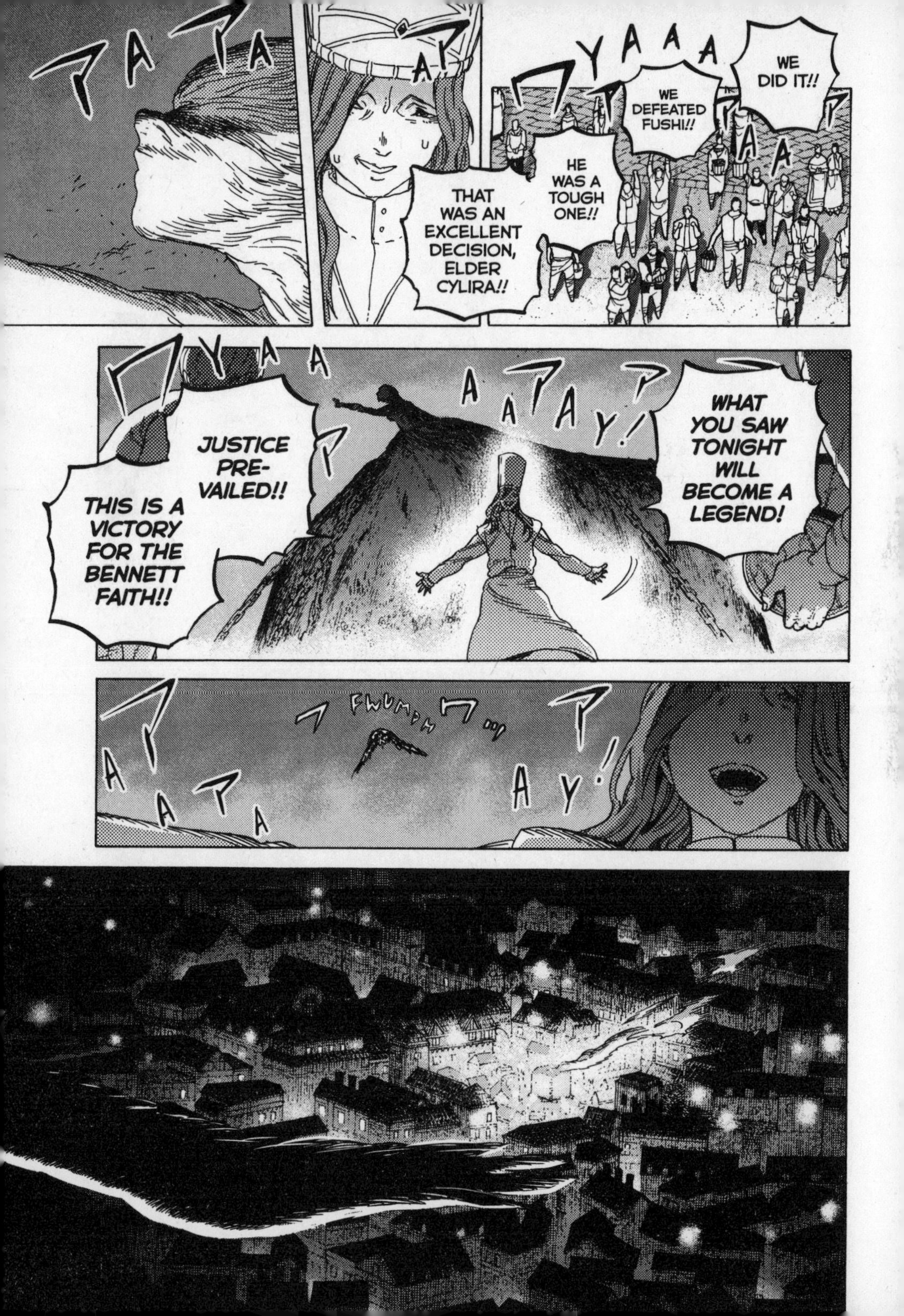
WE DID IT!!
WE DEFEATED FUSHI!!
YAAAA
HE WAS A TOUGH ONE!!
THAT WAS AN EXCELLENT DECISION, ELDER CYLIRA!!
AAA
WHAT YOU SAW TONIGHT WILL BECOME A LEGEND!
AAAAY!
JUSTICE PRE-VAILED!!
YAAA
THIS IS A VICTORY FOR THE BENNETT FAITH!!
AAY!
FWUMPH
AAAA

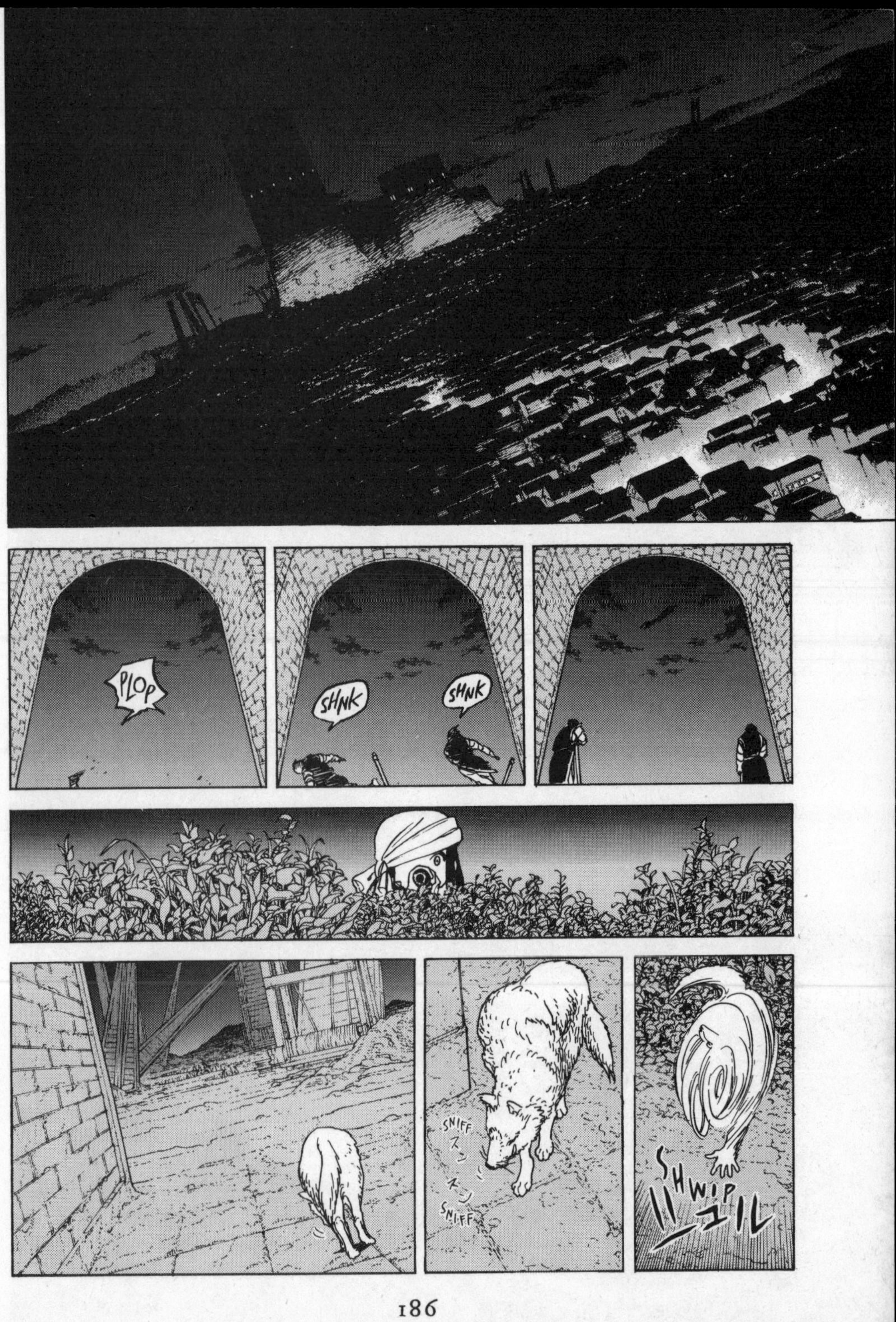
SHNK
SHNK
PLOP
SHWIP
シュル
SNIFF
スン
スン
SNIFF

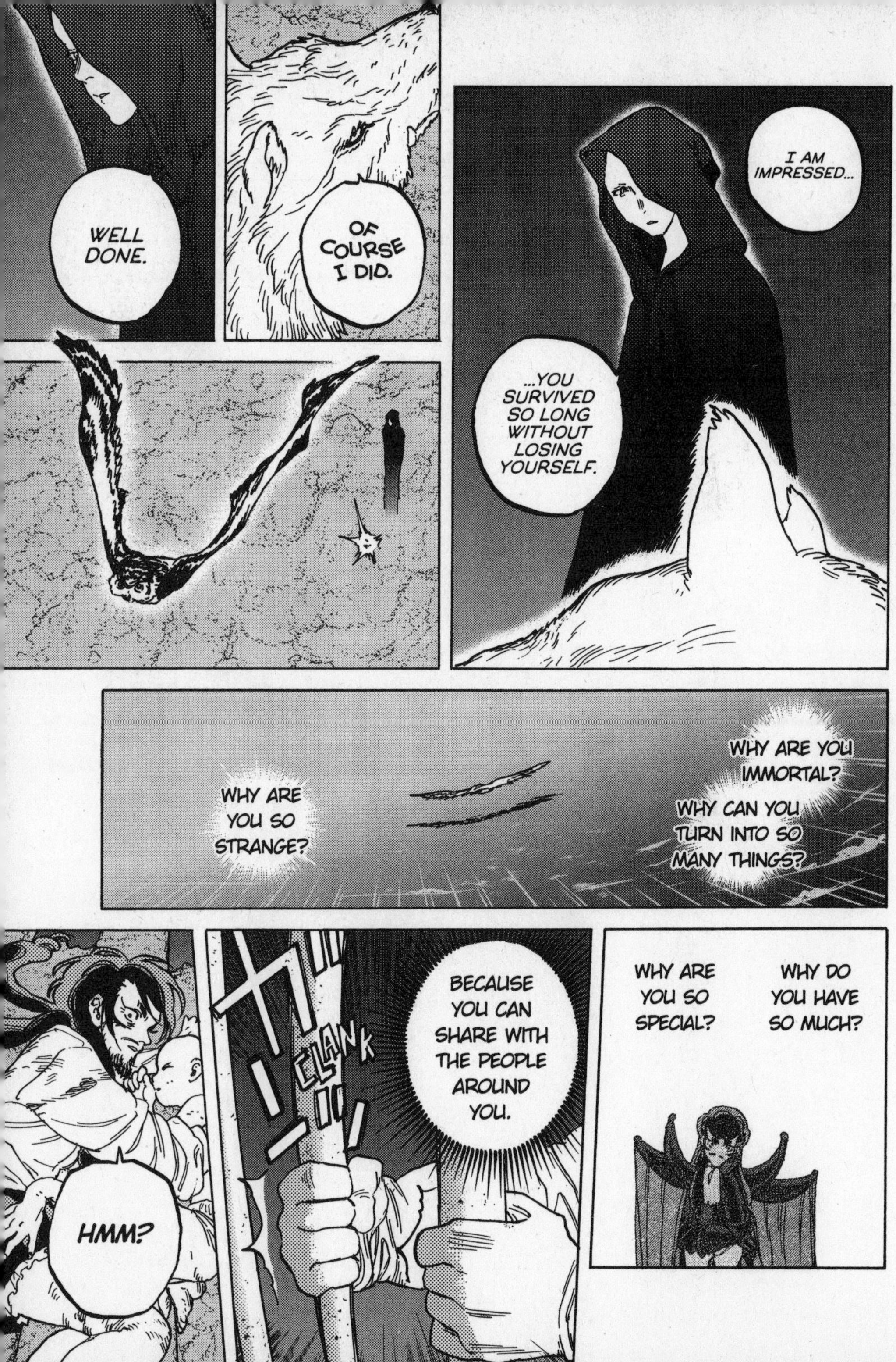
I AM IMPRESSED...
...YOU SURVIVED SO LONG WITHOUT LOSING YOURSELF.
OF COURSE I DID.
WELL DONE.
WHY ARE YOU IMMORTAL?
WHY CAN YOU TURN INTO SO MANY THINGS?
WHY ARE YOU SO STRANGE?
WHY DO YOU HAVE SO MUCH?
WHY ARE YOU SO SPECIAL?
BECAUSE YOU CAN SHARE WITH THE PEOPLE AROUND YOU.
CLANK
HMM?

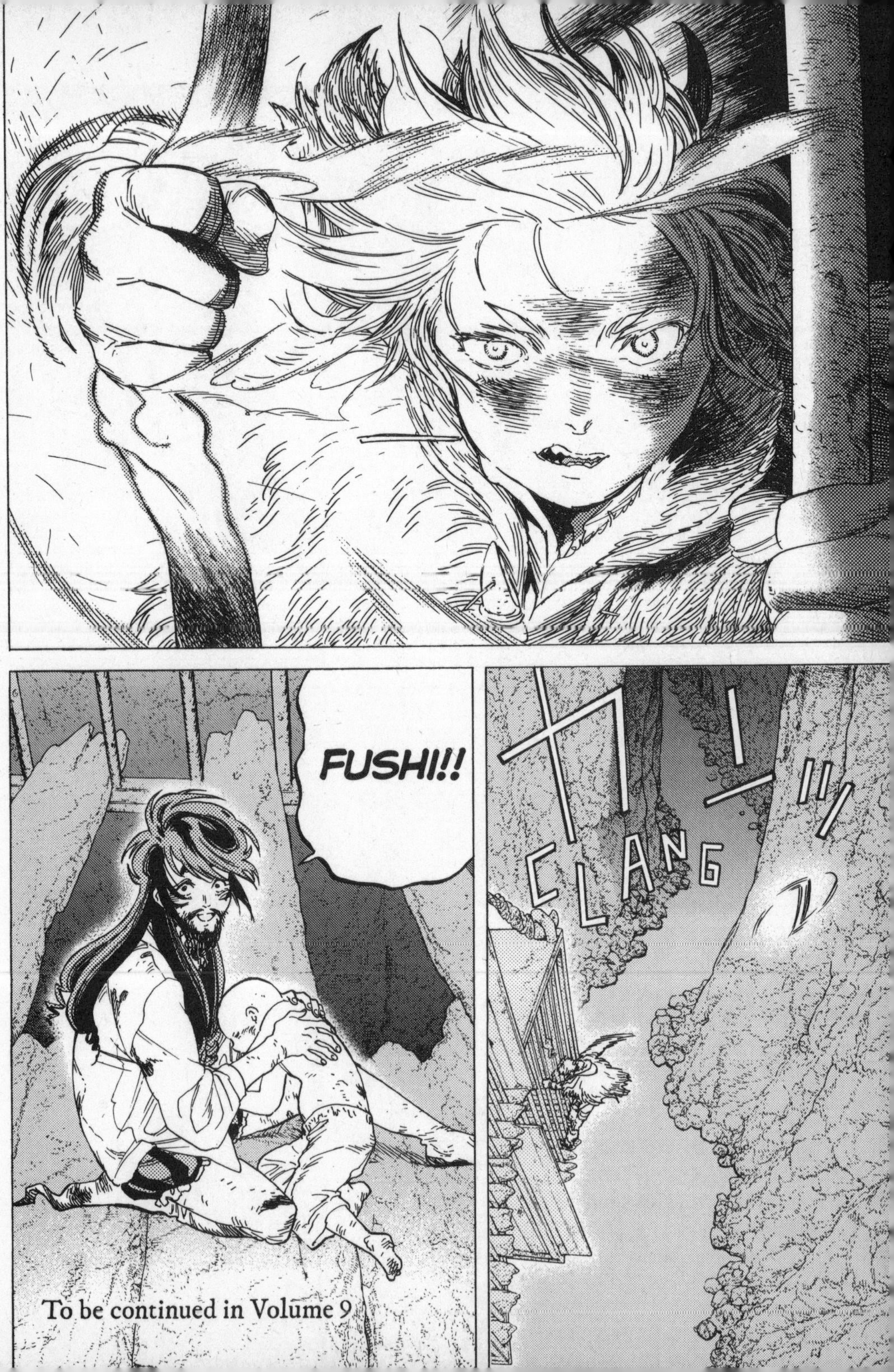
CLANG
FUSHI!!
To be continued in Volume 9

TO YOUR ETERNITY

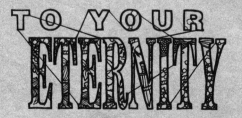

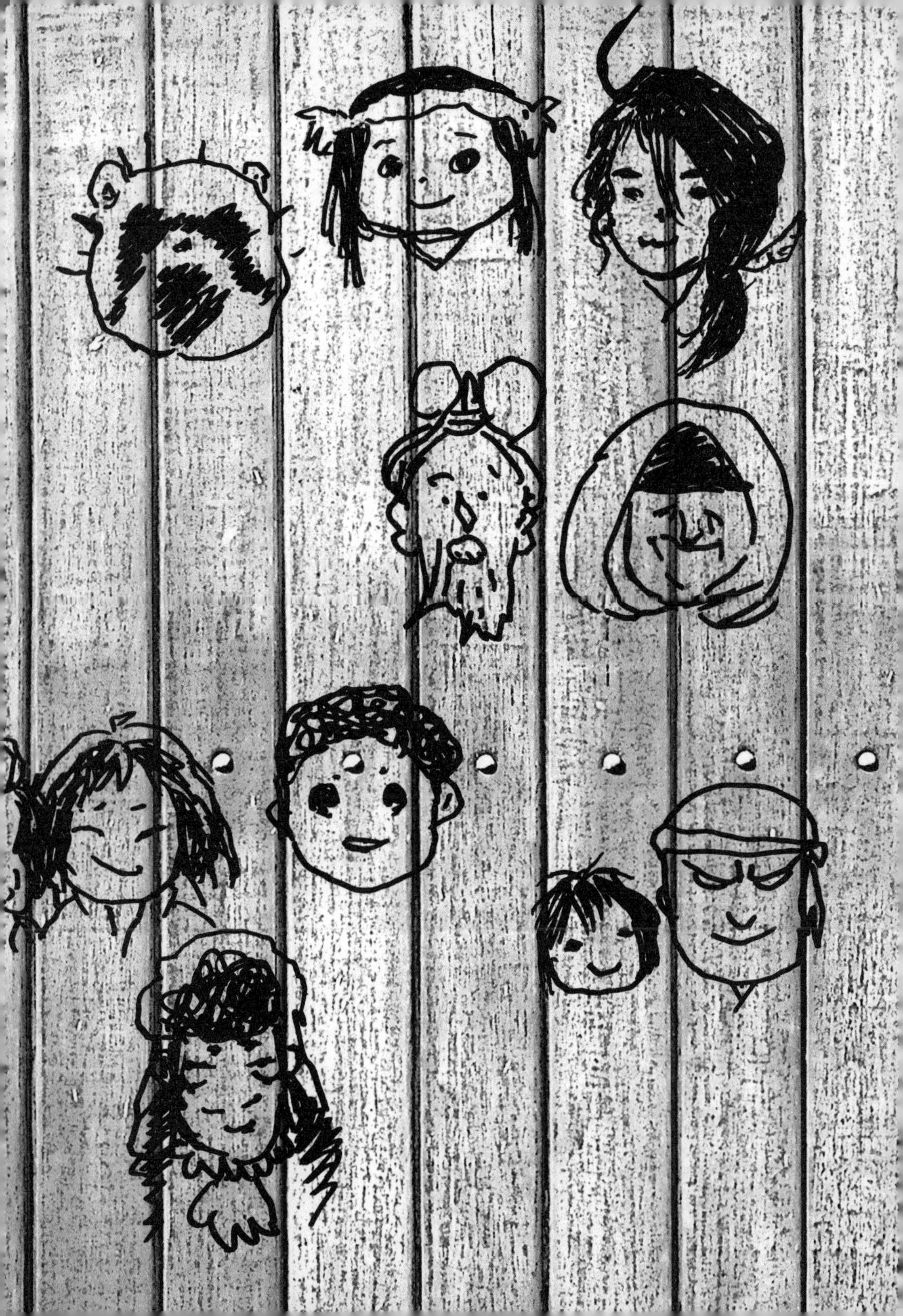

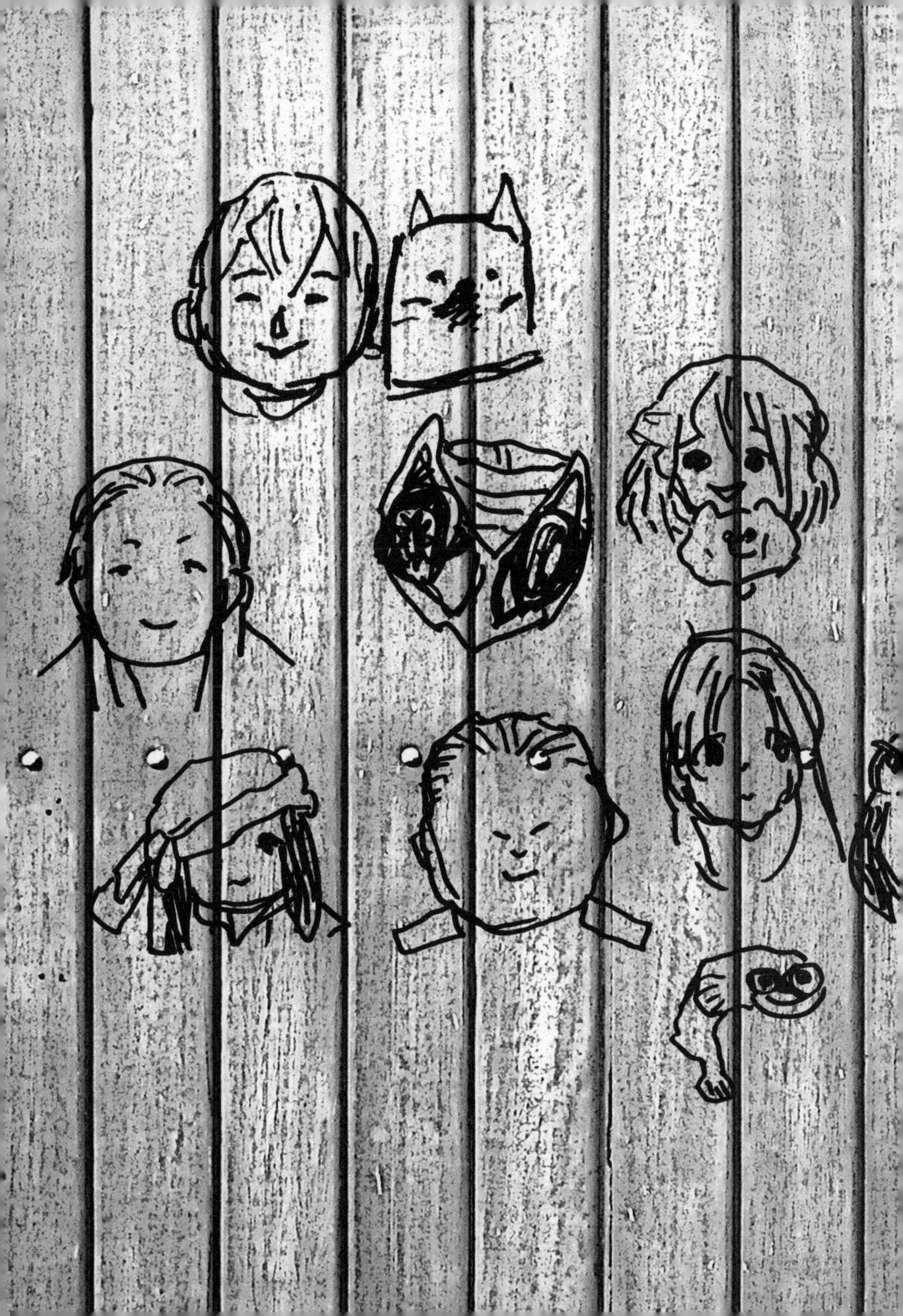

To Your Eternity volume 8 is a work of fiction.
Names, characters, places, and incidents are the products of the author's imagination or are used fictitiously. Any resemblance to actual events, locales, or persons, living or dead, is entirely coincidental.

A Kodansha Comics Trade Paperback Original.

Published in the United States by Kodansha Comics,
an imprint of Kodansha USA Publishing, LLC, New York.

Publication rights for this English edition arranged through Kodansha Ltd., Tokyo.

First published in Japan in 2018 by Kodansha Ltd., Tokyo,
as *Fumetsu no Anata e* volume 8.

Cover Design: Tadashi Hisamochi (hive&co., Ltd.)
Title Logo Design: Shinobu Ohashi

ISBN 978-1-63236-684-9

Printed in the United States of America.

www.kodanshacomics.com

9 8 7 6 5 4 3 2 1

Translation: Steven LeCroy
Lettering: Darren Smith
Editing: Haruko Hashimoto, Alexandra Swanson
Editorial Assistance: YKS Services LLC/SKY Japan, INC.
Kodansha Comics Edition Cover Design: Phil Balsman